Makhmalbaf at Large

Hamid Dabashi is Hagop Kevorkian Professor of Iranian Studies and Comparative Literature at Columbia University, New York. His acclaimed books include *Dream of a Nation: On Palestinian Cinema* and *Close Up: Iranian Cinema, Past, Present and Future*.

Makhmalbaf at Large
The Making of a Rebel Filmmaker

Hamid Dabashi

Foreword by

Mohsen Makhmalbaf

I.B. TAURIS

LONDON · NEW YORK

Advisory Editor: Sheila Whitaker

Published in 2008 by I.B.Tauris & Co Ltd
6 Salem Road, London W2 4BU
175 Fifth Avenue, New York NY 10010
www.ibtauris.com

In the United States of America and Canada distributed by
Palgrave Macmillan a division of St. Martin's Press, 175 Fifth Avenue,
New York NY 10010

ISBN: (PB) 978 1 84511 532 6
ISBN: (HB) 978 1 84511 531 9

A full CIP record for this book is available from the British Library
A full CIP record is available from the Library of Congress

Library of Congress Catalog Card Number: available

Designed and Typeset by 4word Ltd, Bristol, UK
Printed and bound by TJ International Ltd, Padstow, Cornwall, UK

Contents

In memory of my parents

Zahra Parvizi Motlaq (1917–82)
homemaker, mother, herbalist, storyteller

and

Khodadad Dabashi (1910–70)
railroad laborer, father, chef extraordinaire, toymaker

At the Sunset,
Amidst the tired presence of things,
The gaze of an expectant man
Pierced through the volume of time.
On the table,
The commotion of a few fresh fruits
Were flowing gently
Towards the inarticulate side
Of grasping death —
While the wind
Was granting generously
The aroma of the small garden
To the transparent edges of life
Upon the restful carpet —
And as imagination
Was holding the translucent surface of a flower
In hand —
Just like a folding fan —
Fanning itself.

The Traveler
Stepped out of the bus:
'What a beautiful sky!' —
And the continuity of the street
Carried away his lonesomeness.

From Sohrab Sepehri's *Traveler* (1966)

Acknowledgments

I have been working on this book for more than a decade. It took me so long to bring it out for several quite diverse reasons – the most important of which perhaps is the subject of my study, Mohsen Makhmalbaf himself. Makhmalbaf, I believe, defies a simplistic and straightforward understanding and requires a certain degree of critical intimacy rarely afforded these days to major world artists and their phantasmagoric visions of where we are in their universe. As I was traveling around the world to see and spend some time with Makhmalbaf, while I kept watching his films and reading his prose, I was getting far closer to the man himself than completing what I was writing about him. He is in his person a far greater man to know than a filmmaker to introduce to a wider circle of critical readings. For every film that he has made and the world has seen, he has told me (while walking for endless hours in the streets and back alleys of Locarno, Tehran, New York, Cannes, or Paris) at least ten more stories and read me even more scripts that he has written and are yet to be made into movies. The entire world, at times it has appeared to me, is just raw material for him to turn into stories and tell them in a slightly off-centered way. There were times that I had completely sublated the idea of writing this book on him into the exceedingly rewarding fact of my emerging friendship with him. I could just walk with him for hours and days and weeks and chat with him about one thing or another rather than sit down, organize my thoughts, and write something sensible about who and what he was. Without that sense of wonder and that inevitable critical intimacy with him as a person, my feeling is that it is impossible to write about this particular filmmaker.

There were any number of other reasons, however, for this delay. I had written too much on Makhmalbaf, and the mass of my writing reflected the meandering musings of a man in search of something at once at hand and yet elusive. Given the closeness of my relationship with Makhmalbaf and the density of my writings on him, I needed an editor who could cut through the thicket of my meanderings with him and his cinema, and sort out the good, the bad, and the perhaps redeemable. Publishers seldom have that sort of patience with an author anymore. But as the fate would have it, while aimlessly loitering in a bookstore in New York I chanced upon Jeanette Winterson's *Written on the Body* (1992) and spent a couple of splendid hours with her sparkling intelligence and piercing prose excavating the hidden shrills of bodily insurrections against the tyranny of the mundane and the avoidability of the available. As I was putting Winterson's book back on a table, I flipped through its initial pages and my eyes caught the phrase, 'my thanks are due to ... Philippa Brewster for her editorial inspirations.' By then I had approached Philippa Brewster and asked her to look at my manuscript and consider editing it. Once we had made contact Philippa looked at and agreed to edit my work, and I knew I had a book. To Philippa Brewster, and Sheila Whitaker who helped me persuade her to take on my book, I cannot be more eloquent in expressing my gratitude than to reiterate Jeanette Winterson's thanks for her 'editorial inspiration.' Philippa has cut from the shapeless granite of endless writing I handed her the shapely apparition you are about to meet. I am equally grateful to my distinguished colleagues Ella Shohat and Mehrzad Boroujerdi, as well as two other anonymous readers, for their constructive criticism of an earlier incarnation of this book.

My paramount note of gratitude, however, is due to Mohsen Makhmalbaf himself. Ever since I met him in August 1996 in Locarno, he has been a constant source of inspiration in my life. I cherish his precious camaraderie far beyond the point and purpose of this book. It gives me unsurpassed joy that I have been able to write a book on him – the only way I know to tell him how much I admire his art. Over the years my friendship with Makhmalbaf has extended to his family – his wife Marziyeh Meshkini, and their children Samira, Meysam, and Hana. They are all as dear to me as my own family.

Because of this friendship, I have no claim to critical distance from Makhmalbaf and his cinema. However, I hope whatever objectivity I may have lost because of that friendship, I have gained by my privileged proximity to the texture and tenor of his art.

A few of Mohsen Makhmalbaf's closest friends have become my friends too. Mamad Haghighat, Kazem Musavi, Sadiq Barmak, Mohammad Ahmadi, and Nezam Kia'i have been a precious source of solidarity and hope whenever I have had the fortune of seeing them in Makhmalbaf's company.

I have fond memories particularly of Fatemeh Moatamed Arya, one of the most gifted Iranian actresses, ever since I met her at Cannes. I am privileged by her friendship.

I am blessed to be in the vicinity of Richard Peña and Irene Bignardi. The fate of world cinema is very much in their capable hands.

For Nikzad Nodjoumi, Shirin Neshat, Shoja Azari, Ramin Bahrani, and Kouross Esmaili: what a joyous circle of solid friends come together to make New York, New York!

Margaret Parsons of the National Gallery in Washington DC, and Michael Jeck of the American Film Institute, were instrumental in my writing the first version of what is now a major chapter of this book as the text for the catalogue of a retrospective on Makhmalbaf in May 2002. I am grateful to both of them and to Renee Wright of Lens to Lens for making that retrospective and my contribution possible.

Arby Ovanessian and Susan Taslimi, two pillars of Iranian cinema, have taught me many hidden truths about its perils and promises. During a trip to Oslo, Norway, to participate in a conference on Henrik Ibsen made possible by the Ibsen Institute and organized by Farin Zahedi, I much benefitted from my conversations with Arby and Susan. I am grateful to them.

Finally: my love of cinema, and anything I might ever say about any film worth reading twice, I owe entirely to Amir Naderi, my source of inspiration in New York, and my picture-perfect vision of what it means to be an artist. He is my teacher, my mentor, my measure of what is good, what is bad, and what is inconsequential in any film I see. I have been blessed far beyond my deserve by his friendship. How poorer is Iran after his departure; how richer New York by his presence; and how blessed the happy few who can call him friend.

My wife, colleague, and comrade Golbarg Bashi, my children Kaveh, Pardis, and Chelgis, and the extended circle of my friends and comrades at Columbia University and in New York define the center of the universe from which I see the world and for which I put pen to paper.

HAMID DABASHI

NEW YORK

2007

Foreword

The Dinner of 1996

I met Hamid Dabashi for the first time in Locarno. Quite by serendipity. I was rushing to be interviewed by a reporter. I was looking hurriedly around for someone to help me with the translation of what I wanted to say. Exactly at this moment I saw Dabashi:

> 'Are you Iranian?'
> 'Yes.'
> 'Do you know English?'
> 'Yes.'
> 'Would you please help me translate what I have to say?'
> 'Yes.'

He is originally Iranian. But he has lived in the USA for more than three decades – a Professor at Columbia University in New York, teaching sociology of culture and specializing in world cinema, Iranian cinema and the cinema of the Arab world in particular. That year in Locarno they were celebrating Arab cinema, so Hamid Dabashi was there too. He said he wanted to introduce me to Youssef Chahine. He did. But in the course of that meeting I got to know Hamid Dabashi more than I did Youssef Chahine, though I had heard the name of Youssef Chahine earlier.

Dabashi sat at the head of a table; on either side of him sat an Iranian and an Arab filmmaker. The Western world would frame both of us under a category like Middle Eastern cinema. But we did not know one another that well, nor had we seen that many of one another's films to be able to talk about them. Thus our conversation turned to the subject of censorship in our respective countries, Iran and Egypt, measuring the length, width, and depth of censorship, concluding that the most common denominator of our cinema was in their Middle Eastern mode of censorship. Dabashi was falling off his chair with laughter, discovering the common feature of our cinemas – and from behind his bushy beard-full of a face I had a glimpse of his childish innocence. Without prejudice, without judgment, without having already made up his mind, he was searching for truths that were flowing in the details of a conversation around that dining table in Locarno in 1996.

> 'What do you do?'
> 'I ... a critic.'
> 'No!'
> 'Yes!'

I could not believe it. I had always regarded critics as very small people, climbing on the shoulder of big people, in order to claim they were bigger. They are like those finicky teachers bent on finding fault with dictation exercises of artists in order to assign each of them a grade. Each one of them has a couple of favorite students, giving all the rest failing grades. The style and vicissitude of all art criticism consists of nothing other than a few prefabricated notions whose fate is *a priori* and *a posteriori* in the manifesto of these critics. All they do is to gauge the work of an artist against the inventory of these pre-fabricated concepts. That's all. Thus had I always considered critics as being failed and bitter artists. I told him: 'It's a shame you are a critic.'

> 'Why?'
> ''Cause I think you are a good man.'
> 'Good man? What's that?'
> 'Searching for truth and never finding it. Constantly looking into the very essence of a work of art, in a "Rashomon"-like multiplicity of perspectives.'

Throughout that dinner, he changed his chair more than ten times. I remember him giving it up to any newcomer who joined us, fetching another one, every time placing it at some other corner of the table, so that once he was sitting in front of me, then in front of Youssef Chahine, then behind the both of us, and then again next to us. He mediated our conversations without prejudice, adding a question to every question we asked, and yet another question to every answer we gave – all without a trace of showing off his own erudition. I felt he had more questions to ask than answers to give; he had not yet made up his mind about anything; and though a professor he was more eager to learn than to teach. He had come to introduce me to Youssef Chahine, but he ended up introducing me to himself.

They say, 'Always go after someone who is after truth; and stay away from those who have found it.' After Locarno, Dabashi and I met many times in other countries, and I gradually realized that through my work he was trying to find out what had happened to Iran in the past two decades. I wondered if Dabashi did not harbor a certain nostalgia for Iran in his investigation of the social themes of my work, as his courage and sharp tongue had caused him on occasions to be barred from coming back to our country. Might it be that he is after those three damned decades when he was away from his birthplace and yet under the Statue of so-called Liberty worrying about his homeland?

The occasion of his writing a book on my work, of the content of which I am unaware, gradually merged into an excuse for us to become friends. Eventually the book became a rather marginal guise, clearing the way to our conversations and collaborations in lending support to Iranian, Afghan, and Palestinian cinemas. During these years, he once went to visit a physician because of heart palpitations. The cardiologist had not allowed him to leave the hospital and there and then had cut up his chest and performed surgery on his heart. During the two to three months when he was recuperating from his heart surgery, like a condemned man who had been granted the span of a few days to draft his last will and testament, he worked intensely on the book.

'Mr. Dabashi, are you writing a book about me?'

'No.'

'About my cinema?'

'No.'

'Are you trying to understand the social developments of Iran through my work?'

'No.'

'Then why are you wasting so much of your time – not to speak of pen and paper?'

Instead of answering my question, he paused for a while, and began to talk about Palestinian cinema in exile, about the fact that he had been able to locate thirty-five Palestinian films, that perhaps Palestinians themselves did not suspect they had made that many films, that he intended to turn the walls that had been erected around Palestinians into screens on which to show them their own films. And he did precisely that – during a trip fraught with danger inside Palestine itself, he went to become the Lumière of Palestinians.

'Who are you? Are you a professor at a university?'

'Yes.'

'A critic?'

'Yes.'
'An expert on the cinema of the Arab world?'
'Yes.'
'A projectionist?'
'Yes.'
'A political activist?'
'Yes.'
'Someone who hates politics?'
'Yes.'

He does not believe in God, nor does he believe in any religion, nor indeed does he have any faith. He has spent a lifetime in utter disbelief of any religion, or of what he calls 'superstition'. But when he succeeded in projecting Palestinian films on the walls surrounding occupied Palestine, overjoyed and thankful, he prostrated and prayed at Harm al-Sharif, at al-Aqsa Mosque, and at the Dome of the Rock – thanking God like a devout Muslim.

'Do you believe in God?'
'No.'
'So whom did you pray to?'
'To God.'

Hamid Dabashi – this pious atheist friend of mine, the man who loves cinema and hates art, this political activist who abhors politics, this thinking, pondering, critical intellect. To me he is always the same boy whose childish laughter I discovered from under a whole bush-full of beard during that dinner at Locarno in 1996.

He is a strange man. I have learned much from him. Perhaps he too, has learned from me. The times he and I have spent together have been occasions of discovery and illumination. Occasionally in a country, he and I are walking together. We come across a traffic light. We stop. We turn to each other and we say, 'Tell you what, let's see if before the light turns green we can teach each other something.' I presume that this book he has written is also a moment of reflection, in between two traffic lights, for the duration of a pause called life, for the driver who is stuck behind the traffic light, and for the moment when he reaches for a book or a newspaper, opens it up to a page, and after a moment of reading discovers that he has discovered nothing – yet.

Mohsen Makhmalbaf
Tehran

Introduction

Early in July 1997, after an absence of almost 20 years from Iran, I flew from New York, via London, to Tehran and spent about a month with Mohsen Makhmalbaf and his family. I had met Makhmalbaf almost a year earlier in the course of the Locarno International Film Festival in August 1996 and had decided almost immediately that I wanted to write a book on him. We struck up a friendship in Locarno that has lasted uninterrupted ever since.

I spent many memorable evenings into the wee hours of the night talking with Mohsen Makhmalbaf that August in Locarno, as his daughter Hana kept falling asleep on his lap – she was eight years old at the time. After the festival, Makhmalbaf, his wife Marziyeh, and Hana came to Geneva, where we spent a day walking by Lake Geneva, having lunch at a restaurant in Ouchy, and again talking incessantly – about cinema, politics, literature, and his amusement that I had not been to Iran for almost two decades – until we all went to Geneva airport, where they left for Tehran.

'Your Persian is quite good,' I remember him telling me that summer in Geneva while we were having lunch, a reference to my long absence from Iran. 'Your Persian is not bad either,' I jibed back, claiming equal footing in a language he and I both call home. I soon discovered that we shared an almost identical love for Sohrab Sepehri (1928–80), one of Iran's most beloved twentieth century poets, and we kept quoting each other passages we knew by heart. 'The sun had set,' he began reciting from Sepehri's *Traveler* (1966), as we were walking by Lake Geneva near Lausanne, his daughter Hana and my daughter Pardis walking and playing ahead of us. 'One could hear the intelligent sound/Of vegetations./The traveler had arrived/And sat upon a comfortable chair/By the Lawn.' His Persian has a solid, southern Tehrani accent. My own, having lost all but traces of its southern intonations, is Pahlavi-schooling and deliberately out-Tehranis the inhabitants of our capital city. 'I feel sad,' I began from where he had left off from Sepehri's *Traveler*:

I feel inexplicably sad.
And all the way here
I could not but think of only one thing –
As the color of the prairies
Were driving me
Mad with their beauty –
And as the lines of the highway
Were lost
In the sadness of the prairie –
What splendid valleys!
And the horse, do you remember –
It was white –
And just like the word for 'purity'
It was grazing
Over the green silence of the grassland –
And then (do you remember):
The colorful lonesomeness of the villages on the way –
And then: the tunnels –
I feel sad.
I feel inexplicably sad –
And nothing:
Neither these aromatic minutes,
Dying as they do over the Persian Orange branches,
Nor indeed the sincerity of this spoken word in between
The silence that separates the two leaves of the Shab-bu flower,
No – nothing
Can save me from the onslaught of the emptiness
Of the surroundings –
And I think that this melodic whispering
Of sadness will be heard forever.

One of the first things I learned about Makhmalbaf from that initial meeting was his extraordinary forbearance – especially in relation to incidents that might embarrass his friends. While we were still in Locarno, I learned that he had to go to Geneva to catch his flight to Tehran. I suggested to him that he and his family get the train from Locarno to Geneva, the same train that I had arrived by. He liked the idea, so we got him tickets similar to the one I had from Locarno to Geneva a few days earlier. I arranged to pick up him and his family from Geneva station on the day of their arrival. I did so, spent a whole day with them, and on the following day took them to the airport, from where they left.

1   Mohsen Makhmalbaf in Switzerland, during the Locarno International Film Festival, August 1995. It was a year later, in August 1996, during the same festival that I first met Makhmalbaf. Soon after that encounter, I decided I wanted to write a book on him. (Photograph courtesy of Makhmalbaf Film House.)

It was years later and in a completely serendipitous context that I learned what a blunder I had made and what a headache I had inadvertently created for him. The train from Locarno to Geneva exits Swiss territory for about an hour or so, and around Domodossola enters Italy. Traveling on a US passport, I had no clue as to how many times the police would come aboard and ask to see the train passengers' passports, or what country those police officers represented. It transpired that when the train entered Italian territory, the Italian police had boarded the train and asked passengers for their passports, and Makhmalbaf and his family for their visas. They only had Swiss visas. The problem was apparently quite disconcerting, because the Italian police officer had almost got into a fistfight with another visa-less passenger in the same car where Makhmalbaf and his family were sitting. There was a troubling moment of bewilderment and anxiety for the Makhmalbafs which they handled gracefully. Years after I learned about my blunder, I could not believe the patience and grace with which Makhmalbaf handled the crisis and never uttered a word about it to me until much later and in an entirely different context. Over the years I have witnessed many other occasions of an almost mystic patience and forbearance in Makhmalbaf.

Makhmalbaf came to New York the following October for the premier of his *Gabbeh* (1996) at the New York Film Festival, where we met and talked again for days. As he was leaving, we still had much to talk about and so we agreed that I would go to Tehran the following July. I spent the next winter in intensive communication with Makhmalbaf by fax, while watching as many of his films as I could find. While I was in Vermont during the winter vacation of 1996–97, every night I would send him a fax full of questions and queries, and receive a detailed response from him the following day. During the spring of 1997, the exchange of faxes, occasional telephone calls, and repeated viewing of his films continued uninterrupted. This was the year of President Mohammad Khatami's election. I remember when Makhmalbaf returned to Tehran in the following June from a trip to Tajikistan, as he was getting ready to shoot *Silence* (1998), he and I would spend many sleepless nights wondering about the results of the presidential election. He was glued to the television following the election results and faxing them to me, and I dozing off by my fax and phone in New York. For the first and final time in my life I was convinced that I should vote. Useless hopes we had those years.

On 1 July 1997, soon after Khatami's election, I flew to Tehran, and upon my arrival I called Makhmalbaf and arranged to see him at his downtown home. He told me to get a cab to Dowlatabad Square, then ask for a local sports complex. He added, 'Our home is right in front of that sports complex.' I did as he had instructed. The cab I had hired in northern Tehran reached Dowlatabad Square. The cab driver did not know where the sports complex in that part of the city was, so I stuck my head out of the cab and asked a young passer-by if he knew where it was. The man stopped patiently, pointed toward a wide avenue in front of us and said, 'you take that street and go straight for a few blocks, then you come to a fork, take the right side until you reach Mohsen Makhmalbaf's house, right in front of it is the sports complex.'

During that July in Tehran, on many occasions I was witness to the extraordinary love and affection that very ordinary people on the street had for Makhmalbaf: florists giving him free flowers, for example; greengrocers offering him free fruit juice; excited bookstore employees calling their friends from the backroom to come and see him; restaurant owners on the Alborz Mountain north of Tehran refusing to accept money from him; traffic cops on Vali Asr Avenue (what used to be called Pahlavi Avenue before the revolution) stopping the traffic when they spotted him in his car, coming forward to greet him and shake his hand. Years later, I witnessed similar encounters in Paris where young Algerian, Tunisian, Egyptian, Iranian, Turkish, Indian, and Malaysian laborers would stop him on the street, shake his hand, and tell him how much they admired him and loved his cinema. In Cannes, it is almost impossible to walk on Boulevard de la Croisette with him. He is constantly interrupted by his fans, by film critics, by festival directors pleading with him to give them his next film first, and by filmmakers from around the globe.

The presence of Makhmalbaf inside Iran is something of a phenomenon. One of Abbas Kiarostami's most celebrated films, *Close Up* (1990), based on an actual event, is about a man who pretends he is Mohsen Makhmalbaf. Hossein Sabzian goes about his life making people believe that he is someone else, getting himself and others into trouble by doing so. In what many critics believe to be Abbas Kiarostami's finest film, he studies the psychopathology of a man who inhabits the life of a publicly celebrated figure and then turns the film into a reflection on the nature and disposition of identity and alterity, celebrity and desperation, but ultimately of the changing contours of (fabricated) *reality*.

Makhmalbaf himself once told me the story of yet another man who introduced himself to him as Mohsen Makhmalbaf! 'You are Mohsen Makhmalbaf?' Makhmalbaf asked the imposter in bewilderment. 'Yes, I am Mohsen Makhmalbaf,' the man insisted, 'the famous filmmaker.' Makhmalbaf did not tell him who he was. There are many other such stories, some of them assuming the character of urban legends, about men falling in love with young women, asking for their hands and, in order to impress the family of their intended, pretending to be Mohsen Makhmalbaf.

I was away from Iran for too long for Makhmalbaf to have been a cultural icon for me. Six years older than Makhmalbaf, I come from a generation of the Iranian cosmopolitan left that was deeply disappointed with the way the 1979 Iranian revolution had turned religious and ended up in a theocracy. Makhmalbaf was in fact constitutional to the success of a revolution I thought a failure. I had grown up on the cinema of Daryush Mehrju'i, Bahram Beiza'i, Amir Naderi, and Abbas Kiarostami, and like all other Iranian cosmopolitans left I had no clue what an 'Islamic cinema' would look like. My generation grew up admiring Jalal Al-e Ahmad, Ahmad Shamlu, Bahram Beiza'i, Houshang Golshiri, Forough Farrokhzad, Gholamhossein Sa'edi, and Simin Daneshvar. Our heroes were the Fada'ian-e Khalq guerrillas (President George W. Bush would call them 'terrorist' today) – Amir Parviz Pouyan, Hamid Ashraf, Ashraf Dehghani, Bizhan Jazani. These were our heroes, the measures of our truths, the test of our mettle – their heroic deeds we narrated in awe and cherished in secret. Poets we loved had immortalized our guerrilla fighters – Shamlu's poem on Khosrow Ruzbeh, Esmail Kho'i's poems on Siahkal martyrs, named after a heroic uprising in northern Iran by a small band of fighters in 1970. Despite our love and admiration for Ali Shari'ati (whom I was once taken to hear by a religious activist friend at Hosseiniyeh Ershad) and for the Mojahedin Khalq organization, we considered them too religious for our taste. By and large we looked at religious activists as distant cousins of ours whom we felt obligated to meet every once in a while but with whom we really did not have much in common to talk about. People of my generation of student activists liked to watch Fellini and Naderi, listen to Mozart and Shajarian, catch a production of a Chekhov or Sa'edi play at Tehran University, or hike on Alborz Mountain. We occasionally drank, never prayed, knew miles of Ahmad Shamlu, Mehdi Akhavan Sales, Mahmoud Darwish, Faiz Ahmad Faiz, Nazim Hekmat, Vladimir Mayakovsky, Pablo Neruda, and Aime Cesaire's poetry by heart – and had all but forgotten every verse of the Qur'an we had learned in our childhood. This is not to paint too much of a 'secular' society in the capital of our country in the late 1960s and early 1970s. Quite the contrary. We were of course all Muslims, but Muslims in a cultural kind of a way, in a cosmopolitan kind of a way[1] – and every month of Muharram and Safar suddenly a shriveled Shi'i emerged from a hidden side of our soul. Islam might be the opium of the masses. But Imam Hussein was an entirely different matter.

Though only a few years apart in age, Makhmalbaf and I seemed to have come from two different universes – a massive revolution and a bloody war stood between us. 'After the revolution,' he told me in Locarno in August 1996, 'all who had heart went to fight for their homeland and died in the course of the Iran–Iraq war, and all who had brain left Iran. Iran is now a heartless and brainless corpse.' This was too brutal, too definitive, too categorical a pronouncement for me to share. Until I met Makhmalbaf in Locarno I did not realize how much I had been away from Iran – not just physically but emotively, imaginatively, creatively. In Makhmalbaf and his cinema, I have at times thought that I have been seeking an alter ego, telling me what I have missed in my homeland in the more than quarter of a century I have been away from it. In me, I have at times suspected, he has detected the curiosity of a familiar foreigner, a mixed metaphor, a virtual reality, the stuff of which his cinema is made.

Before I met Makhmalbaf in Locarno I did not know much about him. I had seen a couple of his films and very much liked his *Once upon a Time, Cinema* (1992), which I thought was a beautiful love letter to the history of Iranian cinema. But there was much rumor about Makhmalbaf and his harassment of pre-revolutionary filmmakers soon after the success of the Islamic Revolution. There was an obvious rift between Iranian leftist intellectuals living outside Iran and what was happening under the charismatic terror of Ayatollah Khomeini in the 1980s. So it was with some bewilderment that I pondered my attraction to Makhmalbaf's cinema and soon his character and career. When I first saw him in Locarno, his face had an uncanny similarity to a mental picture I had in my mind of a young boy I once saw in the bazaar of the Shah Abd al-Azim shrine near Tehran, which I visited with my mother when I must have been ten or eleven years old. On our way back from Shah Abd al-Azim mausoleum, I noted a police officer giving a dirty look to a small boy almost my age. It was early in the afternoon and the bazaar was quite crowded. I have no idea what the boy had done, or why the police officer was so angry with him. But what I do remember is that the boy returned the police officer's stare and whispered after him with a contemptuous look, 'matarsak-a-ye Mammad Damagh az in behtar nemishan' ('The scarecrows of Mammad the Nose can't be any better'). That was the first time I had heard our king, Mohammad Reza Shah Pahlavi, being referred to as 'Mammad the Nose' (he had quite a big nose). When I told Makhmalbaf this story in Locarno, he laughed: 'Maybe it was me.'

This book is the result of more than a decade of watching Mohsen Makhmalbaf's films repeatedly, reading his writings closely, and getting to know him personally. These encounters have been a precious component of my life and a constant source of hope and aspiration in the course of a particularly troubling decade in world events. The result is the summation of my prolonged reflections on a filmmaker I deeply admire, without (I hope) having totally lost my critical distance from him. There is much to be loved and admired in Makhmalbaf and his cinema, and there is much to be criticized in both. But whether I praise him or criticize him, I do so with an abiding love of cinema. Cinema for us in the colonial edges of its invention is not merely an entertainment, as soccer is not just a sport for us, or poetry something we do in a class on 'creative writing' at college. As an art easily accessible to masses of ordinary and poor people, cinema has assumed the definitive status of an almost religious ritual that we practice with utter devotion, humility, and an abundance of love – the same way we play and watch our soccer, or compose and recite our poetry. Neither the culture industry nor the entertainment business understands the love we colored folks from the former (or emerging) colonies hold for cinema. That love underlines whatever I have to say about a rebel filmmaker I also know as a close friend.

The Major Theme and Scope of this Book

My attraction to world and national cinemas in general, and here to Makhmalbaf's cinema in particular, is definitive to my enduring concern about the nature and function of post/colonial agency – about how, why, and under what specific historical circumstances people pick up arms, sharpen their pencils, or fine-tune their cameras and in an in/audible cry against injustice command 'Action!'[2] My principal theoretical proposition in this book, which reflects my previous work and here sets in the foreground everything I have to say about Makhmalbaf, is that in the historical unfolding of his cinema we witness the creative outline of a critical constitution of an historical subject whose active agency in the material world – when she stands erect and says no to power – is beyond the pale of colonial modernity. Beyond the limits of a post/colonial critic of the postmodern dismantling of the sovereign subject, an apt and appropriate criticism remains valid that by virtue of engaging poststructuralism, postcolonialism in fact remains epistemically bound and thus ultimately loyal to it. I, of course, note with delight the battle between Habermas (defending the cause of European Enlightenment modernity) and Derrida (dismantling the all-knowing and sovereign European subject).[3] But as a colonial, now the subject of an empire, I watch their skirmishes with a little bit of bewilderment and much amusement. My own critical apparatus, meanwhile, is firmly located on the colonial site, where there is an urgent need to generate and sustain a critic of modernity that for those who have received it at its imperial edges has always been a *colonial* modernity – it is a critique that is *not* identical or even tantamount to postmodernity. It only takes a kind of rather perverse delight in watching its imperial and sovereign projects self-destruct. In Makhmalbaf's cinema I wish to show a kind of creative agency in which the worldly presence of post/colonial people, their historical agency, their material subjectness, in short their ability to be the author of their own destiny, are all beyond the reach of what for us on the colonial edges of European modernity – whether we live in Harlem and Bronx, downtown Tehran, or the slums of Cairo – has always been colonially mitigated. I have learned much from Gayatri Spivak's legendary essay, 'Can the Subaltern Speak?'[4] But I believe too much encampment in the domain of the postmodern – a post/colonial critic of the postmodern dismantling of the sovereign subject – robs the historical particulars of our post/coloniality of the terms of our own enchantments with a mode of historical agency that does not replicate the manner, if not the mood, of our coloniality.

My way toward an articulation of the emancipated post/colonial subject is informed by two sorts of rather distant echoes: critical theory from one side and cultural criticism from the other. I am very much aware of the pitfalls of such an uncanny encounter, and quite wary of negative reactions to it. Many fine scholars

I admire have been put on the defensive because of their theoretical language. In a footnote to her wonderful essay on 'Marking Gender and Difference in the Myth of the Nation: A Post-Revolutionary Iranian Film,' Nasrin Rahimieh, for example, states:

> I am conscious of the fact that my use of these theoretical concepts [of those offered by Julia Kristeva and Luce Irigaray] might be interpreted as a form of 'Westomania' (*Gharbzadegi*), a term publicized in the 1960's by the Iranian writer and social activist Jalal Al-e Ahmad to refer to a whole range of social, cultural and political subjugation of Iranians by the West. Yet, like Leila Ahmad, I maintain that the prohibition of such cross-referencing in the name of preserving specificity and authenticity is isolationism at its worst.[5]

Echoing Nasrin Rahimieh is Susan Buck-Morss, who in her wonderful recent book *Thinking Past Terror* (2003) becomes one of the first, serious, critical theorists to have something important to say about militant Islamism, having successfully surpassed the psychological barrier of being a member of the European left and yet engaging critically with matters beyond the domain of her immediate scholarship.[6] In active camaraderie with these distinguished scholars, I no longer even believe in the fabricated binary opposition manufactured between 'the West and the Rest,' because I believe that the colonially manufactured category 'the West' has long since surpassed its historical uses and the terror that it has perpetrated on the globe. As the work of scholars and theorists like Nasrin Rahimieh and Susan Buck-Morss demonstrates, critical thinking about matters of cultural production can no longer remain limited to colonial boundaries manufactured to alienate and separate, in order to divide and rule. So if we have occasion to engage in conversations with thinkers who have thought through problems of modernity, it makes no difference on which side of our library we have kept them. In this book, I have a critical perspective on the project of European Enlightenment. Much of what I have to say about Makhmalbaf's cinema reflects my concern that it has happened under the colonial shadow of that project. It is thus all but inevitable that I ought to have a conversation with people who have had something to say about the matter – whether their name is Martin Heidegger (a philosopher), Edward Said (a cultural critic and a literary humanist), Gayatri Spivak (a poststructuralist and feminist theorist), or Jalal Al-e Ahmad and Ali Shari'ati (two revolutionary polemicists). One crucial thing I have learned from world cinema (with Amir Naderi as my principal guide) is that there is a republic of vision that major filmmakers around the world share and call home, and that republic is entirely beyond the realm of political boundaries and *National Geographic* exoticism. Mohsen Makhmalbaf adores

Yoshijiro Ozu; John Ford admired Akira Kurosawa, while Akira Kurosawa very much liked Abbas Kiarostami; Satyajit Ray was indebted to Jean Renoir, while François Truffaut loved Alfred Hitchcock; Wim Wenders likes Mohsen Makhmalbaf; Michel Khleifi is a great fan of Bernardo Bertolucci; Amir Naderi is a walking encyclopedia of world cinema. The whirling dance is interminable. In the spirit of that dance, my book on Makhmalbaf thrives in the choreography of a creative affinity with the critical constitution of a post/colonial subject beyond the pale of an East–West binary that the globalized capital has now forever dismantled. In short, and above all else, I am a New Yorker – I live by a river from which drink people of all colors and combinations – and above all I write for them.

I set the tone of my book by first placing Makhmalbaf in the first chapter, 'On the Paradoxical Rise of a National Cinema and the Iconic Making of a Rebel Filmmaker,' within the larger context of the rise of Iranian cinema during the last two decades of the twentieth century.[7] Here I discuss the more general question of the rise of national cinemas, which I propose are predicated on severe national traumas: in the Iranian case the cataclysmic events of the Islamic Revolution in 1978–79 and the subsequent eight years of war with Iraq between 1980 and 1988. Here I provide a general outline of Iranian cinema and discuss the apparent paradoxical question usually put forward by those who wonder how a cinema of such significance could emerge in an Islamic Republic. In this chapter, I turn the question around in fact and argue that the rise of any national cinema is predicated on a national trauma. I make this proposition and give examples of other major national cinemas from around the world, before I narrow in on Iranian cinema in particular, its development after the Islamic Revolution of 1979, and the rise of Mohsen Makhmalbaf as a major figure in that cinema. The formation of an anticolonial subject, I argue, is integral to an emancipatory aesthetics that re-signifies the world in a liberating and expansive way.

The second chapter, 'Makhmalbaf at Large: The Making of a Rebel Filmmaker,' is a comprehensive account of his career as a revolutionary filmmaker.[8] In this chapter I begin to outline my reading of the various phases of Makhmalbaf as a filmmaker, identifying five such phases in his cinematic career formed immediately after his political activism, incarceration in Pahlavi prison, and release in the course of the Islamic Revolution: a religious visionary, a social realist, a philosophical relativist, a visual theorist, and a poetic surrealist. In this chapter, I identify the films of each period, give a detailed analysis of why they belong to these phases, and what they represent in conversation with historical events surrounding Makhmalbaf's life as an artist and social activist. In this chapter, I also begin outline a theoretical reflection on the of Makhmalbaf's aesthetics as articulated outside the purview of the Kantian aesthetic dismissal of non-Europeans as incapable of conceiving the notions of the beautiful and the

2   Mohsen Makhmalbaf as director/actor in his own Salam Cinema (1995). Makhmalbaf has assumed a dual character in several of his own films, as both director and actor. He also acted in Abbas Kiarostami's Close-Up (1990), again as himself. His career as a director and his appearances as an actor representing that director often crisscross the boundaries of fact and fiction. The fusion of the two personas has been a principal feature of cultural politics of post-revolutionary Iran. (Photograph: Jamshid Bayrami; courtesy of Makhmalbaf Film House.)

sublime. Here, my concern is to see how the successive phases of a restless artist like Makhmalbaf – sometimes at critical odds with each other – are constitutional to his articulation of agential autonomy and historical character for his nation at large.

In the next chapter, 'Dead Certainties: The Early Makhmalbaf or the Purgatory of a Rebel Filmmaker,' I provide a comprehensive reading of Makhmalbaf's early film and fiction, tracing the origin of his art to his revolutionary disposition.[9] My principal objective here is to trace the origin and nature of a defiant form of subject formation on the evident site of post/colonial aesthetics. My main argument is that the aggressive instrumentalization of *reason* in the course of capitalist modernity was far more evident on the *colonial edges* of the project than in its stated *capital centers*. In both these cases, the aesthetic site remains the singularly significant location of resisting colonial de-subjection of the colonized and restoring agency to their defiant subject. The early work of Makhmalbaf, I wish to demonstrate, is a clear example of how the narrative mutation of anticolonial ideologies will have to go through the hazardous path of mystical flirtations with the *Absolute* before it can begin to articulate a liberation aesthetics. I hope to demonstrate in this chapter the need to bring the critic of post/colonial art closer to the postmodern critic of the European Enlightenment. The underlying argument of this chapter is to link Makhmalbaf's early revolutionary career as a rebel, who was willing to take up arms against tyranny, with the creative disposition of his cinematic will to resist power and posit an historical subject capable and willing to say 'no' to power. In this chapter, as in much of the rest of this book, I take my cues on the question of re-subjection of the post/colonial person very much from Frantz Fanon's essay 'Concerning Violence', especially when he says, 'decolonization is quite simply the replacing of a certain "species" of men by another "species" of men.'[10] That is all I mean by *re-subjection*.

Chapter Four, 'The Rebel Matures: Makhmalbaf's *A Moment of Innocence*,' is a close reading of what I believe to be his most successful film so far: *A Moment of Innocence* (1995).[11] In this chapter, I pick up on the earlier arguments I have made for art as the singular site of resisting de-subjection and restoring agency to the colonially denied subject. My principal argument here is predicated on the proposition that the varied forms of ideological resistance to colonialism cannot but further implicate the colonial subject in its own de-subjection. I examine Makhmalbaf's perhaps most successful manipulation of time and narrative to demonstrate how the creative site of visual and performing arts is in fact the *material* ground for resistance to colonial subjection. I have a tacit conversation with Michel Foucault in this chapter, arguing that while he had to go to 'the Other Victorians' to locate the shadow side of bourgeois morality, on the colonial site such transgressions are in fact the very center of the moral and material imaginary – 'transgression,' though, in a very positive reading of the creative imagination – that is to say, the creative will to resist power. In this discussion, I have sought to demonstrate how, by visually altering the imaginative perception of reality, Makhmalbaf has been able to craft a creative constitution for an historical agency otherwise unimaginable. The principal thesis of my book, namely the outline of the aesthetic space in which Makhmalbaf has crafted a sovereign subject beyond the limits of 'tradition and modernity,' receives a full analytical detail in this chapter.

My fifth chapter, 'Recasting the Subject: The Anticolonial Rebel at Work,' is a detailed reading of three other Makhmalbaf films – *Once Upon a Time, Cinema*; *A Time for Love*; and *Gabbeh* in particular – plus several other scripts that he has never made into film. In this chapter, I pick up from where I left off in the previous chapter on the manner of Makhmalbaf's dismantling of the sovereign subject that we have forcefully received and paradoxically reciprocated in the course of colonial modernity. Instead, I argue, what we witness in Makhmalbaf's cinema is an attempt to reach for *the transparency of the real*, which *ipso facto* mocks and modifies the authority of the *evident*. By mocking reality via an aesthetic of its transparency, through what I will call his *virtual realism*, Makhmalbaf manages to transgress the authorial boundaries of the colonially constituted *modernity* and point toward an emancipatory aesthetics in which the post/colonial subject is let loose on an enabling political domain beyond the debilitating false paradox of 'tradition versus modernity.' For this very reason, the constitution of a defiant subject must be guarded against falling into the trap of a jaundiced nativism. My hope in this chapter is to demonstrate in what particular terms cinema is effectively transgressive by being voyeuristic: as such it robs the politics of the ancestral authority of any claim to essentialized *authenticity*. My principal point is thus to argue that the fate of a post/colonial artist is inevitably cast in resisting an active transmutation of his life-experience into raw material for either useless cultural anthropology[12] or else consumed in the culture industry. Toward that end, I argue, the aesthetics that the post/colonial artist inhabits and thus represents has to cut on two apparently opposed but quintessentially identical fronts: not just on the colonially constituted subservient *subjectivity*, but also on the jargon of *authenticity* that animates the 'traditions' that colonial modernity invents.

In the sixth chapter, 'The Gnostic Simplicity of Silence: Makhmalbaf as an Ascetic Revolutionary,' I pick up the discussion of a cinematic manipulation of the binary opposition colonially projected between tradition and modernity, which I have argued is integral to an emancipation of the subservient subject. I demonstrate Makhmalbaf's cultivated penchant for what I call his *gnostic simplicity* and *ascetic minimalism*, both of which are constitutional to his *parabolic narrative* – as evident in such films as his *Silence* (1998), which in this chapter I read very closely. His *virtual realism*, I then argue, has given Makhmalbaf's mature cinema a Spartan disposition, a rather lean and crisp mannerism that empties his cinema of all superfluous anxieties. An austere precision thus emerges in Makhmalbaf's cinema that is constitutional to the crafting of an agency beyond the pale of 'tradition and modernity,' 'Islam and the West,' or any other such false but powerful binary opposition. The organic link among a virtual realism, a gnostic simplicity, and a parabolic narrative are all diverse manifestations of Makhmalbaf's revolutionary asceticism that extends from the defining moment of his cinema to his personal and private demeanors. That revolutionary asceticism, I suspect, is the *tabula rasa* of the anticolonial subject that cries for freedom in Makhmalbaf's cinema.

In the seventh and final chapter, 'The Beauty of the Beast: From Cannes to *Kandahar*,' I attend exclusively to *Kandahar* (2001), perhaps the most universally famous film of Makhmalbaf, albeit for all the wrong reasons. In this chapter, I in fact take to task my own earlier assumption about the autonomy of purpose of a work of art, independent of the political context in which it is manufactured and contextualized. However, I will show how a work of art can effectively turn around and abuse its abusers. What is particularly important in this chapter is what I identify as Makhmalbaf's visual improvization, which I propose is central to his ability to go inside a political predicament and dismantle it through its own contradictory forces. In this respect I challenge Jean Baudrillard's assumption of a transaesthetics of indifference, and instead argue not just for the necessity but in fact the presence of an emancipatory aesthetics that can very easily tell the difference between entrapment and freedom, not just from forces external to a culture but from those domestic to its predicament – and thus in effect collapse the binary between the internal and the external.[13]

Finally, in my Conclusion, I pick up a few of the ideas I have raised in this Introduction, discuss the most recent films of Makhmalbaf, and thus bring this book to a closure in terms of what I have sought to accomplish by writing on one of the most restless rebel filmmakers of our time.

Years Later, Once in Paris

'Are you at all interested in mysticism?' I cannot remember the reason, nor do I think there were any, when I quite abruptly asked this question of Makhmalbaf while we were walking by Lac Leman late that August of 1996. 'Not really,' he said. 'I am more interested in the mystery of the moment, in the gnostic innocence of the instance, just before it passes us by, and from which we as adults get farther and farther in our lives.' We kept on walking for a few seconds. 'You mean like Sepehri – right?' He did not say anything for a while; then he turned toward me and looked at me with a smile that I have since thought permanently carved on his face, even when he is asleep. 'The traveler looked at the table,' he began quoting from Sepehri's *Traveler*, and I continued:

> 'What beautiful apples!'
> Life is the pure ecstasy of solitude.'
> The host asked:
> 'What does "beautiful" mean?'
> – "Beautiful" means to interpret the forms lovingly and
> Love, only love
> Can acquaint you with the warmth of an apple; and
> Love, only love
> Took me to the vast expanse of lives, and
> Brought me to the possibility of becoming a bird.
> – 'And as for the panacea of sadness?'
> 'The pure sound of elixir gives you that cure.'

Years later, I remember, in Paris once I asked Makhmalbaf who his heroes were – or if he had any. 'First it was Ali,' he said, referring to the first Shi'i Imam known for his chivalry and innocence. Then he added, 'the permanent ascetic.' And he went on, 'Then Che Guevara, the permanent rebel. Then Einstein, Christ, and Buddha. But right now my heroes are little kids, maximum until they reach the first grade – exactly before we start educating them. Kids are the real creatures of the moment. They have no time for prolonged hatred, and need very modest reasons for happiness.' We had come to traffic lights and we had to wait. The sunsets in Paris are always gray. At times I have thought that in Makhmalbaf's cinema I have been looking for the mystery of that magical moment when we trespass the imaginal and porous line separating (and yet connecting) the movie theater from (and thus to) the flickering screen. There is a transgressive ecstasy in that moment that is hard to come by and difficult to convey. More than anything else, I hope in this book I have left at least a trace of that ecstasy, of the joy I have had over so many years of being in the close vicinity of a cinema of festive fury, fresh from the wondrous mind of a rebel alchemist of a defiant happiness.

Published by I.B.Tauris & Co Ltd
in association with
the Iran Heritage Foundation

Long Shot

On the Paradoxical Rise of a National Cinema and the Iconic Making of a Rebel Filmmaker

Mohsen Makhmalbaf is today the single most celebrated filmmaker in the world who has come to complete creative fruition in the immediate context of an Islamic Republic. Other Iranian filmmakers, like Abbas Kiarostami and Amir Naderi, were active and productive long before an Islamic Republic descended upon and dominated the Iranian polity. Many more Iranian filmmakers, like Jafar Panahi and Bahman Qobadi, have received widespread global attention after this Islamic Republic had become an ordinary fact in the annals of its regional history. Only Mohsen Makhmalbaf's name and career coincides with the heydays of the revolutionary crescendo that resulted in the Islamic Republic. This book is dedicated to a reading of this seeming paradox.

First, the simple facts of his life. Born in Tehran on 28 May 1957 to a staunchly religious family, Mohsen Ostad Ali Makhmalbaf grew up in the southern neighborhoods of the Iranian capital. He spent his early childhood in the care of his maternal grandmother and aunt while his mother, Esmat Jam-pour, divorced by his father, Hossein Ostad Ali Makhmalbaf, worked as a nurse. Already married, Makhmalbaf's father had married Esmat Jam-pour in the hope of having a son. Just six days after this marriage was consummated, Hossein Ostad Ali, Makhmalbaf's first wife, found out about her husband's deed and forced him to divorce his second wife – the marriage having lasted just enough for Mohsen Makhmalbaf to be conceived. 'Had it not been for those six blessed days,' Makhmalbaf once told me in jest in New York, 'only God knows what would have happened to Muslims and infidels of this world.'[1]

Makhmalbaf grew up in a religiously devout and politically charged atmosphere in the 1960s. The June 1963 uprising of Ayatollah Khomeini, in which he all but failed to topple the Pahlavi monarchy, constitutes one of his earliest memories. Chiefly responsible for his early religious sensibilities was his maternal grandmother, while his politicization was due to his stepfather, a religiously devout and politically active supporter of Ayatollah Khomeini, whom his mother married soon after Makhmalbaf was born. A mere teenager, in 1972 Makhmalbaf formed his own urban guerrilla group. In 1974 he attacked a police officer, was arrested, put in jail, and brutally tortured. He was not sentenced to death and got away with his life only because he was under age. He remained in prison until 1978, when the revolutionary wave led by Ayatollah Khomeini freed him (having served his full term) and launched his literary and cinematic careers. Soon after his release from Pahlavi prison in 1978, Makhmalbaf married Fatemeh Meshkini, who gave birth to their three children – Samira (or Zeynab, born in 1980), Meysam (or Ayyoub, born in 1981), and Hana (or Khatereh, born in 1988). Fatemeh Meshkini died in a tragic accident in 1992. Makhmalbaf subsequently married Fatemeh Meshkini's sister, Marziyeh Meshkini. Makhmalbaf, his wife Marziyeh, and his three children Samira, Meysam, and Hana now live in Paris. They all make movies.[2]

Three consecutive but inconsequential films – *Tobeh-ye Nasuh/Nasuh's Repentance* (1982), *Este'azeh/Seeking Refuge* (1983), and *Do Chashm-e Bi-Su/Two Sightless Eyes* (1983) – were Mohsen Makhmalbaf's first attempts at filmmaking. By the late 1980s, these early experiments began to yield more fruitful and mature engagements with cinema. *Bycote/Boycott* (1985), *Dastforush/The Peddler* (1986), and *Bicycle-ran/The Cyclist* (1987) are the results of a more serious awareness of the nature and function of cinema as an art form. With *Nobat-e Asheqi/A Time for Love* (1990), *Shab-ha-ye Zayandeh-rud/The Nights of Zayandeh Rud* (1990), *Naseroddin Shah, Actor-e Cinema/Once Upon a Time, Cinema* (1991), and *Honarpisheh/The Actor* (1992), Makhmalbaf entered the most serious stage of his filmmaking, a major contender along with the earlier masters of the Iranian cinema. By this time he could no longer be dismissed as a committed ideologue of the Islamic Republic. Falling into the visual corner of his creative imagination hook, line, and sinker, cinema had entered Makhmalbaf's consciousness and completely transformed him. By the late 1990s, Makhmalbaf's global reputation as a major filmmaker was indisputable. *Salam Cinema* (1994), *Nun va Goldun/Bread and Flowerpot* aka *A Moment of Innocence* (1995), and *Gabbeh* (1995) became trademarks of an Iranian cinema that was now the common staple of major film festivals all over the world. *Sokut/Silence* (1998), *Dar/The Door* (1999) (a short episode in a collection of short films in and about the small island of Kish in the Persian Gulf), *Test-e Demokrasi/Testing Democracy* (2000), and *Kandahar* (2001) consolidated the reputation of Makhmalbaf as a major filmmaker. Makhmalbaf's most recent films – *Sex va Falsafeh/Sex and Philosophy* (2005) and *Faryad-e Morchegan/Scream of the Ants* (2005) – are further indices of his tireless mind, his restless creative soul, always at work in discovering newer visual experimentations.[3]

My interest in Makhmalbaf and his cinema rests precisely in the creative domain defined between his life as a radical rebel who turned to art and the specific terms of his global reception as an artist. In terms domestic to his life as an Iranian artist, I wish to understand the contours of the visual imagery that has made him a global phenomenon. In these terms, I would like to posit and

3 From right: Mohsen Makhmalbaf (age 7), his grandmother, his mother, and sitting on grandmother's lap is Zahra, his younger sister. (Photograph courtesy of Makhmalbaf Film House.)

introduce Makhmalbaf as a post/colonial rebel turned artist and then navigate my way through his films to see in what particular visual vocabulary he has sought to create and craft historical agency for otherwise colonially de-subjected and politically atomized individuals. In short, I wish to read and decipher the communities of collective sentiments he has dreamed in his cinema, and by virtue of which the sparkle of fire that warms his heart and sets his mind creatively aflame shines through the character of the culture he and I call home.

The Making of National Cinemas

Before I address the specific case of Mohsen Makhmalbaf as a rebel filmmaker, I need to place him in the cultural context of Iranian cinema at large. To do so

I will first need to locate the rise of Iranian cinema in the more global configuration of various national cinemas that have emerged over the twentieth century. The rise of a rebel filmmaker in the seemingly paradoxical context of an Islamic Republic points to a more immediate issue of how we understand the appearance of any national cinema. My principal proposition here is that like all other manners of cultural production, national cinemas emerge at moments of national trauma. Here I make a radical distinction between the concocted manufacturing of a 'national cinema' by way of the varied forms of national insignias at the service of a nation-building project (in the same vein as a national airline or a national soccer team), in which case anywhere from Bahrain to Switzerland can have a claim to a national cinema, and the historic emergence of collective traumas at the heart of a national experience (such as a major war, a massive revolution, an anticolonial uprising) that invariably manifest themselves in cultural and aesthetic forms. In this latter respect, very few nations in the world can have a claim to a national cinema – and my suggestion is that Iran is one of them. But first I have to give an outline of the very idea and varied expressions of the phenomenon of 'national cinema.'[4]

The origin of national cinemas as a designated category begins with a Soviet and three European models: Russian Formalism, Italian Neorealism, French New Wave, and German New Cinema. As a category, though, national cinema is a thematic and aesthetic claim that is not exclusively linked to countries that have produced great films and master filmmakers. Though major masters in world cinema with a global reach to their transcultural influences, John Ford, Alfred Hitchcock, or Satyajit Ray have never been identified with any conception of a national cinema that projects generic American, British, or Bengali cinesthetics. Thus nations boasting the possession of great filmmakers does not necessarily amount to their claiming a national cinema.

The mystery of which nations possess and which nations lack national cinemas ultimately rests in the historical evidence that national cinemas emerge out of national traumas and that colonial and imperial countries have never produced a national cinema. The idea of an American cinema is flawed because Hollywood reflects the imperial imagination, the arrested banality of a globalized market and capital, and a bellicose empire that goes with it. It is not possible to talk of a British cinema because on the creative conscience of Great Britain is cauterized the sign of a sustained history of colonial domination of other people – as close as the Irish, as far away as the Indians. One may, however, consider the cinema of David Lean as a particularly powerful visual reckoning with the British imperial past. The French did not have a claim to a national cinema until the social trauma of facing their colonial atrocities in Africa – culminating in the May 1968 uprising. The Germans had no such claim to a national cinema either, until the post-Nazi trauma of German artists beginning to ask themselves how they could send millions of living human beings to gas chambers, and then in return suffer the horrors of the indiscriminate fire-bombing of Dresden by the British and the Americans. Italian Neorealism is a sincere apology sent to the world for the terror that Italian Fascism perpetrated upon it, and then a social reflection on post-war trauma of nation-building in Italy. The unfathomable trauma of the Japanese nuclear holocaust remained at the center of Akira Kurosawa's cinema, single-handedly giving Japan the aesthetic record of the terror that the Americans visited upon them. From the ashes of a catastrophe on a smaller scale than the Jewish Holocaust, Atom Egoyan has crafted a national cinema out of the Armenian genocide, despite the fact that he was born in Cairo and now lives in Toronto. Upon the mass grave of millions of European Jewry, 'Israel' could not create a national cinema (despite the fact that there are a few extraordinary filmmakers who live in that colonial settlement) because the Holocaust industry cashed in on that colossal tragedy to build a colonial state in Palestine on the broken back of Palestinians. Palestinians (denied, denigrated, and destroyed) put a handful of borrowed and broken equipment to work and produced one of the most magnificent national cinemas in modern history.

Several successive national cinemas have followed a similar pattern of national identification to the Soviet, Italian, German, and French cinemas. The Chinese, the Egyptian, the Cuban, the Iranian, and now the Palestinian cinemas are chief among several in the post/colonial world that have either gradually earned (Iran and Palestine) or eventually lost (Egypt) the status of a national cinema.[5] Emergence of national cinemas has a direct correlation to the collective experience of a national trauma. As an art form constitutionally contemporary to our global predicament, cinema has a creative correspondence to conditions of coloniality – both the endemic miseries and the rebellious euphoria caused and conditioned by it.

The first major national cinematic formation was embedded in Soviet socialist realism that emerged in the immediate aftermath of the Russian Revolution of 1917, and dominated world cinema during the 1920s and the 1930s.[6] During the 1920s, a major cinematic culture emerged in the Soviet Union, which in turn gave rise to the aesthetic conception of Russian formalism. At once a radical social revolutionary project and an aesthetic movement, Russian cinema of the 1920s and 1930s generated the astonishing proposition that no revolutionary art was possible without a radical formalist revolution. Sergei Eisenstein emerged as the principal visionary theorist of Soviet cinema. His revolutionary conception of *montage* became by far the most influential aesthetic legacy of Russian cinematic formalism. In one cinematic masterpiece after another – from *Strike* (1924), to *Battleship Potemkin* (1925), *October* (1927), *The General Line* (1928), *Alexander Nevsky* (1938) and *Ivan The Terrible* (1942–46) – Eisenstein mapped out the contours of a revolutionary cinema at once politically engaged and aesthetically adventurous.

Through a process of what he called *shocks and montage*, Eisenstein crafted a cinematic vision that celebrated its infinite staccato capabilities.

Expanding on the ideas of his two predecessors, Lev Kuleshov and Dziga Vertov, Eisenstein paced his way toward a film-truth (what Vertov had called *Kino-Pravda*) that remained influential for much of twentieth century cinema. The dialectical materialism at the root of the Soviet Socialist Revolution soon heavily influenced Eisenstein's manner of editing with effective contrapuntal results. A committed Marxist revolutionary, Eisenstein gave to montage an almost spontaneous dialectical force − fully at the service of the Socialist Revolution. His preference for non-professional actors, who were asked to draw on their own experiences, anticipated much that would later happen in various forms of *realism* in world cinema. Eisenstein's visionary aesthetics soon left behind his political limitations, and Stalin began to lose patience with his cinema, forcing him to leave Russia − first for the USA and then Mexico, where he stayed for almost a decade.

It seems that at the time of major national trauma, cinema becomes far more integral to its social and cultural roots than a mere artistic manifestation of them. The texture of the Soviet cinema that emerged in the immediate aftermath of the Russian Revolution was far more quintessential to moral and intellectual movements present at the time than merely partaking in them. From the historical materialism of Karl Marx to psychoanalytical theories of Sigmund Freud and even the scientific discoveries of his time, Eisenstein's cinema expanded the normative and moral imaginary of the Soviet cinema and connected them to the material basis of a revolution he sought to visualize. This thematic and visual expansion corresponded to the immediate revolutionary project serving the soviet peasantry and the proletariat in whose name it had articulated its thematic and aesthetic ideals. The emergence of a new spectatorship for Soviet cinema (on a massive and unprecedented level) had a major catalytic effect on its expansive cosmovison. Along with a sizable new audience, whereby cinema was taken into the streets and alleys, factories and farms, of history, came substantial governmental funding and other resources, which at once enabled and targeted the Soviet cinema toward specific revolutionary and propaganda purposes.

In the immediate aftermath of World War II in Italy, during the the 1940s and 1950s, a considerable number of films were produced that were gradually designated a globally influential cinema known as *Italian Neorealism*.[7] Real locations shot in realistic long takes, with non-actors given improvisatory liberty to enrich the fantasy of filmmaking with the fact of lived experiences, and a full-bodied topography of the moral and economic problems that post-war Italy faced, became the hallmark of Italian *Neorealism*. The German occupation of *Cinecitta* studios had forced Italian filmmakers to shoot their scenes outside in real locations, thus forcing their cinesthetics toward a far more realistic cinema than was possible in studio filmmaking. Italian Neorealism − perhaps best represented in Vittorio De Sica's *Shoeshine* (1946) and *Umberto D* (1952), and Roberto Rossellini's *Open City* (1945) – connected to literary realism of its own nineteenth-century culture – particularly to the literary *verismo* of Giovanni Verga (1840–1922) – and thus crafted a new kind of *verismo* at once visual and contemporaneous with Italian realities.

By and large, most masterpieces of Italian *Neorealism* have their roots in the national trauma of post-war anxieties. Rossellini's *Roma, città aperta/Open City* (1945) is a hallmark testimony of the Italian national unification in the face of the German Gestapo. It is the central example of a national trauma giving rise to a cinematic vision unprecedented in its immediate context. De Sica's *Sciuscià/Shoeshine* (1946) claims the post-liberation Rome for a future Italy through a depiction of its downtrodden youth; and yet it manages to be a celebration of freedom in midst of chaos and corruption – at once jubilant, realistic, and yet hopeful. De Sica claims Italy – from its anarchic urbanity to the munificent peace of its countryside – for an Italy that can now forget its pains and sufferings and remember itself in peace and with purpose. A masterpiece example of Italian *Neorealism*, the six episodes of Roberto Rossellini's *Paisà/Paisan* (1946) directly narrate the adventures of the Italian liberation forces to expel the Nazi occupation from their homeland. In a stroke of genius, Rossellini began the momentous occasion of extracting life out of the brutalities of a national trauma.

During the 1950s and 1960s, the emergence of such prominent filmmakers as Rainer Werner Fassbinder, Wim Wenders, Werner Herzog, and Margarethe von Trotta brought to full fruition a cinematic adventure in Germany that sought to exorcise the ghost of post-Holocaust German soul-searching in one of the most devastating national traumas of modern history.[8] The German New Cinema emerged in the 1950s in part to address the horrors of a nation that at once gave rise to and suffered from the consequences of a global monstrosity. Almost simultaneously, the French New Wave (*La Nouvelle Vague*) emerged in the course and immediate aftermath of the Algerian war of independence, a national liberation movement that deeply divided French society, forced it to face its brutal colonial legacy, and ultimately led to the widespread social uprisings of 1968.[9] From the intellectual core of the magazine *Cahiers du Cinema* gradually emerged the most prominent young directors – François Truffaut with his *400 Blows* (1959), Jean-Luc Godard with his *Breathless* (1960) – and with them was born the very idea of *auteur* filmmaking.

As German and French cinema was emerging in Europe, the most consequential social revolution in Latin America, the Cuban Revolution of 1952–58, inaugurated a national cinema of astonishing richness and brilliance – again out of the national trauma of a brutalized people rising against tyranny and colonial domination.[10] The birth of Cuban cinema in the 1960s and 1970s is coterminous with the Cuban revolution. In both its revolutionary aspirations and

4   Mohsen Makhmalbaf's mother, Esmat Jam-pour, acting in Makhmalbaf's Do-Chashm-e Bi-su (Two Sightless Eyes, 1984). *Almost all members of Makhmalbaf's family have appeared in his films. (Photograph: Ahmad Tala'i; courtesy of Makhmalbaf Film House.)*

its decidedly anti-Hollywood thematic and aesthetic thrust, Cuban cinema reflected the hopes and aspirations of the newly liberated nation. The emergence of Tomás Gutiérrez Alea and Humberto Solás as two major revolutionary filmmakers placed Cuban cinema on the world map. As a revolutionary art form, the significance of Cuban cinema was not limited to that country alone and soon assumed both symbolic and catalytic significance throughout Latin America. The Cuban Institute of Art and Film Industry emerged as the principal organ of the new Cuban cinema almost immediately after the collapse of the mercenary regime of Batista. The cinematic education of Tomas Gutiérrez Alea in Rome in the 1950s brought the gift of Italian Neorealism directly to the fertile imagination of revolutionary Cuba.

By far the most promising national cinema of global significance today is the Palestinian cinema, deeply rooted in the trials and tribulations of a brutalized nation. Beginning with Mustapha Abu Ali's *They Don't Exist* (1974) in the early 1970s, culminating with Michel Khleifi in the 1980s and now coming to full fruition with Elia Suleiman in the 1990s to the present, Palestinian cinema has been one of the most creative sites of the Palestinian national liberation movement against an intransigent colonial domination.[11] What is particularly powerful about Palestinian cinema is the centrality of a national trauma, the Palestinian *Nakba/Catastrophe*, the enormity of whose historical significance simply cannot be told, and in the creative crisis of that impossibility the Palestinian cinema is born and thriving.

While in the case of Chinese cinema the emergence of the so-called 'fifth-generation' of filmmakers was a direct result of the trauma of the post-Cultural Revolution that brought such directors as Zhang Yimou and Chen Kaige to global attention, in the case of Iranian cinema it was the trauma of a bloody revolution and a devastating war that ultimately coagulated a national cinema.[12] In forming a manner of national cinema, Iranian cinema of the 1980s and 1990s has a remarkable similarity to the rise of Italian Neorealism of the 1940s and 1950s in the immediate aftermath of World War II, when a devastated country began to reconcile with the miseries and banalities inflicted upon it by fascism. In the case of the Iranian cinema, despite its earlier aesthetic and thematic roots, as well as the pre-eminence of a few of its current masters in the early 1960s, it was not until after the Islamic Revolution of 1979 and the start of the devastating Iran–Iraq war (1980–88) that it emerged as a major artistic adventure – revealing both its deep wounds and the varied measures of healing them.

The Rise of Iranian National Cinema

The global celebration of Iranian cinema that began during the last two decades of the twentieth century and has continued unabated well into the first decade of the twenty-first has consistently pointed to a seeming paradox: how could a national cinema of such rich diversity and power flourish in a time of severe theocratic control and systematic censorship of art and culture?[13] To be sure, Iranian cinema had attracted the critical attention of film festivals long before the advent of the Islamic Revolution in the late 1970s. Such prominent Iranian directors as Daryush Mehrju'i, Bahram Beiza'i, Amir Naderi, and Bahman Farmanara had successfully screened their films to critical acclaim throughout the 1960s and the 1970s. The origin of the Iranian cinema goes all the way back to the opening decade of the twentieth century, and as early as the 1950s pioneering filmmakers like Farrokh Ghaffari, Forough Farrokhzad, and Ebrahim Golestan were making films that were featured in major film festivals.[14] But it was not until after the Islamic Revolution of 1977–79 that Iranian cinema became a major staple of film festivals and commercial releases the world over. It was after the Islamic Revolution that the pioneering figures of Iranian cinema like Daryush Mehrju'i, Amir Naderi, Bahram Beiza'i, Abbas Kiarostami, and Mas'ud Kimiya'i were joined by a new generation of filmmakers that included such prominent members as Mohsen Makhmalbaf, Ja'far Panahi, and Marziyeh Meshkini. And it soon gave birth to yet a third generation of directors like Samira Makhmalbaf, Bahman Qobadi, Babak Payami, Mohammad Shirvani, and Ramin Bahrani.

The Islamic Revolution of 1979 and the devastating Iran–Iraq war (1980–88) that followed it do not posit a question but in fact present an answer to the rise of Iranian cinema.[15] It is not *despite* the Islamic Revolution and the republic that succeeded it but in fact *because* of them that we can have a causal insight into the rise to global prominence of Iranian cinema. Despite a brutal censorial policy, the repressive organs of the Islamic Republic are incapable of stifling the creative energy let loose by the Islamic Revolution itself to address the political and moral issues at the root of that cataclysmic event.

Within the censorial limits of the Islamic Republic, what social, economic, cultural, or political forces combined to facilitate the birth of what many observers believe is the most significant national cinema in recent memory? To reverse the proverbial expression, the road to the paradise of Iranian cinema was paved with bad intentions. The official banning of foreign films, of Hollywood in particular, will go a long way in explaining how the Islamic censorship had the unanticipated consequence of creating a considerable domestic market for critically acclaimed films. Upon its success, the Islamic Revolution institutionalized one of the severest forms of political opposition to hegemonic presence of American and Western European art in Iran. From its roots in the ideological articulations by Jalal Al-e Ahmad, Ali Shari'ati, Morteza Motahhari, and above all Ayatollah Khomeini, the Islamic Revolution had a claim to an Iranian and Islamic authenticity against the Pahlavi monarchy's (1926–79) assumptions of state-sponsored modernity. A return to narrative devices and artistic expressions local to the Iranian culture, and yet with an eye to globalizing their appeal, became paramount in the gradually articulated post-revolutionary aesthetics. To be sure, prominent pre-Revolutionary filmmakers like Bahram Beiza'i had a long-standing interest in pre-modern Iranian performing arts, such as *Ta'ziyeh* (Shi'i passion play) and *Pardeh-dari* (public story-telling with visual aids), long before the advent of the revolution. But the ideological predicates of the Islamic Revolution gave added momentum to that return to native sources of visual and performing arts.

Serious demographic changes in the composition of the society at large gave a ready and enthusiastic audience for the rise of Iranian cinema. The Iranian population increased from about 40 million in the mid-1970s to about 70 million in the mid-1990s. The decline of the infant mortality rate, with an absence of any significant increase in the average life expectancy, resulted in an overwhelmingly young population, with close to 60 per cent below the age of 25. The overwhelming concentration of the young population is thus primarily in elementary and high schools. Fewer than 10 per cent of annual high-school graduates are absorbed into the Iranian university system, public and private; about 250,000 students out of three million in 1997. The nature and disposition of the Iranian economy, 85 per cent oil-based and thus capital-intensive and not labor-intensive, does not allow for sizable incorporation of these young people into the job market. Millions of dollars in surplus income from oil revenue in the late 1990s under President Khatami's administration were budgeted for job training, in the feeble hope that it would boost the available amount of skilled labor, but to no significant change in the overall composition of the national economy. If we were to add to this picture the catastrophic consequences of the eight-year war with Iraq (1980–88), with millions of casualties and incapacitated war veterans, we will have a picture of the social predicament in which the contemporary Iranian cinema emerged. A significant number of prominent filmmakers, such as Mohsen Makhmalbaf and Ebrahim Hatami Kia, made their initial impact by addressing these social conditions. They could do so with a minimum of official censorship because they themselves had solid revolutionary credentials and their audience had put their lives on the line for the cause of the revolution. Sympathetic revolutionaries were now among the high-ranking officials of the Islamic Republic and as a result these films had an already positive reception within official circles.[16]

Throughout the 1980s and 1990s cinema emerged as the single most socially relevant cultural production, a function almost exclusive to poetry in the decades before the Islamic Revolution. There was an immediacy to the issues that Iranian filmmakers depicted, whether in the documentaries of Kamran Shirdel, the feature films of Mohsen Makhmalbaf, or the war movies of Ebrahim Hatami-Kia. The almost exclusive control of the press by the government until the death of Ayatollah Khomeini in 1989 had made visual and performing arts the only viable forum for social concerns. After the death of Ayatollah Khomeini, the theocratic control over the press began to loosen up and by the time Khatami was elected president in 1997 an atmosphere of unprecedented press freedom blossomed. The result was that in the course of the student uprising in the summer of 1999, the press was far more aggressive in addressing social issues than cinema. Courageous journalists like Akbar Ganji and Abdollah Nuri risked their lives in exposing the abuses of power in governmental agencies. They in effect forced the confession of the Ministry of Information that their agents were directly responsible for the serial murder of some leading secular intellectuals. But filmmakers soon caught up with events. Mas'ud Kimiya'i in his *Protest* (2000), Mohsen Makhmalbaf in his *Testing Democracy* (2000), and Bahman Farmanara in his *Smell of Camphor, Fragrance of Jasmine* (2000) all addressed the emerging social concerns of the Khatami presidency.

The parliamentary election of February 2000 was a threshold in the rise of a democratic movement in Iran. With the reformists now controlling the legislative branch of the government, and with Khatami as president, the only remaining institutions of the theocracy were the judiciary and the office of the Supreme Leader. In collaboration with two other undemocratic institutions in the fabric of the Islamic Republic, namely the Council of Guardians and the Expediency

Council, the conservative front has been relentless in thwarting the democratic movement. Soon after it convened upon its February 2000 landmark triumph, the parliament sought to enact a press law that would loosen governmental control. Ayatollah Khamenei, the Supreme Leader, used his veto power to prevent that piece of critical legislation. The result was the continued repression of the press, and yet another chance for Iranian filmmakers to address social issues. This they did with remarkable tenacity under the patronage of Ataollah Mohajerani, then the Minister of Culture. President Khatami himself, in fact, made his liberal reputation during his tenure as the Minister of Culture in the course of the presidency of Rafsanjani. Much of the success of Iranian cinema in the 1990s was at the time that Khatami was the Minister of Culture. Thus, despite severe official censorship, many high-ranking officials of the Islamic Republic have been both sympathetic and instrumental in the success of Iranian cinema.

Iranian filmmakers have nevertheless had an uphill battle fighting against one of the most atrocious censorship apparatuses in history. As a rule, Iranian filmmakers have to submit their script for official permission, with no guarantee that when the film is actually produced that permission will continue to be valid. On the pretext that sex and violence are not to be shown in films, much artistic creativity is curtailed and thwarted. Women's bodies are particular objects of severe censorship in Iranian cinema. Moments of adult intimacy are virtually impossible to film. Iranian filmmakers have had to resort at times to ingenious ways of suggesting physical intimacy. Criticism of the government and the state apparatus, or challenging the official ideology of the regime and the state religion, are all forbidden. None of these though has succeeded in preventing the rise to global attention of a magnificent national cinema. Iranian filmmakers have in effect internalized the terms of official tolerance and worked them into their creative process. They do, of course, regularly up the ante in both political and cultural terms. Ja'far Panahi's *The Circle* (2000) was a pioneering effort in addressing the two forbidden issues of prostitution and political prisoners in one brilliant move. His *Crimson Gold* (2003) was an incisive exposé of brutal class differences consolidated after the 'Islamic' Revolution. Bahman Qobadi's *A Time for Drunken Horses* (2000) for the first time placed an Iranian Kurd behind his exceptionally creative camera, addressing the most debilitating predicament of an ethnicized minority. Mohsen Makhmalbaf's *Kandahar* (2001) addressed the status of women in Afghanistan and by extension in other parts of the Muslim world. Earlier, Samira Makhmalbaf's *The Apple* was a damning condemnation of Iranian patriarchy. The same is true of Marziyeh Meshkini's *The Day I Became a Woman* (2000). Usually these films are not screened in Iran until they have won international acclaim, at which point they are given very limited theatrical release. *Faramushi/Forgetfulness*, Makhmalbaf's first feature film after *Kandahar*, was banned from the very beginning by the government refusing him permission at the script level – ultimately forcing Makhmalbaf to leave his homeland, reside in Paris, and do most of his shootings in Tajikistan, Afghanistan, and India.

Iranian cinema caught the world by surprise because the world had already decided and sealed the fate of Iranian culture through the prism of what it understood from an Islamic Revolution – an angry and defiant crowd saying no to a military dictatorship. What the world now sees and celebrates in Iranian cinema is less a contradiction of what it understood of the Islamic Revolution than a confirmation of what it failed to see in that cataclysmic event. The Islamic Revolution was a cry for freedom, sounded from the pulpit of an outdated theocracy. Both the theocracy and the Islamic Republic that it gave birth to were (and are) the obsolete metaphysics of some dead and deadening certainties. But the defiance of the injustice that they articulated in their medieval terms was (and is) not obsolete. They are familiar the world over. In its elegant simplicity, Iranian cinema conceals a rich poetic of resistance to power, and a will to justice. This cinema is the aesthetic rise of taking a culture to task for all the promises it has given, all the hope that it continues to nourish.

My way of accessing the particularities of the paradox that goes into the making of Iranian cinema (as a particularly potent mode of national cinema) is by way of concentrating on one particular Iranian filmmaker, arguably the most globally celebrated artist to have emerged in post-revolutionary Iran with a solid commitment to Islamic Revolution – being the only Iranian filmmaker with a radical revolutionary background, having raised arms against the Pahlavi regime, been imprisoned and tortured in its dungeons, freed by the revolutionaries, and subsequently having served it with full conviction, before he lost hope and turned against its tyrannical institutionalization. Makhmalbaf's prolonged personification of a rebel filmmaker is not limited to his having once been a rebel and then turned into a filmmaker. A rebellious disposition is definitive to his creative character and constitutional to his cinematic culture. In his restless character and culture, he is always on the run, and as such at the cross-current paths of art and politics – come to think of it, the very first time that I saw him in Locarno he was running, running from the Piazza Grande toward the Press Court – and for no apparent reason; and ever since I scarce have a memory of our conversations together except both of us walking and talking, at times having no clue where we were headed. He is something of a peripatetic filmmaker, very much the way Aristotle was a peripatetic philosopher – the philosopher who walked and taught at the same time. Makhmalbaf too is always on the move, from Iran to Afghanistan, from Afghanistan to Tajikistan, Pakistan, India, Turkey, all over the world. The same mobility of the spirit defines his restless and indefatigable cinema – jumping from genre to genre, from location to location, from subject to subject, from cause to consequences, as if he is running from something, or toward something else. Makhmalbaf is a troubadour, a traveling singer and songwriter, though he likes to show and tell what he sees and sings. Is that why he and I have always found ourselves quoting from Sepehri's *Traveler* to each other?

> The night had descended now.
> The light was on.
> They were having tea.
> — 'Why do you feel so sad?
> You seem to be lonely.'
> — 'Oh yes, Lonely, you have
> No clue how lonely!
> — 'I believe
> You are afflicted by that hidden vein of colors.'
> — 'What does "afflicted" mean?'
> — 'To be in love—
> Just think how lonely would the little fish be
> Were it to be afflicted by the blue of the vast seas.'
> — 'What a delicate and sad thought!'
> ...
> 'One has to be afflicted
> Otherwise the murmuring whisper
> That always oscillates between two spoken words
> Will be wasted.'

The Two Polar Opposites

The seeming paradox at the heart of the contemporary Iranian cinema and its location in the current Iranian political culture cannot and should not be explained away, because it is precisely in terms constitutional to that paradox that its significance and appeal will have to be understood. As a national cinema of global significance, Iranian cinema carries within itself the paradoxical roots of its origin and destination. The paradox speaks of the dialectical outcome of the sets of oppositional forces that are competing for dominance in the post-revolutionary Iranian culture at large. This competition – discursive and ideological at times, physically violent at others – is the clearest sign of the final demise of the cultural disposition of public intellectuals in the Pahlavi period and the rise of the new terms of public engagement with the fate of the nation. This epistemic rupture, now in the making for about a quarter of a century, has definitively changed the character and disposition of the Iranian creative culture and the significance of Mohsen Makhmalbaf as a filmmaker and public intellectual who will have to be understood in terms domestic to this culture.

With the collapse of the Pahlavi regime in the course of the Islamic Revolution of 1979, the cosmopolitan culture that was in fact instrumental in toppling it was ideologically outmaneuvered and politically repressed. Mohsen Makhmalbaf represents the rise of an 'Islamic' set of aesthetics and political sensibilities initially squarely at the service of the Islamic Revolution. Prominent members of the Iranian artistic community and literati were immediately persecuted and punished for either their active affiliation with the Pahlavi regime or else because of their cosmopolitan (and thus non-denominational) disposition, which the Islamic Republic would not tolerate. The rise of Mohsen Makhmalbaf as a filmmaker and public intellectual coincides with a brutal, systematic, and far-reaching repression of intellectuals and artists at odds with the Islamic Republic and its theocratic disposition. After the death of the founder of the Islamic Republic, Ayatollah Khomeini, and the start of a reform movement under the presidency of Mohammad Khatami, dissident intellectuals had a slightly better condition under the reign of the Islamic Republic. Despite this, to a measurable degree the character and culture of the Iranian artistic and intellectual disposition changed forever after a period of almost quarter of a century of radical revolutionary agenda and severe political pressure that accompanied it. Makhmalbaf made much of his earlier reputation as a filmmaker and public intellectual at the service of the Islamic Republic, before he too – as he began to find and articulate his own voice and vision – became a victim of it.

The defeat of the cosmopolitan culture by the revolutionary Islamists does not mean that all the ideologues of the Islamic Republic or its publicly celebrated intellectuals were identical in their moral and intellectual dispositions. The paradoxical rise of Iranian cinema to global celebration – competing forces thwarting and advancing it at one and the same time – points to two diametrically opposed forces domestic to the Islamic Revolution and now vying for prominence over the body and soul of the Iranian post-revolutionary culture. The world at large remains oblivious to this cosmic clash because it can only see one side of it and is unable to read the other. No two terms, ideas, sentiments, or institutions represent the polar opposites of this internal paradox better than the two prominent intellectuals who have emerged in the aftermath of the Islamic Revolution in Iran and assumed national and international stature: one of them is Mohsen Makhmalbaf, the other Abdolkarim Soroush.[17] Soon after the success of the Islamic Revolution, Abdolkarim Soroush emerged as the most prolific public intellectual of his generation, publishing a succession of very learned essays and books on a variety of subjects, most famously on what he called *Qabz-o-Bast-e Teoric-e Shari'at/The Theoretical Expansion and Contraction of Religious Law*. His principal argument is that historical circumstances and hermeneutic disposition of scholars can potentially alter the juridical articulation of religious laws and thus make them variable from one generation to another – a rather modest theoretical proposition which nevertheless made an extraordinary impact on the overtly anxious custodians of the Islamic Republic. Soroush suddenly emerged as the most prominent member of a new category called 'religious intellectuals,' at odds with the Islamic Republic and yet paradoxically committed to it. Thus, in the immediate aftermath of the Islamic Revolution, both Makhmalbaf and Soroush became the two most famous public intellectuals of their generation not only at odds with the Islamic Republic, but also at odds with each other (and yet equally paradoxically reflecting the mirror image of one another). As such, Makhmalbaf and Soroush (both in their similarities and their differences) represent the cataclysmic consequences of the Islamic Revolution in Iran and mark a radical epistemic shift in the Iranian moral and intellectual imagination.

At the height of their success and reputation, Mohsen Makhmalbaf and Abdolkarim Soroush have effectively left behind the patently cosmopolitan disposition of their predecessors and launched their respective projects from the Islamic angle of their vision. However, that angle both opens and closes their similarity. In their divergence dwells the quintessential paradox at the heart of contemporary Iranian culture – a paradox that gives it its effervescent nature and creative disposition.

In their defiant character and dissident disposition, both Makhmalbaf and Soroush are the moral and intellectual by-products of the Islamic Revolution, which was launched to topple a monarchy squarely at the service of imperial and colonial interests in the Iranian market, as well as its cheap labor and natural resources. The Islamic Revolution and the Republic it engendered ultimately failed to secure either the Iranian national interest or sustain economic autonomy from the overwhelming globalization of capital. Political resistance to the classical colonization of Iranians as the potentially sovereign subjects of their own historical destiny, which in effect amounts to the atomization of the individual in the globalizing project of capital, soon assumed metaphysical (other-worldly) proportions in Soroush's case and artistic (aesthetically emancipatory) terms in Makhmalbaf's. A critical reconstitution of the colonial subject in the creative act charted out Makhmalbaf's emergence as an historical agent, with himself carrying the rest of his nation out of their post/colonial predicament. For both Makhmalbaf and Soroush, as two Muslim intellectuals, the question of moral and political agency was critical in a post-revolutionary era that had to articulate the terms of its cultural resistance – for one artistic and for the other intellectual – to the planetary domination of capital and its increasingly globalizing culture. Their mutual success and failure, yet to be assayed, points to a more enduring problem in how political resistance to globalization can assume a degree of cultural autonomy.

It is crucial to trace in Makhmalbaf's cinema, from the earliest films to the latest, the path that has now become evident toward an aesthetic emancipation of the colonial subject and the creative autonomy of an historical agent that is always contingent on it. The global attraction to his cinema is because of this creative mutation of *the verbal entrapment in the possible* into *a visual release toward the ideal*, a radical sublation in which we can see pollinating the terms of a global re/subjection of the colonial subject far beyond the territorial limits of an Islamic Republic. For all its debilitating entrapments in an Islamic imposition, Makhmalbaf's art has had the critical element of having arisen from the very depth of his society, the perils and promises, impediments and aspirations, of his nation at the tip of his pen, around the frame of his camera. Even in its crudest moments, Makhmalbaf's art has restored dignity of place to the impoverished segments of his nation, organicity to its intellectuals. Makhmalbaf is drawn increasingly away from the revolution, its ideological convictions, and even its metaphysical certainties. What he sees in his characters, which he portrays with unflinching realism, is the persistence of moral, cultural, and social malaise beyond any political predicament or ideological cure. Makhmalbaf's revolutionary outbreak of a moral emancipation from the predicaments of his culture are powerful precisely because and not despite these prejudices. As best exemplified in his (perhaps) absolute masterpiece *A Moment of Innocence* (1997), when history and memory begin to change place and tango to a different tune than they are wont, the open-ended nature of Makhmalbaf's cinematic cross-coding of the evident posits the most stubborn of all realities pertinent to his society as factually fungible. Thus the very claim of realism to democratic hermeneutics, which ordinarily thrives on strategically mobile interplay of tropes, becomes definitive to the poetic playfulness of his most mature cinema.

The difference that I detect and suggest here between Makhmalbaf and Soroush is the difference between two modes of creative emancipation not just from the claws of a godforsaken theocracy but far more importantly from the colonial trappings of agential de-subjection – where the more the colonial subject seeks to liberate his/her mind and soul the more they are trapped in a dialogical conversation with the very condition of coloniality. The Islamic Revolution of 1979 politically liberated, but epistemicly trapped even deeper, the Iranian political culture from, and yet in, the paradoxical predicaments of Enlightenment modernity. As I have documented the phenomenon in some extended detail elsewhere,[18] the very idea of an 'Islamic ideology' further entraps the doctrinal foundation of the faith into a locked interlocution with 'the West,' a fictive nemesis that is as much the figment of its own collective imagination as the colonial fabrication of a mighty abstraction. My argument is that while Soroush's monumental attempt at resolving the paradoxes of Islam in modernity has in fact plunged his ancestral faith even deeper into the dialectical paradoxes of Enlightenment modernity in its colonial shadows, the creative outbursts that filmmakers like Makhmalbaf represent posit a far more emancipatory track out of that cul-de-sac. However learned and erudite, Soroush's metaphysical interface between what he continues to call in a grand metanarrative 'Islam and the West' cannot but further plunge the metaphoric tropes of his faith into a dialectical interlocution with an abstraction ('the West') that has long since lost its historical claim to authority, authenticity, or moral and normative primacy. Meanwhile, not by any sustained intellectual engagement or theoretical design, but by virtue of a creative effervescence over which they have no total control or awareness, Makhmalbaf and filmmakers like him are busy with a far more defiant semiotic rebellion against the de-subjected servitude of the postcolonial person.[19]

As with all other creative and critical thinkers and practitioners, Makhmalbaf and Sorush do not have complete control or even awareness that in their respective works they are dealing with epistemic and aesthetic parameters beyond the limits of any specific (Islamic) culture. From the vantage point of two revolutionary intellectuals, they are both seeking moral and political agency for a colonially de-subjected community of moral sentiments and normative behavior. In doing so, while Soroush is engaged in a conversation with the European Enlightenment modernity (decades after its global implosion), Makhmalbaf is critically oblivious to it – and yet both are charting the moral disposition of their nation in dialectical opposition to each other. They have both, of course, long since lost hope in the promises of the revolution they once wholeheartedly endorsed, and are now active in opposition to its political beneficiaries. However, in their mutual opposition they posit two different post/colonial responses to a radically more significant issue than their respective turn against the Islamic Republic. One (Soroush) is seeking moral and political agency via a *hermeneutic* encounter he posits between Islam and Enlightenment modernity, whereas the other (Makhmalbaf) configures a manner of moral and political agency that is navigated *artistically*. Between the *metaphysical* disposition of Abdolkarim Soroush and the *aesthetic* temperament of Mohsen Makhmalbaf there is a dialectical space on which the paradoxical nature of contemporary Iranian culture is mapped out and assayed.

My principal interest in Makhmalbaf's cinema, and the point of this book, is detecting and arguing precisely this creative restoration of historical agency in the post/colonial subject. I have no grand metaphysical trust in that subject – nor do I believe it to be sovereign. But I do consider its strategic emancipation from the domain of its colonial predicament critical for any course of permanent revolutionary disposition. I have been attracted to Makhmalbaf's cinema far beyond its political origins in an Islamic Republic or its aesthetic vicissitude by Makhmalbaf's own genuine but still whimsical distractions to social and political issues tangential to his art as a filmmaker. My principal theoretical question in this book is rooted in a much more enduring concern in the fate of the post/colonial subject, its revolutionary disposition, political prowess, cultural agency, and emancipatory possibilities. I am principally interested in Makhmalbaf because he was a rebel – a revolutionary, an urban guerrilla who took up arms against tyranny – who turned into an artist, but who is now in the aftermath of the post-9/11 Afghan War back to his social and political concerns – not having made a film for over five years, a remarkable record in his otherwise crowded career. As a rebel, Makhmalbaf emerged from the very depth of his society, with endemic poverty, religious convictions, political dogmatism, and a rather permanent revolutionary disposition. As a filmmaker, Makhmalbaf sustained a consistently radical temperament in his creative urges. These two qualifications are critical in any creative defiance one might detect or articulate in a post/colonial subject. The purpose of this book is to navigate the contours of Makhmalbaf's creative outbursts – from his earliest films that were in fact at the service of the Islamic Republic, to his latest that are after a far more visceral aesthetic disposition – all set against the endemic entrapments of a post/colonial subject otherwise unable to say 'I' without uttering a contradiction.

The Cosmopolis and its Shadows

The paradoxical rise of Iranian cinema to global celebration is predicated not only on oppositional forces integral to the contemporary Iranian culture, but also in terms evident in the portrayal of Tehran and all its cinematic opposites. In the universe of sentiments identified with the Iranian capital as a cosmopolis, Tehran is subconsciously contrasted with a subterranean oasis that it dreams in Iranian cinema. If Soroush and Makhmalbaf represent the two polar opposites of the post-revolutionary Iranian critical and creative culture (one entrapping it, the other liberating it), Tehran and its reflective shadows in the Iranian cinematic imagination correspond to the topographical landscape of that culture.

Tehran is the city where Makhmalbaf was born and in which he came to full religious, political, and creative maturity. The cinematic topography of the Iranian capital is cast on the very soul of Makhmalbaf's creative consciousness. Between this site and the binary sentiment that separates his creative energy from Soroush's persistent metaphysical predicament, Makhmalbaf's cinema has creatively visualized and narrated itself. To understand his cinema, we must trace the binary opposition of these enduring sentiments to the cosmopolitan disposition of that urban site.

The Tehran of Mohsen Makhmalbaf's birth and breeding is mapped around several major squares and divided along its vertical axis, coming down from the southern slopes of the Alborz Mountain to the north and spreading itself lazily south toward the lowlands. The north of the city is more modern, and the south more ancient. Citizens of Tehran have a soft spot for public parks, where anything from an innocent family picnic to aggressive drug pushers, from heated political debates to bewildered prostitutes may on occasion be caught in one glance. The mayor of Tehran, Gholam Hossein Karbaschi, until his fall from grace in spring 1998, had become something of a legendary figure in the 1990s for his aggressive policies of creating public spaces from abandoned lots. He was able effectively to eradicate much of the cultural divide that had for long separated the north and south of the city by seeking to unify it around common definitions of public spaces – parks, libraries, museums, shopping complexes, etc. But despite Karbaschi's imaginative, albeit at times heavy-handed, projects, the city still carried its tormented historical memory of a radical division between its northern and southern claims and climes.

Tehran, bloodied by the grass-root revolutionary mobilization in the late 1970s, dispirited by the puritanical reign of Ayatollah Khomeini and the long and dark years of the Iran–Iraq war in the 1980s, now boasting more than 12 million residents, seemed hesitantly to regain its urban vitality in the 1990s, as it was getting ready to inaugurate the presidency of Mohammad Khatami. After the Arab oil embargo of 1973, in which Mohammad Reza Pahlavi did not participate, annual income from Iranian crude oil reached an unprecedented level, some 20 billion US dollars a year. A good portion of that income resulted in a substantial increase in the size and substance of the Iranian modern bourgeoisie. This in turn became materially evident in a rising urban vitality in the 1970s. A systemic influx of the peasantry into the city gave an atmosphere of fervor and zest to the capital. Much of the migrant peasantry was absorbed into the workforce, but many more could not make it into the institutional fabric of the rising urbanity and were living in shanty houses in the vicinity of the capital. Those who did make it into the workforce contributed to a noticeable change in the demographic composition of the city. When in 1974 Mohsen Makhmalbaf formed his own band of urban guerrillas in the southern part of Tehran, he had every reason to believe that a substantial revolutionary support would come his way – but that was not to be.

Tehran of the 1970s was a rich and fulfilling urban environment for those who had made it. Movie theaters and cafés, bookstores and restaurants, colleges and shopping districts, a crazed traffic and a labyrinth of new highways wove together the fabric of a cosmopolitan urbanity. With a population of about five million inhabitants in the mid-1970s, Tehran was the dreamland of the nation at large. Every year some 100,000 high-school graduates participated in a national entrance examination to compete for only 10,000 seats that the entire Iranian university system could offer. Those who were smart and/or lucky enough to make it were particularly fortunate if they were accepted at the prestigious Tehran University, which was the Mecca of young Iranian students from all over the country – Sorbonne, Oxford, and Harvard all put together. An impressive array of bookstores lined up in front of Tehran University was a major point of attraction for Tehran-based intellectuals, literati, and their young admirers and followers. This row of large and small bookstores, ranging from Amir Kabir – a major conglomerate – to modest bookstands, stood five-blocks strong right in front of Tehran University on (what was then called) Shah Reza Avenue. Persian translations of literary and critical texts from American, European, Latin American, Asian, and African sources were on display and in demand – Steinbeck, Sartre, Che Guevara, Gandhi, and Fanon were the common staple. Original Persian works of fiction were equally popular – Sadeq Hedayat, Sadeq Chubak, Ebrahim Golestan, Simin Daneshvar, Mahmoud Dowlatabadi, and Houshang Golshiri all came together. In the vicinity of these bookstores were a whole slew of art exhibitions, playhouses, and movie theaters. *Talar-e Rudaki*, the Rudaki Hall, was the crowning achievement of this cultural urbanity. Here the annual Tehran Film Festival, along with European opera, Russian ballet, and American Pop made the scene at once artistically exciting and yet rubbing the Iranian upper middle class too closely against the deeply resentful poverty of the southern part of the city – precisely at the time that Mohsen Makhmalbaf had already landed in the Pahlavi prison for having raised arms against the reigning monarchy.

Attending these cultural icons of a cosmopolitan urbanity were thousands of college students from Tehran and the provinces, negotiating their time between attending college, working full time, and catering to their political activities. With civil servants and factory workers, young urban professionals and military personnel, Tehran was composed of classes and dispositions representing the nation at large. By the end of the 1970s, a combination of Pahlavi corruption, social unrest, ideological mobilization, and religious agitation culminated in the Islamic Revolution of 1979. While the smoke screen of the US hostage crisis of 1979–80 was diverting everybody's attention, the ideologues of the Islamic Revolution took their cue from Ayatollah Khomeini, drafted an Islamic constitution and founded a theocracy, brutally silencing all other alternatives. This dark winter of discontent turned out to be the bright spring of Makhmalbaf's freedom. He came out of jail, let loose to cultivate his creative career precisely at a moment when Iranians as a nation – Makhmalbaf included – plunged deeply into the subterranean dungeons of a theocracy. He took advantage of his revolutionary credentials to begin his literary and cinematic career precisely at a time when the masters of his chosen craft were paralyzed by the censorial policies of the theocracy he had helped to bring to power, and now endorsed by propagating its metaphysical underpinnings – a phase and aspect of his early cinema that can be categorically cut off from his creative career without much being lost, for there is a lot there to be regretted.

As Makhmalbaf started his creative career in earnest, the 1980s was a decade of sacred rage – when from the mountain retreat of Jamaran to the north of the city Ayatollah Khomeini ruled over Tehran with an iron fist, reminiscent of Calvin's

Geneva in the 1550s. Throughout the 1980s, every day busloads of mesmerized admirers and entranced devotees, young soldiers on their way to the battlefield of the Iran–Iraq war and the families of those who had already perished there, would all drive up north to the slopes of Alborz Mountain to pay their respects to the aging sovereign and receive his blessings and revolutionary instructions. By the late 1980s, when much of the world's attention was diverted by the Salman Rushdie affair, Khomeini managed to resolve a major constitutional crisis that faced the succession to his autocracy. By the time the revolution was successfully institutionalized and the Iran–Iraq war over, Khomeini dead and his successors dividing up his charismatic legacy, Tehran as the very soul of the nation, flattened in its spirit, was ready to rise. By the time Khomeini died in 1989, Makhmalbaf had also buried all his political devotions to a religious ideology, exorcised his pious anxieties in such films as *Nasuh's Repentance* (1982) and *Two Sightless Eyes* (1983), and was about to embark on a far more joyous ride of his cinematic career – where eventually a poetic realism would replace his political fervor.

On 21 June 1990 a major earthquake devastated northern Iran. Some 40,000 people were reported killed in the disaster. A few days later, Abbas Kiarostami took his Spartan camera crew to the wasted landscape and started shooting what later became the second of his celebrated Koker trilogy, *And Life Goes On* (1992).[20] In it, Kiarostami, at the height of his visual poetics, excavated the particulars of hope from a universal site of despair. In something of a miraculous way, that film was a premonition of what would happen in Iran of the 1990s, center-staged in the capital of all its hopes and fears.

On the surface of its veiled apparition, Tehran of the 1990s exuded a quieted down version of the overwhelming fear that had been visited upon it, a muted violence waiting upon its soul. Men were hurried and distracted, women veiled and preoccupied. There was an eerie silence about public parks and movie houses, bookstores and theaters. Even in the suburbs, where the foothills of Alborz Mountain were turned into recreational spots, full of open-air cafés and restaurants, there was an uneasy air of emptied silence about the surroundings (this is July 1997, when I spent a month in Tehran roaming its north and south with Makhmalbaf). No music, no noise, not even children seemed to be breathing a sound of defiance. In downtown areas, huge murals of the religious leaders dwarfed the height and compromised the character of the passers-by, while revolutionary graffiti dared the normalization of life. One entire side of an apartment building would be painted with the US flag, captioned with a prominent 'Death to America.' Names of streets, highways, squares, and public parks were all reminding the citizens of the martyrs who had given their lives for the cause of the revolution and the war that had followed it. An officially pronounced Qur'anic Arabic was categorically imposed on the soft-spoken whisperish Persian of the public. Religious commemorations were loud and clear.

Civil ceremonies were nowhere in sight. The city was wrapped in a religious aura. Tehran was Qomified. Qur'anic recitations broadcast from television and radio, mosque minarets, and their courtyards – a thick yellowish smog covered the noisy atmosphere of the impatient clutter in and about the city. Buses were impossible to ride. You could only grab cab drivers' attentions by yelling at the top of your voice, in a rapid Tehrani Persian that would test the limit of your speaking speed in combining the code-name of your destination and three times the official fare. Veil, violence, and martyrdom underlined congestion, greed, and despair, and painted the city dark, dense, and agitated, making it up to look crowded, cruel, and indifferent.

The desolate landscape of Amir Naderi's *Water, Wind, Dust* (1989) responds to this atmosphere of post-revolutionary predicament. With his usual fury, Amir Naderi in one mesmerizing sweep wipes out all signs of humanity and urbanity in the film. Filmed in its entirety in the desert, under unforgiving sandstorms, *Water, Wind, Dust* in sound and sight captures the drama of desolation and despair that was the repressed negation of a lost civility. In its entirety reminiscent of the central scene of Akira Kurasawa's *Dersu Uzala* (1975), *Water, Wind, Dust* searches for salvation in the heart of a desert Naderi now saw writ large in his country at large. By the late 1980s, Tehran was the deserted soul of the nation it was supposed to represent. What Amir Naderi had captured in such films as *Water, Wind, Dust* was the soul of Tehran in the nightmare of its subterranean desert. A decade into an Islamic revolution, and as Makhmalbaf is emerging out of his ideological commitments to the nature and disposition of that cataclysmic Armageddon of fear and fury, Naderi's desolate landscape is the picture of a nation replete with despair, at loss for hope. Eight years of devastating war with Iraq had depleted the nation of all its moral and political imagination – precisely at a time that Makhmalbaf was ready to re-cast its imaginative topography.

What a contrast between Amir Naderi's *Water, Wind, Dust* (1989) and Majid Majidi's *Color of Paradise* (1998)! In about a decade, the sandstorm desolation of Naderi had given way to Majidi's luscious landscape, the water that Naderi had discovered and sprinkled like sparkles of grace over the hope of resurrection and renewal at the very last scene of *Water, Wind, Dust* was now in effect feeding the growth of a rising urbanity. Majidi used the occasion of telling the story of a blind boy at the mercy of his relatives, kind or cruel, to take his camera to the most beautiful landscapes of his country and reclaim the land for his nation at large. The blindness of the young protagonist dramatized the eye of the camera and sharpened the focus of its visions. What had happened between Naderi's desolate landscape in 1989 and Majidi's luscious hope in 1998 was the election of Seyyed Mohammad Khatami to presidency on 23 May 1997, with some 69 per cent of the popular vote, a spring of desperate hope against winterloads of despair. Khatami's election in 1997, and after that his (perhaps genuine, perhaps false) promise of a resurrection and renewal, radically changed the landscape of Iranian polity – and much in Iranian cinema of this period, including the best in Makhmalbaf's turn to poetic realism, reflects that hope.

Between *Water, Wind, Dust* and *Color of Paradise*, the hope of resurrection and renewal of Tehran as the imaginative center of the nation was mapped out. Abbas Kiarostami's *Taste of Cherry* (1996) narrowed in on the city from its suburban landscape. The vision of Tehran in *Taste of Cherry* is circumambulatory. The lead character, in his inarticulate reflection on the text and texture of suicide, in effect accentuates life. 'Had it not been for the possibility of suicide,' E.M. Cioran had once proposed, 'I would have committed suicide a long time ago.' Kiarostami took that phrase as the topic of *Taste of Cherry*. It narrates the tale of a man on the verge of committing suicide around a city on the verge of coming back to life. Kiarostami's glorious, courageous, long-shot long-takes on and about the winding roads in and around Tehran ooze out the extenuating urbanity that informs its surroundings – an urbanity at once political and memorial, as if Kiarostami had to go to the desolate landscape at the periphery of the cosmopolis to remember and remind its repressed cosmopolitanism. The lead character, Mr. Badi'i, drives in and about Tehran in his Range Rover, picks up even and odd characters, propositions them to come and cover a hole in which he plans to lay down and die if he in fact goes ahead and kills himself. But instead, from the suggestive combination of Kiarostami's patient long takes, the claustrophobic enclosure of Badi'i's car, and the enticing hustle-bustle of life in and about Tehran, emerges the implied urbanity of a life about to re-emerge and surface.

The massive influx of the rural peasantry into Tehran had already reached a critical point in the early 1970s, when the Shah's developmental plans translated into rapid urbanization and an almost total neglect of the agricultural sector of the economy. The Islamic Revolution, in need of militant supporters, simply aggravated this trend. Hundreds of thousands of single males flooded the capital from around the country, where many of them joined the revolutionary militia, the Pasdaran, the Basijis, and the Hezbollah, all paramilitary coteries at the service of the revolution. Before the Islamic Revolution was successfully institutionalized, these militia groups were effectively mobilized to crack down on all secular opposition. By the early 1990s, the influx of the peasantry into the capital had already subsided, but the effect of the preceding decades was harshly evident on the face and in the fabric of the city. An under-appreciated Kiarostami masterpiece, *Fellow-Citizens* (1983), has long set the standard for capturing the soul of Tehran in the midst of its maddening traffic jams. Kiarostami's patient camera narrows in with a caring close up on traffic police trying to restore and sustain order in the confusion that seems to threaten the very fabric of the urbanity that surrounds it. By the mid-1990s, the accumulated tension of veiling, violence, and martyrdom seemed to rupture that urbanity. The face of the city was visibly

5   *Mohsen Makhmalbaf, his late wife Fatemeh Meshkini, and their children Hana and Meysam. (Photograph: Aziz Saati; courtesy of Makhmalbaf Film House.)*

rusticated. Millions of middle-class Tehranis had either left the capital for Europe and North America or else retreated to the privacy of their home, rarely part of the urban landscape. This was particularly evident in Tehran's infuriating traffic, where no sign of any regulated conception of saving the bewildered pedestrians from the crazed motorists was evident. In front of Tehran University in particular, the cosmopolitan elegance of its self-assured urbanity had given way to the crowded and confused busyness of a refugee camp.

This confusion was the direct result of a collapsed urbanity that had failed to re-articulate itself in a post-revolutionary logic. The influx of millions of Afghan refugees, especially after the Taliban take over, did not particularly help either them or the Tehranis' perception of them. In the summer of 1997, a serial murderer, code-named 'Nocturnal Bat,' had plagued Tehran and the surrounding cities. Urban legends immediately blamed the murders on Afghan refugees (the murderer turned out to be an Iranian). Meanwhile, scores of Iranian films featured a solitary Afghan figure in their narratives. Mohsen Makhmalbaf's *The Cyclist* (1987), Abbas Kiarostami's *Through the Olive Trees* (1994) and then *Taste of Cherry* (1996), Ja'far Panahi's *White Balloon* (1998), Hasan Yektapanah's *Jom'eh* (2000), Majid Majidi's *Baran* (2001), and then Mohsen Makhmalbaf's *Kandahar* (2001), all included the fate and foreign familiarity of an Afghan character in their midst. In 1998, Iran almost went to war with the Taliban-dominated Afghanistan. There was always a fear of proto-Taliban takeover in Iran by the religious right, betraying the hopes and aspirations of the reformists.

The economic embargo that the USA imposed on Iran in the mid-1990s only aggravated anti-US sentiments, reiterated in every Friday prayer on Tehran University campus. The site of those routinized anti-US slogans was what used to be the campus soccer field. In the late 1970s, that soccer field had immediately turned into the principal site of political demonstrations, mostly by radical revolutionaries opposing the rapid Islamization of the revolution. After a major rally in July 1979 by anti-Islamic Republic leftist revolutionaries (I was there), the soccer field was savagely attacked by a handful of mercenary thugs, employed by the official organs of the Islamic Republic and led by a certain Zahra Khanom, a militant woman mercenary hired by the Islamists. Soon after that the field was completely taken over by the Islamic militants, categorically silencing the cosmopolitan left. Zahra Khanom proceeded to become a major force, effectively used by the nascent Islamic Republic to disrupt demonstrations and intimidate the participants. She would march into any demonstration with her chador wrapped around her waist and knotted behind her neck, screaming at the top of her voice, surrounded, like a field marshal, by a band of club-wielding lieutenants. After her effective role in the soccer field of Tehran University campus, she was equally ruthless in breaking a demonstration by women judges and legal aides protesting in the main Tehran courthouse against the mandate of the Islamic Republic prohibiting them from practicing their profession (I was present at both these events).

From the purgatorial bonfire of these atrocious mayhems gradually emerged Mohsen Makhmalbaf's *poetic realism* – at once defiant and emancipatory. Makhmalbaf's *A Moment of Innocence* (1997) captures the wintry mood of the city and appropriates its pre-Revolutionary history. Shot in the winter of 1996, *A Moment of Innocence* is Makhmalbaf's re-inscription of his youthful revolutionary zeal when he was almost killed trying to disarm a police officer, steal his gun, rob a bank, and launch an urban guerilla movement against the Pahlavi regime. Some 22 years after the event, Makhmalbaf re-narrates that youthful act of defiance with a disarming satire against the background of a snow-covered Tehran. His picture-perfect shots in *A Moment of Innocence* are recuperative in their memory, forgiving in their generosity, and cosmic in their embracing love for the city he then called home. It is in this film, arguably his best, that Makhmalbaf teaches his camera how to open up and reciprocate, rather than cover up and dismiss, the feminine embrace. Makhmalbaf's alter ego in *A Moment of Innocence* represents the soul of the capital in its renewed hope. The character of Makhmalbaf's youth refuses to heed the directorial instructions of Makhmalbaf and offers bread instead of a knife, as his police officer counterpart puts forward a flowerpot instead of pulling a gun, both embraced within the caressing warmth of a feminine hold.

While Makhmalbaf's *A Moment of Innocence* is snow-white forgiving, Ja'far Panahi's *Circle* (2000) is laser-beam critical, unrelenting in its going straight for the emergent pockets of poverty, prostitution, and muted violence in Tehran. Prostitution is rampant in the Iranian capital. But it is an entirely taboo subject and few people dare to address or even admit it. City-center parks and boulevards are filled with young women having either just arrived from rural areas or else from the poorer sections of the city. *The Circle* is a critical contemplation on the manner and matter of mutated violence against women. Narrated around the fate of several unrelated women and their dire circumstances under an Islamic Republic, *The Circle* captures the effervescent energy of a bewildered cosmopolis – rambunctious, noisy, agitated, disorderly, defiant, barely holding itself together.

Beyond the violent or forgiving face of the city sits the dispirited middle class, surpassed by the revolution, condemned to concealment behind their closed doors and tall walls. Daryush Mehrju'i's *trilogy* is the most significant post-revolutionary attempt at capturing the soul of the Iranian middle class harassed and disheartened by the advent of the Islamic Revolution. The *trilogy* is a reactionary re-appropriation of the middle class as the upholder of the moral apparatus of a lost urbanity. *Sara* (1993), *Pari* (1994), and *Leila* (1996) test the limits of official censorship and dare to articulate the discrete c/harm of the Iranian bourgeoisie. Beleaguered and belabored, the Iranian middle class never surpassed its colonially mitigated composition, contingent as it has always been on facilitating, rather than initiating, the operation of globalizing capital.

A sad and rather pathetic outcome of the dispirited Iranian bourgeoisie's loss of confidence and spirit has been its strange flirtation with what it gathers from Persian Sufism, accompanied by an inordinate number of middle-aged members of the intelligentsia turning to opium, invariably coupled with a belated attraction to a bourgeois version of Persian mysticism. It has always been disturbing to see giant literary and artistic figures, cosmopolitan heroes of an entire generation, now left behind by an Islamic Revolution, sit or lie down by a small brazier huffing and puffing at the tail end of an over-abused pipe. To see that mise-en-scène of abject resignation sublated into attempts at literary and visual art is positively hideous.

By far the most striking example of how a bourgeois flirtation with Persian mysticism can collapse into a dangerous seduction of a metaphysical culture of bodily denial is to be seen in Mehrju'i's *Pari* (1995) – loosely based on J.D. Salinger's *Franny and Zooey* (1961). The two central characters of *Pari*, the deliriously beautiful Pari and her brother Dadashi, stand on the opposite sides of a deadly attraction to mysticism. Dadashi had started his moral and intellectual quest with mysticism and is now an actor who sees the entire world as a big theatrical scene. Pari, on the other hand, starts as an actor and now is deeply and almost violently mystical. Pari and Dadashi have had two older brothers, one of whom has committed suicide by setting himself on fire, having reached the end of the rope in his futile quest for 'Absolute Truth,' while the other leads a pathetically isolated and empty life in a remote village. The memory of a dead idol and the shadow of a lesser ideal now loom large over the mutually contradicted lives of Pari and Dadashi.

Balancing Pari's debilitating fixation with 'Truth' is not any conception of reality that might challenge the absolutism of that quest. Balancing the absolutism of that quest is Dadashi's utter denial of any 'Truth' and immediate collapse into the world of acting. There was a time when Dadashi was seeking the 'Truth' and Pari was acting. Now they have switched roles. Caught between the oscillating extremities of these two poles, Pari and Dadashi, *ipso facto*, complement by contradicting each other; they thus deny any other possibility, any other occasion on which the illusion of 'Truth' and the fictive reality of 'Acting' might indeed serve the purpose of celebrating life as it is: truth-less but good, act-full but real. In *Pari* and the other two components of this *trilogy*, Mehrju'i chronicles the moral collapse of Tehran-based bourgeoisie, cut off from any meaningful connection to the material production of reality, thrown off to the most retrograde elements of a distorted past.

Late in July 1997, the Tehran police sent a social worker to a downtown neighborhood, where an old man had been reported by his neighbors to have incarcerated his twin daughters for all their lives. Samira Makhmalbaf's *Apple* (1997) is only a slightly fictionalized version of this incident. 'That's the story of our nation,' said Makhmalbaf, Samira's father, who wrote the script for his daughter's debut. 'We have been kept in protective custody by our fathers for the longest time. It is time to get out of our dungeon. But we are not used to looking at the sun. It blinds us.'

The May 1997 election of Mohammad Khatami ushered in a new generation of hopes and aspirations that Samira Makhmalbaf best represents. But the sudden revelation that, throughout 1998, the Ministry of Information was directly responsible for the serial murder of several dissident intellectuals, whose dead bodies were discovered in their homes or thrown to waste in highways and under bridges, demonstrated the criminal extent to which the clerical clique would go in eliminating any sign of opposition to its rule of fear and intimidation. It became evident that during the preceding decade many other dissident intellectuals were subjects of assassination plots, including the deliberate attempt to crash a bus-full of prominent writers into a ravine. A courageous journalist, Akbar Ganji, began to investigate these murderous activities in the capital and pointed his finger at high-ranking officials of the Islamic Republic. By July 1999, as the pro-reform newspapers were being officially banned by the clerical judiciary and unofficially attacked by mercenary gangs, the streets of Tehran were the sites of fierce confrontations between stone-throwing students and the militant paramilitary. With the suspicious death of an author at the center of its narratives, Bahman Farmanara's *Smell of Camphor, Fragrance of Jasmine* (2000) captures the political battleground of the city after all these horrific events. This is not a 'political' film in the ordinary sense of the term, but it sublates the political dead-end of this period into an elegiac pause. By far his most personal film so far, *Smell of Camphor, Fragrance of Jasmine* traces the meditative reflections of Bahman Farjami, played by Bahman Farmanara himself, as he navigates through the sur/real preparations of his own funeral. Wise, wondrous, contemplative – Farjami carries in his quiet demeanor the tired memories of his generation of Iranian intellectuals, intelligentsia, literati, and of course filmmakers. Part autobiographical, part nightmarish, *Smell of Camphor, Fragrance of Jasmine* often captures its principal character sitting by the window inside a train car, looking quietly outside and letting loose a melodious recollection of his collective memories.

By February 2000, Tehran was the scene of yet another enormous mobilization of hope when Khatami was given a boost by the parliamentary election in which 170 of the 290 seats were won by pro-Khatami reformists.[21] But the religious right and its vested economic interests would not relent. On 12 March 2000, an assassination attempt on Sa'id Hajjarian, a major reformist theorist, marked the alarming alacrity of the militant mafia. In April 2000, several prominent intellectuals who had participated in a conference in Berlin were officially persecuted by the revolutionary court as soon as they returned to Tehran. An all-out crackdown against the press ensued. The parliament sought to ratify a press law that would restrict the hand of the judiciary in cracking down the pro-reform papers. But on 6 August 2000, the Supreme Leader Khamenei forbade the parliament from passing a more liberal press law. Nevertheless, Khatami was re-elected for a second term on 8 June 2001 with some 77 per cent of the popular vote. However, by July, the Islamic Republic faced a constitutional crisis when the parliament refused the ratification of a new set of reactionary members to the undemocratic Council of Guardians, nominated by the judiciary. As usual, the Supreme Leader Khamenei interfered on behalf of the reactionary forces and prevented the inauguration ceremony of the newly re-elected president on the pretext that the Council of Guardians had to preside over this event. Through further creative accounting, the votes of the members of parliament were re-tabulated, the reactionary nominees approved, and the progressive but beleaguered president inaugurated.

None of these pathologies of power could repress the indomitable spirit of the citizens of Tehran, historically poised to gain their fateful share of freedom. In the course of the qualifying games for the soccer World Cup in the fall of 2001, as the Iranian national team was getting ready to battle the Republic of Ireland, the custodians of the sacred terror declared that only the Irish female fans were allowed to enter the stadium. The young Iranian women fought back for their historic right of watching their national team parade in full soccer gear. About five years later, Jafar Panahi would direct yet another masterpiece in his brilliant career, *Offside* (2006), in which he would gracefully bring to world attention the horrors of a gender apartheid system that denies half of its citizens the full and legitimate rights to citizenry.

Aspects of Kiarostami's cinema that are rural, plus the recent films of Makhmalbaf and Bahman Qobadi, have given a false impression to the outside world that Iranian cinema is essentially rural. It is not. All the major Iranian filmmakers are born and bred in major cities – most of them in Tehran. Even when they move to rural areas, their camera remains quintessentially voyeuristic (if not outright touristy). The urban dispositions of Iranian filmmakers have invested in all of them the paradoxical forces of their birth and breeding. The more recent attention of Makhmalbaf to Tajikistan, Afghanistan, Pakistan, and Turkey, or Kiarostami's attention to Africa, have not much changed the urban disposition of their visions – at once investigative and condescending, visually curious, and verbally arrested.

If national cinemas are predicated on national traumas, and if national traumas are the registers of a nation's rise and response to (colonial) modernity, then Tehran as the principal site of that trauma carries the paradoxical contradictions that have informed all Iranian artists who are either born and bred to that paradox or else aspire to its creative energy. From the earliest encounters of Iran with colonial modernity, Tehran provided the universal imagery of the nation – and in the paradoxical turmoil of that imagery was coined the visual vocabulary of Iranian cinema.

Toward an Aesthetics of Emancipation

The paradoxical rise of Iranian cinema in the course of an historic revolutionary movement and the iconic making of Mohsen Makhmalbaf as a rebel filmmaker posit a critical question in the predicament of all the cultural manners of national liberation movements in the face of predatory globalization. While the very bread, bone marrow, and blood of a people's struggle for pride and dignity, the art that emerges from that tumultuous site is invariably mutated into a transnational transaesthetics of indifference, as Jean Baudrillard has called it,[22] where the European and North American film festivals, film critics, and film scholars can effectively turn the cries and whispers of people around the world into matters of seasonal entertainment and useless theoretical speculation. The European and North American venues of film festivals and distributions (and the critical apparatus of film criticism and scholarship that emerges around them) have a catalytic effect on degenerating the effective politics of the films they thus showcase into a liberal transnationalism that robs them of their revolutionary form and rebellious function. The same transformative effect on revolutionary art is of course evident in the economics of financing such films by European and North

American cultural institutes, governmental agencies, and benevolent financiers. These deeply corrosive forces are bound to have their collective impact on the rising generation of filmmakers from around the world. Before they know it, their aesthetics and politics begin to cater to the flamboyant expectations and short attention span of the transnational bourgeoisie and their seasonal entertainment, in which a Russian circus may hold their attention for a week in Cannes or some other seasonal resort, before they turn to a telecast of a summer Olympic Game, while waiting for an international film festival by their nearest lake or seashore.

The result of this paradoxical matching of Third World miseries as spectacle with transnational bourgeoisie as spectator is the journalistic manufacturing of a liberal transaesthetics of indifference that corresponds to the logic of the military globalization it represents. The manufacturing of a transnational civil society and the military expansion of economic liberalism are both conducive to the globalization of an audience for world cinema that amounts to the effective disappearance of an immediate audience that politically matters. The paradoxical origins of various national cinemas have now been confounded by the equally paradoxical privatization of the spectatorship and the effective disappearance of a public audience. The image of a single viewer or at most a couple sitting in front of their television set and watching a rented or purchased video or DVD while having dinner is now the paramount reality of the privatized spectatorship in Euro-North American cosmopolis. Major film festivals are not events of public consequence. They are exclusive to a very select and limited group of people, while film critics writing for their respective newspapers and magazines can claim no organic link with people who are actually going to watch these films. The equally troubling picture of North American or Western European anthropologists or scholars of film studies sitting in front of a small screen watching bootleg copies of films produced thousands of miles away from their homes and offices, then turning to their laptop and writing excruciatingly erudite but astoundingly irrelevant theoretical speculations about those films, is now equally definitive to much public knowledge that is produced about masterpieces of world cinema.[23] The privatization of spectatorship in the so-called 'First World' is bound to have a catalytic effect on the privatization of public predicaments – wars, social revolutions, colonial occupations, anticolonial resistances – in the rest of the world. The US invasion of Afghanistan coincided with the release of Mohsen Makhmalbaf's *Kandahar* (2001), and the film will forever be assimilated into the propaganda machinery of an Empire – quite irrespective of the intent and purpose of the filmmaker himself.

Contingent on the rapid privatization of world cinema for seasonal entertainment of the transnational bourgeoisie is the inevitable manufacturing of several lenses through which world cinema is seen – chief among them is a radical over-aestheticization of arts whereby visual pleasure is derived from the factual miseries of other people. There is an endemic and pervasive Orientalization of various national cinemas in the major film festivals and their more minor subsidiaries. This overwhelming exoticization of the world, the (*National Geographic*) anthropologization of artistic endeavors in telling terrifying stories, robs art as much of the politics of its production as it does of the aesthetics of its commercial consequences. There is also a prevailing cinematics of the current affair – where the attention of the major film festivals chases after the military conquests of the United States and the colossal catastrophes contingent on them. Thus Bahman Qobadi's *Songs for my Motherland* (2002) turns into *Marooned in Iraq* (2003) as soon as the USA invades Iraq, or Samira Makhmalbaf's *Five in the Afternoon* (2003) or Sadiq Barmak's *Osama* (2003) are assimilated backwards into an *ex post facto* reflection on the miseries of Afghanistan after the US invasion. National cinemas may temporarily benefit but will ultimately suffer from this sporadic, whimsical, and corrosive attention of the major European film festivals to the miseries that these films portray. In the heart of the Empire itself, Michael Moore's *Fahrenheit 9/11* receives the 2004 Palme d'Or as a European (French) political gesture against George W. Bush. Bush, of course, deserved to be reminded that the world is watching what he does. However, this award equally neglected that Michael Moore in fact took commercially clever advantage of pervasive anti-Muslim and anti-Arab sentiments in the USA and Europe by linking Bush to the Saudi Sheikhs – and thus in a patently anti-war film blatantly corroborated the racist assumptions of his fellow Americans.

The perils of globalization, however, hide varied promises. Binary oppositions have collapsed between the West and the Rest, opening a space for modes and manners of solidarity unimagined before. An international film festival can potentially be the principal site of this dismantling. There is an emergent and aggressive cross-metaphorization of cross-national sentiments that is rescuing an otherwise crippling mimetic crisis endemic to these cinemas – as for example between Palestinian cinema and American rap music, as best used by Hany Abu Assad in his *Ford Transit* (2002). In more theoretical terms, however, Jean Baudrillard has diagnosed this cross-metaphorization negatively and as amounting to a 'transaesthetics of indifference,' declaring in resignation at some point, 'perhaps we ought to consider art solely from an anthropological standpoint, without reference to any aesthetic judgment whatsoever.'[24] Quite to the contrary, in this cross-metaphorization, the achievements of one national cinema can in fact inform and invigorate the promises of another – and the global space generated by the recognition and distribution of world cinema is the best location of such a cross-national conversations – always already evident and visible in all cinema of all national origins.

The liberating consequences of art know no geographic boundaries. Gillo Pontecorvo's *Battle of Algiers* has been more effective as a text of revolutionary mobilization than ten political manifestos put together in any language. Liberation movements in art are more the *ex post facto* results of an accidental congregation of aesthetic events (in film, photography, video installation, painting, drama, poetry, literature, etc.) than a conscious decision on the part of the artists to concoct a conspiracy of premeditated moves. The Tehran of Mohsen Makhmalbaf's cinematic imagination – somewhere between the fact of its political brutality and the fiction of its cinematic reconciliation – is the geographical site of an artistic liberation movement set to emancipate the Iranian subject from the claws of its imperial, colonial, or tyrannical mediations. In the post-revolutionary Iranian cinema, Abbas Kiarostami, Mohsen Makhmalbaf, and Marziyeh Meshkini (as examples of a more generational shift in Iranian cinema) represent three distinctly different cinemas that nevertheless move in an extraordinarily similar emancipatory direction: liberating the Iranian cultural modernity from its most debilitating forces. While Abbas Kiarostami's cinema is the aesthetic vision of an emancipated *future*, free from all the received and enduring entrapments of an ancient culture, Mohsen Makhmalbaf's cinema is the singular semiotics of one daring effort to shed the thick and thickening layers of a *past* that refuses to let us forget. In contrast to these two contrasting/complementary visions, the younger generation of filmmakers that someone like Marziyeh Meshkini – or Samira Makhmalbaf, Jafar Panahi, or Bahman Qobadi – represents is the rich topography of a *present* at once brutal and beautiful.

The aesthetic expediency crafted for a concerted liberation in the work of these filmmakers is conducive to a singular recognition of the Iranian culture as an historical product of its own conceptions, in dialogical conversation with the crosscurrents of its history. The *truth* evident in the cinema that these filmmakers represent, however, speaks not to a universal or atemporal objectivity, but instead to a reality that needs *re-defining* (Abbas Kiarostami), *re-historicizing* (Mohsen Makhmalbaf), and *re-signifying* (Marziyeh Meshkini *et al.*). Truth, Nietzsche once said, is a 'mobile army of metaphors ... illusions about which one has forgotten that this is what they are.' To mobilize an army of metaphors to liberate represents a truth at once historical and liberating. The truth evident in Iranian cinema never approximates a grandiloquent claim to a reality that transcends time and space. It breaks through all layers of cultural conditioning and reaches for those moments when a culture begins to dream in its art the terms of its own potential emancipation. As a result, there is a revolutionary aesthetic about this cinema of liberation, a provocative abandoning of all cultural clustering of extraneous meaning and intention. Reality is re-invented in them, remembered, and re-signified in a newly modulated fashion, in an imaginatively realistic language.

Three distinct modes of cinematic realism now divide the Iranian scene. The *actual realism* of Abbas Kiarostami is particular about the terms of relentlessly reducing reality to its ephemeral constituents. As perhaps best represented in his

Koker Trilogy, Kiarostami's *actual realism* begins to peel off reality, which his camera picks up from its bare minimal registers, until it is cleared of all its pretensions to metaphysical reality, right there and then for Kiarostami to deliver them to a different mode of meaning. Right next to Kiarostami's *actual realism* we witness Makhmalbaf's *virtual realism*, a mode of seeing the world that attends to reality only to see it mutated into its virtual matter-of-factness, there to tease out of its thick darkness the terms of its emancipation. As perhaps best represented in *A Moment of Innocence* (1995), *Gabbeh* (1995), and *Silence* (1998), Makhmalbaf's virtual realism takes the very same surface of reality familiar in Kiarostami's cinema, and yet in Makhmalbaf's case he vacates it of all its factual and actual connectedness to history and then lets it loose to roam in the realm of a poetic memory of itself. The result is a manner of realism that is at once connected and yet paradoxically released from history. Deeply rooted in Kiarostami's actual and Makhmalbaf's virtual realism is the *parabolic realism* evident in the cinema of Marziyeh Meshkini, Bahman Qobadi, Samira Makhmalbaf, and in some of its most spectacular cases Jafar Panahi's cinema. This mode of *parabolic realism* captures the presential disposition of that same reality that Kiarostami and Makhmalbaf take to divergent directions; yet without allowing it either to collapse into its sub-atomic energies (*a la* Kiarostami) or sublate to figurative suggestiveness (*a la* Makhmalbaf) sublates it into a manner of parabolic storytelling, where the story is at once mimetic in its dramaturgy and yet miasmatic in the range of meanings it exudes.

Mohsen Makhmalbaf's *virtual realism* is the *modus operandi* of the *paradox* that creatively constitutes his cinema. He is a *realist* through and through, from the earliest phases of his film and fiction to their latest. But the particular *mood* of his realism vacates from reality all its superfluous extravaganza and reaches for its quintessential brevity – there *virtually* to allow it to negotiate its alternatives. The *virtual realism* that results remains unfailingly loyal to the politics of its origin, but moves toward an aesthetics of its own emancipation. In the location but not in the culture of his cinematic imagination, Makhmalbaf has moved from Iran to Turkey, and from there to Pakistan, Tajikistan, and now most comprehensively to Afghanistan – where he and his family have become almost natives to its predicament. The geographical expansion of Makhmalbaf's cinematic location has now reiterated his creative dissemination into the voices and visions of his own progeny – his daughters Samira and Hana, his wife Marziyeh, the young Afghan filmmaker Sadiq Barmak whom he has adopted and trained, and scores of other filmmakers whose creative characters he has helped to shape. A ventriloquist at large, Makhmalbaf is narrowing in on the beleaguered and belabored matter-of-factness of the colonized subject – reviving its moral imagination and giving it historical agency.

What I have set out to do in this book (as site, sight, and citation) goes against the grain of everything that is said and sought in Iranian cinema – all the manners of writing about its rise and significance that seek to subsume and pacify its subversive forces for habitual indifferences. In the politics, aesthetics, and epistemics of his cinema of emancipation, Makhmalbaf has done something worth noting, watching, and theorizing beyond its immediate citations. I have a set of multiple targets: a transaesthetics of indifference that is the staple of major international film festivals; a transpolitics of bourgeois banality to which they cater; the intransigence of power that in the form of an Islamic Republic seeks to turn this cinema into its ideological foregrounding; a pathological transnational bourgeoisie that in the form of Iranian expatriate culture seeks to read and modulate it in a racially identified manner to generate and sustain credibility for itself in the blue eyes of its white interlocutors; and ultimately career opportunism of all sorts that seeks to benefit from the temporary global attention to Iranian cinema. These are all the principal target of my criticism when I read Makhmalbaf in a language and a diction that they cannot decipher – tell its tail from its head. I celebrate and thrive in that language because my purpose is to read Iranian cinema to a transaesthetics of liberation that offers it as a gift to national liberation movements and the arts that attend to their revolutionary agenda throughout the world – and in that goal the miserable meanderings of either an Islamic Republic or all the transnational bourgeois pathologies it has generated (from antiquarian monarchists to postmodern secularists) are of no concern to what I have detected and wish to share in Makhmalbaf's cinema.

The result amounts to my varied accounts of the points of contact where Makhmalbaf's cinematic career meets the challenge of the post/colonial subject and lets it loose historically to redeem itself. I have been primarily attracted to Makhmalbaf because he was first a rebel and then he turned to cinema. The manner of creative agency evident in his cinema – navigating the topography of its landscape is the principal task of this book – is constitutional to his character as a rebel filmmaker. In him and his cinema I have detected the aesthetic domain of constituting and crafting historical agency for the colonially de-subjected in a visual vocabulary unprecedented in his cinematic culture. I see this historical agency as articulated principally outside the paradox of colonial modernity, where were it not for our poets and artists we post/colonial agents of our own destiny could not be modern without being *ipso facto* colonized. It is the modernity of that agency beyond the paradox of colonial modernity that concerns me most in any foray I have made into revolutionary ideologies or aesthetics of emancipation. In Makhmalbaf I believe we witness the first fusion of both. In the very same creative agency I detect and propose two modes of emancipation quintessential to a revolutionary aesthetics: first, *a critical agency* that is outside the political paradox of colonial modernity; and second, *a creative effervescence* that is outside the epistemic paradox of a bifurcated aesthetics and politics. In Makhmalbaf's character and culture I detect and propose a manner and a mood of creative and critical agency that liberates his post/colonial audience from the cul-de-sac of colonial modernity – as there is a manner of seeing and reading that cinema that does not collapse into a bifurcated reading of aesthetics and politics as two separate or even opposite propositions. In Makhmalbaf's cinema, I propose in this book, the two are fused, the subject is actively freed, the agent is historically alerted, the artist is autonomously creative, and thus the moral imaginary of the nation is revolutionary beyond the outdated boundaries of the nation. And in that paradox dwells our freedom.

Chapter Two

Makhmalbaf at Large:
The Making of a Rebel Filmmaker

In the previous chapter I provided a reading of the making of national cinemas as a cultural manifestation of major national traumas, within which idea I then placed the rise of Iranian cinema in the aftermath of a massive social revolution in 1977–79 and an even more destructive Iran–Iraq War (1980–88). By predicating my reading of Iranian national cinema on the paradoxical conception of a debilitating event that generates an invigorating art form, I placed Makhmalbaf's aesthetics against Abdolkarim Soroush's metaphysics, as I did the physical reality of Tehran as a cosmopolis against the backdrop of its cinematic representations. I then used this pretext to articulate my theoretical interest in Makhmalbaf's cinema as a particularly poignant site where the post/colonial subject can see, watch, internalize, and creatively manifest its agential autonomy. My purpose in this second chapter is to provide a comprehensive view of the entirety of Makhmalbaf's cinema, from his earliest films and fiction to his latest. Here I wish to give a sustained, thematically connected, and analytically thorough reading of his films set against the backdrop of post-revolutionary Iranian social and cultural history.

An Aesthetics of Wonder

Soon after the events of 11 September 2001, and by sheer historical serendipity, Makhmalbaf's *Kandahar* (2001) suddenly became the center of a global sensation – audiences throughout the world were watching this film in an urgent context vastly different from the one in which it was made. People were desperately looking at Makhmalbaf's *Kandahar* for an alternative vision of Afghanistan, different from what they were being fed on an hourly basis by CNN, Fox News, and the conglomerate of a news and entertainment industry that they now represent and overwhelm. The result was to throw Makhmalbaf himself into a spotlight much brighter in its focus than he had experienced before – even as a world-renowned filmmaker. Throughout his long and adventurous career, Makhmalbaf has been no stranger to controversy. He is not exactly the average film school graduate who makes a few short films on borrowed money and then goes on waiting tables until s/he gets a big break from some producer or a studio. Things do not work quite that way in his neck of the woods. His art is of an entirely different disposition, of the sort that one cannot turn to Immanuel Kant's *Observations on the Feeling of the Beautiful and the Sublime* to understand or theorize it. He, and all other artists in the neighborhood of his creativity, class, and culture (in Asia, Africa, Latin, and Native America), were categorically dismissed and barred from Kant's universe of imagination and the Enlightenment modernity that he theorized.[1] Makhmalbaf's art, now emblematic of an entirely different universe of imagination, is rooted in the tyrannical reign of the monarchy to which he was born; in the poverty-stricken neighborhood of his childhood; in his precocious politicization; in his youthful indiscretions; when he took up arms to oppose and end tyranny; in his years in Pahlavi prison; in his devotion to an Islamic Revolution, with all its hopes and horrors, asseverations and atrocities; and more than anything else in his deep political disappointment, soon to be translated into a pervasive philosophical disillusionment with any revolution, any and all acts of violence, paving his way – impatiently, pointedly, persistently – toward a poetic sur/realism that would become definitive to his cinema. His art is equally rooted in the private cast of his memories; in having been born to a marriage that lasted only six days; in having been raised in fear of being hunted by a father intent on kidnapping him; in having been dearly loved and cared for by three women in the incarcerated privacy of their household; in his single mother providing for him; in his grandmother's deeply religious sensibilities and nocturnal storytelling about prophets and demons, saints, sinners, and saviors; in his maternal aunt's exposing him to the magic of literary humanism; in his stepfather's piety and politics. There, in the midst of the hustle-bustle of Pahlavi monarchy and mendacity, and the social upheavals and revolutionary fervor that they entailed, Makhmalbaf was born and bred into the most enduring traits of his creative imagination. His cinema is not the well-polished flower of some greenhouse seclusion from reality. It is tough, the rough cut of a rambunctious effervescence that throws the gauntlet at a world that has historically denied his class and denigrated his consciousness, repressed his aspirations and incarcerated his agencies, his confidence and courage – and thus his daring imagination, his early revolutionary violence, his fanatical commitment to an Islamic revolution he later detested and deserted for good, for art. Throughout his life and career, Makhmalbaf seems to have been on the run, afraid that he might be caught.

Makhmalbaf is a nomadic filmmaker, a traveling troubadour, in the cast of his creative character, in the texture of his impatient imagination. Itinerant, migratory, evasive, he can never be cornered or settled. He is a fugitive, from his own fears, toward his own hopes, indeterminate – attractive because he alienates, repellent because he attracts. He is blinded. He is insightful. His wife and children are the extension, the letting loose, of his creative ego. He is a ventriloquist. He is spasmodic in his aesthetic choices, erratic in his politics, sporadic in his output. He is unpredictable, capricious, whimsical in his disposition. He is fanciful in his aesthetics, urgent in his creativity, miasmatic in his mind. His is an aesthetics of wonder. When he wants to concentrate, he bends over on the floor with a pen and paper and pulls a blanket over his head – and does not come out until he has finished writing what is on his mind. 'Can you breathe in there?' I once asked him in a hotel room in Paris, where we were spending a week talking politics and watching foreign films. He did not hear me. I looked at him and I remembered Sepehri:

> I am a Muslim.
> My Qibla is a red rose –
> My prayer rug a fountain.
> On Light I prostrate, and
> On the prairie I place my face down.
> I take my ablution
> With the palpitations of windows.
> In my prayer the moon flows and
> Thus flows a magnetic charge.
> I can see
> The stone from behind my prayers
> And all the particles of my prayers are crystallized.
> I whisper my prayers
> When the wind has recited
> The Adhan on the minaret of the cypress tree.
> I recite my verses
> When the tall grass has called for prayers,
> When the wave has commanded me to stand up.
> My Kaaba is on the waterfront,
> My Kaaba is under the acacias,
> My Kaaba is just like a breeze,
> Moving from garden to garden,
> From town to town.

The Political Activist

Representing a whole culture of creative effervescence from the colonial corner of modernity, Makhmalbaf's cinema has always been controversial because in his art and in his persona as a revolutionary filmmaker he collapses the customary separation between art and politics, cinema and society – forcing the two into negotiating a new space for their coexistence. The division of intellectual labor between the *creative* and the *critical* is a Platonic paradox that was later uncritically assimilated forward in the course of European Enlightenment modernity and as such holds no water on its colonial edges. The rest of the world has no reason to abide by that Platonic paradox, nor by its Aristotelian re-modulation into poetics that theorize operative logos in the heart of the aesthetic cosmos; nor indeed, *a fortiori*, by a European modernity that in its very Kantian origin excludes the colonial peripheries of the bourgeois Enlightenment from participating in an articulation of 'the beautiful and the sublime.'[2] The collapse of Aristotelian logic into instrumental reason in the course of the European bourgeois revolution and the implosion of the Weberian conception of charismatic causality into rationalized directions mean nothing on the colonial edges of that modernity – except as a *modus operandi* in which that very charismatic resistance to routinization of instrumental and instrumentalizing reason, aka 'Modernity,' is at once a creative *and* a critical proposition. The result is that a creative work of art is as much critical in constituting historical agency as a critical work ought to be creative in theorizing that work of art precisely in the same direction. On that ferocious frontier line, the creative work of art is as much co-critical in soliciting theorization as the critical work ought to be co-creative in responding to that need. This is not a matter of creative choice. This is a matter of critical necessity. To the degree that creative works of art on the colonial edges of European modernity partake in the bourgeois instrumentalization of reason and the separation of the creative and the critical, they betray the aspirations of their local needs to address global concerns. Makhmalbaf's cinema is one of those rare moments in contemporary art where an artist not only rises from the colonial corner of power but remains true to its defiance of the categorical separation of the critical from the creative. His is not a 'transaesthetics of indifference,' as Jean Baudrillard thinks our globalized fate to be in postmodernity. Makhmalbaf's is an aesthetics of choice; however, he may himself regret the choices he has made in the earlier phases of his politics and cinema.

No-one in Makhmalbaf's generation could be born in 1957, four years into the British- and American-engineered coup that toppled the government of Prime Minister Mohammad Musaddiq and restored the tyranny of the Pahlavi monarchy, and not be political in every aspect of their creative and critical character. Children of Thomas Jefferson had conspired with the Mother of all Parliaments and robbed an entire nation of the mere possibility of a democratic life.[3] Musaddiq's democratically elected government was ruthlessly toppled, the fugitive Pahlavi was restored to power, and a monstrous secret police was fortified to frighten a whole nation into obedience to a medieval monarchy. All modes of resistance to that tyranny – from political to cultural – were brutally eliminated. Only under

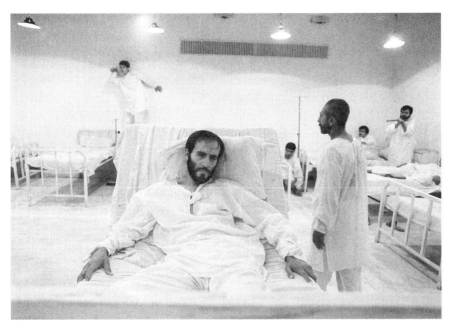

6   *Mahmoud Bigham as Haji in Mohsen Makhmalbaf's* Arusi-ye Khuban (Marriage of the Blessed, 1989). *With this film Makhmalbaf breaks away from the organs of the Islamic Republic and reconnects with the social basis of his cinema — a move that effectively challenges the promises of the Islamic Revolution. (Photograph: Bahram Jalali; courtesy of Makhmalbaf Film House.)*

the mantle of the Shi'i clerics could cries and whispers of dissent be voiced and heard. The dissident left opposed the Pahlavi terror at great risk to their lives and liberty. The religious opposition to the Pahlavi and the cosmopolitan left had a common enemy. Their constitutional differences remained largely potential. Within that historical context, Makhmalbaf's personal life accentuated the general condition of his early upbringing.

The June 1963 uprising, led by Ayatollah Khomeini, left an indelible mark on the young Makhmalbaf because by then his mother had married the lawyer who had helped her in her divorce proceedings, and the young lawyer was a devout Khomeini supporter. Between 1963 and 1974, Makhmalbaf increasingly grows in his political awareness of his environment. Precocious, presumptuous, and over-confident by the maternal care of three, instead of one, mother-figures, and the total absence of a father, Makhmalbaf forms his own small band of urban guerillas by 1974 and attacks a police officer to steal his gun, rob a bank, and launch a revolution. He, of course, botched the plot and was almost killed in the process. At the age of 17, Makhmalbaf landed in jail, where he spent the next four years of his life. His years in jail were brutal and formative. He was viciously tortured and maimed. Wounded by a bullet in the course of the aborted plot, he was hospitalized, cured, and cared for, and then subjected to mind-numbing torture.

He in part exorcised the horror of those years in a short story he wrote, *Surgery of the Soul* (1987). But he still carries the scars of the cruelty that Pahlavi jailers perpetrated on his body and soul. His walking is permanently impaired. He cannot wear a regular pair of shoes and usually walks in sneakers, otherwise he has to bend the back of his heels. He limps along when he walks. When you walk with him you can hear the monotonous rhythm of his right heel sliding on the ground. The cables with which he was beaten, varying in thickness and size, have disfigured the soles of both his feet. The same is true of his spinal cord. He cannot sleep on a bed and must toss and turn on a thin blanket on the floor, for a few hours of Spartan nap. Even while asleep, he unconsciously folds his feet over his belly, bending one from the knee and making an arch over it with the other, to lessen the pressure on his back. His elastic fibrous disks have been irreversibly damaged. His torturers now live in the United States, where they have received political asylum. 'Physical pain under torture,' he once told me walking uphill in a back alley of Cannes, 'means nothing. You forget it almost immediately. It's like pangs of pain when giving birth to a child. Soon after the child is born, women go ahead and have sex with their husband and get pregnant again.' He then made his habitual bend on his left foot, pushed forward in the dimly lit walkway, and added, 'I kept screaming Ayn al-Qudat's name out loud when they were beating me with those cables.' Years before I had met Makhmalbaf, I had started working on (and later published) a book about Ayn al-Qudat, the medieval mystic who was brutally tortured and murdered at the age of 33 in Hamadan.[4]

Makhmalbaf was released from prison in 1978 in the wake of the Islamic Revolution. Soon after, he married Fatemeh Meshkini and the young couple joined the revolutionary mobilization almost instantly. As their first two children were born, Zeynab Samira on 15 February 1980 and Ayyub Meysam on 3 July 1981, the Makhmalbafs joined the Iranian national radio where they devoted themselves to revolutionary propaganda on behalf of the nascent Islamic Republic. These were not ordinary years. The millennia-old Persian monarchy had just collapsed. The Shah had fled the country. The Islamists had effectively used the American hostage crisis and out-maneuvered all their political rivals. The radical left and the liberal nationalists were out to claim their share of the political pillage. Makhmalbaf's years in Pahlavi prison had made him particularly hostile to the organized left. To this day, the Iranian progressive left and the Mojahedin-e Khalq Organization, an Islamist guerilla group, share the sentiments of the monarchists outside and the religious right inside; and they all collectively condemn Makhmalbaf with a litany of bad memories from his early years as a militant Muslim activist. Various groups on the left still remember how his films were shown in the dungeons of the Islamic Republic to harass and horrify them. The Mojahedin still carry their bad memories of his solitary activism against their organizational mobilization. The monarchists outside Iran have no love for an early Muslim revolutionary, whereas the religious right inside Iran is utterly disgusted with his having betrayed their cause. There is of course a ring of truth about all these sentiments and grievances. But they are all barking up the wrong tree. Makhmalbaf never climbs a tree twice. He is always somewhere else, somewhere present, presential, instantaneous, memory-less. There are times that I think he has no memory of anything at all and that history means nothing to him more than mere material for stories he wraps around and spins off for yet another script. He has tucked away myriads of them in various neatly organized folders and files in his basement in Paris – only a small fraction of them has he managed to cast, project and show to people around the world.

The Religious Visionary

Controversy being constitutional to that site where Makhmalbaf's emergent cinema and his tumultuous society fade in and out of each other, we need to break such controversial moments to their opposing ends, attending to the centrifugal forces that at once pull apart and *ipso facto* constitute his aesthetics. The earliest public record of Makhmalbaf as a filmmaker and a novelist is between 1981 and 1983. Before he went to jail he had written a few plays. While in jail he had written some stories. But soon after his release he went on a rampage, organizing reading and writing groups. While working for the revolutionary radio, his writing skills were put to backbreaking test. By 1981, he was convinced that art satisfies far more when it ennobles politics, not politics when it kills all truths and ideals. Now fully at the service of the nascent Islamic Republic, he, his wife Fatemeh Meshkini and their two children Samira and Meysam, bundle up together to serve the beleaguered revolution. The hostage crisis of 1979–80 is now over, its smokescreen cleverly used by the clergy to ratify a theocratic constitution, and the repressive regime of Ayatollah Khomeini is in full power. Iraq invades Iran in September 1980, and the revolutionary land plunges into a combative mobilization, when millions of Iranians are dispatched to the front and hundreds of thousands of dead and maimed bodies return home as the martyred witnesses to the sacred rage that now burned their homeland to the ground.

Between 1982 and 1983, Makhmalbaf makes three films: *Nasuh's Repentance* (1982), *Seeking Refuge* (1983), and *Two Sightless Eyes* (1983).[5] This is Makhmalbaf the religious visionary. He attends to his camera with the innocent passions of a revolutionary zealot. He does not know cinema from a hole in the wall. But he is determined, unwavering, resolute in his vision to make an 'Islamic cinema' a legitimate proposition. He has experience with writing fiction even from his teenage years, before he was arrested and during the time that he was in jail. He is particularly adamant that the pre-revolutionary cinema was categorically implicated in the cultural agenda of the Pahlavi monarchy. He dismisses with one broad and damning brush the entire pre-revolutionary cinema, including its master practitioners like Bahram Beiza'i. He pontificates loudly on the virtues of an 'Islamic cinema,' and the revolutionary zealotry of the time makes an even more dogged fanatic out of him than is warranted by his actual positions. He goes so far as to write a book, *An Introduction to Islamic Art*, in which he theorizes the parameters of an 'Islamic cinema.' His films from this period are the pious practices of a revolutionary zealot at best, frightful propaganda pieces on the merits of metaphysical beliefs at worst. These films are the product of a group of Muslim artists that Makhmalbaf helped organize, 'The Artistic Branch of the Organization for Islamic Propaganda,' in order to Islamicize the very practice of art as a revolutionary project. Before he made his own first features, Makhmalbaf wrote a couple of plays that his friends turned into films. Manuchehr Haqqani Parast's *Explanation* (1981), and Mohammad Reza Honarmand's *Fortress in Fortress* (1981) and *Someone Else's Death* (1981) are all based on Makhmalbaf's plays. These films are squarely at the service of the Islamic regime and a feeble attempt at the Islamicization of the emerging revolutionary art. *Someone Else's Death*, for example, is a visit between Death and a general who is about to order an attack that will result in massive casualties. Here Makhmalbaf condemns militarism but celebrates an unexamined afterlife. In his own films, the issues and their treatment are not any better. *Nasuh's Repentance* condemns a greedy and covetous man but celebrates the fear of death. *Two Sightless Eyes* denounces the horrors of war casualties but glorifies the virtues of a blind faith. *Seeking Refuge*, the most dangerous collapse of Makhmalbaf into metaphysical abstraction with deadly political implications, frightens the wit out of reality by postulating Satan as the source of evil temptation against good.

What we see in Makhmalbaf's early cinema is more than the predilections of a religious visionary determined to cast a metaphysical shadow on reality. Makhmalbaf is very much the creature of his age, the representative of a cultural rupture in the moral disposition of a society. At the height of its power, the Pahlavi monarchy seemed interminable. The Iranian cinema came of age in the 1960s and 1970s, either under the suzerainty of the Pahlavi cultural agenda or in such clandestine opposition to it that was brutally repressed and cut off. The early masterpieces of Iranian cinema, such as Daryush Mehrju'i's *Cow* (1969) or Amir Naderi's *Requiem* (1972), had to be either smuggled out of the country to be screened in international film festivals or else they would collect dust and gradually whither away without being seen. Makhmalbaf's early cinema represents a filmmaker with the sentiments of the disenfranchised classes, people who were denied even the agency of trusting their own creative impulses. Makhmalbaf doggedly exacted a creative agency for himself, and with himself for the disenfranchised classes he represented. In the revolutionary zealotry of the time he would go overboard and make flamboyant remarks about pre-revolutionary filmmakers. But in doing so he was also creating confidence and cultivating a pride of place for a whole nation of discouraged hopes. It is a fact of Iranian society of his generation that destitution and religious sentiments went hand in hand. Many revolutionary activists came from impoverished families and communities with a strong presence of religious sentiments among them. The Pahlavi monarchy was principally responsible for disallowing any alternative form of critical judgment to be institutionally cultivated. Religious mobilization was the most viable form of political opposition left operative at a vast societal level. It is also a fact of Iranian society of Makhmalbaf's generation that most (but by no means all) Iranian filmmakers came from relatively affluent families. Bahram Beiza'i, Abbas Kiarostami, Daryush Mehrju'i, Bahman Farmanara, and Ebrahim Golestan were the leading filmmakers of the Pahlavi period and all of them came from moderately to lucratively affluent families – rich enough to send their children to film schools in Europe and the United States. A filmmaker of Amir Naderi's monumental brilliance and deep roots in impoverished communities (who would dare his poverty, defy his fate, and prove his brilliance) was rare among Iranian filmmakers. And Amir Naderi, a poor, provincial lad eager to join the emergent filmmakers, would sit for days at the door of prominent filmmakers like Ebrahim Golestan and not be admitted for an audience. (This I know from Amir Naderi's own account to me.)

Makhmalbaf's early career as a filmmaker was far more seriously implicated in the atrocities of the Islamic Republic than a generation before him whose filmmakers were framed within the Pahlavi regime. This is not to say that such prominent pre-revolutionary filmmakers as Daryush Mehrju'i, Bahram Beiza'i, Abbas Kiarostami, or Bahman Farmanara were active instruments of Pahlavi propaganda, an inexcusable suggestion that Makhmalbaf made at the time. Quite to the contrary. Mehrju'i's affiliation with Gholamhossein Saedi's drama, Kiarostami's with Sohrab Sepehri's poetry, Farmanara's with Houshang Golshiri's fiction, and Beiza'i's unrivalled creative mastery of Iranian literary and artistic heritage made them immune to any active abuse by Pahlavi propaganda. But all these great artists came from relatively affluent and cosmopolitan families. There was not a single serious filmmaker among them (Amir Naderi the exception that proves the rule) who either came from disenfranchised communities or shared their religious sensibilities. Makhmalbaf did. He jolted the Iranian cinematic scene because he erupted in it with the full, repressed confidence of a whole spectrum of Iranian society that was denied its creative agency because it did not corroborate the Pahlavi's presumptuous 'modernization' agenda. It might be difficult to accept. But the fact is that though exceptionally important in bringing Iranian cinema to the center stage of world cinema, the Tehran Film Festival was also an unseemly spectacle for the Tehrani bourgeoisie from which was systematically denied a whole spectrum of Iranian society. The headquarters of the Tehran Film Festival at the Rudaki Hall was so obscenely class-conscious that it denigrated and alienated millions of disenfranchised Iranians living in the vicinity of its very location. The Shiraz Art Festival was an even more atrocious spectacle of disregard for a people's dignity. The Pahlavi monarchy presided over such wanton acts of humiliating an entire nation. The fact that today the Islamic Republic has a sustained record of even more ghastly and criminal deeds in other directions should not be allowed to eradicate the memory of those years of horror. Alienated from themselves, estranged from their own society, humiliated by exclusion, this angry population could not but burn to the ground those movie theaters into which they were denied access the instant the revolutionary uprising took momentum. The ordinary, poor, and religiously inclined people equally could not but wholeheartedly celebrate the first serious filmmaker that emerged from the depth of their deprived creativity, the very heart of their disallowed agency, their denied dignity, their repressed place in the world: from the Makhmalbaf universe of their imagination.

This, however, is not to excuse Makhmalbaf's early, religiously charged, ideologically loaded, and politically frightening cinema. He was a young revolutionary just released from prison. His side of the political fence had just won. The overwhelming majority of the recognized masters of his chosen profession were frightened and paralyzed. Both in his personal relationship to them and in the texture of his cinema, Makhmalbaf was integral to the reign of terror that the Islamic Republic perpetrated on an entire nation.

The Social Realist

The division of creative and critical labor implicit in the presumed bifurcation between cinema and society – that in cinema we create and toward society we apply our critical faculties – does not hold at the colonial corner of aesthetic modernity. At that corner, artists are denied this division of labor and privileged by seeing creativity and criticism as integral to each other. In their criticism, post/colonial artists are creative, in their creativity critical. This is the only way artists can dodge colonial subjugation and cultivate agential autonomy. The conclusion of Makhmalbaf's cinematic career as a religious visionary, a short period that lasted only two years from 1982 to 1983, was marked by a turn to writing fiction. Two of his novellas, *Hoz-e Soltun* (1984) and *The Crystal Garden* (1985), stand out as two crucial moments in post-revolutionary Persian fiction.[6] Because of the language barrier, the outside world scarcely notices Makhmalbaf's contribution to contemporary Persian fiction. But even critics inside Iran usually do not consider his works of fiction in their general assessment of Makhmalbaf's work. The unfortunate reason for that dismissive attitude again is the religious disposition of his early cinema. The modern Iranian creative universe, almost from its very inception in the early nineteenth century, has had an overriding cosmopolitan disposition with little or no room for religious sentiments. Even recently, when there was a symposium of literary figures in southern Iran, religious writers were not invited to the gathering. The violent Islamist appropriation of the 1979 Revolution has categorically cornered the critical disposition of creative writing as 'secular' in texture and disposition. The serial murder of some dissident intellectuals by agents of the Ministry of Information in the mid-1990s has in fact aggravated this dismissal of being at once religious and critically creative. Makhmalbaf's early works of fiction, however, are integral to the Iranian cosmopolitan literary heritage, and yet they have suffered from a categorical neglect by Iranian literary critics. To be sure, such prominent members of the Iranian literati like Houshang Golshiri (died 2000) and Mahmoud Dowlatabadi represent an entire history of literary modernity in which religious sentiments scarcely have a role or place. And certainly compared with them, Makhmalbaf's work remains amateurish and accidental. But still in the general composition of his creative output that literary aspect is quite significant and noteworthy.[7]

What is astonishing about Makhmalbaf's short-lived career as a fiction writer is that there is not a trace of religious sentiment or even ideological conviction in his two novellas. Both in *Hoz-e Soltun* and in *The Crystal Garden* the chief protagonists are women, in the first drawn into political activities without any solid convictions and in the latter completely lost in the mundane realities of their daily predicaments. *Hoz-e Soltun* is an account of the June 1963 uprising from the perspective of Ezzat, a poor woman from the working class. She has lost her husband and soon loses her young son too. She survives by doing all kinds of odd jobs until she marries again, this time a revolutionary seminarian. In the character of Ezzat, Makhmalbaf obsessively narrates the personal account of a public predicament. Not for a second does Ezzat's account of her life collapse into either self-pity or political pronouncements. She is a survivor, and precisely in her relentless pursuit of a living does she exude affirmation of life, without losing its sight to a grandiose idea. The same is true of *The Crystal Garden*, narrated around the servants' quarters of a rich family's house, the owners of which have fled the country after the revolution. Here too, Makhmalbaf portrays his characters, most of them women, with ease, grace, and empathy. His childhood proximity to three women gives Makhmalbaf a critical intimacy with the fate and disposition of his female characters. Among an array of memorable women that Makhmalbaf portrays in *The Crystal Garden*, the character of Khorshid stands out as one of the most colorful creations of contemporary Persian fiction. She is a rambunctious woman with a worldly wisdom beyond any faith or ideology, and yet steadfast in her own version of moral propriety. Having been born to poverty, she is like Ezzat a survivor. She has also mastered the art of surviving the maladies of a patriarchal culture. She is a vibrant epitome of shrewdness, marrying men left and right, using the patriarchal practices against themselves and for her survival. In Makhmalbaf's vividly sympathetic portrayal of Khorshid, we see an incorrigible, dyed-in-the-wool woman who refuses to collapse into sentimentalism and yet has her romances with a panoply of men she has married to survive. As Makhmalbaf creates the character of Khorshid, the character of Khorshid saves Makhmalbaf from his ideological convictions, cleanses his creative character, and rinses every wrinkle of rancor from his tortured body.

That tortured body, though, has its own enduring logic and lunacy. It is not until Makhmalbaf exorcises the anger and horror of his years in Pahlavi prison in *Boycott* (1985) that he can open his eyes and look critically at the revolution for which he all but lost his life. The central character of *Boycott*, Valeh Ma'sumi, is Makhmalbaf's wishful thinking of converting a committed Marxist into a Muslim revolutionary. There are reports by Marxist revolutionaries incarcerated in the dungeons of the Islamic Republic (some of whom I have interviewed) that they were forced to watch Makhmalbaf's *Boycott* in jail repeatedly on closed-circuit television by way of forcing them to repent and convert. 'To this day,' one of these former prisoners told me, 'every time I hear the sound track of that film I have a nauseous node forming in my belly.' Makhmalbaf's short story *The Surgery of the Soul* (1987), which is an account of his own torturous experiences in the Pahlavi dungeon, is said to have been given to leftist prisoners to be read by way of psychologically breaking their will to resist. 'That short story of Makhmalbaf was like a stab in my heart,' one Marxist revolutionary, whose husband was murdered by the Islamists in jail and who herself was brutally tortured in the dungeons of both the Pahlavi regime and the Islamic Republic, told me. 'As much as a poem of Ahmad Shamlu would lift our spirit and strengthen our will, *The Surgery of the Soul* would do exactly the opposite.' The purpose of the exercise, as these former prisoners report, was to subject them to psychological pressure, weaken their will, and turn them to Muslim converts. The term 'Tawwabin' ('those who have repented') was used in prison for those who had converted, or pretended to have converted, to the religious convictions of their jailers. Makhmalbaf himself is reported to have regularly visited Qezel Hesar prison, talking to 'converted' prisoners, organizing them in writing classes, giving them guilt trips, encouraging them to marry the survivors of martyred soldiers. That most of these former prisoners carry the scars of their wounds quietly, and scarcely anyone hears of them or knows their stories, does not wipe out that particularly criminal phase in the continued atrocities of the Islamic Republic.[8] Nothing can excuse Makhmalbaf for whatever share he had at the time in such atrocities, or forgive him such horrid abuses of power. Thousands of political activists were cold-bloodedly murdered in the dungeons of the Islamic Republic,

7   Shiva Gerede as Gozal in Mohsen Makhmalbaf's Nubat-e Asheqi (A Time for Love, 1991), a film that carries Makhmalbaf away from Iran and marks his signature preoccupation with relativism. Shot in Turkey, the film was banned in Iran. (Photograph: Bahram Jalali; courtesy of Makhmalbaf Film House.)

others were severely tortured in the same cells and torture chambers where these jailers were themselves once jailed. Those were days of revolutionary terror, and they continue to haunt the moral imagination of a nation that once produced and endured them.[9]

Having finally exorcised the pains of his years of torture and isolation out of himself in *Boycott*, Makhmalbaf turns his attention to the enduring social malaise that had made him a religious revolutionary in the first place. Between 1986 and 1988, he makes three films: *The Peddler* (1986), *The Cyclist* (1987), and *Marriage of the Blessed* (1988). Not a trace of a religious visionary or a revolutionary ideologue is now detectable in this phase of his filmmaking. It is as if he has peeled off a former self, casting, shedding, excoriating himself into a whole new creative courage. To trace these films in Makhmalbaf's creative career, we need to go to his works of fiction, to *Hoz-e Soltun* and *The Crystal Garden* in particular. Otherwise, nothing in his early cinema could anticipate this social realism up his sleeve. By attending to poverty and destitution in *The Peddler*, to the Afghan refugee predicament in *The Cyclist*, and to the veterans of the Iran–Iraq war in *Marriage of the Blessed*, Makhmalbaf retrieves his initial social concerns before they were distorted into ideological warfare and thus forever breaks ranks with the Muslim revolutionaries now in power.

Needless to say, Makhmalbaf's tenure as a social realist brought him unparalleled fame as one of the leading public intellectuals of post-revolutionary Iran, reminiscent of the fame and popularity of such intellectuals as Jalal Al-e Ahmad (died 1969) and Ahmad Shamlu (died 1999), at the peak of their prominence in the 1960s and 1970s. He was the public intellectual of the poor and of the downtrodden, the denied, and the denigrated. He was a Muslim intellectual, and nobody since the now-legendary figure of Ali Shari'ati (died 1977) had restored dignity to that patently oxymoronic expression, and doing so at the height of an Islamic Revolution. To be sure, Muslim intellectuals were now in power and were brutal in their abuse of power and the persecution of secular intellectuals. Abdolkarim Soroush, another major public intellectual of the period, was instrumental in 'cleansing' Iranian universities of those members of the faculty deemed at odds with the Islamic Republic and thus helped to aggressively 'Islamicize' the curriculum. Ahmad Shamlu, the most celebrated public intellectual of his generation and the poet laureate of his nation, was forced to silence and seclusion at the peak of his creative effervescence. Muslim intellectuals had stopped speaking the truth to power. They were in power. But soon after the success of the Islamic Revolution, though not before he had been directly implicated in some of the most atrocious abuses of power by the Islamic Republic, Makhmalbaf broke rank with the revolutionary activists now turned into politicians and bureaucratic functionaries. Having broken ranks with power made Makhmalbaf even more popular among his admirers. Abbas Kiarostami's masterpiece, *Close Up* (1990), depicts the most famous, but not the only, case of young men impersonating Makhmalbaf. But ultimately Makhmalbaf's fame and popularity did not survive his artistic integrity. The more his flamboyant creativity took him into unchartered territories, the farther away he grew in taste and disposition from the initial base of his early popularity. The more global he became in his fame and aesthetics, the more his local constituency faded into the emerging politics of a post-revolutionary indifference. What Makhmalbaf still had to see and say, shoot and show, was pregnant with a different audience altogether.

The Philosophical Relativist

Makhmalbaf's social realism phase cures him of his religious visions but leaves him empty. He sees the same atrocious social circumstances of destitution and depravation that led him to pick up arms to launch a revolution still afflicting his society. The revolution for which he had almost lost his life had succeeded but not much had changed in the condition of the poor and the disenfranchised. As the Iran–Iraq war is drawn to a bitter end, and as Khomeini dies and his charismatic violence releases a whole nation from its suffocating grip, Makhmalbaf spends that year (1989) making no film but reading extensively and systematically in philosophy and psychology. The positive result of this year of philosophical reflection is a necessary distance from being dragged into a suffocating hermetic seal of factual problems; its not so positive consequence are two films that are only of archival interest in Makhmalbaf's multifaceted career. *A Time for Love* (1990) and *The Nights of Zayandeh Rud* (1990) are excellent exercises in philosophical relativism but as 'films' entirely useless, trite, and prosaic. *A Time for Love* narrates three versions of a tragic love story, a menage-a-trois with a deadly end, to reflect the relativity of a person's position in his or her view of things. *The Nights of Zayandeh Rud* does the same relativity turnover on political and amorous relations before and after the Islamic Revolution. These two films add nothing to Makhmalbaf's cinematic career, but they do rescue him from the trap of falling back on a kind of social–realist cul-de-sac that would have forever buried him under the heavy burden of documenting *the evident* and never detecting the subterranean inroad toward *the possible*. Both films were banned in Iran, one because it dealt with marital infidelity, the other for equating the Islamic Republic with the Pahlavi monarchy.

The Visual Theorist

The purgatorial passage out of a jaded philosophical relativism, which after Makhmalbaf's initial phase as a religious visionary could equally have terminated his career as a serious filmmaker, came in the form of an aggressive theorization of the visual, paving his way toward his poetic sur/realism. The project begins with his phantasmagoric *Once Upon a Time, Cinema* (1991), continues with his flirtatiously flamboyant *The Actor* (1992), comes to a sudden and tragic halt with the death of his wife Fatemeh Meshkini in 1992, goes into a deeply repressive hibernation and reflective reading and writing in 1993, and finally resumes with a biting vengeance in his sardonically poisonous *Salam Cinema* (1995).

Once Upon a Time, Cinema (1991) is a love letter to (Iranian) cinema. It is wise, spacious, endearing, a celebration of tolerant wisdom, with the visual vastness of being-in-the-world all around its sagacious sight. This festive occasion of reason, configured in the character of Amir Kabir, the nineteenth-century champion of salvaging a nation from medieval feudalism, is told as a history of the Iranian encounter with colonial modernity, when the autumnal patriarchy of the dying Qajar dynasty sees itself in the mirror of the newly invented miracle of the moving picture. Makhmalbaf's *Once Upon a Time, Cinema* is a loving pastiche, quoting and honoring most memorable scenes in Iranian cinema, carrying them on his shoulder into the festive occasion of the birth of his own cinema. Whatever nasty thing Makhmalbaf may have said against the masters of his chosen profession, here he more than apologizes by paying joyous homage to their pioneering wisdom, sagacious insights, honored memory. The result is a festival of light, a joyous fiesta in praise of the indomitable spirit of cinema, singing, dancing, moving to the rhythm of reasoned hope, laughing at the banality of evil. No rancor, no anger, no resentment, no bitterness, nothing but a cascade of love pours over and dignifies the master practitioners of an art to which Makhmalbaf now knew defined his own calling. It is as if *Once Upon a Time, Cinema* is the baptismal cleansing of Makhmalbaf's perturbed soul, now confident in his full membership in a vocation as sacred to him as his once held his ancestral faith. The original title of the film, *Naser al-Din Shah, the Cinema Actor* is given in deference to the very first Iranian feature film ever, *Haji Aqa, the Cinema Actor* (1933), Avanes Oganian's pioneering manifesto championing the cause of cinematic modernity in a visual culture blinded in public by moral bigotry and ossified fanaticism. From its deferential title, *Once Upon a Time, Cinema* anticipates its concluding sequence, a magnificent cross-cutting of embraces, borrowed from across the Iranian cinematic culture, all along the topography of its emotive universe, mental notes, and projected pictures of Makhmalbaf himself – hugging and being hugged, forgiving and asking for forgiveness. Particularly privileged is the homage he pays to Bahram Beiza'i, apologizing in public for any disrespect, in a language common to both of them, the visual vastness of signs signating their emotive universe.

As an orchestral celebration of cinema itself, *Once Upon a Time, Cinema* sparkles with an aesthetic intelligence that is rarely so pure and simple. It is the festive gathering of all the boisterous frivolity of cinema as a visual take on history, reality, and humanity. Here, Makhmalbaf thrives in showing what it means to show. Spending all that time with the masterpieces and major landmarks of Iranian cinema, cutting and pasting his pastiche together, Makhmalbaf effectively makes love to Iranian cinema, in the broad daylight of his vast and voluptuous

8   Mohsen Makhmalbaf on the set of Honar-Pisheh (Actor, 1993) – a flamboyant, Felliniesque experimentation with notions of acting, madness, and eroticism. It marks a major transition in Makhmalbaf's cinema. (Photograph: Mitra Mahasseni; courtesy of Makhmalbaf Film House.)

screen, enticing and cajoling it, kissing and cuddling it, embracing and holding it, inserting himself lovingly in between its teased out spaces. He more than apologizes to Iranian cinema for his having insulted some of its master practitioners. The result is a visual grasp of reality unprecedented in his earlier cinema. There is a scene from Sohrab Shahid Sales' *Still Life* (1974) that Makhmalbaf quotes in which the old woman is trying to thread a needle; it takes her a very long time – one of the most brilliant long takes of Shahid Sales' masterpiece. His Majesty the Qajar monarch watching this film (anachronistically of course, and thus the power of the image) gets really bored and incensed with this masterpiece of Shahid Sales' long takes, and in a moment of absolute creative brilliance Makhmalbaf has one of his characters, Malijak (for we are now in the late nineteenth century), walk into Shahid Sales' scene and help the old woman thread the needle, so the show can go on. Malijak in that scene becomes Makhmalbaf, placing himself in front of Shahid Sales' camera, touching the visual wisdom of his master to be anointed in his chosen vocation. Very few people other than Makhmalbaf could have made that film, with that audacity of spirit and quickness of wit, to cut and caress his way into the bosom of Iranian cinema.

Soon after *Once Upon a Time, Cinema*, Makhmalbaf made *The Actor* (1992), the rambunctious alliteration of visual inconsistencies, Felliniesque in its crazy defiance of narrative logic, imaginatively boisterous, insolent and quarrelsome in its unabashed celebration of *acting* as an act of foolery, make-believe, phantasmagoric folly. It is the least of Makhmalbaf's own favorites, because he says he made it formulaically. What he means by this is in an essay he once wrote on how to make a film and make it sell well. To put the formula he theorized in that essay to the test he made *The Actor*, and it sold massively! But like all works of art, *The Actor* defies its own creator. The sur/realism that is generated around the threesome of an actor, his barren and mad wife, and a voluptuously enticing gypsy girl exudes a visual energy unparalleled in any of Makhmalbaf's other, categorically boisterous, films. The actor's room, the barren wife's madness, and the physical energy of the gypsy girl feed on each other, and nourish the phantasmagoric vision that defies Makhmalbaf's own intention and carry his imageries into uncharted territories.

The emergent sur/realism of *The Actor* remained a major component of Makhmalbaf's cinema almost despite himself. An understanding of the nature of this sur/realism must begin here in *The Actor*, whose creative spontaneity has the evident traces of Federico Fellini's *8½* (1963), while its measured mannerism is deeply indebted to the nightmarish self-consciousness of Joseph K (Anthony Perkins) in Orson Welles' adaptation of Frantz Kafka's *The Trial* (1963) – one of the best examples of how an imperceptible sur/realism can begin to sneak out of a perfectly realistic setup. The morning that Joseph K wakes up and faces the bizarre accusation that he has committed an unidentified crime begins like every other day, and in the very familiar surroundings of his vacated bedroom. Throughout his ordeal until his demise, Joseph K is depicted in nothing that cannot be seen as the logical (rhetorical) extension of his real employment inside a bureaucratic machinery. Makhmalbaf's *The Actor* is very similar in its having layers of the sur/real emerge from the surface of reality. Whether it is through Welles' vernacular uses of camera angle or Anthony Perkins' jittery and nervous Joseph K, the shimmering palpitation of the surface solidity of reality soon succumbs in *The Trial* to the hidden terrors it thinly disguises – and thus slips through the appearance of normalcy the gory phantasm of the unreal. Beginning with Welles' contorted camera angle of the opening sequence in *The Trial*, in which the head of Joseph K and the two inspectors have come to pick him up – Inspector A (Arnoldo Foá) and Second Assistant Inspector (Jess Hahn) – the entirety of the film is a kinetic setup to implicate the viewer in the uncanny teasing of the unreal out of the prosaic realities of Joseph K's pathetic life. The same result, the same inching toward the realization of the sur/real from the evident fact of the real, is evident in Makhmalbaf's depiction of the decline and collapse of Simin (Fatemeh Moatamed Arya) into madness – framed and formed within the phantasmagoric setup of her husband Abdi (Akbar Abdi)'s kinetic roomful of movie pictures. Whether or not Welles' (or Kafka's) Joseph K has actually committed a crime becomes entirely irrelevant in the face of the paralyzing flow of his unconscious overflow of anxiety that in and of itself overwhelms his being. That overpowering presence of the unmitigated subconscious of a bureaucrat, now standing for Man as such, is the machinery that animates this unfolding of the sur/real, as indeed in the case of *The Actor* the evident lunacy of Simin becomes inconsequential once Makhmalbaf, in one of his most imaginatively daring moments in *The Actor*, depicts a homoerotic scene between Simin and the Gypsy (dumb) girl (Mahaya Petrosiyan) – from which Simin becomes miraculously (fictively) pregnant.

The year that Makhmalbaf made *The Actor* was also the year that he lost his wife to a tragic accident, when she inadvertently caught fire while trying to turn on a gas water-heater. Fatemeh Meshkini was Mohsen Makhmalbaf's soul-mate soon after he was released from Pahlavi prison. She was the mother of Makhmalbaf's three children and his principal assistant in all his films, even acting in a few of them. For more than a year, Makhmalbaf mourned the death of his wife and partner. He did not make any film throughout the following year. He read and wrote, attended to his three children, and later married his sister-in-law, Marziyeh Meshkini, now a filmmaker of extraordinary promise.

Salam Cinema (1994) begins as a salutation to cinema (this it shares with *Once Upon a Time, Cinema*), then innocuously mutates into a psychopathology of tyranny (this is the bereaved Makhmalbaf remembering the revolutionary zeal he shared with his late wife), and thus reveals the madness at the heart of this thing called *acting* (and this it picks up where *The Actor* left off). *Salam Cinema* is the nightmare of the dream that was *The Actor*, where *acting* is no longer the endearing detour into the nature of *being* but the horror that is hidden in its subterfuge. In *The Actor* all the actors are professionals. In *Salam Cinema* none of 'the actors' are actors. They are all real people who storm into a venue where Makhmalbaf has announced he wants amateurs to audition for his next film. Between acting by actors and non-acting by non-actors, Makhmalbaf frames the enigma of being in the crisscrossing of two distorting surrealities, broken mirrors that reflect in full pictures of the real. In both *The Actor* (1992) and *Salam Cinema* (1993), interrupted tellingly by the death of Makhmalbaf's lifetime soul-mate in 1992, he, still unknown to himself, is paving his way toward his own version of poetic sur/realism, where he will make reality yield, unwillingly, to madness on one side, nightmare on the other. What does it exactly mean to act? In *The Actor*, we see the rambunctious edge to the left of reality, and in *Salam Cinema*, the tyrannical nightmare to its right. Deviance from the real in *The Actor* is flamboyant and endearing. Mutation of the real in *Salam Cinema* into tyranny is the very banality of evil, as Hannah Arendt would say. Thus *The Actor* and *Salam Cinema* are the two dangerous edges that embrace and outright authenticate the real, one into madness, the other into tyranny. The two edges, though, do not ossify into concrete solemnity of two absolutes. They fade into the miasmatic recesses of an atmospheric mistiness that caresses and thus corrodes into the concrete claims of the *real* to reality. Predicated on *Once Upon a Time, Cinema*, jolted by the death of his wife, and framed in between *The Actor* and *Salam Cinema*, Makhmalbaf breaks the code of the *real* and dismantles its claim to absolutist authenticity. Thus by 1994 and at the conclusion of *Salam Cinema*, Makhmalbaf's hallmark sur/realism is born. The death of his wife occurs smack in the middle of the birth of his indissoluble cinematic vision, from the throws of his pain the soul of his cinema.

The Poetic Sur/realist

At the conclusion of *The Actor* and *Salam Cinema*, interjected by the tragic death of his wife, *reality* had become entirely miasmatic for Makhmalbaf, and the metaphysics of *the real* had totally lost its grip on the violence it perpetrates on the *all-but-evident*. These abstract shades and shadows of what we categorically call and dismiss as 'reality' had assumed concrete significance by the time Makhmalbaf had finished making *Salam Cinema* and began to wonder how to see and render the evident matter-of-factness of cinematic realism. In his last, mature phase of filmmaking, Makhmalbaf learns how we should not be fooled by the bogus claims of *reality* to truth, and through the instrumental facility of *the real* he gets ever so closer, without being afraid, to *all-but-evident*. This simple and elegant insight is the soul of Makhmalbaf's poetic sur/realism – what his sagacious cinema ultimately had in store for him and his audience. *A Moment of Innocence* (1995), *Gabbeh* (1995), and *Silence* (1998) – the gap between the first two films and the last covered in 1995–98 by Makhmalbaf's turn from a filmmaker into a filmmaker-maker (as he put it to me once in Cannes) – are the elemental birth of Makhmalbaf's mature poetic sur/realism. At the pinnacle of his mature cinema, the factual evidence of *the real* has been joyously emancipated from the violent grips of any metaphysical claim on their authenticity, leading their neighborhood into the vicinity of *all-but-evident*. In mythic immoderation with in/nocence, in/sight, and ultra/sound, *A Moment of Innocence*, *Gabbeh*, and *Silence*, respectively, are the three giant steps that finally lift Makhmalbaf up and place him among the greatest filmmakers of his generation. His confident, caring, and creative camera now comes to full fruition and steals the light of freedom from the incarcerated heart of tyrannical darkness – where *reality* used to have a claim to *authenticity*. Himself having arisen from the heart of that darkness, Makhmalbaf knows exactly where to look for the light: not in the Platonic Beyond casting its shadow on a cave-wall, not in the Aristotelian Reason placed beyond the reach of human means, not even in an Enlightenment modernity that has categorically denied him agency by putting him beyond the folds of reason, the fusion of the sublime and the beautiful.[10] Light in the very heart of darkness. *All-but-evident* in the midst of *the real*, *the real* in the heart of *reality*, *reality* authenticated in and by the metaphysical violence that gives it its aura of *Truth*. Reality is no longer authentic for Makhmalbaf's poetic sur/realism, because *the real* is freed from any metaphysical claim on it and has led his camera into the vicinity of *all-but-evident*, there to tease out the light of its emancipation from the heart of its own darkness.

In these three films of the mature Makhmalbaf, the narrative of his poetic sur/realism is confidently parabolic, his visual phrasing creatively spasmodic, his charismatic diction self-assuredly spontaneous – extemporaneous filmmaking of an artist at his best. This is the fully blown Makhmalbaf: minimalist in his visual diction, calm, quiet, and composed in his creative effervescence, brevity the very soul of his wits. *A Moment of Innocence* remembers Makhmalbaf's youthful indiscretion with an anamnesis of cultural forgetfulness, a recollection of guilt writ forgivingly large. Here Makhmalbaf remembers how he once wanted to stab and disarm a police officer to pick up his gun and to launch a revolution. The result is the fourfold splitting of two characters, Makhmalbaf himself and his would-be victim, both in their injudicious youth, the resulting four now in creative conflict. The almost 40-year-old Makhmalbaf at odds with his almost 17-year-old youth, the almost-killed police officer at odds with his almost-forgotten youth. At the center of the fourfold mirroring of the real is a young woman, the juvenile revolutionary Makhmalbaf's comrade, the sweet summation of every woman he has ever loved now made into the young police officer's object of affection. The last frozen shot of the film, the open invitation of the young woman's face graced even more by a flowerpot (instead of the police officer's gun) and a piece of bread (instead of the young Makhmalbaf's knife), is the variegated field of a poetically surreal salutation to life.

Gabbeh does for sight what *A Moment of Innocence* does for guilt, freeing it from the controlled tyranny of *the real*, as it blesses it with the emancipatory force of *the surreal*. As a love story, *Gabbeh* is more a celebration of color in an Islamic Republic of fear and darkness than a mere tapestry of the emotive universe it seeks to reverse. The protagonist of *Gabbeh* is neither the young girl nor the object of her affection, neither the carpet nor its story. It is color. The sheer galaxy of shades, shapes, and shimmering sensations that colors create and convolute to stir e/motion in the universe constitute the text and texture of *Gabbeh*. The scene in which the teacher pushes his punch out of camera's frame and reaches for the blue in the sky, the green in the pasture, the red of the flowers, and the yellow of the wheat field is pure cinematic joy. There Makhmalbaf has his hands on the very pulse of the *all-but-evident*, right before the *real* has any claim on it, way ahead of that catastrophic moment when *reality* has unleashed its metaphysical claim on its authenticity. Makhmalbaf is elemental in that moment, his frame throbbing with the beat of life before it is narrated, theorized, pigeonholed into one metaphysics or another culture.

Silence does for sound what *Gabbeh* does for sight, freeing it from the controlled tyranny of *the evident*, as it blesses it with the emancipatory grace of *the possible*. In *Silence*, Makhmalbaf blinds the sight to hear the sound. *Silence* thus will not only have to be heard with the blind boy's perfectly pitched ears but also seen with his totally dark sight. *Silence* is extraordinarily beautiful to look at because it is imagined from a blind boy's mind, with Makhmalbaf's camera planted in his head. Add to that the poetic Persian of the Tajiki dialect, which is pure music to an Iranian set of ears, and the result is the idyllic lyricism of elemental sounds in *Silence* echoing the elemental colors of *Gabbeh*. Cut down to its primeval forces, the site of *the evident* is now the open field of *the possible*, and we are at the primordial pulse of simply *being-in-the-world*, where all its symbolically ordered elements melt down and absolve into their originary signations, long, very long, before they are acculturated into one violent metaphysical claim on them. Khorshid imagines the world anew, in his blind insights, in his hearing the super-sonic sound of the real, to which the rest of the world is deaf. He is blind but in his mind he sees for and in the world another universe. He has perfect pitch and in his ears is echoed the melodic harmony of a universe. His singular mission in life is to restore the cacophonic confusion of the world to that perfect harmony that he sees in his mind's eyes. This is Makhmalbaf the religious visionary, turning his blindness into insight, his musical infirmity to visual strength, his metaphysical malady to cultural cure. When he was a young child walking past a record store, his grandmother would tell him to stick his fingers into his ears so he would not hear sinful music. That infantile inhibition of forbidden music in the maturity of Makhmalbaf's forgiving of his tyrannical culture sublates into restoring harmonic order to a universe of emotive dissonance he has inherited in his world. The conclusion of *Silence* is an orchestral celebration of cacophonic dissonances collectively contributing to the making of a harmonic melody – a culture that does not demand categorical conformity, but which fuses differential discord into creative concord.

Makhmalbaf at Large

In his critique of Immanuel Kant's constitution of a critical reason for the European project of Enlightenment modernity, Theodore Adorno points out that Kant's purely theoretical human being is completely isolated from his material reality, that he does not exist except in the pages of *Critique of Pure Reason* (1781).[11] What Adorno leaves out in this assessment is that this isolation of reason from reality in the European Enlightenment is conceived precisely in the same way that the global operation of capital is understood in a fabricated isolation from its colonial consequences. It is in fact the defining moment of European Enlightenment modernity that it dismisses colonialism as accidental to the operation of capital. But on the colonial edge of the very same project, the two are lived and experienced, though never theorized, as integral to each other. Reality is as co-terminous with reason as colonialism with the global embeddedness of capital. If we were to restore reason to reality, in the way Adorno criticized Kant, but also place the operation of capital in its globally colonizing context, the way Adorno as all other European intellectuals has failed to do, then the logical consistency of the European subject will be constitutionally compromised, as indeed the absence of that agency in the colonial context is opened up for an enabling criticism. In other words, restoring reality to reason and incorporating the colonial into the capital will produce a global blueprint for an emancipated subject that is no longer divided along the power-basing access of 'the West and the Rest' – the very condition under which the assumption of 'the West' has been imperially fabricated to denigrate and dismiss the colonial site capital thieveries.

In Kant's categorical constitution of both moral and ethical agency to the European subject, calling it Enlightenment (Modernity), Adorno detects a critical paradox whereby 'the metaphysical inspiration is shifted onto the concept of reason.'[12] Adorno traces this paradox to his assessment that what they have in Germany is not Enlightenment but Enlightened theology, of the sort evident in Kant's celebrated attack against Swedenborg in his *Dreams of Spirit-Seer*. It is the illogical translation of that metaphysical element into Kant's constitution of 'pure reason' that allows for the unreal postulation of theoretical consistency in the subject at the expense of its material context. Because the rest of the world received the European project of Modernity through the gun-barrel of colonialism, it never assumed that its reason had any transhistorical validity. There, the colonial could see through the bogus claims of that reason long before the Holocaust and much sooner than Adorno and Horkheimer theorized it in their *Dialectics of the Enlightenment*.

On the edges of the colonial context we could clearly see that beyond the collapse of the aristocratic longevity and ecclesiastical order that preceded it, the European bourgeoisie went about inventing an Enlightenment modernity for itself with such a metaphysical confidence that we could never share or trust. No Enlightenment confidence informs the colonial comprador bourgeoisie (or its inorganic intellectuals for that matter), nor indeed has a systemic philosophical aesthetics ever theorized our works of art. Such works of art, as a result, *are* the theories of post/colonial cultures, all articulated at the colonial periphery of the European Enlightenment. In retrospect, in our works of art, we in fact celebrate, not lament, our marginality to an Enlightenment modernity that – as Adorno and Horkheimer demonstrated – had the Holocaust up its sleeve. From that marginality, there is a subterranean access to a form of subjection that is not power-basing, panoptic, or exclusionary. We the subjects of European colonies were lucky to have been excluded and exiled from Kant's aesthetics. He aesthetically theorized the beneficiaries of capital by constituting the European bourgeois (which he cast as a universal *Homo sapiens*) as an autonomous subject in full control of his critical faculties and universally in charge of the objective world. His critical philosophy – from *The Critique of Pure Reason* (1781), to *The Critique of Practical Reason* (1788), to *The Critique of Judgment* (1790) – is categorically geared toward an enabling of the European subject and the authorization of historical agency to him. It is not just by omission that the colonial person is made subject of European agency in Kant. The Kantian constitution of the European subject – as knowing and conquering – is in fact integral to, coterminous with, and entirely contingent on a simultaneous de-subjection of the colonial subject. The two effectively implicate each other. At the conclusion of *Observations on the Feeling of the Beautiful and Sublime* (1763), a key pre-critical text in which Kant's philosophical guards are down, he goes out of his way to articulate and argue the non-European out of his conception of the beautiful and the sublime, the critical site on which the autonomous European subject is put to critical test in his command over the objective and knowable world. We need to read the passages at the end of *Observations on the Feeling of the Beautiful and Sublime* not merely as the textual record of Kant's mind-numbing racism, which goes without saying and is rather commonplace among all his European contemporaries. We need to read these passages as Kant's philosophical argument denying the Orientals (which for him meant the world in its entirety minus Western Europe) the autonomy of a knowing subject, and thus their *ipso facto* delegation to the knowable world. It is not that we as Orientals are incapable of the sublime and the beautiful to Kant. In Kant's philosophy, we as Orientals are incapable of the sublime and the beautiful because he has already catapulted us to the realm of the knowable world, to objects that need to be conquered and deciphered – and thus the fundamental and organic roots of European Orientalism in Kant's epistemic foregrounding. The entire nonsensical proposition that European Enlightenment is a universal project with which the rest of the world must catch up and become modern flies in the face of the textual evidence of the European project itself, which *ipso facto* enabled the European subject by not just disregarding the rest of the humanity but was in fact predicated on the global denial of any agency for it. To Kant the Orientals could not share that agential autonomy of the knowing subject because he had already delegated them to passive objectivity of the knowable world, where they waited for the European officer – authored and authorized by Kant – to discover and conquer them. To Kant, we Orientals are *things*, waiting to be discovered, known, and thus conquered and owned. We are not human beings who can – even on borrowed European terms – get to know, understand, or, *a fortiori*, possess.

Makhmalbaf represents a mode of creative explosion at the post/colonial edges of capitalist modernity that is both disallowed by Kant and disenfranchised by capital, an aesthetics that collapses the creative and the critical together, and that as such is rooted in pain and branched out to hope. My principal argument throughout this book and in whatever reading of Makhmalbaf's cinema I suggest, is that on the site of his cinema there is the evidence of a creative constitution of an anticolonial agency entirely autonomous of Kant's (and by extension European) denial of that possibility in the post/colonial artist, and by extension person. In the aesthetics of emancipation that Makhmalbaf's searching cinema, poetic sur/realism, and restless creative consciousness represent, we can detect a site of anticolonial agency that opposes the definitive de-subjection of the colonial person by successive colonial projects, both in discursive and institutional terms. Outside the citadel of the metaphysics of any certainty and disallowed to have a claim in Kant's categorical imperatives, in between those two sites of power and domination, artists like Makhmalbaf have had to fend and fare well for themselves and for nations of negations their art represents. There upon that site, and perforce, he has had to become spontaneous: he has had to go back into his own history and invent his own Omar Khayyám. His aesthetics, as a result, are impulsive, his creativity impetuous, his awareness of the world awaits no theorization, his being-in-the-world is circumambulatory. He is rash in his articulation of the beautiful, reckless in his notions of the sublime, extremely sketchy in the cut-and-paste quickness of his artistic whereabouts. But all these are definitive to an aesthetics that is grounded and material, rather than theoretic and abstract. To be sure, there is nothing specific about Makhmalbaf's cinema that lends itself to such modes of anticolonial theorization. One could easily argue the same through the cosmopolitanism of Abbas Kiarostami's cinema, Sohrab Sepehri's poetry, Houshang Golshiri's fiction, or Gholamhossein Saedi's drama.

What is (perhaps) peculiar to Makhmalbaf, and thus my concentration on his cinema in this book, is that in the course of a single cinematic career he exemplifies and historicizes in macrocosmic terms the microcosmic unfolding of colonial conquest and anticolonial resistances in creative and critical terms – at one and the same time. The fact that he first was a militant revolutionary activist and then he becomes a world-renowned filmmaker mirrors this artistic history and corroborates the choice of his cinema as the site of my investigation and argument.

Makhmalbaf's poetic sur/realism is his final sublation as a religious visionary. He has now come full circle, from religious revelation to poetic inspiration. Turning his full attention to his family and training them as fully fledged filmmakers occurred exactly at a time when his poetic sur/realism had peaked and paradoxically plateaued. By 1995, when he made both *Gabbeh* and *A Moment of Innocence*, his creative effervescence hit yet another cul-de-sac exactly at a time when his elder daughter, Samira, quit school at the age of 15 and vowed never to go back. By then she had already assisted her father on several of his projects and had also made a couple of short films – a precocious pattern that was later followed by Makhmalbaf's youngert daughter, Hana, who at the age of nine made her first short film, *The Day My Aunt Was Ill* (1997). Makhmalbaf abandoned his initial idea of starting to shoot *Silence* in India, remained in Tehran, and turned his attention exclusively to Samira and his other children, teaching them the tools of his trade. The only other thing he did in 1996 was to take stock of his creative career and then publish three volumes of his selected writings, both creative and critical. *Gong-e Khabdideh/A Dumb-man's Dream* gives a summation of Makhmalbaf's relentless work of close to two decades.[13] That year was a time of creative hibernation so far as his own work was concerned.

In the following year, Makhmalbaf was itching to get back behind the camera. During the summer of 1997, he visited Dushanbe in Tajikistan for location scouting for *Silence*. He was about to pack up and go when the daily press in Tehran reported that two young girls were found incarcerated by their over-protective father for the entire duration of their young lives. Samira Makhmalbaf immediately became attracted to the story and demanded that her father give her the negatives he had just obtained to go to Dushanbe and shoot *Silence*. By the following summer, the world premier of *The Apple* (1998) took place in Cannes, where people watched Samira Makhmalbaf's debut (then aged 17) shot on a negative that was meant to picture her father's *Silence*.

The set of *Silence* (1998) in Dushanbe was a field trip for Makhmalbaf's family to practice their newly acquired skills. The following year (1999), Makhmalbaf took his family around the country, location scouting and collecting local music for their next projects, Samira's *Blackboard* (2000) and Marziyeh Meshkini's debut film, *The Day I became a Woman* (2000), shot in Kurdistan and on Kish Island in the

9   Moharram Zeinalzadeh in Mohsen Makhmalbaf's Bicycle-Ran ('The Cyclist,' 1989), the first film that Makhmalbaf made about Afghan refugees in Iran. From this film forward he will remain consistently concerned with the fate of the Afghans and Afghanistan. Turkey, Tajikistan, Afghanistan, Pakistan, and India will soon emerge as the alternate sites of his cinema. (Photograph: Aziz Saati; photo courtesy of Makhmalbaf Film House.)

Persian Gulf, respectively. While on Kish, Makhmalbaf shot a short film called The Door (1999). The officials in charge of tourism and the free-trade zone on Kish asked six prominent filmmakers, including Makhmalbaf, to make six short films to be put together and released as Tales from the Island of Kish. By February 1999, in time for the Fajr Film Festival in Tehran, one of these six was not yet ready, while another did not make it through the Islamic Republic censorship. The remaining four were put together and submitted to the Cannes Film Festival. Cannes, at the time still directed by Gilles Jacob, accepted three of the four, including Makhmalbaf's The Door, but rejected Bahram Beiza'i's entry, Goft-o-Gu ba Bad/Conversation with the Wind (1998). The producer of the film, Mohsen Gharib, accepted the cut and the three-episode Stories from Kish Island (1999) – Nasser Taqva'i's The Greek Boat, Abolfazl Jalili's The Ring, and Mohsen Makhmalbaf's The Door – was accepted at Cannes in 1999. This incident created considerable controversy in Iran, in the course of which Bahram Beiza'i publicly accused everyone involved, including Makhmalbaf, of bigotry, bias, and even charlatanism. Angered by the incident, Makhmalbaf went so far as to sit for a long interview responding to these charges, but at the very last minute prevented the publication of that interview. The sum result of the event was the public discrediting of two major public intellectuals, and all that at the time of a massive social uprising spearheaded by students against the atrocities of the Islamic Republic, including the bloody suppression of a grass-roots movement defending freedom of expression by mercenary thugs at the service of the theocracy. While globally celebrated around the world, major voices in Iranian cinema were effectively discredited at a time of critical importance for their homeland. Journalists like Akbar Ganji and reformists like Said Hajjarian took center stage and became far more important for the future of their homeland than the whole array of Iranian filmmakers and the fancy footwork of their international festival circuit. It was in part in response to this event that while in Kish, helping his wife with the script for *The Day I became a Woman*, Makhmalbaf made *Testing Democracy* (2000), a fantastic tale of cinematic self-reflection by a filmmaker concerned that he was losing public relevance in his own homeland.

The balance of Makhmalbaf's work since 1995 has tilted far more toward his family than himself. With *Gabbeh* (1995) and *A Moment of Innocence* (1995) he peaked and plateaued in his poetic sur/realism, and in *Silence* (1998) he simply completed this trilogy. *The Door* (1999), *Testing Democracy* (2000), and *Kandahar* (2001) have been sporadic forays, on the same level of poetic sur/realism, without adding or subtracting anything significant to or from what he had achieved in the three masterpieces that initiated and culminated this last period of his filmmaking. The same holds true for his latest features, *Sex and Philosophy* (2005), *Scream of the Ants* (2006), and one short, *Chair* (2006) – three quite personal reflections on love and life that were both critical and commercial flops. Far more critical has been his role in making three filmmakers out of his wife and his two daughters. Though a photographer of extraordinary talent, and despite the fact that he has made a behind-the-scenes documentary about his sister Samira, Makhmalbaf's son Meysam has now assumed control of financial matters for the House of Makhmalbaf.

As in his childhood, when he grew up in the protective custody of his grandmother and her two daughters, Makhmalbaf is once again surrounded by three women: his wife and his two daughters. In between these sources of his inspiration and aspiration, he has now successfully escaped the cul-de-sac of any creative phase he has crafted for himself. Mature and fruitful at the last, poetically sur/real phase, he intuitively and as a matter of obligation to his family turned to them and to making 'filmmakers instead of films.' He has now successfully sublated his own person into a polyphonic ventriloquist. As he speaks his mind and pictures his imagination, his wife and children now have a subterranean inroad to both – with a distinct and pronounceable twist of their own. From soliloquy to ventriloquy, Makhmalbaf has delivered his poetic sur/realism into the inventive impersonation of his creative ego – making filmmakers over whose cinematic vision he has no complete control. He kept moving from phase to phase, and when he ran out of phases, he mutated and multiplied and thus gave birth to creative surrogates of himself, letting them loose upon a world whose unpredictability requires unpredictable responses. Makhmalbaf is no longer. Makhmalbaf is now his family. But like all great artists he is not in full control of his own creations. Marziyeh Meshkini, Samira Makhmalbaf, and Hana Makhmalbaf will each go their own way. In doing so, Makhmalbaf has perpetuated his proverbial unpredictability in the unpredictability of three women, three feminine sub-versions of his masculinist culture. He has thus planted three seeds of uncertainty in the uncertain soil of an unknown future for himself and his family, for his family and his nation, for his nation and the world.

Medium Shot

Chapter Three

Dead Certainties:
The Early Makhmalbaf or the
Purgatory of a Rebel Filmmaker

As I pointed out in some detail toward the end of the last chapter, one of my principal concerns in this book is to see in what particular aesthetic terms we ought to watch Makhmalbaf's films and relate to his art. This concern is predicated on my conviction that the sort of art that we produce on the post/colonial site is not to be assimilated backward (without major damage to its nature and function) into the dominant aesthetic terms of European Enlightenment modernity. This is not out of any *a priori* hostility toward that modernity, which has done splendidly well for Europeans, but because of its own deliberate and specific exclusion of us Orientals, as Immanuel Kant and his Orientalist progeny call us, from the possibility of the sublime and the beautiful. The rapid globalization of spectatorship – particularly through the intermediary function of the major European and North American film festivals, art exhibitions, and biennales – places these works of art at the receiving end of manners of reading and 'appreciation' inevitably dominated by film critics and film scholars either steeped in or else beholden to the aesthetics of European post/modernity. One can read the entire French reception of Kiarostami and Makhmalbaf, as perhaps best represented by the journal *Cahier du Cinema*, as the best representative of this sort of assimilation backward of an art form otherwise demanding the manners of its own articulation, in terms at once global to its spectatorship and yet domestic to its production. In everything I have said or written on art and cinema, I am very particular about the intersection of artistic production in a particular domesticity and its subsequent global interface. This is not an altogether accidental issue, given the fact that a monumentally brilliant and productive filmmaker like Bahram Beiza'i never received the global attention he has always richly deserved, and yet other Iranian filmmakers like Abbas Kiarostami or Mohsen Makhmalbaf have. My point of contention here is to find out what dialectic of reciprocity between artistic production and global reception is at work that makes such discriminations possible.

If we are not particular about the specifics of that interface, before we know it, the very alphabet of our reading these works of art either assimilates them into

European post/modernity or else anthropologizes them into a sort of Third-Worldist object of curiosity – a manner of reading Iranian cinema perhaps best represented in Michael M.J. Fischer's learned book *Mute Dreams, Blind Owls, and Dispersed Knowledges: Persian Poesis in the Transnational Circuitry*. My contention here is that these works of art ought to be saved from both these traps, and let loose to breathe in aesthetic terms global to the audience they have earned (and that is not limited to those in the Western European film festivals) and yet domestic to the poetic disposition that has generated them. But equally dangerous to a theoretical articulation of this aesthetics is the blindfold cultural reductionism that leads to the cul-de-sac of an inconsequential *nativism* – arguing, for example, that Makhmalbaf's films are exclusively 'Islamic' or 'Iranian,' and as such are to be understood in specifically (and thus entirely vacuous) Islamic and Iranian terms. This too is a bogus claim. Makhmalbaf, as all other globally celebrated artists, is a creature of his chosen craft. There are traces of the masters of his profession in his work far beyond and above his immediate geographical and cultural vicinity – ranging all the way from the Japanese Ozu to the Italian Fellini to the Bengali Satyajit Ray. Makhmalbaf himself is a great admirer of Andrei Tarkovsky, Yasujiro Ozu, and Vittorio De Sica, for example. By his own admission, when he saw Wim Wenders' *Der Himmel über Berlin/Wings of Desire* (1987) for the first time in London (his first trip ever outside Iran), his life was changed forever. These filmmakers are as important to him as the poetry of Forough Farrokhzad and Sohrab Sepehri, and the cinema of Sohrab Shahid Sales and Amir Naderi. The only legitimate site of working toward an articulation of his aesthetics, as a result, is his own cinema, without assimilating it backward to any culture domestic to his birth and breeding or else an aesthetics alien to them.

The task of articulating that aesthetics is a long and diligent proposition. What I will try to do in this chapter is to link the moral imagery of Makhmalbaf's early cinema to a particularly acute moment in the European crisis of technological modernity, as best, in my judgment, articulated by Martin Heidegger in his essay 'The Question Concerning Technology.' I have detected in that moment of philosophical crisis of European modernity a particularly critical blind spot, which I wish to explore here and show that it is precisely from that blind spot that the post/colonial art can begin to see, articulate, and reveal its aesthetic predilections. My strategic departure from Heidegger's essay, via a detour through Stanley Kubrick's *Eyes Wide Shut*, takes us directly to the moral imagery at the heart of Makhmalbaf's early film and fiction. On that site, I propose to articulate the start of Makhmalbaf's career as a rebel who has just turned to art – and thus in his art dwell the manners and modes of aesthetic liberation from the epistemic cul-de-sac of colonial modernity. Makhmalbaf's life as a revolutionary and the art that he has produced in continuation of his politics deserve careful attention, not despite his Islamist roots but in fact precisely because of them. His revolutionary disposition is as much constitutional to the metaphysics of his erstwhile absolutist convictions as it is definitive to his restless and agitated mind and soul: homeless, always, where it is at home, a way station for where he is going next. His mobile life and volatile career beacons from the heart of danger – and in the heart of that danger dwells the aesthetic pharmacon that were it not to kill his instincts it was meant to save his nation of sentiments, and with those sentiments any claim to truth and reconciliation that is embedded in his cinema.

The Question Concerning Technology

Toward the end of his essay on 'The Question Concerning Technology' (1955), Heidegger begins cautiously to introduce the hidden and forgotten meaning of the Greek word *technê* as a way out of the cul-de-sac of the *Enframing*, as *Destining*, which is the most pernicious danger, as he saw it, constitutional to technological modernity: 'But might there not perhaps be a more primally grounded revealing that could bring the saving power into its first shining forth in the midst of the danger, a revealing that in the technological age rather conceals than shows itself.'[1]

This is a critical point in the European self-reflection on the crisis of technological modernity and only a slight modification of its evident Euro-centricity makes this passage extraordinarily revealing for the state of art in the rest of the world at the receiving end of the selfsame project. The *concealing* against which Heidegger sees this 'primally granted revealing' launched is itself the technologically constituted *revealing* of *standing-reserve* (when humanity is mutated into a thing) as the characteristic *Enframing* essential to the technological projects. Technological modernity is the carrying forward to logical conclusions the Greek sense of *technê* as *bringing-forth*, as a *presencing* that reveals itself as *destining* (the poetic possibility at the heart of things). Heidegger calls this entire calamitous conclusion of the technological modernity 'Enframing' (*Ge-stell*), which means that 'challenging claim,' or that inevitability of technological conditioning, which 'gathers man thither to order the self-revealing as standing-reserve.'[2] Here is precisely where and when everything reveals itself, shows itself as being nothing but useful, useable, dispensable, expendable, integral to the line of production, everything, even, or particularly, man *itself*.

Against the *danger* of this kind of concealing reality in the form of revealing it as useful, Heidegger sought to detect a *saving power*, which is evident in technological modernity itself and as such rooted in the self-same Greek conception of *technê* that this time around is more akin to *poiêsis*.[3] Seeking the antidote of turning man into an irresistible agency of useful ordering in that ordering itself, Heidegger postulates a primal time 'when it was not technology alone that bore the name *technê*. Once that revealing that brings forth truth into the splendor of radiant appearing also was called *technê*.'[4]

This 'once' of Heideggerian nostalgia is a Hegelian trace, here translated into a theoretical anti-technological device, which no one at the colonial end of the project trusts. On the colonial site, technology did not come out of the Greek *technê* but from the long and extended colonial barrels of European vernacular guns. For Heidegger, Greece was 'the outset of the destining of the West.'[5] For the rest of the world such Hegelian illusions, surviving the axe of the Heideggerian *destruction*, have been catastrophic because precisely by virtue of such illusions it has been far more nakedly incorporated into the *Enframing* that has gathered the post/colonial person to be in his and her very body instrumental in *ordering*, by *being-ordered-to*, *self-revealing* itself as *standing-reserve*. No one has stood in reserve more than the colonial person has. Literally.

Subtract from Heidegger's hermeneutics of Hegelian fixation with *Origin* its unexamined predicating on the 'Western' *Destining*, and then his 'art was simply called *technê*' assumes a significance far beyond its European vicinity. For those at the receiving end of technological modernity, the brutality of its colonial reception has been constitutional to creative revolt against it. Consider the evident materiality that Heidegger ascribes to art at this presumed primal moment. He could very well be speaking of art as it is created and conceived on the harsh scorches of colonial outposts: 'The arts were not derived from the artistic. Art works were not enjoyed aesthetically. Art was not a sector of cultural activity.'[6]

This is post/colonial art, the state of the art as the saving power against the danger of *Enframing* constitutional to technological modernity. But whereas Heidegger has to go back to a fictive Greece and impregnate an innocent or willing *technê*, all the post/colonial artists have to do is to place themselves where they are, at the receiving end of technological modernity, at the colonial site of capitalist modernity, at the tropical outpost of the polar centers of the European Enlightenment. For all 'traditions' in pre-colonial arts that they may have invented, there is no understanding their art, as there is no escaping their politics, without a preliminary reading of this modernity.

'Why did art bear the modest name *technê*?' Heidegger asks and then responds, 'Because it was a revealing that brought forth and hither, and therefore belonged within *poièsis*.'[7] That too is the post/colonial artists, at their poetic best, when Mahmoud Darwish, Nazim Hekmat, Pablo Neruda, Ahmad Shamlu, or Faiz Ahmad Faiz revolt against the colonial consequences of technological modernity. The moment that Heidegger has called 'the frenziedness of technology'[8] is the colonial site, the location of its most naked accomplishments, yet invisible at the polar centers of technological modernity until the horrors of the Holocaust. The Jewish Holocaust was the scattered and invisible atrocities at the colonial peripheries of technological modernity 'coming home to roost,' as Malcolm X put

10   *The desolate landscape of Mohsen Makhmalbaf's* Tobeh-ye Nasuh *(Nasuh's Repentance, 1982) revealed
the emergence of a young filmmaker deeply committed to an Islamic Republic and its metaphysical underpinnings.*
(Photograph: Ahmad Tala'i; courtesy of Makhmalbaf Film House.)

it upon hearing of President Kennedy's assassination on 22 November 1963. The 'frenziedness of technology' has wreaked havoc on the colonial world *en masse* and thus post/colonial art artists could not but speak in the naked anxiety of that frenziedness. For colonial artists the *technological* was also the *mysterious*. They may not have known how it worked and yet they were at its mercy. On the post/colonial site the non-Europeans (by the very fact of the diversity of their cultures and contexts being thus leveled to the status of the 'non-European') are at the mercy of the technological twice removed in terror from 'the European.' The European (thus designating itself) had unleashed the monster and was *riding* it, while it was *feeding* on 'the non-European' – thus designated and dismissed by the founding father of Enlightenment modernity, Immanuel Kant.

Heidegger is very particular on the link between technological modernity and art: 'Because the essence of technology is nothing technological, essential reflection upon technology and decisive confrontation with it must happen in a realm that is, on the one hand, akin to the essence of technology and, on the other, fundamentally different from it. Such a realm is art.'[9] What exactly does it mean that the essence of technology is not technological? If we bracket for a moment Heidegger's proclivity to trace everything to its Greek origin – in this particular case the tracing of technology to a mis/reading of the Greek *technê* – and place the German philosopher himself squarely in the context of the post/Enlightenment anxiety against which he launched his philosophical project, then it is precisely that European project which is the ideological foregrounding of capitalist modernity and which is the essence of technology, and thus not technology itself.[10] Heidegger is correct that the essence of technology is not technological. But it is not a mis-reading of the Greek *technê* either. That *essence* is to be detected in the cataclysmic changes in the very subjectivity of human agency ushered in during the course of the European Enlightenment and its twin project of capitalist modernity. Once we go that far, there is only one step we need to take toward the colonial conclusion of the project of capitalist modernity. And once on that site, the essence of technology as the categorical reduction of things, including the human, to their use-value need not be persuasively argued. It is there. Colonialism *is* the essence of technology, directly consequential to the twin projects of the European Enlightenment and the capitalist modernity that occasioned it.

Heidegger postulates both an 'essential reflection' of and a 'decisive confrontation' with the essence of technology. 'Essential reflection' on the essence of technology is of course an entirely European proposition. The deceptive monster was born there and can only be *essentially* reflected upon precisely on that site. But when it comes to 'decisive confrontation' with it then the site cannot be *but* the colonial realm, its categorical denial, its civilizational Other. Heidegger is right that the realm of this confrontation must be akin to the essence of technology *only* so far as 'essential reflection' on technology is concerned. But

11   *Unmarked and abstract landscape was the defining moment of Este 'azeh (Seeking Refuge, 1984), which continues with Makhmalbaf's preoccupations with a metaphysics of dead certainties. (Photograph: Ahmad Tala'i; courtesy of Makhmalbaf Film House.)*

when it comes to 'decisive confrontation' with it then we must be on a site that is 'fundamentally different from it.' As an imperially imagined idea, 'Europe' is not that site. Colonial territories are. But even so far as 'essential reflection' on the nature of technology is concerned, where Heidegger sees the essential function of art, it is crucial to keep in mind his stipulation that it can only happen if art 'does not shut its eyes to the constellation of truth.' This is a warning only appropriate to and in place at the heart of technological modernity where the luxury of such a 'shutting of the eye,' a conditioned ignorance, exists. On the colonial frontiers, meanwhile, there is no such luxury. The art crafted on the colonial site has never had the option of shutting its eyes 'wide open' – as Stanley Kubrick's last failed masterpiece exemplifies – on the constellation of truth, the technological constitution of modernity as the premise of the revealing of things as *standing-reserve*, ready to be used.

Heidegger rightly saw the problem of art in achieving the task he was stipulating for it: 'In our sheer aesthetic-mindedness we no longer guard and preserve the coming to presence of art.'[11] The radical theorization of the *work* of art into *aesthetics* is almost exclusively an act of post-Enlightenment practice. Cultural modernity, as Max Weber realized and Habermas underscored it,[12] broke down what Weber had called 'substantive reason' – and placed it within the prerogative of the sacred imagination – into three autonomous spheres of *truth,* *normative authenticity,* and *beauty*. As science claimed the 'truth' and morality 'normative authenticity,' aesthetics assumed an exclusive jurisdiction over 'beauty,' autonomous of both truth-claims and morality. It is only in reaction to the catastrophic consequences of the Enlightenment that Adorno later tried, in his *Aesthetic Theory*, to retrieve for the work of art its inherent truth-claims. Thus Heidegger's diagnosis of the super-imposition of aesthetics between the post-Enlightenment European and the work of art is exclusively limited to that polar center of technological modernity and entirely absent in the case of post/colonial art and confrontation with the work of art. Here, we need to avoid by all means the categorical trap of the so-called 'traditional art' that both technological modernity and its nativist detractors, strange bedfellows but nevertheless in active coalition with each other, have concocted for post/colonial art. What artists have produced on the post/colonial site is *not* 'traditional art,' but a perfectly contemporaneous response to the predicament of their place at the colonial end of the twin projects of the European Enlightenment and capitalist modernity. Precisely because of the colonial nakedness of creative expression on this site, post/colonial art is particularly resistant to European aestheticization. Kant's assertion that people in the African and Asian outback of his Enlightenment modernity were lacking in their grasping of the sublime and the beautiful in fact helps in keeping that art at the necessary arm's length from the European aesthetics that as Heidegger rightly suggests is an Enlightenment proposition. The naked nature of technological aggression at its colonial ends, one might thus argue, has made post/colonial art particularly immune to European aesthetics. European aesthetics, as a colonial (and of course self-alienating) proposition, in turn, has been the necessary distancing measure that technological modernity has exacted in order to keep the eyes of the European 'wide shut' on the truth of the Enlightenment.

What is particularly applicable to the colonial site in its creative moments is Heidegger's suggestion that 'the closer we come to the danger, the more brightly do the ways into the saving power begin to shine and the more questioning we become.'[13] But while he tried philosophically to persuade a *simulation* of presence in that danger for the European, for the post/colonial no such *simulation* is necessary. S/he has *lived* that danger, and thus s/he *is* that danger. There is no site closer to the danger of technological modernity than its colonial consequences where the brutalities of the fatal attraction to the *Enframing* as *Destining* as *standing reserve* (all Heidegger's terms) had no sugarcoating of the Enlightenment. In fact quite to the contrary, the post/colonial has been the civilizational Other of the project of the Enlightenment – the shadow that has made its light possible, the 'grotesquery' (Kant's choice adjective for 'Orientals') that has made the European feel beautiful and sublime.

Closest to the Danger

On the site of the post/colonial production of material reality, artists have been the closest to the danger constitutional to technological modernity. At the best moments of their emancipation, they have managed ideologically to resist the colonial extension of the inner logic of technological modernity while artistically constituting a mode of subjectivity beyond the reach of that colonially conditioned subjectivity. But ideological resistances to colonialism have been, *ipso facto*, a negational reflection of the colonial project itself. We could not resist colonialism except with ideologies that it made possible. Islamism, as a liberation theology, has been one particularly poignant form of ideological resistance to the colonial extension of the project of technological modernity. Both the saving power *and* yet itself the very nature of the danger, Islamism was a particularly powerful ideological apparatus not because it was so radically *different* from colonial modernity but, quite to the contrary, because it was so thoroughly *rooted* in it.[14] What then is an 'Islamic art,' as in 'Islamic cinema,' in the context of this ideological Islamization of resistance to colonialism? In this context, 'Islamic art' is nothing but a further Islamization of ideological resistance to colonialism as the extended arm of technological modernity, an art in the service of Islamism as an ideology of resistance. It is to this notion of 'Islamic art' that Makhmalbaf, along with any number of other Muslim activists, squarely belonged when he began to take pictures with his camera, stick close ups to long shots, and try to tell an 'Islamic' tale. Neither the Islam that was conducive to the reign of the Pahlavi monarchy nor the Islam that was in the Orientalist production of subservient subjectivity on behalf of colonialism meant anything to this generation of Muslim activist. 'Islamic art' of the sort useful to them was conceived and executed on the ideological site of a David-and-Goliath battle against the onslaught of capitalist modernity, a helping hand given to the cultural constitution of resistance as *ipso facto* 'religious,' 'traditional,' or 'authentic' in its claims to ideological legitimacy.

At the start of their activities, such Muslim ideologues-turned-artists as Makhmalbaf did not recognize that their ideological *mode* of resistance to cultural colonialism is *itself* the most effective form of self-colonization. From Fanon to Shari'ati, a fundamental feature of counter-colonial resistance has been this categorical failure to recognize the formation of the so-called 'native' or 'traditional' mode of resistance to colonialism as something in and of itself deeply colonial. Fanon went so far as to consider veiling for Muslim women a counter-colonial barrier, guarding a territory that colonialism could not transgress.[15] Shari'ati went even further and sought radically to ideologize his received conception of 'Islam' into nothing but an anti-colonial ideology.[16] But an 'anticolonial ideology' is a colonial ideology. It is the colonial subjects, in their most agitated moments of political anxiety, that go to the memorial remembrances of their ancestral legacies in order to concoct an ideology of resistance to the colonial onslaught. The colonial subjects, so long as they remain 'ideologues' of their own liberations, cannot but be colonial in all their acts of compliance *and* resistance. In the acts of ideological resistance in particular, their militated subjectivity having been constituted by the very act of colonization, they cannot but further colonize the traces of their ancestral memory in search of an ideology of resistance.

When as a post/colonial subject a Muslim activist like Makhmalbaf turns into an artist he cannot but *initially* further cultivate the site of resistance to colonialism (and its varied mutations into global imperialism or regional tyrannies) in what he now considers to be 'artistic' terms. He may have thought that he is an artist but he was still too much in the sun of ideological resistance. The first phase of Mohsen Makhmalbaf's cinema, roughly from 1981 when he wrote *Marg-e Digari/ Someone Else's Death* until 1983 when he made *Do Chashm-e Bi-Su/Two Sightless Eyes*, a period of about two years, is squarely at the service of the Islamic ideology as a site of revolutionary resistance to both imperialism and its domestic political and cultural consequences. Makhmalbaf's early cinematic endeavors are entirely devoted to substantiating the metaphysical foundations of the theocracy he had helped to bring to power. His turn to art was a continuation of his ideological commitment to the cause of the Islamic Revolution. Now that the revolution was politically successful, he saw its achievements threatened by the cultural forces of the *ancient regime*, as well as by more cosmopolitan revolutionary forces that were brutally cut off from having a share in the fate of their nation. So he began his artistic career with the stated purpose of helping buttress its cultural foregrounding. Early in his artistic career, Makhmalbaf joined the propaganda machinery of the young Islamic Republic with the expressed intention of preventing 'non-Islamic' art to be used against the revolution. He soon joined *Howzeh-ye Andisheh va Honar-e Islami* ('The Center for Islamic Thought and Art'), to be re-named *Howzeh-ye Honari-ye Sazeman-e Tablighat-e Islami* ('The Art Center of the Organization for Islamic Propaganda'), in short *Howzeh*, and was organizationally brought directly under the jurisdiction of the chief propaganda machinery of the Islamic Revolution. Makhmalbaf became the chief artistic ideologue of the *Howzeh*, in a search for translating ideological concepts into 'artistic' expressions. At this time, Makhmalbaf believed that there was no theoretical statement about the nature of an Islamic art and he was single-handedly after creating it. He squarely denounced pre-Revolutionary art in general, cinema in particular. He believed that when people were burning the cinemas in the course of the revolution they were expressing their categorical condemnation of pre-Revolutionary art. A 'Muslim artist' was his preferred mode of identification, viscerally dismissing all those who failed to meet his revolutionary piety – and thus shooting himself and his chosen profession in the foot, living to regret these dark and damning days.

Makhmalbaf's turn to art was generic and yet experimental. He wrote short stories, novels, plays, scripts, and even critical essays on the nature and disposition of 'Islamic art.' His target, first and foremost, was artists at ideological odds with the Islamic Republic, filmmakers in particular, whom he categorically identified with the 'evil' monarchy and even demanded for them to be publicly tried. In his *Moqaddameh-'i bar Honar-e Islami* ('Prolegomena to Islamic Art'), he sought to give the outlines of a new and revolutionary description of what exactly constituted the nature and function of 'art' in an Islamic context. Makhmalbaf's writing in this period is prosaic, sophomoric, simplistic, bordering on banality. But there is an urge in him, a relentless pursuit to reach for something that his blind dedication to an *Islamic* ideology prevents him even to articulate let alone to probe.

Tojih/*Justification* (1981), the first feature film that Manuchehr Haghghani-parast directed on the basis of a play by Makhmalbaf, reveals the types of issue that preoccupied the young rebel turned filmmaker. The play/film is about an urban guerrilla organization that during the reign of Mohammad Reza Shah assassinates an American diplomat and plans a series of explosions in the capital. The disagreement between two of the guerrillas and their doomed fate is all centered on the cliché-ridden debate whether the end justifies the means. In both *Hesar dar Hesar/Fortress in Fortress* (1982) and *Marg-e Digari/Someone Else's Death* (1982), which Mohammad Reza Honarmand directed on the basis of Makhmalbaf's script, we do not see much of a change. Makhmalbaf is still embroiled in flat ideological investigation of Death and Destiny. In *Someone Else's Death*, Makhmalbaf depicts an encounter between Death and a General. At its best moments, this film becomes a moment of anti-military reflection. But Makhmalbaf is still too raw, too flat, too much visually pleonastic to see anything. He is very much like that General, imprisoned in the bunker of his ideological limitations, convictions, and certainties. Makhmalbaf's principal problem at this point is that he is after the wild goose chase of an 'Islamic cinema,' so much a figment of his perturbed ideological imagination that even he himself does not quite know what it is. He knows that an 'Islamic cinema' has to be revolutionary, anti-status quo, against secularism. But these are all the negational aspects of this 'Islamic cinema.' What precisely this cinema is to be in positive terms neither he nor his revolutionary cohorts know. However, what is still lurking beneath all this pompous emptiness is a restless mind. Makhmalbaf's creative body is captivated by a spell. He does not know it. But he is in labor.

In *Tobeh-ye Nasuh/Nasuh's Repentance* (1982), Lotf Ali Khan, a bank employee reminiscent of Scrooge in Dickens' *A Christmas Carol*, is taken for dead but arises from his death and – guided by his benevolent friend Us Yahya – seeks to remedy his past evil deeds. The 25-year-old director who has spent his life fighting for a just 'Islamic' society is now after pontificating about the morality of a pious life. He is bewildered by this cinematic medium. But like a sleepwalker he is attracted

12 *A filmmaker in the making: The young Makhmalbaf (on the right reading the script) behind the scene of* Tobeh-ye Nasuh *(Nasuh's Repentance, 1982). (Photograph: Ahmad Tala'i; courtesy of Makhmalbaf Film House.)*

to it almost involuntarily. In the depth of this prosaic banality, of celebrating a vacuous piety, something is brewing in Makhmalbaf. It is true that all of these early films, up to *Bycote/Boycott* (1985), can be safely thrown into the trashcan and nothing will be missed of Makhmalbaf's cinematic career. But there is much archival evidence in them to justify their existence and relevance to how a post/colonial artist rises from the perils of a colonized mind to meet the promises of an embattled wisdom. Lotf Ali Khan, the chief villain of *Nasuh's Repentance*, is an evil character that Makhmalbaf must exorcise from his own creative imagination before he can dig deeper and wider and begin to be more serious about his art. More than to any critic, to Makhmalbaf himself will these characters later appear as empty, shallow, flat, and pointless. And yet they are the signs of the growing pains in the groins of his creative body.

In *Do Chashm-e Bi-Su/Two Sightless Eyes* (1983), Makhmalbaf continues to exorcise the political demons inhabiting his still agitated imagination since his prison years. A leftist teacher and a greedy merchant are now the target of his pontificating anger. Salvation is to be found in two pious Muslims, Mashhadi Iman and Seyyed Abdollah, their names crudely reminiscent of what Makhmalbaf wants them to represent. The teacher lacks any principle; the merchant is sub-human. The puritanical sentiments evident in *Two Sightless Eyes* is equally evident in Makhmalbaf's oft-quoted statement from this period that he was not willing to be caught 'even in a long shot' with pre-revolutionary filmmakers, Bahram Beiza'i chief among his targeted anger, whom he categorically dismissed as 'satanic' (*Taghuti*).

Este'azeh/Seeking Refuge (1983) is by far the most catastrophic product of Makhmalbaf's early cinema, imbued with a formal mysticism that had he not immediately cured himself of, he would have ended up with the most malignant case of cine-mysticism (the mutation of cinema from creative doubts into mystical convictions), to which fatal disease we have lost one of our best filmmakers, Daryush Mehrju'i. As evidenced in this early symptom, Makhmalbaf would have contracted a far more deadly case of cine-mysticism than Mehrju'i's had he not put up a tough resistance to the fatal attractions of the deadly disease. In *Seeking Refuge*, Makhmalbaf completely abandons the social scene and opts for what he terms 'Philosophical Men,' vastly empty abstractions that he constructs in order to examine the nature of Evil. Five Philosophical Men encounter Evil in five convergent episodes, each trying to simulate the pitfalls of the Carnal Soul. It is nothing short of a frightful nightmare to imagine the effect of a film like *Seeking Refuge* being screened in Iran in 1983, right under the puritanical terror of Ayatollah Khomeini. The culture was tip to toe plunged into a pool of martyrdom and mysticism, the Iran–Iraq war was raging full blast, Iranian youth in their thousands were perishing on battlefronts, and then this ghastly metaphysical examination of the 'nature of Evil' was indeed the very nature of evil itself. Five nameless, shapeless, characterless Men get into a forsaken Boat and sail to an abandoned Island in the middle of Nowhere. Four of them perish in a fictive battle with Satan, and the Fifth man survives by rectitude and righteousness. Makhmalbaf's Manichean mind is still dividing the world between a shapeless Evil and an afflicted Good, engaged in a fateful, cosmic battle. It is nothing short of a miracle how Makhmalbaf could save and salvage himself after such malignant catastrophes – the rosters of a metaphysical registry of mental malaise with which not just Makhmalbaf but a whole culture has been afflicted for eternities. What Makhmalbaf gives to these mental afflictions, this psycho-pathological impotence to face reality with all its calamities and glories, is a new lease on life, a fresh radical contemporaneity. There is such a vertiginous anthropophobia in the fake Biblical/Qur'anic narrative of *Seeking Refuge* that makes the film simply unwatchable. Was it necessary for Makhmalbaf to pass through these valleys of dead certainties to reach for the saving power of living doubts?

The Decisive Moment

The fate of *Islamic Cinema* has been co-terminous with the demise of *Islamic Ideology* itself, both colonially mediated responses to the onslaught of technological modernity, both incapable of coming to terms with the overriding logic of a

13 *The young Makhmalbaf (on the right reading the script) behind the scene of* Este 'azeh (Seeking Refuge, 1984). (*Photograph: Ahmad Tala'i; courtesy of Makhmalbaf Film House.*)

phenomenon unprecedented in human history. The decisive moment comes, however, when art as a phenomenon *sui generis* gets hold of the ideologue and transforms the site of his resistance from merely political to one that is substantially poetic. Having emerged from the very heart of *danger*, Makhmalbaf has within him the *saving power* constitutional to the colonial extension of the project of *capitalist modernity*. He, of course, does not recognize the mutation in specifically transitional terms. That a relentless dissatisfaction with what he achieves constantly agitates him is the key factor. From the heart of the *danger*, from the ancestral faith of a people colonially occasioned to turn into an ideology of resistance to colonialism, emerges first an art, an *Islamic cinema*, which is in effect the birth-channel delivering the Muslim ideologue's subjectivity from a colonially constituted identity into an emancipatory direction. It is constitutional to the very nature of the post/colonial poetic to resist over-aestheticization. It cannot afford it. Makhmalbaf's art is particularly powerful *because* it emerged out of the *Islamic* ideological response to a sustained and prolonged course of colonialism. That art has been closer to its *danger*. Makhmalbaf's cinema is the light of hope having just emerged from the darkness that colonialism and anticolonial reduction of reality to politics posit and projects – the tree of its *poetics* is rooted in anticolonial *politics* but moves away and in the opposite direction. It is a saving grace always reminiscent of the danger at its bosom – the dialectic of its own emancipation, and with it the people that have dreamt and interpreted it.

Eyes Wide Shut

Makhmalbaf has had to pass through that danger in order to reach for the *saving* power of the poetic now paramount in his cinema. An historical collapse into essentialist mysticism, of the sort evident in Makhmalbaf's early cinema, is not limited to a young and inexperienced filmmaker. Far more seasoned and accomplished filmmakers in Iran have fallen squarely into that trap and never emerged from it. Daryush Mehrju'i, whose last films, concluding with *Derakht-e Golabi/The Pear Tree* (1998), exemplify the catastrophic consequences of a fatal attraction to cinematic mysticism. The crucial difference between Makhmalbaf and Mehrju'i, however, is that Makhmalbaf *commences* his cinematic career with this affliction with cine-mysticism and very quickly recovers from it, whereas Mehrju'i has pretty much *concluded* his oeuvre with this disease and evidently opted to sign his final signature on his otherwise extraordinary cinematic career in the jaundiced color of this affliction. Quite obviously the Islamic Revolution in Iran, which is in effect one massive, colossally orchestrated, ideological Islamization of a constitutionally polyvocal culture, is chiefly responsible for this artistic turn to the metaphysical. The difference between Makhmalbaf and Mehrju'i, again, is that while Makhmalbaf by ideological breeding was born into a metaphysics of mystical convictions and gradually allowed the aesthetic realities of his art to lead him to autonomous judgment, Mehrju'i, quite to the contrary, was artistically born into that mutlivocality but gradually degenerated into a jaundiced submission to the overwhelming authority of the mystical, now fully supported by a triumphant theocracy. The best films of Mehrju'i were all the results of his close collaborations with one of the most brilliant Iranian dramatists of his time, Gholamhossein Sa'edi. The suicidal urges of Sa'edi in the aftermath of the Islamic Revolution, which resulted ultimately in his deliberately drinking himself to death in exile, undoubtedly left Mehrju'i morally and psychologically depleted. Practically all of Mehrju'i's films after the death of Sa'edi in 1985 have had a penchant for a fatalistic mysticism. But whereas superior artists like Bahram Beiza'i have been able to rein in this urge and with impeccable creative discipline channel it into constructive directions, in weaker hands and minds the fatal attraction has been quite catastrophic. The case of Makhmalbaf is one critical example of a brutal honesty with *the real* literally pulling the artist out of the bewildering misery of casting a mystical gaze on the world.

To understand these *false* moments of ideological liberation from the onslaught of technological modernity on its post/colonial outpost, we need also to understand the *genuine* moments of despair at its polar centers – and there is no better place to look for that than in Stanley Kubrick's *Eyes Wide Shut* (1999). This example from outside the purview of Iranian cinema both illuminates the case of the early Makhmalbaf and points to a larger attraction to cine-mysticism as a particularly powerful pathological trait, albeit for different but nevertheless symptomatic reasons. Stanley Kubrick's *Eyes Wide Shut* should now be seen as the last, most spectacular, failure of a cinematic genius. By trying to transform Arthur Schnitzler's *Traumnovelle* from fin de siècle Vienna to fin de siècle New York, totally disregarding the cataclysmic century in between, Kubrick miscalculated the set up and missed the entire high bourgeois foregrounding of Fridolin and his wife Albertine by cross-breeding them into the yuppie consumerism of Bill and Alice Harford. A catastrophic confusion of what exactly happens to bourgeois subjectivity once it is subjected to 100 years of useable solitude is at the root of Kubrick's failure in *Eyes Wide Shut*. In Schnitzler's original *Traumnovelle*, Fridolin and Albertine live in the golden age of European high bourgeoisie, the full recipients of the bourgeois revolution still nowhere near its catastrophic consequences that were still not even on the European horizon – except in the criminal atrocities they perpetrated far and away in 'the colonies.' The Veblenian leisure class[17] that the couple represent gives them the full freedom of delving deep into the dream-life of temptation that lies disturbingly under the surface of civility they intimate. The whole point of the novella is this barely hidden ocean of temptation lurking under the veneer of Victorian civility they represent. This is far from the case of the two New York yuppies, Dr. William and Mrs. Alice Harford, who are deep into their useful reduction into mere consuming agents, long after the century of global wars, genocidal holocausts and massive colonial catastrophes marking the project of European modernity. The first thing that Stanley Kubrick and Frederic Raphael's Bill Harford can think of to say to a prostitute is 'So, do you, do you suppose we should talk about money?'[18] This is what Heidegger meant by technological modernity 'expediting' (Fördern) everything toward its use-value, 'toward driving on to the maximum yield at the minimum expense,'[19] toward reduction of man himself to the 'standing-reserve,' to be ready to be useful. But this is far from Fridolin's nocturnal adventures into his subconscious where on the bourgeois borderlines of a decadent aristocracy that has lost all its authority but none of its privileges (yet) he can see and reveal exactly on what precarious premises Victorian morality presides.[20] We can see the sandcastle of that morality precisely because Fridolin is the emerging high bourgeois European, at the last fin de siècle, who has a very direct access to his transgressive subconscious. 'So, do you, do you suppose we should talk about money?' is not the first thing that Fridolin would have said to a young and very attractive woman invitingly looking at him in the privacy of her kitchen. Bill Harford would do so and he does and thus the glacial sea that separates the two end-of-the-centuries from each other. The case of Alice Harford is even more catastrophic. In Kubrick and Raphael's narrative, she does not even work. The fact that she *used to* run an art gallery, as she says ever so deceptively to Sandor Szavost, the Hungarian philanderer who is trying to seduce her, and is now reduced to a 'home-maker' flies in the face of the contemporaneity that Kubrick wants to give to the Austrian novella.

'Think it's dated?' Kubrick is reported to have asked his co-scriptwriter Frederic Raphael. 'That's part of the ... challenge,' Raphael hesitates to tell the truth, hides it in the three-dot elision, and camouflages it in the euphemism 'challenge.' 'Dated in what way?' Kubrick continues. 'No cars, no phones, but that's not a problem,' Raphael seesaws, fearing to upset the master filmmaker. But that is *exactly* the problem. Cars and phones are precisely the most visible insignia of the technological spectrum on one end of which lived and dreamed Fridolin and Albertine, and on the other consume and go to parties Bill and Alice. In the course of these 100 years of technological frenzy, Fridolin and Albertine of the high European bourgeoisie have collapsed and degenerated into the Bill and Alice of New York yuppie consumerism. Of course Fridolin and Albertine had voluptuous access to their dream-lives. This is the Vienna of Dr. Freud himself, a friend in fact of Arthur Schnitzler's. A whole continental landscape of the unconscious is laid open and accessible to Schnitzler's fiction and Freud's theorization. Only one generation earlier, Dostoyevsky and Nietzsche had paved the way for this charting of the unconscious. But by the time we get to Dr. and Mrs. William Harford of Central Park West, New York, at this *fin de siècle*, nobody reads Schnitzler any more and Freud's theoretical elegance has degenerated into a multi-billion-dollar, Prozac-punctuated, therapeutic industry. That logic of the therapeutic, brilliantly diagnosed about halfway between Schnitzler/Freud and Raphael/Kubrick by Philip Rieff in his prophetic *Triumph of the Therapeutic*,[21] has made of the Bill Harfords of the world a consuming agency devoid of a creative subjectivity independent of his use-value as a professional physician. In his St Albans solitude and secrecy, Stanley Kubrick had remained frightfully ignorant of all these changes and asked his co-screenwriter 'what's the problem' with adopting Schnitzler for New York. 'The underlying assumptions,' Raphael responds in a moment of brilliant accuracy, 'which are dated, aren't they? About marriage, husbands and wives, the nature of jealousy. Sex. Things have changed a lot between men and women since Schnitzler's time.' Raphael could have added pre- and post-nuptial agreements, gay marriage, living will, Jack Kevorkian, genetic engineering, cloning, artificial intelligence, *ad infinitum*. 'Have they?' Kubrick retorts to Raphael, 'I don't think they have.' Raphael collapses under the summoned authority of Kubrick and drops his raised guards and thus succumbs his insight to what he believes to be the superior intelligence of Kubrick and consents: '(After thought) Neither do I.'[22]

But the superior intelligence of Kubrick has already collapsed into a blinding mysticism that seeks to rescue his historical blindness via the most magnificent sequence of the whole film, the central orgy sequence, which can only document, precisely in its metaphysical certainty, the final loss of Kubrick to cine-mysticism.

What happens in the central orgy sequence? Kubrick tries to fill the gap that separates the Fridolin/Albertine pair from Bill and Alice with the overwhelmingly mythical tonality that animates the orgy *sequel*. 'He wanted to escape into myth and inhabit an alien character who, nevertheless, would be close to him.'[23] A combination of critical factors – including Joycelyn Pook's haunting music, Barbara del Greco's Venetian masks research, and Marit Allen's costume design – makes the sequence, from the moment that Bill puts his mask on in the pillared hallway of 'Somerton' and begins to hear the strange music, until the Red Cloak discovers and dismisses him, particularly haunting because in it we are in the midst of one spectacular ritual of atemporal orgiastic foreboding, which is Spaceless, Timeless, and Ethereal in its sheer mythological narration. We are at the very Dawn of History, men and women doing in the ceremony of their at once sacred and sacrificial innocence the most spectacular acts of ritual sex. Here, Kubrick's camera is far closer to Schnitzler's narrative than is his script. Visually Kubrick does penance for all his narrative sins in misreading a psychological masterpiece. The monotonous, solemn, and frightful music has its best description in Schnitzler's own narrative: 'In place of the harmonium a piano had struck up a more impudent and earthly note, and Fridolin immediately recognized Nightingale's wild and rousing touch, while the female voice, hitherto so noble, culminated in a shrill, lascivious screech which seemed to take off through the roof into infinity.'[24]

The difference, however, between Schnitzler's scene and Kubrick's is that in the former it is part and parcel of the dream narrative, in perfect harmony with the realm of fantasy that Fridolin and Albertine help each other create to the point of breaking their barely holding together marriage. Whereas in Kubrick's, the scene assumes phantasmagorically mythical proportions precisely because the rest of it is so end-of-the-twentieth-century consumer industry. The faster the calamities of technological modernity have degenerated human subjectivity to ready-to-hand usefulness, the more Kubrick has to compensate for them with the mythical narration of the orgy sequence. Only by resorting to ritual mysticism can Kubrick approximate the voluptuous access that Fridolin and Albertine so naturally had to their dream-world and Bill and Alice so sadly lack in theirs. In effect, the high bourgeois life at the end of the nineteenth century is something of a mythical era for the generation of Bill and Alice Harford. The result, however, is identical: 'What I dread and cannot help probing is the possibility that the Kubrick myth will perish under close inspection.'[25] Raphael is absolutely correct. Kubrick's myth does perish precisely because it is, in all its splendid majesty and visual defiance of the real, un-real. The sad and spectacular fate of art at the end of the twentieth century, at the polar center of technological modernity and as evident in one if its greatest visual theorists, is precisely this turn to false mysticism at a moment of genuine despair.

The cumulative result of that orgy scene in the middle of the most repressed visual analytic of bourgeois banality is nothing more than a spectacular verification of Michel Foucault's enduring insight that talking incessantly about (or showing) sexual repression is in fact the best stratagem for the solid operation of capital and its unquestioned logic. What links the lurid (nocturnal) conversation between Bill and Alice (casting the infinite superiority of Nicole Kidman's Alice to Tom Cruise's bewildered and lost Bill) and the orgy scene is their mutual participation in a voyeuristic confirmation of the logic of capital. 'If sex is repressed,' Foucault observed, 'that is, condemned to prohibition, nonexistence, and silence, then the mere fact that one is speaking about it has the appearance of a deliberate transgression.'[26] That deliberate transgression is a mere simulacrum of defiance, as Foucault noted, effectively confirming the operation of the successful repression: 'What sustains our eagerness to speak of sex in terms of repression is doubtless this opportunity to speak out against the powers that be, to utter truths and promise bliss, to link together enlightenment, liberation, and manifold pleasures; to pronounce a discourse that combines the fervor of knowledge, the determination to change the laws, and the longing for the garden of earthly delights.'[27] *Eyes Wide Shut*, as a result, and its orgy scene in particular, becomes only a superior cinematic version of yet another episode of the HBO Original Series *Sex and the City*, where Carrie Bradshaw (Sarah Jessica Parker) publicly visualizes her relentless (tasteless and entirely asexual) monologue on her and her friends' sexual fantasies. Talking about and visualizing repression – from *Eyes Wide Shut* to *Sex and the City* to Eve Ensler's *Vagina Monologues* – are all capitalist consumerism sold *en masse* – and from art to entertainment. By vicariously participating in a visual or verbal orgy, the consumer is publicly sustained in the logic of the reigning capital.

What can we learn from this turn to cine-mysticism by the early Makhmalbaf and the late Kubrick? The genuine moments of despair at the polar center of technological modernity corresponds to false moments of liberation at the tropical peripheries of the post/colonial outposts.

The Crystal Garden (1984–85)

Makhmalbaf's emergence from his stint with cine-mysticism is not abrupt, but miasmatic, maneuvered through a much-neglected aspect of his oeuvre, namely his works of fiction. By the summer of 1984, one year into his success as an 'Islamic' filmmaker and four years into the brutal Iran–Iraq war, Makhmalbaf is ready to be born again, and he is, though not in a film but in a work of fiction he begins to write. *Bagh-e Bolur/The Crystal Garden* (1985) begins with the painful description of an excruciatingly torturous childbirth.[28] The birth of Setareh to Layeh, the birth of an orphaned child even before her birth, might as well be the birth of an artist in Makhmalbaf, from the very depth of his religious and revolutionary convictions. Setareh was conceived before her father Mansur was dispatched to the Iran–Iraq war fronts and killed in action. Layeh is now a martyr's wife. It is noteworthy here to remember that Makhmalbaf himself was conceived to his mother in the course of a marriage that lasted only six days. His parents were separated and divorced before Makhmalbaf was born. Like Setareh, Makhmalbaf was born to an absent father – a child of his own making, as it were. This is how he described his own birth in the course of a conversation with me in the fall of 1996:

> My father becomes acquainted with my mother. He had a wife, from whom he'd had two daughters, and not having a son, he made some excuse about wanting a son even though he'd actually fallen in love with my mother. They were more or less living in the same district. But my father was illiterate ... And so my father comes along and marries my mother, and after six days his first wife comes and grabs him by the ear and takes him back, and the story so ends. I'm the outcome of those six days ... which is to say, if my father hadn't fallen in love, and they'd not spent those six days together, well, who knows what really would have happened to Islam and blasphemy ... After I was born, I lived with my mother ... and my mother would go to work everyday ... after my birth, I was looked after by my grandmother as my mother worked nights in the operating room at the hospital. She paid our bills. My father refused to get a birth-certificate for me, and the two of them fell into the sort of petty games of humiliating and holding grudges against one another ...[29]

In *The Crystal Garden*, the description of Layeh giving birth to Setareh is unusually detailed and poignantly graphic. Makhmalbaf describes a childbirth as if he were giving birth himself, in himself, to himself. By the summer of 1984, Makhmalbaf had been married to Fatemeh Meshkini since 1978 and had witnessed the birth of two of their children, Zeynab (Samira) in 1979 and Ayyoub (Meysam) in 1981. His mother was also a nurse by profession. But something far more enduring, far more significant, is also taking place in this chapter and in this entire book. To come from those ideologically overburdened films to this gem of a short novel is something of a revelation. In the pages of *The Crystal Garden* we are reading an artist in the making, and here there is no Makhmalbaf the religious and revolutionary ideologue in sight. What happens in *The Crystal Garden* is Makhmalbaf's metaphoric return to an *internal* birth-point. In the first two chapters of the book he recreates not just the world of Layeh, a widowed mother of three young children, but the cosmic expanse of a universe of emotions to which he is born and from which he can now draw. In this book, he goes back to the basics and there in the simplicity of poverty and the brutality of the reality that he sees, feels, and lives, he gives birth to his own poetic self.

Already by the third chapter of *The Crystal Garden*, the surreal Makhmalbaf is in full, fantastic view. His description of the nightmarish insomnia of Layeh – her fears and tribulations in facing the prospect of caring for three young kids single-handedly – is the premonition of the later Makhmalbaf of *Once Upon a Time, Cinema* and *Gabbeh*. It is hard to believe that the author of *The Crystal Garden* is the same ideologue who about a year ago had made *Este'azeh/Seeking Refuge* (1983). There is not much of a plot to *The Crystal Garden*. The narrative alternates around the fate of four families gathered in the servants' quarters of the house of a rich family who have fled the country in the aftermath of the Islamic Revolution. These houses were typically confiscated by the revolutionary government and given to the families of those who had perished in the course of the revolution and the war. Khorshid and her husband Qorban Ali were the servants of the house before the revolution and now continue to live there. Layeh has just given birth to Setareh and has two other children, Sarah and Meysam. The third household is that of Mashhadi and his wife Aliyeh. Their son Akbar has perished in the war. They now live with their daughter-in-law, Akbar's widowed wife, Souri, and her two children, Samira and Salman. The other son of Mashhadi and Aliyeh, Ahmad, the younger brother of the martyr Akbar, also lives with them. The fourth household is that of the young Maliheh and her husband Hamid. Hamid has been paralyzed from the waist down in the war. Maliheh has married Hamid *after* his partial paralysis and out of her religious convictions to care for a hero of a just war. Because of Hamid's partial paralysis, they cannot have any (sex) children.

Writing fiction, as opposed to making a film, puts an entirely different set of creative urges to work for Makhmalbaf, reflective venues that will soon transform his entire imaginative mood. If we consider the scene of Layeh going to a public bath, after her childbirth, in the company of her friends and neighbors, the way Makhmalbaf describes it in patient and analytical details, the ritual ceremony is almost touchable in its physical and unburdened realism. Here Makhmalbaf's descriptive power leaves no room for any intrusion by ulterior motives. It is as if in the *privacy* of these pages, Makhmalbaf has no chip on his shoulder. He does not have to prove himself to Beiza'i or any other prominent filmmaker of the pre-Revolutionary period. Not a single trace of a committed revolutionary, or the dead certainties of a political activist, or the blind convictions of a fanatic Muslim, is remotely evident in *The Crystal Garden*. Quite to the contrary. Everything is here torn open, layer after layer, in an almost archeological introspection. There is thus a kind of moral *retreat* in *The Crystal Garden*, a reversal back into the robust busyness of the rambunctious life of women Makhmalbaf knows best – wives, daughters-in-law, mothers-in-law, nieces, sisters – where life is crowded, complaints are constant, few things are actually said, and yet that is all that there is. In this novel, Makhmalbaf gets himself lost in the bosom of the women-folk, young wives who have lost their husbands in the war, bitter mothers mourning their martyred sons, pious young women who marry maimed war veterans. In the midst of such miseries, however, neither Makhmalbaf nor any one of his characters is remotely ideological, revolutionary, committed, or even political. Politics is almost absent from *The Crystal Garden*. But the *consequences* of politics are not. These people just live, and their lives are crowded, lost to all grand illusions, major highways of salvation, monumental solutions, abstract convictions, metaphysical certainties. These women are Makhmalbaf's way back to the insurmountable ephemerality of *the real* in its magnificent cruelties, in its detailed minutiae of small hopes, long before and beyond its distortions into one grand illusion or another.

In *The Crystal Garden*, Makhmalbaf reaches for the hidden corners of cultural catastrophes. His description of the inner anxieties of Hamid, the young war veteran paralyzed from the waist down, for example, is brutally suggestive, reaching for paralyzing pains beyond name and recognition. Though not a single word is mentioned about sex in this description, Makhmalbaf's awareness of Hamid's sexual paralysis and his anxieties toward his young wife are culturally cataclysmic. Hamid is almost obsessively aware of the religious reasons for which Maliheh has agreed to marry a half paralyzed and totally useless man. Makhmalbaf gives full narrative swing to the young veteran's anxieties without ever collapsing into any moral evaluation about the reasons for his sacrifice or its consequences. He simply dwells on the paralyzing anxieties of a perished life, a wasted youth. The result is a tortuous passage through an awareness of realities that defy categorical ideologies, political pronouncements, banal formulations. Mundane realities that Makhmalbaf has to face in order to describe in effect *force* him to abandon all ideological formulation and reach for earthly and material details that collectively make a mockery of straightjacket edicts. Practically all the criticism of the early Makhmalbaf has concentrated on his naïve and flat films and totally disregarded what is happening, almost at the same time, in his fiction.

Not much is happening in Makhmalbaf's fiction. He is not much of a storyteller. He is a well-digger, an archeologist of latent emotions, forgotten anxieties, hidden horrors, inarticulate hopes. What he is doing in *The Crystal Garden*, in Chapter Five for example, when he unfolds the inner trepidations of the young widow Souri, is mapping out the topography of conflicting, at times eloquent, at times mute, emotions. The flat certainties of Makhmalbaf's characters in his early, *Islamic*, cinema here give way to a universe of painstakingly sculpted characters, the living memories of a culture in crisis.

Many of the characteristic features of Makhmalbaf's later films are already evident in *The Crystal Garden*. The narrative movement is always *virtual* – both here and in the best of his films. This short novel is of central significance in detecting the earliest moments of Makhmalbaf's later cinematic penchant for *virtual realism*, a characteristic that has been chiefly responsible for his global celebration as a filmmaker.[30]

The reason for the rise and the constitution of Makhmalbaf's creative character in fiction rather than cinema is initially sociological before it transmutes to other possible factors. Makhmalbaf came from a poor and a fiercely religious family. He was neither highly educated nor had the air of a deeply cultivated intellectual. The most prominent members of the Iranian cinematic establishment, coming from upper middle class families, were given a highly cultivated demeanor by their cosmopolitan upbringing, which created a certain kind of awe and a degree of anxiety among the class that Makhmalbaf best represented. The Islamic Revolution of 1979 had, of course, a profoundly class-based component to it. Many of the so-called *Islamic* codes of conduct brutally imposed on the general public at large were the expression of a lower-class resentment against the upper-class air of presumed superiority. To this day, this profoundly class-based cultural distinction is paramount in Iranian cultural politics – a distinction that is often distorted by the bogus bifurcation posited between the *Traditional* and the *Westernized* components of the society. The schism is far too serious to be represented by any such fallacious dichotomy. Entirely economic in base and cultural in disposition, this schism was rooted in the semi-colonized state of Iran during the nineteenth and the twentieth centuries. Makhmalbaf's search for an *Islamic* cinema is rooted precisely in this categorical search for an alternative cultural expression that defied the dominant self-raising, other-lowering air about the pre-Revolutionary filmmakers. Makhmalbaf's derogatory and dismissive attitude toward the pre-Revolutionary filmmakers rests precisely on this sentiment. The term 'Taghuti' (evil) that was applied to the pre-Revolutionary filmmakers also had this bitter attitude of *ressentiment* (sour grapes) against everything that had survived the brutal cut of the revolution. In his early cinema, Makhmalbaf was after proving that there is such a thing as an *Islamic* cinema. By that thoroughly codified term he meant far more a *revolutionary* cinema than a religious cinema. But the historical fact of the Iranian polity at this particular juncture was that a *revolutionary* cinema had also to be a *religious* cinema. It is crucial to remember that quite a considerable part of the revolutionary anger early in the course of the event was manifested in bombing and burning the movie-houses. It was in one such attack that hundreds of innocent spectators perished in the southern city of Abadan. In the 1970s, the Tehran International Film Festival was headquartered at Rudaki Hall in the posh, northern neighborhoods of the capital. The festival had enduring and positive consequences for the Iranian cinema of the 1970s but, at the same time, it was profoundly alienating to millions of the poorer residents of the capital. It is a sad but nevertheless undeniable fact that much of the cosmopolitan culture of the Iran of the 1960s and 1970s, as expressed not just in the Tehran International Film

Festival but even more offensively in the Shiraz Art Festival, was sponsored by and incorporated into the propaganda machinery of the Pahlavi monarchy. To be sure, pre-Revolutionary Iranian filmmakers like Bahram Beiza'i or Daryush Mehrju'i were entirely innocent of being accomplices in Pahlavi tyranny. Quite to the contrary: they were the very source of hope for emancipation – the moral architects of a progressive and cosmopolitan culture. Nevertheless, the Pahlavi monarchy sought to whitewash its criminal atrocities against its own citizens by taking advantage of the artistic achievements happening on its watch, very much in the same vein that the Islamic Republic does today. This observation should not be confused with a categorical dismissal of the robust Iranian cosmopolitan culture[31] that for over 200 years has cultivated its emancipatory tenets in active and heroic battle against tyranny of all sorts; colonial, monarchic, or theocratic.

Makhmalbaf very soon realizes the absurdity of his position and begins to paint himself out of that unseemly corner. But the result of this passage through a revolutionary determination against the *ancient regime* is that in Makhmalbaf's creative imagination there is a solid material base in Iranian realities that at once defies the colonial constitution of all revolutionary ideologies, *including* Islamism, and reaches for a kind of creative emancipation that does not issue imaginative checks that it cannot materially cash. The fundamental problem with the Iranian art of the twentieth century, which has been its quintessential *inorganicity* to its material conditions, is here solved through an excruciating passage through the material hell of that society. To be sure, the pre-Revolutionary art against which Makhmalbaf had revolted had not altogether yielded to either the colonial or the nativist parameters alternatively placed in its path. The modernist poetry of Nima Yushij, the dramatic stage of Gholamhossein Sa'edi, and certainly the cinema of Bahram Beiza'i and Amir Naderi (among others) all had profoundly liberating and emancipatory thrusts in the larger context of Iranian artistic modernity. But as an artist Makhmalbaf had not emerged from our *cosmopolitan* responses to cultural colonialism. He had been specifically and with insistence a *Muslim* activist and as a result his art had to survive its own particular demons.

The political tide of a massive, radically Islamicized, revolution had given Makhmalbaf the historical opportunity to express his at once Islamic *and* revolutionary charge against pre-Revolutionary art. When, on 1 February 1979, Ayatollah Khomeini returned triumphantly to Iran and millions poured jubilantly into the streets to welcome him, Makhmalbaf had already been released from prison and felt it incumbent upon himself to give that revolutionary moment what it artistically deserved. Less than a week after his return to Iran, Khomeini had appointed Mehdi Bazargan as the Prime Minister of the transitional government, and less than two weeks into his return he had forced the last remnants of the Pahlavi monarchy in the form of Bakhtiyar's government to resign and go into hiding. By the end of March, Khomeini had seen to it that millions of Iranians had come to the polling boxes and given their unconditional support for an Islamic Republic. The failure of the cosmopolitan left and liberals to resist the radical Islamization of the revolution in Makhmalbaf's eyes must have been the categorical condemnation of the whole universe of corruption with which the *ancient regime* was now identified. By the summer of 1979, the constitution of the Islamic Republic was already being drafted, and under the smoke screen of the Hostage Crisis that began in November it was finalized. Now everyone, religiously inclined or otherwise, was living in an *Islamic* Republic. Makhmalbaf was triumphant. This is the revolution for which he had fought all his life. By September 1980, a far more serious and bloody process of Islamicizing the revolution began. The Iran–Iraq war (1980–88) was by far the bloodiest and most enduring act in consolidating the Islamic Revolution as the defining moment of Iranian political culture. The explosion at the headquarters of the Islamic Republic Party on 28 June 1981 showed the degree of violence prevalent in this period. On 30 August 1981 the newly elected President Mohammad Ali Raja'i and Prime Minister Mohammad Javad Bahonar were killed in yet another bomb blast. These violent forms of opposition to the Islamic Republic while the Iran–Iraq war was raging could not but further strengthen the Islamists' grip on power and crush any form of opposition. Under these circumstances, artists with a more cosmopolitan disposition to their work were frightened, isolated, and under siege.

By far the most visible sign of the active Islamicization of the revolutionary Iran was the status of Iranian women. Almost half a century into their active incorporation into state-sponsored modernization under the Pahlavis, they were now forced to assume far more restricted public presence. Women are also of central concern to Makhmalbaf in *The Crystal Garden*. The novel is in fact dedicated 'to Women, the tyrannized women of this land' – widowed at a very young age and having infants to care for with no steady source of income, at the mercy of the revolutionary zeal to which their young husbands, brothers, or sons have lost their lives. In these women is evident the enduring stigma of being a widow and the ephemeral respect of having been married to a *martyr*. Makhmalbaf is acutely clear in his diagnosis of the enduring calamities of being a woman and totally dismissive of the momentary *respect* they are offered. Layeh, whose husband has died in the course of the war with Iraq, has three children to raise. Souri, who also lost her husband to the war and who has two children, has to endure the indignity of living with her in-laws. Maliheh, who married a partly paralyzed war veteran out of pity and religious piety, now mourns her wasted youth and her natural desire for having children. These are the women who in their lives represent realities that persist through revolutions and wars. These women, smack out of the post-Revolutionary, war-torn Iran, are in effect curing Makhmalbaf of his ideological convictions. While people with far fewer revolutionary credentials are now holding high-ranking offices, Makhmalbaf is drawn increasingly away from the revolution, its ideological convictions, and even its metaphysical certainties. What he sees in these women, whom he portrays with astonishing realism, is the persistence of moral, cultural, and social malaise beyond any ideological cure.

Far more simple and palpable realities are now revealing themselves to Makhmalbaf, realities that both in their enduring miseries and their promising hope have a ring of truth in them that no ideological movement in contemporary Iran has addressed, let alone changed. In Sarah and Salman, the orphaned children of Layeh who at a very young age lose their father to the war, Makhmalbaf invests the vast innocence of birth, wonder, and discovery. 'What is this Layeh?' asks the little Sarah:

> 'It's an earring.'
> 'What's an earring for?'
> 'It's to hang on your ear. It's for beauty.'
> 'Beauty?'
> 'Yes dear. Beauty.'
> 'What's beauty for?'
> 'Beauty? It's for happiness.'
> 'Happiness?'
> 'Oh for God's sake leave me alone my dear. I don't know. Put it back where it belongs. You're going to ruin it.'[32]

In *The Crystal Garden*, Makhmalbaf is almost clinically aware of this irreducibility of the real and disarmingly analytical in his unraveling of the tyranny that is perpetrated on Iranian women, as one particularly poignant example of such realities. The novel, as a result, can be read like an archeological account of grave injustices that culturally and socially have conditioned the status of women in all patriarchal societies. It is not just the cultural construction of femininity that becomes evident in *The Crystal Garden*. By examining the inner anxieties of Hamid, a half-paralyzed man married to a young woman, a marriage that has not been consummated because Hamid is paralyzed waist-down, or the masculinist trepidations of Karim Agha, a second husband to Layeh, Makhmalbaf assays the whole topography of gender-constitution, both in masculinity and in femininity. By placing these deeply wounded and permanently scarred adults next to children like Sarah, Salman, Meysam, and Samira, Makhmalbaf's story becomes a panoramic view of the very process of socialization through which culture and society cultivate their enduring miseries in young and impressionable children.

Over all his characters, without any exception, Makhmalbaf pours a cascade of love and affection, understanding and sympathy, and *that* is the singular superiority of his auto-didactic pulling up from the depth of his shallow ideological convictions. He takes a look at Mashhadi, for example, Aliyeh's husband, father-in-law to Souri, father to the martyred son Akbar and his younger brother Ahmad, grandfather to Samira and Meysam, and he unpacks this pious, prematurely old man into the diverging sum of emotions that makes him possible and prompts him to act. It is precisely this love that Makhmalbaf has for his characters that enables him to reach out and grasp a far richer and much more fulfilling conception of them and their moral and cultural predicaments. He could no longer have this grasp of reality and continue to issue those ghastly ideological statements about the Fate of Man or the Battle of Good against Evil. By and through The Crystal Garden, Makhmalbaf is freed from the dual Manichean dungeon of his Persian prison, freed from the labyrinth of Islamic meandering that his fight against Pahlavi monarchy, and through it the very constitution of colonial subjectivity, had made all but inevitable. In that freedom, Makhmalbaf does not pull any punches. There is something of that youthful 17-year-old revolutionary who dared to pull a knife on a police officer about Makhmalbaf's art. One of the most powerful moments of the novel is when Mashhadi arranges for the marriage between Souri, his young daughter-in-law, and Ahmad, his son. Souri used to be married to Akbar, Mashhadi's oldest son who was killed in the war, and now has two children from that marriage, Meysam and Samira. The moment is transgressively powerful. Souri's husband, Ahmad's brother, was alive; she was like a sister to her brother-in-law, and yet now that her husband is dead her brother (-in-law) is both religiously and socially eligible to marry her. The match is so logically perfect that it loads the transgressive moment with a daunting sexual overtone, without the slightest narrative suggestion to that effect.

In The Crystal Garden, Makhmalbaf has had an uncanny ability to penetrate into the deepest thoughts, doubts, and anxieties of his female characters. His portrayal of Layeh, the widowed wife of the martyred Mansur, mother of three young children and re-married to Karim Agha, is particularly powerful. Makhmalbaf spent years of his early childhood at home in the protective care of his mother, his aunt, and his grandmother. Partly because of these early experiences, Makhmalbaf's female characters come straight out of the Iranian urban working class. The autobiographical narrative of Khorshid in Chapter Eleven is a sparkling piece of monologue where the life of a young peasant girl married first to a tribal chieftain, then to a wandering pilgrimage leader, and finally left to her own devices in a succession of countless temporary marriages (mut'ah) is a perfect portrayal of the terrors and tribulations of her gender and class. By far the most colorful and courageous character of the entire novel, a woman who constantly defies her fate and turns the tyrannically abused status of a woman in patriarchal cultures to her advantage, is Khorshid. In effect engaged in one religiously sanctioned act of prostitution after another, Khorshid has the extraordinary character of turning her fate upside down. Within her limitations, she is an exceptionally resourceful and assertive woman, changing as many husbands as a slight improvement of her lot may require. She has now become something of a philosopher and has a profoundly perceptive conception of life in general, men in particular:

> But what can I say? As they say, a woman with no husband is like pure gold, but hidden in a drawer. Unless you put her on display behind the window no customer will notice her. Someone has to tell the rat what's in the barn you know. But say what you will, eyes deceive before the ears can hear. In my case it was the landlady who kept my market hot. She was a noble lady, she was. But wasn't I? Of course I was. Thanks be to heaven that not once did I lay hand on a forbidden good. Not once did I look at a man in a sinful way. Don't you believe for a moment that I was particularly happy. No. I married about a hundred men, one worse than the other. When a woman is put on and off like a piece of garment even her soul becomes worn out. Just like her body it becomes old. I have never lived in comfort. But, hey I saw the world and pretty much figured it out. The whole world is run by men. The whole world has been created for bastard men. Whoever they want they marry. Whoever they don't want they divorce. If they are good they collect every good thing for themselves. And if they are bad they do the same with the bad things. All over the world men want women only for one thing and for one thing only: To play doll with them and have them serve them, mother them. Once I married this fellow ... [33]

Khorshid also has the great virtue of being in love with cinema. The highest expression of her piety is always the most sincere moment of her love for cinema: 'In the mornings I used to go to the movies. In the evenings I went to the sacred shrine as a humble pilgrim.'[34] The Indian musicals are her favorites. Speaking of one of her favorite husbands, she says: 'When he came home that night, again he had made himself up to look like Raj Kapour ... He said to me, he said, "Let's go out to see a movie." He used to put a comb and a piece of paper in his mouth just like a harmonica and then sing in this nasal voice: "*Gunia, Guni, Gunia, Gunia mo Saghia.*" I said to him, I said, "what madness is this? You mourn 'O My Martyred Lord Abolfazl!' one day and then you sing '*Gunia Guni Gunia!*' another."'[35] In Khorshid, Makhmalbaf invests a manifesto for the veracity of cinema as an art. Speaking of yet another husband, Khorshid reports:

> We used to go to the cinema too. But I went to see the movies mostly by myself. Once every blue moon he would take me along with him to see a movie. 'Ali Baba and the Forty Thieves,' we saw, 'The Famous Amir

Arsalan,' 'Joseph and Zoleikha,' 'The Return of Abu Antar.' Only God knows how terrified I was when Abu Antar used to put this pair of dark sunglasses on and do all weird kind of tricks. When I left the movie houses I saw the world differently. Once I had made it a condition of my temporary marriage with the fellow. I said to him, I said, 'Your rights and privileges as my temporary husband are all good and dandy. But I have to have my rights to the movies.' He said to me, the bastard, he said, 'I won't marry a woman who doesn't care about what's forbidden and what's permissible by the holy Qur'an and goes to the movies.' I said to him, I said, 'You can go to hell. I won't marry you.' The ugly bastard! ... Once I saw a movie, there was this man in it, a kind of foreign spy, you know. He had come to another country to have a temporary wife, I am quite sure of it. Then he was secretly putting her up to all kinds of tricks to report to him about this, that, and the other thing. Finally they were both caught. They killed the poor woman. But the man who was from some other part of the world was returned to his country. When I tell you all over the world women folk are just plain stupid here is the example. The hell with the bastard! He didn't deserve me anyway. ... [36]

Khorshid's attraction to cinema cannot be passed over quickly given Makhmalbaf's own increasingly serious investment in the art and craft of filmmaking. There is a dialectical relationship between Makhmalbaf and Khorshid, constitutional to the rest of his career as a filmmaker. Khorshid, in short, is the real mother of Mohsen Makhmalbaf the filmmaker.

All of Makhmalbaf's religious and revolutionary convictions, evident and flaunted in his early cinema, come to a head-on collision with his portrayal of the wedding night of Ahmad and Souri. The im/possibility of these two young people consummating their marriage is what keeps everything Makhmalbaf holds sacred in balance. The memory of Souri's martyred husband, Akbar, haunts and paralyzes the newly weds. Makhmalbaf, of course, cannot see them having sex under the gaze of the dead martyr, even if Aliyeh, Souri's vigilant mother-in-law, has wisely taken her son's picture to her own room. Makhmalbaf's way out of this impasse is to send the newly weds off on a pilgrimage to Mashhad, there to absolve themselves of their 'sin' and who knows what else.

The sudden, bewildering, news that Akbar is alive and a prisoner of war in Iraq jolts not just Mashhadi and Aliyeh with a paralyzing combination of joy and fear, but throws Makhmalbaf's own narrative off balance:

It is as if Aliyeh did not hear. She was sitting down and talking to her shadow on the wall. Suddenly she would just get up and run away from

her shadow to the other side of the room. As for Mashhadi, he didn't
even have a shadow. He was standing in the dark, behind the window,
looking at the courtyard that was again covered by snow. Overnight he
had been cut thin. He was going mad with sadness and joy: 'What's
right. What's wrong? The Day of Judgment. Akbar. Ahmad. O my God!
Souri. Aliyeh I am leaving.[37]

Mashhadi has been instrumental in giving his daughter-in-law to his young son,
thinking that her husband, Akbar, his elder son, is dead. Ahmad and Souri were
now in Mashhad on some sort of a honeymoon, and now the news that his son
is actually alive! The combination of joy of this news and the terror of the 'sin'
that he has committed by giving his daughter-in-law to his other son and now
what was he to tell his first son paralyzes the old man. He leaves for Mashhad to
prevent a catastrophe.

Meanwhile in Mashhad, Ahmad and Souri, in the company of Souri's children
Samira and Meysam, are trying to redefine their relationship from brother-and-
sister (in-law) to husband and wife. They succeed. They break the barrier. They
make love. Souri becomes pregnant and begins to learn to love her new husband.

There are very few chapters in the history of modern Persian fiction that can
compete with Chapter Fifteen of Makhmalbaf's *The Crystal Garden*. Mashhadi,
Aliyeh, Ahmad, and Souri are, of course, completely paralyzed. They don't know
whether they should be happy that their son, brother, and husband is alive and
will be coming home soon or petrified at the thought of what to tell him when
he comes back to see that his younger brother has married his wife, and she is
now pregnant. Makhmalbaf's depiction of this moment of moral and emotional
paralysis is mesmerizing. The Persian ethical universe and Shi'i morality are here
held at bay. Juridically, Souri and Ahmad are just fine. According to Islamic
religious law, a woman whose husband is presumed dead can of course marry.
Marrying one's brother-in-law is not a problem either. In addition, they have the
added social approval of Ahmad having assumed responsibility for his brother's
family and Souri not having married outside her dead husband's family. But the
mere possibility of her first husband being alive and soon coming home to see
what has happened puts the whole spectrum of male–female and male–male
relationships off balance. It literally jolts the system.

If this were not nerve-racking enough, they soon learn upon further
investigation that there are two Akbar Soleimanis among the enlisted soldiers at
the front. One is dead and buried in Iran and the other is alive and a prisoner of
war in Iraq. Now what? Is Akbar dead or is he alive? The relationship between
Ahmad and Souri immediately reverts back to its former formality, something of
a brother–sister (in-law) relationship. But what is even worse is that they do not
know whether they should hope for Akbar to be alive and in Iraq or dead and

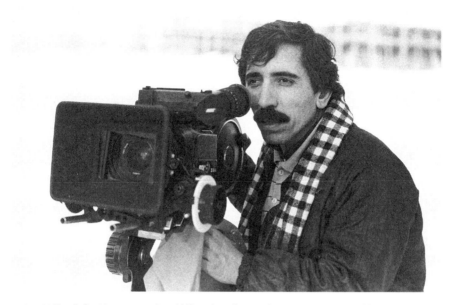

14   *Makhmalbaf and his camera – the indelible markers of post-revolutionary Iranian cinema.* (Photograph: Mitra Mahasseni; courtesy of Makhmalbaf Film House.)

buried in Iran. This moment puts to the test the brutal balance between familial affection and moral propriety. The moment, opening a vast universe of ethical conflicts, is one of those rare occasions when the whole textural integrity of a culture is brutally tested and let loose from its presumed angle of legitimacy. All emotions, relations, convictions, moralities, laws, social norms, and cultural proprieties are brutally and summarily suspended. For the duration of a few days that is an eternity, Ahmad and Souri are head-to-toe de-humanized, cut off from all their vital signs of cultural character, social membership, familial identity, and moral integrity.

Mashhadi is furious with all his friends and family who did not let him see the face of his son when they buried him. But what can he do now? 'We'll exhume the body!' he announces to his son Ahmad. There is only one way out of this debilitating misery. They have to dig out the body that they thought was Akbar's and see if it is he. Even if the face is not recognizable, they can measure the length of the body. If it is 170 cm, it is Akbar. If it is 153 cm, it is the other Akbar Soleimani. The commotion in convincing a grave-digger to disinter the body is only the tip of the phantasmagoric nightmare of social and religious taboos that the family have to transgress in order to resolve their predicament one way or another.

The scene of the actual disinterring of the body is horror incarnate. Makhmalbaf's eye for detail is frightfully descriptive. Everybody is present at the exhumation. Mashhadi, Aliyeh, Souri, Ahmad, and even the half-paralyzed Hamid have come along. By midnight they have done all the bribing that they had to and have mobilized all the courage that is left to them and brought themselves all together for one final and resolute look at the body of their loved-one – maybe he is, maybe he is not – in order to resolve the catastrophe one way or another. They fear and they dig and they reach the body only to tear its shroud and expose the decayed flesh and exposed bones of a skeleton that resembles nothing but the very picture of death. It is the wrong grave.

Is there an end to this calamity? They move to another grave, read the name of Akbar on it a million times and they start digging again. It is Akbar's. There is no way to describe the condition of Aliyeh when she sees and recognizes the body of her dead son. No way to know what Mashhadi feels when he is at once destroyed and relieved to see the dead body of his son. No way to reach for the depth of Ahmad's relief and sorrow or Souri's frightful relief. No way to know any of these. But Makhmalbaf's electrified narrative has something of a possessed diction about it here – mournful and resigned at the same time.

They all go home. They are ... what? Happy? Sad? Relieved. Soon after, Ahmad goes back to the war-front. Souri is hospitalized for manic depression. Mashhadi and Aliyeh get busy raising their grandchildren. But before long Mashhadi cannot take the sedate pace of his wintry life any longer and joins his younger son on the battlefront. The news of Ahmad and Mashhadi's death soon reaches their family and nearly destroys Aliyeh and Souri. But the two ravaged women return from the edges of madness to take care of their children.

At the end, Makhmalbaf disperses these four households that were brought together in this servants' quarters of a confiscated house by the common misery of having had a young martyr in their family. The revolutionary government returns the house to its original owner, who has now returned from abroad to claim his property. Khorshid, her opium-addicted husband now dead, initially stays with them as their servant. The other three families are all given one room in a hotel until proper housing is arranged for them. They divide the room into three sections: one for Hamid, Maliheh, and their adopted daughter Najmeh; one for the old Aliyeh, the pregnant Souri, and her two rambunctious children; and the third for Layeh and her three children. Karim Aqa, Layeh's second husband, disappears. But Khorshid returns to live with the rest after the owner of the house sells his property to the first buyer he finds, gets his cash, and leaves the country for good.

Makhmalbaf concludes his story and exits the narrative with two enduring marks: one the promissory note of how art saves reality; the other, one of the most haunting scenes in modern Persian fiction, how reality saves art. In the first scene, the young Samira is falling asleep while listening to her grandmother Aliyeh telling her and other children a bedtime story:

> One by one children were all falling asleep. All except Samira who had
> noticed that the Grandmother was actually telling them her own life
> story. She had just changed the names. She even knew that the person
> who in the story was called Nasim was really she. But she could not
> quite understand why the people in the story were more lovable. She
> could not understand why the grandmother in the story was much
> more beautiful than Aliyeh herself.
> 'Why Grandma?'
> 'Why what my dear?'
> 'Be quiet Sarah. Go to sleep!'[38]

The second scene is one of a miracle. To end the novel, Makhmalbaf is ready for
one of his most surreal moments in print, a premonition of what later will
become the chief characteristic of his best films. The four households are now
completely dismantled. Mashhadi and his two sons Akbar and Ahmad are now
dead. Souri has given birth to a baby boy from her second husband, Ahmad, but
is now half-crazed and committed to a mental asylum. Meysam and Samira are
growing up like wild weeds. Khorshid has come and taken Layeh and her children
away – no-one knows where. Hamid and Maliheh and their adopted daughter
Najmeh are busy making a meager living. At the center of this collapsing colony
of revolutionary misery, death, and destruction remains Aliyeh and her youngest
grandson who has no name, no father, and a mother in a mental asylum. The
nameless baby boy is used to being breast-fed after the few times that Layeh
played a wet-nurse to the helpless thing. Now that she has gone, he does not take
any infant formula substitute no matter how many times Aliyeh and Maliheh try
to force-feed him. Maliheh is petrified and helpless. The infant cries and screams
ceaselessly, incessantly, then he cries even harder, harsher, acrimoniously, edging,
second by second, his short and fragile life to the brink of a premature death.
Aliyeh, the grandmother, the oldest surviving woman of this small clan of
calamity, the widowed survivor of an olden warrior, the aged mother of two
valiant martyrs, grandmother to three surviving children, herself having just
celebrated her – heaven only knows how old she is – birthday, the sole surviving
pillar of this collapsed tent, grabs her nameless, fatherless, mother-crazed,
youngest grandson and runs in desperation into the middle of the courtyard,
frantic, wild, bewildered, mad with rage, confusion, despair:

> In the half-dark, half-lit courtyard of the hotel, there was no single soul
> in sight. The sky was full of stars. The moon was sliced thin, a narrow
> crescent of light. The infant was irascible. Aliyeh was walking him and
> tapping him on his back. 'La la la la la la, Ala la la la la, Ala la la la la
> ... .' The infant was not getting any calmer. Aliyeh was incensed. Angry

and furious, she began to lacerate her face with her own fingers. She sat down on the ground and tore her dress. She put the baby down and began to beat herself up. Her veil fell off from her head. She was now beating herself up incessantly. The baby was about to pass out again. Aliyeh reached for the dust on the ground and began to strew fistfuls of dirt over his head. She was beating her knees and her chest. Her legs and her breast were hurting. The infant's voice was about to die out again. In the midst of this brutally cold night she was on fire. Suddenly she grabbed the baby and almost involuntarily put one of her breasts into his mouth. She grabbed the infant's two legs from the middle and began to squeeze them. The baby grabbed Aliyeh's nipple in his mouth and started to suck. Crying and sucking began to give his voice a rhythmic tone. Excruciating pain was running wild from the surface of Aliyeh's skin to the very depth of her heart. The baby was chewing on her. Aliyeh was aflame and burning. Her heart and her guts were twisting, turning together. The baby let go of her breast and began to cry again:

'Un na. Un na.'

'Calm down my dear. Calm down! For heaven's sake calm down! That's enough darling.'

It was not enough. Aliyeh grabbed her scarf from her head and put her breast once again into his mouth. The baby was refusing to take the nipple. He would not be fooled. Aliyeh stood up. She raised her head towards the sky, her lips squeezed under her teeth. Blood gushed to her face and she roared:

'Where are you God? Are you there?'

Something in her began to flow. Her heart began to palpitate. She stood up involuntarily and jolted to a run. The infant had put all his remaining strength into his lips and began to suck her breast. Aliyeh's heart was pumping madly. The veins in her neck were swollen in fury. Something, burning her from within, began to swell from the very depth of her heart and gushed forth towards her breast, burning and cutting through the nipple. Fresh milk streaming into the infant's mouth.

The entire earth was becoming young. What is the time? Where is this place?[39]

View from the Edge

With *The Crystal Garden* as the major marker of Makhmalbaf's imaginative disposition at this point, the compelling humanity of the characters he creates in this work of fiction becomes the birth channel of retrieving his own humanity beyond his deadly and dangerous ideological convictions. The detailed disposition of his characters, their fragile and incontrovertible humanity, and the brittle frailty of their ordinary circumstances all come together to save Makhmalbaf from the grotesque grandiosity of his metaphysical predilections. The result is a passage through the purgatory of the ordinary, away from the dead certainties of useless abstractions, and toward an open and inviting space where he can re-imagine the universality of his worldly predicament in free and emancipatory terms.[40]

This view of a poetic visionary from the post/colonial end of the project of modernity that I detect and suggest in Makhmalbaf's early work gives the Heideggerian critique of the Enlightenment an added momentum. Heidegger's critique of technological modernity is placed within the context of German reaction to the immediate consequences of the project at one particularly acute moment and a vulnerable spot at its center of gravity. Heidegger was part and parcel of Weimar Culture, 'haunted,' as Pierre Bourdieu once put it, 'by the "discontents of civilization," fascinated by war and death, and revolted by technological civilization as well as by all forms of authority.'[41] Bourdieu has further demonstrated that Heidegger's prevalent anti-modernity was predicated on similar sentiments of such figures as Oswald Spengler, who were calling for an end to the 'alienation' rampant in the very 'spirit' of their time, while lamenting the 'uprooting' of Germanic culture. Bourdieu singles out Fritz Lang's *Metropolis* as 'that virtual summary of all their fantasized problematics, ... a graphic retranslation of Jünger's *Der Arbeiter/The Worker*.'[42] Bourdieu extensively demonstrates how the anti-technological modernity that finally finds its most elaborate philosophical expression in Ernst Jünger and reveals its culmination with Heidegger had its origin, in fact, in the economic and social circumstances of post-war Germany, where the under-employed professorate became the mouthpiece of a whole generation of dissatisfaction with the catastrophic consequences of technological modernity. The passage from Oswald Spengler's *Man and Technics*[43] that Bourdieu quotes gives a full description of the ideological mood of the era:

> The Faustian thought begins to be sick of machines. A weariness is spreading, a sort of pacifism of the battle with nature. Men are returning to forms of life simpler and nearer to nature; they are spending their time in sport instead of technical experiments. The great cities are becoming hateful to them, and they would fain get away from the pressure of soulless facts and the clear cold atmosphere of technical organization. And it is precisely the strong and creative talents that are turning away from practical problems and sciences and towards pure speculation. Occultism and spiritualism, Hindu philosophies,

> metaphysical inquisitiveness under Christian or pagan colouring, all of which were despised in the Darwinian period, are coming up again. It is in the spirit of Rome in the Age of Augustus. Out of the satiety of life, men take refuge from civilization in the more primitive parts of the earth, in vagabondage, in suicide.[44]

Bourdieu's sociological explanation of the ideological atmosphere that engulfed and animated Heidegger's critique of technological modernity is squarely rooted in his assessment of the class structure of post-war Germany:

> The 'conservative revolutionaries,' whether they were bourgeois who were excluded by the nobility from the prestigious posts of State administration, or petty bourgeois who were frustrated in the aspirations aroused by their educational success, found a magical solution to their contradictory expectations in the 'spiritual renaissance' and the 'German revolution.' 'The spiritual revolution' which was supposed to 'revitalize' the nation without revolutionizing its structure is what allowed these actual or potential déclassés to reconcile their desire to maintain a privileged position in the social order and to rebel against the order denying them this position, with their hostility to the bourgeoisie who excluded them and their repugnance for the socialist revolution that threatened all the values which helped to distinguish them from the proletariat. Their regressive yearning for a reassuring reintegration in the organic totality of an autarchic agrarian (or feudal) society is simply the counterpart of a hostile fear of anything in the present which announces a threat for the future, whether that threat is capitalist or Marxist; they fear the capitalist materialism of the bourgeoisie as much as the godless rationalism of the socialists.[45]

The problem though with Bourdieu's critique of the ideological atmosphere that contextualized Heidegger's critique of technological modernity is that it analytically isolates and then sociologically explains away the German crisis as a unique phenomenon. Both the catastrophic consequences of technological modernity and the 'conservative revolutionaries' response to them were endemic to a constitutional crisis in the very nature of the project, as Horkheimer and Adorno were first extensively to articulate, and which had become evident on the German scene. Both Heidegger's critical stance vis-à-vis technological modernity and the economic and social conditions that were conducive to that response were integral to the project of capitalist modernity and its endemic moments of crisis, whether in Germany or anywhere else. The result is that no sociological explanation can diminish the significance of Heidegger's critique of the whole project of technological modernity.

What both the liberal humanist critique of Heidegger's involvement with Nazism[46] and its sociological explanation[47] totally disregard is what his critique of capitalist modernity has made possible. The misplaced critique of Heidegger's critique of modernity and Enlightenment humanism, which invariably collapses into the perfectly legitimate critique of his Nazi affiliation, has given the liberal humanists strange ideological bedfellows of such fascist ideologues of capitalist modernity as William Bennett, Alan Bloom, and Dinesh D'Souza. The critique of Heidegger's fascism is the very predicate of fascism of equally sinister possibilities. If for nothing else, at least for its reminding everyone of the tremendous critical potency that Heidegger's critique of modernity has made possible, William V. Spanos' corrective move ought to be heeded very carefully:

> What has been obscured in the dramatization of this 'scandal,' especially by those liberal humanists in the United States who have imported the European debate into the North American intellectual milieu, is the ideology informing the attack on Heidegger's personal adherence to the practice in behalf of German National Socialism. Whatever its intention, this negative renarrativization of the itinerary of Heidegger's thought in terms of historical anecdote has as its ideological subtext the discrediting of Heidegger's powerful interrogation of the discourse of humanism as such. More important, it also is at some level intended to delegitimate those later, more radical, demystifications of the privileged concept of Man that Heidegger's interrogation catalyzed.[48]

What even Spanos does not pay attention to are the consequences of the emancipation of the subject at the post/colonial end of the game. The Eurocentricity of this entire enterprise is evident even at its most self-critical moments. To be sure, the freedom of the colonial subject has been *earned* on the backbreaking experience of having been located at the receiving end of the project of modernity. But the destruction of the project internally, whether manifested in the German crisis that gave rise to Nazism or in the monstrous consequences of the movement, has added theoretical zest to the factual evidence of post/colonial emancipation of the subject. But at the globalizing center of modernity, beginning with the publication of Victor Farias' *Heidegger and Nazism*,[49] the numbingly Eurocentric controversy over Heidegger's involvement with Nazism has been caught in a claustrophobic hermetic seal that categorically disregards, as a psychologically conditioned blind spot, the colonial consequences of the Enlightenment humanism and capitalist modernity. The terror that Nazism perpetrated on Europe, European colonialism has been inflicting on the world at large – on a steady, historical, consistent, global, and infinitely more terrorizing scale.

In between the *Authenticity–Traditions* binary opposition that the European project of Enlightenment modernity has invented in order to believe itself, and the colonial constitution of the subject, the post/colonial art that filmmakers like Mohsen Makhmalbaf best represents liberates the subject in divergent and unanticipated directions. But since the post/colonial poetics must, *ipso facto*, pass through the very essence of the danger that technological modernity has constituted, it harbors no illusion for the *Authentic*, as Heidegger did. Makhmalbaf at his best is that defiant subject, the post/colonial poet of the vision of the possible. The fact that he emerged from an *Islamic Ideology*, with all the atrocious implications of that historical force, makes him particularly important as a defiant subject. The very formation of the *Islamic Ideology*, not just in Iran but in the whole spectrum of counter-colonial gestures we have made over the past two centuries in the colonial world, is very much similar to post-World War I German reaction to the project of modernity. Because much of the world at the colonial end of the game was not the beneficiary of the project, and indeed because it was at the receiving end of its most calamitous consequences, it too, just like the Germans of the first two decades of the twentieth century, was attracted to mystical notions of *authenticity*, *collectivity*, *tradition*, etc. Consider the following assessment of Bourdieu about the German condition that bred Heidegger:

> Their regressive yearning for a reassuring reintegration in the organic totality of an autarchic agrarian (or feudal) society is simply the counterpart of a hostile fear of anything in the present which announces a threat for the future, whether that threat is capitalist or Marxist; they fear the capitalist materialism of the bourgeoisie as much as the godless rationalism of the socialists.[50]

And see how perfectly it matches with the rhetoric of *Islam-e Nâb-e Muhammadî* ('The Pure Muhammadan Islam') that became the dominant passion of the Muslim ideologues. This search for *mystical purity* from the real, Bourdieu aptly calls 'the desperate effort to overcome a set of insuperable alternatives through a kind of headlong flight, whether heroic or mystical.'[51] Even more to the point, consider the rhetoric of alternatives available to the German ideologues:

> ... it is no coincidence that the book where Möller van den Bruch, one of the prophets of 'revolutionary conservatism,' preached the mystical reunion of the Germanic past and the ideal Germany of the future, together with the rejection of bourgeois society and economics and the

return to corporatism, was first called the 'Third Way,' and then The Third Reich.[52]

And compare it with the leading mobilizing slogan in the course of the Islamic Revolution of 1979 – *Na Sharqi Na Gharbi, Jomhuri-ye Islami* ('Neither Eastern, nor Western, [but] the Islamic Republic').

Notice the structural similarities of these diversionary tactics, and there remains no difference between the center and the periphery of the project of capitalist modernity. The aggressive instrumentalization of *reason* in the course of capitalist modernity was far more evident in fact in the *colonial edges* of the project than in its presumed *capital centers* – an intensity pointing to a similarity of abuse between capital and labor that collapses any notion of center-and-periphery. *Art* in both cases remains the singular site of resisting de-subjection and restoring agency to the colonially ravaged subject. Whereas anticolonial ideologies – such as *Islamism* – cannot but replicate the strategies of de-subjection endemic to the project of colonial modernity, post/colonial art is *ipso facto* the sight and sound of restoring historical agency to the decolonized subject. The early work of Makhmalbaf is a clear example of how the narrative mutation of anticolonial ideologies will have to go through the hazardous path of mystical flirtations with the *Absolute*. But the perilous uncertainties of art are the cure of all absolutist ideological convictions – as Makhmalbaf's early fiction was to his early cinema: and in that fact dwells the need to bring the critic of post/colonial art closer to the center of the post/modern critic of modernity.

Chapter Four

The Rebel Matures:
Makhmalbaf's *A Moment of Innocence*

I concluded the previous chapter on Makhmalbaf's early film and fiction by suggesting that art is the singular site of resisting de-subjection and restoring agency to the colonially compromised subject. My contention throughout this book is that the imperial manufacturing of the colonial subject is *ipso facto* an act of agential de-subjection, where the person of the colonial lacks any semblance of historical agency – and thus a mere raw material to be incorporated into the moral and material foregrounding of the colonial project. I have also suggested (and elsewhere demonstrated)[1] that the varied forms of ideological resistance to colonialism – ranging from militant Islamism to liberal nationalism and including Soviet-style socialism – cannot but further implicate the colonial subject in its having been always already de-subjected, imaginatively compromised in the dominant ideologies of colonialism. Meanwhile any critical encounter with the European critic of the sovereign subject, such as Gayatri Spivak's conversations with Foucault and Derrida in her 'Can the Subaltern Speak?' (1988),[2] may have to begin with, but cannot remain limited to, the critical apparatus of both post-modernism and post-structuralism. Contrary to both revolutionary ideologies that choose 'the West' as their principal interlocutors (and thus effectively trap the colonial subject in her/his own further de-subjection) and head-on collisions with European post-structuralist implosion of the soverign subject (which in effect do the same), the actively and imaginatively anticolonial production of historical agency (as I articulate and suggest it here) is a manner of creative subjection always in defiance of colonial power – and as such articulated on the creative site of visual and performing arts.[3]

Michel Foucault's assertion at the end of The Order of Things that 'man is an invention of recent date. And one perhaps nearing its end'[4] is perhaps the most notorious sound bite on the question of the deletion of the subject. In his History of Sexuality, too, Foucault has identified the discourse of sex as the quintessential site of subject formation, where 'causality in the subject, the unconscious of the subject, the truth of the subject in the other who knows, the knowledge he holds unbeknownst to him, all this found an opportunity to deploy itself in the discourse of sex.'[5] If sex was the principal site of subject formation, deviance and transgression were for Foucault the major manners of resisting it. Foucault consistently talked about the varied forms of resistance that individuals as the objects of discursive subjection put forward in order to alter the authority of that power. In his studies of Pierre Riviére and Herculine Barbin, for example, Foucault identified creative manners of resistance to technological modernity and its dominant manners of discursive subjection.[6] My contention here, following Spivak's inroad into questioning the European version of dismantling the soverign subject – by her introducing a feminist and a postcolonial critique into it – is that the colonial site has a far more material grounding for imaginative resistance to colonial subjection than limited to transgressive 'criminality.' Whereas Foucault had to go to 'the Other Victorians' (the oppressed, the denied, and the criminalized), as Steven Marcus (Foucault's principal reference) called them,[7] to locate the shadow side of bourgeois morality, on the colonial site such transgressions are in fact the very center of the moral and material imaginary. Yet 'transgression' here is modulated on the simulacra of a creative imagination – a creative will to resist power.[8]

In this chapter, I wish to dwell on what I believe is Makhmalbaf's most successful film, *A Moment of Innocence*, in order to demonstrate how, by visually altering the imaginative perception of reality, he has been able to craft the temporal whereabouts of that creative subjection. Throughout his cinema, but in this film in particular, Makhmalbaf manages to do so through the spatial manner of manufacturing and maintaining agential authority beyond the power or control of colonial de-subjection, as indeed beyond the pale of the limiting binary defined between 'Tradition and Modernity.' My principal contention here is that by altering the *timing* of reality, he has managed to alternate the *narrative* that is embedded in that timing – and by extension, once *time* and *narrative* have lost their customary, fixed, and coagulated correspondences, then the space that is thus generated is open for all sorts of creative conversations and defiant articulation of the subject that is imagined in between them.[9] Contrary to first constituting and then challenging the constitution of a 'sovereign subject' (the way it is done in European modernity and subsequently in its poststructuralist critique), what here in Makhmalbaf's cinema, and elsewhere in my other work, I am after is the constitution of a 'defiant subject' – happily and purposefully busy at the creative corners of colonial modernity.

The Saving Grace

Here is the tale – of the saving grace, of when cinema saves.

Mohsen Makhmalbaf made three films in a row. These are his most epigrammatic films, most personal, most privately narrated, most universally parabolic, orbital in their range and thrust of signification, parable-like in their manner of storytelling (a feature of his cinema that later becomes definitive to that of Marziyeh Meshkini). They may be read, as in this chapter the first of them is, as the three parts of a parable, or one parable in three moves. They are *A Moment of Innocence* (1995), *Gabbeh* – which is a kind of carpet that nomads make – (1995), and *Silence* (1998).[10] In narrating these three parables, Makhmalbaf has found ways of redeeming himself of his early career as a militant Islamist and an ideological filmmaker, fully at the service of an Islamic Republic. In them he has sought absolution. *A Moment of Innocence* is his public confessional.

A Moment of Innocence, or *A Piece of Bread and a Flowerpot*, to be more exact (for that is the name Makhmalbaf himself had originally given to his film before his distributor, MK2, once the French patron of Iranian cinema, decided, right before it was premiered in August 1996 during the 49th Locarno International Film Festival, that 'Un Instance d'Innocence' sounds and alliterates better in French, not knowing that 'Nun-o-Goldun' (Bread-and-Flowerpot) can put up a splendid competition on that score, too ...), is Makhmalbaf's un-telling of his own time in the double-time of modern Iranian history; or, to be even more exact, of the modernity of Iranians *being* in their history.

In *A Moment of Innocence*, Makhmalbaf un-tells, that is to say de-narrates, with a benign kind of self-forgetfulness having been visited upon him by the deuteronomical number of punishment, which is the number of '40' years that he has lived, wandered, and more, the story of his youthful political indiscretions, as it were. When he was 17, as everyone now knows, he wanted to change the world for the better. He is still trying to do it in his forties. But on that first occasion he thought that the way to do that was to attack a policeman, disarm him, get his gun, then go and rob a bank, use its money to form an urban guerrilla network, and bomb the living daylights out of the Pahlavi regime. Makhmalbaf screwed-up the plot, was almost killed, landed in jail, was tortured and tormented, until he was released by the revolutionaries in the wake of Ayatollah Khomeini's return to topple the Shah in 1979.

That is the story. But that story will take no-one anywhere. It is neither here nor there. It is too obvious, too real, too narrowly jaundiced by the factual ferocity of the evident, the pointlessness of the prosaic, a fleeting experience that instantly dies in and on itself.

Toward the end of his essay on 'The Relevance of the Beautiful,' Hans Georg Gadamer suggests that 'the work of art transforms our fleeting experience into the stable and lasting form of an independent and internally coherent creation. It does so in such a way that we go beyond ourselves by penetrating deeper into the work.'[11] The notorious two decades of Makhmalbaf's early childhood and youth, the 1960s and 1970s, witnessed many attempted or successful political assassinations. Many of Makhmalbaf's generation joined militant Islamist,

15   *Mohsen Makhmalbaf, his camera, and his daughter Hana, behind the scene in his* Nun-o-Goldun (A Moment of Innocence, 1996). *Both Makhmalbaf and his daughter acted in* A Moment of Innocence. *An autobiographical account of a turning point in his life, '*A Moment of Innocence*' brings Makhmalbaf's parabolic filmmaking to a new height.* (Photograph: Mohammad Ahmadi; courtesy of Makhmalbaf Film House.)

16   *Mohsen Makhmalbaf and two of his actors – Moharram Zeinalzadeh to his right and Ammar Tafti to his left –* in Nun-o-Goldun (A Moment of Innocence, 1996). *The director as actor underlines the transgressive borderline between fact and fantasy, between filmmaking and realism, whereby the front and back sides of the camera become effectively transparent.* (Photograph: Mohammad Ahmadi; courtesy of Makhmalbaf Film House.)

socialist, or nationalist movements and fought against the Pahlavi regime. On those at times heroic and at times foolhardy darings were ultimately predicated the advent and the success of the Islamic Revolution of 1979. An unjust and deeply corrupt political regime collapsed and gave way to yet another cycle of barbarity and abuse in modern Iranian history. The post-revolutionary Iranian cinema that Makhmalbaf and a handful of other filmmakers represent is the aesthetic sublimation of these repeated cycles of violence into a visual poetic of hope. The transformative power of art, of which Gadamer speaks with a hermeneutic wisdom whose balanced judgment is not marred either by a search for *authenticity* or by a fear of the new, is a gift that an artist makes not just to his audience but first and foremost to the creative moment in which is rooted the artist himself.

When Makhmalbaf was making *A Moment of Innocence*, he was almost 40 years old. When he attacked that police officer he was 17. What happens to an Iranian between the ages of 17 and 40? Born to an historically constituted religious fanaticism when the whole world is going to hell and seeming to enjoy the ride, bred to political activism by a religiously devout, pro-Khomeini stepfather when his heart and soul is drawn to art, put to jail when he should have gone to college, tortured when his body is just beginning to mature, married when barely out of prison, directing films when he still does not know which side of the camera he is to look through – *that* can happen to an Iranian, to any Iranian, to Makhmalbaf.

Makhmalbaf brings that checkered history to his cinema. The perils and promises of his vision are, as a result, symptomatic and symbolic of a world that sustains his creative energy. Reading his art in its immediate context informs the range of possibilities and pitfalls of Iranian history from its semi-colonial (or proto-colonial) modernity to its present and future, including its implications in a global economy of cultures beyond its control. What precisely is the function of aesthetics in the politics of that future is where Makhmalbaf's cinema has set its visual registry.

The parameters of that future, so far as they are to be read in aesthetically relevant terms, are currently negotiated on the no-man's-land of creativity where ferocious facts have to accommodate the workings of a noble fantasy. The trademark of the post-revolutionary Iranian cinema, as a result, has now been squarely established on a widening borderline between *fact* and *fantasy*. This crossbreeding of *fact* and *fantasy* – the making of a *factasy* that teases out both – is the location where the present and future of Iranian *reality* is being re-negotiated. Kiarostami and Makhmalbaf, as the two most globally celebrated representatives of the Iranian cinema, are the master-practitioners of this *factasy*. But their cinemas, vastly different as they are, share this *factasy* as a sign of what is happening on a wider spectrum of cinematic vision. The animating parameters of this mode of *looking* and *being* are yet to be sufficiently theorized, because not even its practitioners are not in full control of its operative measures.[12] Yet it is precisely the active and immediate theorization of this crossbreeding of fact and fantasy, *seriousness* and *frivolity*, which is where the future of Iranian aesthetic culture has a rendezvous with the historical unfolding of the Iranian reality. 'I consider myself to be a solemn figure,' Fellini once told Costanzo Costantini, 'but also a white clown.'[13] Between *solemnity* and *clowning*, between the fear that visits a nation on a cyclical terror of violence and the frivolity that is to sustain its spirit, the artists hang their pictures and tell their stories, imagine the otherwise of being and restore reality to its otherwise than being.

In Zhang Yimou's film *To Live* (1994), there is a scene when the neighborhood communist leader, Mr. Niu, comes to Fugui Xu and his wife Jiazhen's house to collect their metal wares to send to chairman Mao's army in order to make bullets. The family gives all the metal pots and pans they have, and in answer to Mr. Niu's question whether there are any more metal objects left in their possession they say no. Right at this moment, Youqing, the young son of the Xus, drags out his father's box of puppets, and objects that yes there are plenty of pieces of metal left on his father's puppets. 'You are less politically aware than your son,' Mr. Niu admonishes Fugui. There is enough metal on the box and the body of the puppets 'for two bullets,' he points out. And then he adds, 'We are just two bullets short of liberating Taiwan.' As he orders his comrades to take the box of puppets and extract the metals, Jiazhen notices the look of desperation on her frightened husband's face and pleads with the communist comrades, 'don't the soldiers need entertainment?' Fugui joins his wife and reminds Mr. Niu that when he was with the liberating army he staged a puppet show for them and as a result in two days they captured a mountain, two mountains, he adds, in four days. Mr. Niu is good-hearted and is convinced, leaving the puppets with the puppeteer. As he and his comrades are leaving the Xu's house, the young Youqing calls after them, 'so we are not going to liberate Taiwan?'

Makhmalbaf is the Iranian puppeteer whose shadowy figures spare two revolutionary bullets to mobilize an army of hope for future. But here, the first thing that he and generations of Iranian intellectuals who have come out of the atrocious hell of wars, occupations, revolutions, and coups d'état will have to face is their constitutional limitations ever since their colonial encounter with the project of modernity some two centuries ago. Even with the presence of such artists as Makhmalbaf, the fact remains that pre- and post-revolutionary Iranian intellectuals are categorically inorganic to the very marrow of their social presence – that is to say uprooted from any definitive disposition in their class or gender consciousness. We will not understand why an aesthetic of factual modification by fantasy is taking place in modern Iranian cinema, those of Kiarostami and Makhmalbaf in particular, unless we understand the genetic

17 Maryam Mohammad-Amini (as the young Makhmalbaf's cousin and accomplice) and Ammar Tafti (as the young Makhmalbaf) in a scene from Mohsen Makhmalbaf's Nun-o-Goldun (A Moment of Innocence, 1996). Makhmalbaf's framing is quintessential in his manner of iconic realism, whereby the borderline between reality and allegory becomes porous. Framed formally in sacred precincts, familiar faces exude the ordinary from the metaphoric. (Photograph: Mohammad Ahmadi; courtesy of Makhmalbaf Film House.)

18 Ammar Tafti, as the young Makhmalbaf, refusing to follow the instructions of the older Makhmalbaf in re-enacting a youthful crime in Mohsen Makhmalbaf's Nun-o-Goldun (A Moment of Innocence, 1996). Architecturally, Makhmalbaf's framing and mise-en-scène intimates the tragic passage of time, a central theme in the understated mood of 'A Moment of Innocence.' (Photograph: Mohammad Ahmadi; courtesy of Makhmalbaf Film House.)

engineering of this inorganicity. The process of economic production and urbanization in Iran over the past two centuries has been such as to have produced an effectively *comprador* bourgeoisie, almost totally contingent on oil revenues, predicated on massive export of oil and of equally wholesale import of consumer goods.[14] This has been a persistent trend from the earliest decades of the nineteenth century to the threshold of the twenty-first. Neither the Constitutional Revolution of 1906–11 (when a constitutional monarchy succeeded an absolutist monarchy), nor the Reza Shah coup d'état in the late 1920s (which brought the Pahlavi dynasty to power), nor the entire period of the so-called modernization of the Pahlavi period, nor indeed the Islamic Revolution of 1979, and the subsequent decades of its empty rhetoric have made the slightest change in this state of affairs. Iran continues to be, now as in the entire course of its proto-colonialist subjugation to the capitalist logic of *modernization*, an oil-producing, single-product economy, its process of urbanization contingent on the formation of a retarded, *comprador* bourgeoisie. The colonial project of modernity has thus remained only a theoretical proposition in Iran, as in much of the colonized world, always contingent on the changing whims of either state-sponsored *modernization*, which were always to facilitate the incorporation of the Iranian economy into the global capitalist system, or those of an entirely inorganic and amorphous body of intellectuals, never predicated on the solid site of either a self-conscious bourgeoisie or a progressive labor movement that were politically aware of their class interests. In the absence of that historical necessity, the panorama of Iranian intellectuals has been one of episodic cults of individuals, with Ahmad Kasravi (died 1946), Jalal Al-e Ahmad (died 1969), Ali Shari'ati (died 1977), and now Abdolkarim Soroush as the most recent signposts of this genealogy of desperation.[15]

It is thus not accidental that in the best and most promising that the Iranian creative imagination has produced in the course of the nineteenth and twentieth centuries, not by any theoretical awareness but by sheer creative impulse, the turn has been toward an active re-negotiation of how *reality* is to be *perceived*. In the absence of any tangible possibility of changing the material conditions of that reality, of creating the historical possibilities of a civil society – of parliamentary democracy, of the most rudimentary parameters of liberty, human rights, civil rights, women's rights, freedom of the press, of voluntary associations, and the whole apparatus of democratic modernity – what is left is a rhetorical negotiation with reality. This is so that in art one can begin to dream the forbidden thought, perceive the impossible solution, and not only resist colonially constituted subjectivity, but in effect subvert the rhetoric of *authenticity* that animates the *traditions* that that very logic of colonial modernity has instigated, fabricated, and legitimized. What is potential and has at times materialized in this art is the aesthetic resistance to the active transmutation of the consciously colonized individual into the raw material for the globalization of the economic production of reality.

The making of an aesthetic counter-metaphysics of emancipation, while still in the full grip of the logic of a globalizing economic production of reality, is the site of a critical reading of Iranian cinema. The active theorization of Iranian cinema – as the first form of an Iranian art that has received a critical global attention and audience – in these terms is the first step toward a richer realization of the particular terms of its aesthetics. Central to our concern in reading this cinema is to see in what particular ways it is negotiating a way out of the cul-de-sac of a colonially constituted subjectivity in the imperial course of the European project of modernity. To ask those kinds of questions, we need to know what it exactly means when a member of a quintessentially inorganic body of intellectuals, in the classical Gramscian sense, needs to re-define his/her organicity and begin to negotiate a new, materially significant, borderline between fact and fantasy.[16]

How can this cinematic negotiation have any effect on the lived *reality* of the audience that goes to watch it performed? Watch it, that is, not in Cannes, Venice, Berlin, or Locarno, but in Tehran, Shiraz, Isfahan, Tabriz, Ahwaz, and Mashhad, where people actually speak the language of the Iranian cinema, or in Dushanbe, New Delhi, Johannesburg, Fez, Cairo, Mexico City, or Sao Paolo, where that language matters. There is a potential dialectic of reciprocity between the global audiences that the Iranian cinema is attracting, not just in the major film festivals but in the increasingly wider commercial releases throughout the world, and its domestic reception, which unless realized and articulated will have no global consequence. The realization of that dialectic of liberation is contingent on a wedding of the aesthetic potentials of this cinema to its wider social implications.

The inorganic disposition of the colonial artist is conducive to the larger aesthetic task at hand of working toward a critical constitution of the defiant subject via a creative alteration of reality. Makhmalbaf never ceased to be a rebel when he began to be a filmmaker. He just changed his venue – from normative to creative, from ideological to aesthetic, from political to moral. The texture and function of reality in his cinema, thus circumscribed, becomes pliable, amorphous, miasmatic – and for precisely that reason Makhmalbaf's *virtual realism* is the cinematic inroad into that psychosocial surreality where things can meander to mean and mind far beyond the limits of their inherited manner of signification. That realism is virtual and thus pliable in any which way that the artist wishes to move it and let it meander – a crucial aspect of Makhmalbaf's mature cinema, but perhaps best evident in *A Moment of Innocence*. In the far-reaching domains of that virtual realism, reality does not have a tyrannical reign over what it means, and by altering its meaning one can anticipate it is otherwise than evident.

Making the Foreign Familiar by Making the Familiar Foreign

Very few Iranian filmmakers match Makhmalbaf in the twin-pregnancy of his cinema with that aesthetically modulated reconfiguration of reality that can tease out of it its otherwise than being. Reality in Makhmalbaf's cinema, in other words, is merely the raw material (bricks and mortar) for the making of a wide and far-reaching highway out of the cul-de-sac of what it otherwise imposes with finality and inevitability. Like Kiarostami's, Makhmalbaf's cinema at its best is visually re-narrating a new angle on reality, a re-narration that forces *reality* to yield to alternative modes of being, perception, signification. In his case, and when he is at his best, as in *A Moment of Innocence*, we always begin with the *real* and before we know it we have followed him into the *true*. Consider now the trajectory of the *real* leading to the *true* as evident in *A Moment of Innocence*. We know biographically, do we not, that at the age of 17, Mohsen Makhmalbaf, the now-famous Iranian filmmaker, formed a small band of Muslim revolutionaries and planned to attack a police officer in order to steal his gun and use it to rob a bank and launch an urban guerrilla offensive against the Pahlavi regime. This is reality as we know it. We also know that Makhmalbaf's ill-fated attack on the police officer was unsuccessful, that he instead got himself shot and subsequently captured and spent a few years in jail before he was released by the revolutionaries who toppled the Pahlavi regime. We know all of these things – but we know them at a cerebral level of self-evidence that amounts to no emancipatory conclusion. We know this in fact as a piece of rather embarrassing, perhaps disconcerting, biography about a globally celebrated filmmaker who perhaps prefers such nasty biographical data about his youthful indiscretions hidden and forgotten. Then the question is what do we do with the fact that Makhmalbaf not only does not hide this event but actually flaunts it – in a surreal, phantasmagoric, almost autistic, and one could even suggest specious, way.

So let's try it again. There is this film called *A Moment of Innocence*, made by one of the leading Iranian filmmakers about a filmmaker who is now in his early forties but who in his late teens had planned to attack a police officer and steal his gun for revolutionary purposes. His accomplice in this ill-fated attempt was his young cousin, with whom the Muslim revolutionary has also an amorous relationship. Right? Re-narrating reality has the nasty habit of making the whole world look like a sequence in Akira Kurosawa's *Rashomon* (1950).

Maybe it is something else? Let's try it this way: Mohsen Makhmalbaf, who is a famous Iranian director, decides to make a film about a police officer whom he had once tried to kill and whose gun he had tried to steal to rob a bank and then launch a revolutionary war against the Pahlavi regime so that he could bring peace, justice, and prosperity to the world. He decides to do that because one day the police officer, who now after the revolution has realized that this famous director Mohsen Makhmalbaf is none other than the same rascal who had once

19 Maryam Mohammad-Amini as the cousin and accomplice of the young Makhmalbaf in a scene from Mohsen
Makhmalbaf s Nun-o-Goldun (A Moment of Innocence, 1996). A Shi'i shrine, the incidental urbanity of
a sacred space, and the vacated spatial echoes of Makhmalbaf's shots all come together to set the mood of his cinematic
vision. (Photograph: Mohammad Ahmadi; courtesy of Makhmalbaf Film House.)

20 *A scene from Mohsen Makhmalbaf's* Nun-o-Goldun (A Moment of Innocence, 1996). *One can almost hear the vacated resonances of consecrated spaces in Makhmalbaf's mise-en-scène. Throughout* A Moment of Innocence *he spatially contemplates a hidden piety that is architecturally inter-textual with the general landscape of cosmopolitan Shi'ism, in which poverty and destitution are integral parts of the visible. (Photograph: Mohammad Ahmadi; courtesy of Makhmalbaf Film House.)*

tried to kill him, pays him a visit and asks him to let him act in one of his films. 'No,' says Makhmalbaf to the middle-aged former police officer whom he had once almost killed, 'you cannot act in my film but let's go and find our youths, your youth and my youth (the younger version of ourselves), and ask them to re-enact what we did when we were young.' So they go and they find their respective youth and take them to the scene of the incident and tell them to re-enact the event. Mohsen Makhmalbaf the famous director directs his own youth, and the police officer, whose only claim to fame and talent is that the now-famous Makhmalbaf once tried to kill him, directs his own youth. The trouble starts when the younger Makhmalbaf and the younger police officer simply refuse to do as they are told as directed by their own elder versions. Talentless actors, or else conscientious objectors, this couple of young lads cannot, will not, and dare not repeat the stupidities of the youth of these two adults who have nothing better to do than find their youth and ask them to re-enact their youthful imbecilities. So we in effect have a crisis, a conflict, between what Makhmalbaf and the police officer did when they were younger, and the youngsters who now refuse to do what they had actually done in the past – trying to kill people.

Right? That's the story. Isn't it? Or can we read it another way? Maybe Makhmalbaf is tired of directing and wants to become an actor. He acted for Kiarostami in *Close Up*. He acted in his own *Salam Cinema*. And now he has also acted in *A Moment of Innocence*. But he always acts as himself. How exactly does one *act as oneself*? In *Close Up*, Kiarostami directed Makhmalbaf, both the fake Makhmalbaf, Mr. Sabziyan, and the real Mr. Mohsen Ostad Ali Makhmalbaf. But in *Salam Cinema* and *A Moment of Innocence*, Mohsen Makhmalbaf directed himself. How does one direct oneself *as* oneself? What exactly happens when Makhmalbaf checks through the visor, approves the framing, gives the exact instructions to his director of photography for the camera movement, then goes and stands in front, and not behind, the camera and says, 'Action!' Then what? Is he still Mohsen Makhmalbaf the famous filmmaker we know, or is he someone else? Who is this man acting as Makhmalbaf directing Makhmalbaf to act as Makhmalbaf directing his youth to act as his youth? There's the rub.[17]

There is a creative confusion about *A Moment of Innocence*, a quiet erosion of the dead certainties, that separates the *real* from the *make-believe*, and that is precisely the trademark of the best of the post-revolutionary Iranian cinema. This creative confusion disregards facts by subjecting them to a multi-significatory set of fantasies.[18] When facts are constituted by history, then they ought to be reversed by art, re-constituted, re-negotiated, let loose to hunt for their alternatives, all in a creatively multi-focal thrust that no author or filmmaker, let alone a censor official, can control.

What precisely is the nature of that *fact* that needs to be renegotiated via an interface with fantasy? The most foundational of all historical facts of modernity for Iranians and their neighbors in the (post-)colonial world is precisely their colonially mitigated subjectivity, their slanted angle onto the world, and their truncated location in their own culture. The generation that Makhmalbaf represents is at once the culmination of a whole history of colonially constituted identity and the catastrophic collapse of all hopes in political resolutions. The colonially mitigated reception of modernity is conducive only to a specific kind of subject-formation, to a trapped trajectory of (im)possibilities, that colonialism – economic or cultural, classical, or reconstituted for the late globalizing capitalism – as the extended arm of capitalist modernity has grafted on the colonized. The specific parameters and (im)possibilities available in the colonial condition obviously have their authorial roots in the project of capitalist modernity itself. Subject-formation constitutional to that project, even before its colonial extensions which stripped it of all its Enlightenment ideologies, has the epistemic and ontological proclivity of a metaphysics of dis-closure which is, and here we have no choice but to see Heidegger's logic, *productionist* and manifests things as raw material in the economic production of reality. In the colonial outpost, the mutation of individuals into things and things into raw material was a matter of observational evidence and in no need of post-metaphysical theorization and revelation.

If we follow the Heideggerian re-modulation of the Platonic (which he calls *Western*) metaphysics, then the project of modernity would become evident as the last stage of the metaphysics of representation, of dis-closure; that is to say, for something *to be* means for something *to be manifest*. This is predicated on the assumption that temporality, or the timely bound being-in-the-world, is the only viable range of vision within which things can manifest themselves. Foregrounding his phenomenological conception of *Das Man* [the *any-person-self*] on a philosophical tradition that ranged from Hegel and Marx down to Dilthey, Heidegger consciously opted to root his conception of *man* in the everyday experiences of the person's social presence. The *any-person-self* is so constituted by a web of interrelated affiliations – as Georg Simmel would call them – that there is not even a conscious awareness of its full inventory of social and cultural informants. To be *human*, in Heidegger's view, is to be constituted by a public language, a mass entity into which he is located. In the Heideggerian critique of modernity, *the any-person-self* had completely taken over and constituted the self-productionist subjectivity of the individual, facilitating the conception of things as raw material, all facilitated by an instrumental logic that was the chief product of an economic production of *manifestly being-in-the-world*.

In Heidegger's own words:

> In utilizing public means of transport and in making use of information services such as the newspaper, every other is like the next. This being-with-one-another dissolves one's own Dasein completely into the kind of being of 'the others,' in such a way, indeed, that the others, as distinguishable and explicit, vanish more and more. In this inconspicuousness and unascertainability, the real dictatorship of the

'they' is unfolded. We take pleasure and enjoy ourselves as they [man] take pleasure; we read, see, and judge about literature and art as they see and judge; likewise we shrink back from the 'great mass' as they shrink back; we find 'shocking' what they find shocking. The 'they,' which is nothing definite, and which all are, though not as the sum, prescribes the kind of being of everydayness.[19]

In Michael Zimmerman's reading of this passage:

> One of the basic features of everyday life was its 'publicness' [*öffentlichkeit*], a term often used in connection with 'civil society' [*bügerlichen gesellschaft*], i.e., the business world. Heidegger did not emphasize the bourgeois connotation of this term, possibly to avoid revealing the extent to which his analysis of everyday life was in fact an analysis of life in degenerate commercial society. In such a society, nothing truly original can be revealed because language has degenerated to the state of idle talk [*gerede*], the passing around of ungrounded opinions.[20]

All of this is still within the operative parameters of the theorists, practitioners, and the beneficiaries of the joint projects of the European Enlightenment and capitalist modernity. The colonial extension of the selfsame project of modernity and of subject-formation was doubly effective in the aggressive transmutation of the colonial subject into raw material. While in the metropolitan capitals the productionist metaphysics of capitalist modernity was mutating the individual into an instrument of production, its project of Enlightenment was busy giving him (and it was a *him*) the dignity of a place in a universal claim to victory. This was far from the case in the colonial outpost, where the mutation of the individual into raw material was concomitant with his equally aggressive constitution as the colonized other of the civilizing mission of the colonizer. The fate of the post/colonial artist, as a result, has been cast in a poetic, performative, and carnivalesque emancipation from that colonially constituted subjectivity in which individuals, the artist and his audience, are reduced to *things* and *things* are revealed as raw material.

On the site of the visual, how is that poetic shattering of the real possible? Here is where Makhmalbaf's daring imagination has found many inroads. *A Moment of Innocence*, seen on the site of this poetic shattering, is the rhythmic slowing down of time, the narrative re-modulation of the living, the chronic crafting of an alternative possibility to be. In *A Moment of Innocence*, Makhmalbaf re-crafts his own history as the story of a people to whom he wants to, but cannot, belong. By virtue of the poetic intrusion of that possibility, *A Moment of Innocence* is the wintry tale of a people who are not, but whom Makhmalbaf wishes them to be, visually narrating them into existence. Next time you see *A Moment of Innocence*, notice the wintry feeling of nostalgia, the snowy sensation of a hinterland, the quiet calmness of a deadly beauty, that underlines the temperament and mannerism of the film. How is that possible? How did Makhmalbaf craft that calm and yet disquieting serenity of a paradisiacal coldness? Time here is no time, space no space, movements slowed down, frame-by-frame, thus to frame the passage of an unnerving flow of a parable that demands an unearthly attention.

A Moment of Innocence is a love story. In between two young revolutionaries who want to kill for their ideals breaks through the splitting personae of a director, Mohsen Makhmalbaf. The historical Makhmalbaf who is now a director directs his young version to kill. The ahistorical Makhmalbaf who is now a director teaches his young actor to love. The historical Makhmalbaf who is now a director and used to be a rebel directs his police officer to kill. The ahistorical Makhmalbaf who is now a director pleads with his victim to forgive. The 17-year-old actor who is Makhmalbaf acts the way the 40-year-old director who is Makhmalbaf wants and wishes him to act. The 40-year-old actor Makhmalbaf directs the way he wishes he had acted when he was 17. The result of this narrative re-crafting of the crooked timber of a person's life is a poetic of parousia, a parable told at the *pre-moment* of being.

There is a story in the Qur'an that has been the dearest tale to all mystics of the past 1,400 years. According to this story, when God is about to create man, He summons him in His mind. This is the *pre-moment* of creation – the time before time. Man is not yet created. But he *exists* in God's mind. God summons him in His mind and asks him: 'Am I not thy Lord?' Man says: 'Yes you are.' The Muslim mystics call this the day of 'alast,' from the Arabic 'alastu?' 'Am I not?'

> And (remember) when thy Lord brought forth from the children of Adam, from their loins, their seed, and made them testify of themselves, (saying): Am I not your Lord? They said: yea, verily. We testify ... [21]

It is to this passage that Muslim mystics refer in a state of utter self-forgetfulness:

> 'alast' az azal hamchenanshan begush,

Sa'di, the most eloquent spokesman of the Persian classical culture (in the thirteenth century), says about the mystics, and then he adds:

> be faryad 'qalu bala' dar khorush.

The reference is emphatic:

> The call of 'am I not thy Lord' is continually in their ears,
> The cry of 'yes you are' is perennially on their lips.[22]

In *A Moment of Innocence*, Makhmalbaf visually re-creates that pre-moment, but this time in the mind of his camera. Emerging in his wintry paradise are an Adam and an Eve, the bride and bridegroom of a whole new attendance on reality. Through the camera of Makhmalbaf comes forward the visual apparition of a new coupling of innocence and faith, transmuted from the depth of a man's belief in a metaphysics that can no longer sustain him or the culture he calls home. In his youth, and in the image of a virginity he imagines in the woman that his youth ought to have loved, dwells the sanctity of a hope, the bewildered piety of a place that one must call home. What are hidden behind the gaze of this budding innocence are all the promises of a future that must hold, and all the fear of a past that must let go.

How does he do that? Where precisely is the narrative access of the *real* into the *true*, of *reality* unto *truth*, of the *ordinary* sublimating to the *significant*? For a glimpse we may look at *Greeting the Sun*, a script Makhmalbaf wrote and published in 1993 but never made into a film.[23] Khorshid and Mehraban are in love – Khorshid the daughter of a pottery-maker and Mehraban the novice at the service of the master. Khorshid's father acknowledges their love, proclaims them husband and wife and takes them on a pilgrimage to Mecca. On the way bandits attack them. The father is killed, Mehraban is injured and lost, and Khorshid is taken hostage by the bandits. From here starts a whole journey of misery that submits Khorshid to a succession of indignities until she finally finds Mehraban, just for them both to be stoned to death by the order of a religious judge who finds them accused of adultery.

Time and narrative are contracted in *Greeting the Sun*, and so are the visual and the aural. The result is the metaphoric constitution of a fictive reality in which salvation is attained neither through human misery nor by the grace of God, neither by the banality of Evil nor by the sanctity of the *Everlasting*. In the transmuted authority of the *fictive truth*, Makhmalbaf has narratively reconstituted a new mode of reading reality. First the mechanics: time in *Greeting the Sun* is no-time, the double-time of now-and-never, the early Islamic, the early Shi'i, the medieval Iranian, just the day before yesterday, or maybe hundreds of years from now. Space is no-space, the double-space of here and nowhere, maybe Iran, Iraq, and Arabia, maybe another planet, or maybe the hinterland of no-matter-where. The visual here is narrative – the narrative visual. One reads what one sees – as one sees what one reads. The language is archaic – the diction alive. The camera moves in the pen – as the pen sees with an eye. Khorshid is chaste but Khorshid is sold to a bordello-house. Mehraban is brave but Mehraban watches with impotence and destitution his bride being violated by the bandits.

Between his mature cinema and his best works of fiction, Makhmalbaf is a restless manipulator of what is evident into what is important. A lapsed Muslim, a disillusioned revolutionary, a sojourner into the vast and variegated field of creative possibilities – Makhmalbaf is the magician who makes the foreign land of hope familiar by making the familiar land of despair foreign. The Brechtian notion of *Verfremdung* (distancing) here works through a deliberate liberty that Makhmalbaf takes with reality itself – thus instead of making his own presence as a director felt and evident, he reverses the angle and makes the manufactured disposition of reality entirely fictive by making the fictive disposition of fiction real. In this regard, not just Makhmalbaf, but the entire *pararealism*[24] of Iranian cinema is deeply indebted to the self-conscious realism that is best evident in Sepehri's disarming poetry – particularly where he at one and the same time constructs and dismantles the beauty that is at the heart of his fragile perception of reality. Notice, for example, in the following stanza how Sepehri posits the truth and beauty of his painting and poetry precisely at the time that he is in fact announcing their manufactured disposition as the simulacrum of what they are purported to be:

> I am from Kashan.
> I paint for a living.
> Every once in a while
> I build a cage
> With my colors and
> I sell it to you –
> So that your solitary heart is lightened up
> With the song of the red anemone
> That is trapped inside it.
> What delusions, what delusions!
> I know quite well
> That my canvas has no life – and
> I know quite well
> That the pond in my painting
> Has no fish.

The Defiant Alternation of Reality

There is a scene in *A Moment of Innocence* where Makhmalbaf brings the young man who is to act as his own youth (as the younger Makhmalbaf) to the home of Makhmalbaf's cousin to ask her to allow him to take her daughter to make a film.

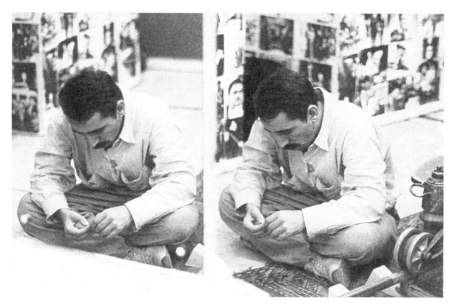

21   *Makhmalbaf mirroring himself, in a shot from behind the scene of his* Honar-Pisheh *(Actor, 1993). The image and the body, as reality and representation, are interchangeable in his cinema. (Photograph: Mitra Mahasseni; courtesy of Makhmalbaf Film House.)*

The story, as told in the film, is that Makhmalbaf and his cousin used to be comrades in arms (this is biographically not true). She is now married and has a daughter. Makhmalbaf wants to ask the young niece to come and act as her own mother, opposite Makhmalbaf's youth, in the film that Makhmalbaf is making. The cousin disagrees, while her daughter is trying desperately to convince her mother to allow her to go with Makhmalbaf and his youth to make this film. We are now in present time, watching the mature Makhmalbaf regretting his youthful violence and trying to make a film about the futility of his youthful deeds. While Makhmalbaf and his cousin (whom we never see and thus her characterization is entirely through her voice) are negotiating back and forth to have her daughter come and make a film, the young girl appears and brings a bowl of soup for the young man who is going to play the role of the young Makhmalbaf. She greets the old Makhmalbaf and proceeds to the car where the young man is preparing himself to act, as the mature Makhmalbaf is waiting. Their conversation is quite formal and in the present. 'Hello. How are you? Please have a little bit of this soup,' and such. As we are all gently led to believe that this is the present time when Makhmalbaf is trying to make a film in the 1990s about something he did in the 1970s, suddenly the young girl, whom Makhmalbaf wanted to act as the youth of his cousin, slips a book to the young Makhmalbaf and makes arrangements to see him in order to carry on the plot of assassinating the police officer. Within the span of the present time, suddenly a temporal cocoon is created that sucks the present back into past. Without the slightest change in location or even the mise-en-scène, and by virtue of a couple of simple lines, Makhmalbaf generates and sustains a veritable past in the middle of an evident present. Nothing has changed except the cinematic manufacturing of a time warp, within which the performed past comes to mark the enacted present.[25]

In its entirety, *A Moment of Innocence* is a constellation of variations on this theme of de-telling the time, as if Makhmalbaf is reaching out to the past to change its course. This temporal abnegation of reality – making time effectively go against its own logic – comes to a climactic conclusion at the end of the film when the young Makhmalbaf, goaded by the old one, is approaching the police officer to assassinate him. The young cousin, now acted by some other young woman (because Makhmalbaf's cousin did not agree for her daughter to act), approaches the police officer to ask him a question in order to distract him, so that the young Makhmalbaf can come and stab him. Meanwhile the older police officer has told his youth that she is not really in love with him but is in fact the accomplice in an assassination attempt to kill him. He has given his own youth a gun and told him that instead of giving the young (treacherous) girl the flowerpot he has brought for her, he should kill her as soon as she comes near him. The camera here becomes curatorial, choreographic, stylistic, ponderous, curious. The young girl comes near the young police officer, turns her (very beautiful) face toward the camera, lifts her veil in a way that blocks the police officer but hugs the camera, and asks in a close up of heart-stopping suspension, 'What time is it, sir?' The whole point and purpose, of course, at this moment is precisely 'time' and its whereabouts, but in more than one sense. The lifting of the veil here returns us to the opening shot of *A Moment of Innocence*, when the police officer comes looking for Makhmalbaf's house and rings a bell. A woman opens the door and tells him he has the wrong door, that the Makhmalbafs live a few doors away. The way that the woman holds her veil is entirely dis-inviting to the camera and dismissive of the audience (we thus never see her face, just hear her voice), paving the way for here at the end of the film where the veil is receptive of the camera and embracing of the audience. The camera freezes on the face of the young girl, the music soars, as she repeats again, 'Excuse me sir, what time is it?' The time is now no-time, ever, never, always. The camera stands still. The young woman holds her veil tightly, hugging the camera, as two hands enter the inner sanctity of her face, one offering her a flowerpot (instead of a gun) and the other a piece of bread (instead of a knife).

This is a cinematic will to rewrite history, to remake the world, to revise its destiny, re-adjust its lenses, revisit its vision, modify its verdict. Makhmalbaf the rebel here is in full control of a cinematic will to dismantle and dismember (by mis-remembering) the fate of an entire nation. Makhmalbaf himself (the person) may wish to apologize here, to seek forgiveness, to solicit absolution. But

Makhmalbaf the filmmaker is after a much bigger fish to fry here. Makhmalbaf the filmmaker here is in possession of a history much more significant than his own – history with a purpose, a point, a vision. Here, in the span of this film, Makhmalbaf the filmmaker manages to overthrow what in his wildest dream he could not have imagined overthrowing when he picked up a knife to launch a revolution. What he is doing here is dismantling the government of the subservient (we on the colonial ends of Kant were never allowed to be sovereign) subject – turning his will around, making her defiance of a colonial fate evident, trustworthy, historical. No form of subject-control is operative here on the site of this cinematic vision to will a subject with full (arrogant even) control over what has been made into a pliable world – time, space, and destiny together. Through the wintry woods of Makhmalbaf's revision of our history emerge the Adam and Eve of a completely new notion of our humanity.

In providing a 'correlative history of the modern soul' in *Discipline and Punish* (1975), Foucault included 'the colonized' among a gyration of subjects that the governing disciplines of the body manufacture.[26]

> It would be wrong to say that the soul is an illusion, or an ideological effect. On the contrary, it exists, it has a reality, it is produced permanently around, on, within the body by the functioning of a power that is exercised on those punished – and, in a more general way, on those one supervises, trains and corrects, over madmen, children at home and at school, the colonized, over those who are stuck at a machine and supervised for the rest of their lives.[27]

At the colonial marshlands of this cosmopolis of discipline and punishment, humans are not attached to those machines. They *are* those machines. If Foucault in his philosophy sought to write a history of that soul through a history of the body it incarcerates,[28] on the colonial edges of the same theoretical truth, artists like Makhmalbaf have intuited a defiance that liberates that body from the tyranny of that servile soul.

Chapter Five

Recasting the Subject:
The Anticolonial Rebel at Work

Toward the end of the last chapter, I concluded my reading of Makhmalbaf's *A Moment of Innocence* by suggesting that in such films his vision is representative of something far more significant than the specifics of his own biography. As a controversial filmmaker in a very tumultuous time in the history of his country, Makhmalbaf has always been at the center of many contentious issues that have had an inevitable impact on his cinema. But his cinema also possesses a life of its own, a kind of history with a purpose, a point, a vision. I also suggested that by creatively manipulating the temporal disposition of narrative[1] in *A Moment of Innocence*, Makhmalbaf manages to overthrow the tyrannical government of the subservient subject, passively received and actively corroborated in the course of colonial modernity.

What I will argue in this chapter is that the fate of a post/colonial artist is inevitably cast in resisting an active transmutation of his life-experience into raw material for the culture industry, facilitated via the colonial extension of the global project of capitalist modernity. The aesthetics that the post/colonial artist inhabits and thus represents, however, has to cut on two apparently opposed but quintessentially identical fronts, not just on the colonially constituted subservient *subjectivity*, but also on the jargon of *authenticity* that animates the 'Traditions' that colonial modernity invents. The *Tradition* invented to face *Modernity* has its own overwhelming weight to impose. But here, the impediments of one enemy can be used as a weapon against the aggression of the other. The metaphysics of modernity is quintessentially ocularcentric,[2] whereas that of the Islamic faith is predicated on a rhetoric of blindfolded faith, of concealment-for-revelation. To conceal and to believe in the concealed is canonical to Islam. Muslims are distinguished from non-Muslims by virtue of believing in the unseen. 'Those who believe in the unseen and keep up prayer and spend out of what We have given them' is the principal cornerstone of defining a Muslim according to the Qur'anic revelation.[3] In the matrix of this im/balance, while the post/colonial artist dismantles the politics of the *ancestral* via the ocularcentrism of the *modern*, s/he also ups the ante and subverts the very same ocularcentricism of the *modern* by the cinematic *transparency of the real*. *The transparency of the real* mocks and modifies the authority of the *evident* – and thus by mocking reality via an aesthetic of its transparency, the post/colonial artist transgresses the authorial boundaries of colonially constituted *modernity*. This metaphysics of dis-closure is quintessential to the project of Enlightenment, and to its *productionist* epistemic, rooted in the material demands of capitalist modernity. Modernity is re-presentational and ocularcentric. Cinema is *ipso facto* transgressive by virtue of being voyeuristic. By revealing, cinema exposes what is to be concealed, and thus robs the politics of the ancestral claim to *authenticity* in its assertion of authority.

Mohsen Makhmalbaf, Director of Cinema

What I am suggesting here is that the aesthetic overthrow of the colonially compromised subject is a double-edged sword, positing a fabricated 'Tradition' and an overriding Modernity against each other, discrediting their colonially manufactured binary opposition, and freeing the defiant subject from the midst of its ruin. As a good case study of what I propose here, I would like now to dwell on one of the best examples of a cinematic manipulation of the history of the Iranian encounter with colonial modernity, namely Mohsen Makhmalbaf's *Nasser al-Din Shah, Actor-e Cinema/Once Upon a Time, Cinema* (1992). In this film, Makhmalbaf depicts Ebrahim Khan Akkasbashi, the first Iranian cinematographer, making a cinematic record of this encounter. Soon after the invention of the first cinematographer by the Lumière Brothers, Louis and Auguste, in 1895, Mozaffar al-Din Shah of the Qajar dynasty (1853–1907; reigned 1896–1907), the reigning Iranian monarch, traveled to Europe and brought back with him the first camera. His own personal filmmaker, Ebrahim Khan Akkasbashi, had just shot a scene of His Royal Highness, as it were, in the course of the Festival of Flowers in Ostend, Belgium. Makhmalbaf uses this historic incident, the very original moment of Iranian cinema and a landmark event in the course of the Iranian encounter with modernity, to re-narrate the history of that colonial encounter in a phantasmagoric torpedo of creative historiography.[4]

The cinematic manipulation of colonial modernity in *Once Upon a Time, Cinema* gives Makhmalbaf an unprecedented opportunity to mock reality – through a creative manipulation of time, space, shape, and color. This is one effective way to alter the metaphysical assumption of *the evident*. The result of this visual poetic is that reality is made to look strange, unfamiliar, always subject to re-negotiation – again through the Persian passion play mimetic version of the Brechtian *Verfremdung*. This in turn leads to an ever-stranger re-discovery of what Hans Blumenberg calls 'the absolutism of reality,'[5] which is here in effect restored via the poetic of the visual. Restoration of the absolutism of reality in this case means

22   Ezzatollah Entezami in the lead role in Mohsen Makhmalbaf's Naser al-Din Shah, Actor-e Cinema (Once
Upon a Time, Cinema, 1992). *A cinematic take on the history of modernity in Iran, Makhmalbaf's take on the
origin of cinema in Iran became a simultaneous commentary on the saving grace of his chosen profession. (Photograph:
Mitra Mahasseni; courtesy of Makhmalbaf Film House.)*

the release of colonially constituted subjectivity, where the individual can no longer be reduced to things, and things to raw material.

Makhmalbaf's *Once Upon a Time, Cinema* creatively reconstitutes that *absolutism of reality*, which is at once frightening and exhilarating, because it renews the world and makes it once again receptive to what Max Weber would call a 're-enchantment of the world'[6] – a task delegated in this film to the central character of Akkasbashi, the prototype of all future Iranian filmmakers. Makhmalbaf's Akkasbashi is based on the historical character of that name. Mirza Ebrahim Khan Akkasbashi (1874–1915) was the son of Mirza Ahmad Sani' al-Saltaneh, the official photographer at the court of Nasser al-Din Shah (1831–96; reigned 1848–96). Akkasbashi (his last name means something like 'Mr. Official Photographer') was born in Iran but raised and educated in Paris as a photographer. His father had gone to Paris without official permission from Nasser al-Din Shah, causing the royal ire and being denied permission to return to his homeland. Nasser al-Din Shah finally forgave the over-eager photographer and allowed him and his son Ebrahim to come back to Iran. On his arrival, Akkasbashi was commissioned as the official photographer of Nasser al-Din Shah's Crown Prince Mozaffar and sent to his court in Tabriz, where he stayed until the assassination of Nasser al-Din Shah in 1896.[7] In the company of the new king, Mozaffar al-Din Shah Akkasbashi came to Tehran and became the official photographer of the court. During Mozaffar al-Din Shah's first visit to Europe in 1900, Akkasbashi accompanied him to the Paris Exposition. It was at this point that five years into the Lumière brother's invention of the first cinematographic camera, Mozaffar al-Din Shah saw a film in France and fell madly in love with the invention and immediately ordered Akkasbashi to buy one for his court. And it was thus that on 17 August 1900, a Gaumont camera at hand, Akkasbashi shot a scene of the reigning Iranian monarch watching a parade in Ostend, Belgium.

Akkasbashi, as depicted by Makhmalbaf, has become an extension of his camera, a visionary witness to the tumultuous history of Iranian modernity. What is paramount about Akkasbashi is his absolute and undivided attention to his profession. His presence at the Qajar court is entirely accidental to his existential identification with his newly found instrument. It is as if he has effectively transmigrated in body and soul into the transparent soul of his cinematographer, unified in voice and vision, creative and critical imagination, with his camera. The scene of the mock execution of Akkasbashi under the guillotine, with an obvious visual pun on 'cutting,' both his neck and his rushes, is one of the most memorable in *Once Upon a Time, Cinema*, in which the cinematographer and his cinema are cross-identified. As the supreme sign of tyranny in the course of the French Revolution, Dr. Joseph Guillotine's invention assumes less ominous and more frivolous significance in Makhmalbaf's hands. As an agent of visually re-enchanting the world, Akkasbashi's presence at Nasser al-Din Shah's court is of course ahistorical. In Makhmalbaf's film, a court magician, Farrashbashi, misunderstands Mozaffar al-Din Shah's command and instead of sending Akkasbashi to the reigning monarch's son Muhammad Ali Shah (1872–25; reigned, 1906–09), dispatches the cinematographer and his camera back in history to the court of his father Nasser al-Din Shah (1831–96). 'May you rot in hell,' Mozaffar al-Din Shah says to Farrashbashi with a thick Turkish accent to his Persian, 'where did you dispatch our photographer, you cursed magician?' Upon hearing the magician say that he dispatched the photographer to His Royal Father, Mozaffar al-Din Shah exclaims: 'What calamity! I said send him to my son! Now what would dead people do to our photographer?'[8]

The cutting edge of the guillotine does not come down to chop off Akkasbashi's neck, but the cut from Mozaffar al-Din Shah's court to Nasser al-Din Shah's cuts the thick course of history – in two complementary ways. Through such emancipatory splicing of *History*, colonially constituted subjectivity is released from the predicament of being cornered by the temporal logic of modernity. It is now possible to be present at and emancipated from not just colonialism and its consequences, but even more importantly from the *productionist* metaphysics contingent on it, from reality as representation, and from the whole calamitous consequences of foundational thinking. Such thinking includes a jargon of *Authenticity* and *Tradition* invented by *Modernity* in order to believe itself.

What Makhmalbaf's *Once Upon a Time, Cinema* does in that simple move of creatively reversing the course of history is to have the paralyzing false dichotomy of 'Tradition and Modernity' eat each other out, and dismantle the authority of each other once and for all. This is a critical move if we are not to fall into the trap of essentializing 'Traditions' as we launch a movement against colonialism. Both in his conception of women's veiling and in his understanding of the Algerian family, and too much in a legitimate haste to oppose colonial modernity, Frantz Fanon fell into the trap of this rhetoric of *Authenticity*. 'Every rejected veil,' he believed, 'disclosed to the eyes of the colonialists horizons until then forbidden, and revealed to them, piece by piece, the flesh of Algeria laid bare.'[9] In similar haste, and in order to demonstrate the socio-pathology of colonialism, Fanon tended to essentialize, authenticate, and traditionalize the nuclear family. In this respect, Fanon was blinded to his own superior wisdom that 'decolonization, which sets out to change the order of the world, is, obviously, a program of complete disorder.'[10] That 'complete disorder' is not limited to the dismantling of the colonial domination. The experience of the Islamic Revolution is an historic lesson in how a cross-essentialization of an authentic nativism can degenerate liberation movements into disastrous mockeries of themselves.

In the figure of Mozaffar al-Din Shah, he invests a benign benevolence, with an almost childish delight in the new toy he has found in Europe and brought with him to Iran – entirely oblivious of the revolution he has inadvertently initiated.[11] It is critical here to keep in mind that the historical Mozaffar al-Din Shah was the Qajar monarch who was finally forced by the revolutionaries to sign a constitution – and to this day the phrase *Adl-e Mozaffar/The Justice of Mozaffar* adorns the gate of the Iranian parliament. Makhmalbaf's Mozaffar al-Din Shah is the figure of vanity transmuted into an unsuspecting visionary. One of the most beautiful and memorable scenes of *Once Upon a Time, Cinema* is when the heavy and majestic monarch begins to dance, with all his ludicrous frivolity, to a whirlwind of film rushes, as the magician is transmigrating Akkasbashi and his camera back in history.

The characterization of Mozaffar al-Din Shah as an unsuspecting visionary rewrites the history of colonial modernity against itself. Makhmalbaf transforms Mozaffar al-Din Shah, who like most other Qajar kings was a bantering buffoon particularly fond of European hot spring spas, into a benign and even loveable character. The colonial plundering of Iranian oil in fact started during the reign of Mozaffar al-Din Shah, when in 1901, a year after he went to Paris and ordered Akkasbashi to buy a Gaumont camera, Mozaffar al-Din Shah granted the British financier William Knox D'Arcy a lucrative contract (more an economic capitulation than a contract, really) to excavate Iranian oil. The Anglo-Persian Oil Company that D'Arcy eventually established became what is now known as British Petroleum (BP).[12] It is in this *bona fide* accomplice in the thievery of Iranian natural

23   *Mohsen Makhmalbaf directing Ezzatollah Entezami in* Naser al-Din Shah, Actor-e Cinema *(Once Upon a Time, Cinema, 1992). Searching for the soul of Iranian cultural modernity in the heart of a decadent aristocracy, the young Muslim revolutionary is teaching himself the art and mystery of paradox. (Photograph: Mitra Mahasseni; courtesy of Makhmalbaf Film House.)*

resources that Makhmalbaf finds a redeeming factor, an unsuspecting visionary, who despite all else was instrumental bringing cinema to Iran, albeit for his own personal entertainment and initially for the recording of royal wedding and circumcision ceremonies.

Some observers of Makhmalbaf's cinema in Iran have noted the dramatic changes in his career, but generally they have attributed these to his whimsical disposition.[13] It would be instructive to pause for a moment and compare *Once Upon a Time, Cinema* with the inauspicious registers of Makhmalbaf's early (religiously charged) films. One can speculate on many factors pertinent to this fundamental change. But, again, I believe it is crucial to note that a simultaneous or successive attraction to either mystical entrapment or poetic emancipation is characteristic of being at the receiving end of the ravages of technological modernity. Heidegger's critique of technological modernity, which ultimately results in his uncanny turn to the operative force of the *poetic shattering of Dasein*, has a decidedly European but uncontrollably global implication above and beyond his immediate sociological reasons in the Weimar Republic to share his contemporaries' fear of the machine. Germany of Heidegger's time had but a taste of the colonial conditions constitutional to the peripheries of the capital. The anti-technological sentiments of Heidegger's generation are instrumental in any understanding of the similar turn to *mysticism* and *traditionalism* on the colonial site of the project of modernity. In Heidegger are simultaneously present *both* the most critical awareness of the catastrophic consequences of the project of technological modernity *and* the seeking of a poetic of emancipation from the cul-de-sac of that historical entrapment. At the same time, Heidegger's own turn to Nazism points precisely to the accuracy of his assessment of the catastrophic consequences of technological modernity. His final turn to a poetic emancipation harbors at the same time the way out of that dead-end *and* the endemic danger of the re-mystification of the world in retaliation to its carnivorous technologization.[14] The crucial distinction is between a *poetics* of emancipation and a *mysticism* of double entrapment. But closing in on Heidegger's critique of technological modernity – on his way to the poetic shattering of the real – we may learn much in the post/colonial possibilities of the poetics of our emancipation, as we are also warned of the deadly consequences of our endemic mysticism.

Makhmalbaf's turn to visual poetry, his increasing facility with the tools of his chosen trade, and ultimately his investing in Akkasbashi the re-inventive imagination of the Iranian encounter with colonial modernity have a vastly liberating impact on him, whereby he himself begins to be cleansed of the terror he has experienced in the dungeons of the Pahlavi monarchy. Makhmalbaf's treatment of Nasser al-Din Shah as exceptionally tender and kind is an only slightly camouflaged version of publicly projecting Mohammad Reza Shah Pahlavi back to Nasser al-Din Shah, and then by forgiving him seeking to cleanse the soul of a nation. This is 1992, almost a decade and a half after the overthrow of Mohammad Reza Shah and his subsequent death in exile in ignominy – the Shah that Makhmalbaf wanted overthrown. That accomplished, Makhmalbaf is now in a vastly different mood than when he was a revolutionary rebel. This, again, is 1992, more than a decade into the charismatic terror of Ayatollah Khomeini reigning supreme over the destiny of a brutalized nation. The tender treatment of Nasser al-Din Shah, the king *par excellence* on the course of Iranian encounters with colonial modernity, has a liberating impact beyond being just a prisoner forgiving his tormentor. This is a filmmaker re-writing a history to liberate a nation from its own self-defeating memories.

Akkasbashi's travels back to the time of Nasser al-Din Shah, the most consequential monarch in Qajar dynasty, recall and recast the medieval monarchy's long and languid encounter with colonial modernity in a liberating and empowering manner. Nasser al-Din Shah's repeated trips to Europe, the legendary premiership of Amir Kabir (1807–52), the champion of Iranian modernity, the last and most devastating feudal revolutionary movement known as the Babi revolt led by Ali Muhammad Bab (1819–50), the rapid intensification of colonial interests in Iran, and ultimately the assassination of Nasser al-Din Shah by a militant Muslim activist in 1896 all mark the prolonged reign of the Qajar monarchy. In the figure of Nasser al-Din Shah, the prototype of all subsequent

Iranian monarchs, Makhmalbaf re-imagines the entire history of Iranian monarchy. He remembers the very king who captured and imprisoned him, then reverses the hatred that was the defining moment between him and Mohammad Reza Shah and mutates it into love, by having Nasser al-din Shah fall madly in love with the first fictive woman character in the history of Iranian cinema, the Golnar of Abd al-Hossein Sepanta's *Dokhtar e Lor/The Lor Girl* (1934). Out of love for Golnar, Nasser al-Din Shah wishes to become an actor (and Makhmalbaf fulfills his wish).

By turning the most proverbial Persian monarch of the nineteenth century into a movie fan, in love with a leading lady, who wishes to become a movie actor, Makhmalbaf conflates two critical moments in the history of Iranian cinema to mutate a collective hatred of tyranny into a communal yearning for freedom. The original title of Makhmalbaf's *Once Upon a Time, Cinema*, namely *Nasser al-Din Shah, Actor of Cinema*, is borrowed from the second Iranian film ever made, Ovanes Oganians' *Haji Agha, Actor-e Cinema/Haji Agha, Actor of Cinema* (1933); while Golnar, the object of Nasser al-Din Shah's affection in Makhmalbaf's film, is taken from the first-ever Iranian talkie.[15] By having a transhistorical mutation of the title character of the last Iranian silent movie (made almost simultaneously with the first Iranian talkie) fall in love with the leading lady of that first talkie, Makhmalbaf points to an historical serendipity by which cinema as an art form becomes definitive to Iranian (cultural) modernity. This is cinema at its best, when it can tease and turn history against its own tormented memories. Keep in mind also that the subtitle of *The Lor Girl* when it was first screened in Iran was *Iran of Yesterday and Iran of Today*, and it was projected as a propaganda piece in support of Reza Shah's 'modernization' projects. It was shown in Mayak Theater in Tehran almost in the same breath as a whole series of propaganda documentaries showing the accomplishments of Reza Shah.[16] Makhmalbaf's ahistorical recasting of these inter-textual references effectively abuses history in order to liberate it from its own debilitating domain.

Makhmalbaf's playfulness throughout *Once Upon a Time, Cinema*, and with such inter-textual references in particular, effectively uses the instrumentality of cinema as an art form to de-instrumentalize the servile subjectivity that was bequeathed to us by and through colonial modernity. If our colonized history could not but assign to us a servile subjectivity, via a vicarious participation in the filmic version of that history, we can re-imagine ourselves otherwise not in a servile but a subversive subjectivity, when we become the agents of our own history. By projecting the spectacle of a re-imagined encounter with modernity, Makhmalbaf, *ipso facto*, de-instrumentalizes the spectator who sits in front of his film – turning him/her around from an object of European colonial gaze into an agent of historical change. Here is a good point to remember, that Heidegger sought to trace the essence of technology, as 'contrivance,' to its Latin root as *instrumentum*: 'The current conception of technology, according to which it is a means and a human activity, can therefore be called the instrumental and anthropological definition of technology.'[17] The key to Heidegger's critique of modernity, through an instrumental reading of technology, is its critical location within the context of the bourgeois revolution – which has resulted in what he considered a constitutional change in the very conception of what technology implies today. Heidegger's principal objective here is a critical awareness of the irresistible power of modernity to instrumentalize not just the idea of technology but also the anthropology that is contingent on it. Close and necessary attention to Heidegger's critique of modernity need not be tantamount to falling into the Hegelian trap of teleological constitution of *Origins*. Whatever the Greeks meant by *technê*, it is the active and rapid instrumentalization of the idea and practice of *technology* that is the key characteristic force of its presence in modernity.[18] What I mean by using the instrumentality of cinema to de-instrumentalize the servile subjectivity is precisely the creative constitution of a defiant disposition that uses the force of that technology against the logic of that anthropology.

We can now investigate this rebellious defiance of technological instrumentalization one step further. What does it exactly mean for Heidegger to reduce the four Aristotelian spectra of causality – *causa materialis*, *causa formalis*, *causa finalis*, and *causa efficiens* – to a singular event of 'occasioning'?[19] In itself quite a revelatory language of Heidegger, 'occasioning' is identified as 'bringing-forth,' and that as 'presencing,' and that as 'bringing out of concealment,' and that as 'revelation,' which is then read as the equivalent of the Greek *alêtheia*, the Roman *veritas*, and thus the German 'Warheit' and the English 'Truth.' This is the hermeneutic passage that Heidegger establishes and follows between *instrumentality* and *Truth*, between the instrumentality of the evident fact and its instantaneous claim to veracity, to having-been-revealed, to being-True. For something to be True, the road begins with being instrumental. 'Bringing out of concealment' then becomes the essence of technology as the mode of its self-revelation. But why is Heidegger so particular in linking the technological act, or the very *essence of technology*, as he prefers to call it, to 'revealing, i.e., to truth'?[20] As early as Aristotle, Heidegger insists, *technê* at the root of *technikon*, at the root of *technology*, was a kind of 'bringing-forth' which was akin to *epistêmê* and thus had something to do with knowledge and understanding and not with manufacturing, with revelation and thus with Truth. Today, however, as the consequence of technological modernity, through the *technê* of technology we do not just get to manufacture things but to reveal things. We occasion and bring-forth *meaning* and *revealing* and *out-of-concealment* in them. It is as if it, i.e., the thing that technology occasions, existed but was concealed, and yet now through technology a veil has been lifted from its existence and its reality and being is now occasioned. Technology occasions the *dis-closure* of things in existence, having just been revealed, as *instrumental*. So if the only way that things can be revealed is for them to be revealed as instrumental, then technological modernity has spread its instrumental epistemics beyond mere technology and into the realm of life as a whole, including, indeed in particular, the realm of the aesthetic. Now imagine if the instrumentalized aesthetics were to use that very instrumentality – essentialized to its core by technological modernity – to de-instrumentalize the subject (both sovereign and servile) that is co-terminous with that technology. This categorical reversal of the technological logic, I propose here, is possible only at its colonial corners because there the colonial instrumentalization of reason, and with it the instrumentalization of the person of the servile subject, is not sugar-coated with the ideological enchantment of the Enlightenment – because the Enlightenment has *ipso facto* dismissed, denigrated, and thus turned a blind eye toward it.

What I am suggesting here amounts to the detection of a ripple effect on the colonial edges of the Enlightenment project of capitalist modernity over which the presumed center of the capital – from its politics to its aesthetics – has no effective control, and yet in its philosophical crisis now dubbed 'postmodernity' has had a glimpse of the terror it has perpetrated on the rest of the world. I am also suggesting that in artists like Makhmalbaf, we witness a facility with turning the metaphysical certainties embedded in such claims as Reality, History, Authenticity, etc. on their heads. Consider, for example, how in *Once Upon a Time, Cinema*, Makhmalbaf reserves his greatest affection for Amir Kabir (1807–52), the champion of Iranian modernity. What is paramount in Makhmalbaf's depiction of Amir Kabir is the panoramic portrayal of the legendary Qajar minister as a visionary reformist anticipating much that was to happen in the future of Iranian history. The result of Makhmalbaf's phantasmagoric injection of fact with fantasy, however, is this loving fictionalization of the factual figure of Amir Kabir, assimilating him into a cinematic trope, safe from the sorrows of a brutal history that had Amir Kabir murdered, on the orders of (the historical) Nasser al-Din Shah, in the Fin Bath of Kashan.

When facts thus become fictionalized, and fiction effective, the work of art assumes a reality *sui generis* and becomes an end unto itself, projecting a self-referential organicity that can affect history without being neutralized by it. This definitive moment of the work of art at the colonial edges of modernity goes against the grain of what at its center Heidegger called *Herausfarden*. Heidegger's assumption about the original meaning of *technê* is technologically *aufgehoben* to accommodate the instrumental exigencies of modernity. Heidegger notes the revolutionary nature of technological modernity but insists that 'it too is a revealing.'[21] But it *reveals* something constitutionally different in modernity, namely *Herausfarden*, or 'determining-forth' something, that is to say, a *challenge* to nature to do something beyond its visible dexterity. What this in effect means is the distinct quality of technological modernity in 'expediting' (*Fördern*) two

24 *Mohsen Makhmalbaf directing Mehdi Hashemi as Akkasbashi, and an attentive cat, in Naser al-Din Shah,*
Actor-e Cinema (Once Upon a Time, Cinema, 1992). By going back to the very first Iranian
cinematographer ever, Makhmalbaf came forward to write a long and endearing love letter to the history of Iranian
cinema. (Photograph: Mitra Mahasseni; courtesy of Makhmalbaf Film House.)

simultaneous things: (1) the unlocking and exposing of the hidden constituents of the visible dexterity of nature; and (2) by virtue of that unlocking and exposition, nature is then demanded-forth to further something else: 'Air is now set upon to yield nitrogen, the earth to yield ore, ore to yield uranium ... uranium is set upon to yield atomic energy, which can be released either for destruction or for peaceful use.'[22] The specific feature of technological modernity is then in its 'demanding forth' a deconstructive and reconstituting chain of unlocking, re-inter-locking, thus exposing, and ultimately furthering-something-else. This *Herausfarden* feature of technological modernity is something entirely new and the direct result of the instrumentalized reason, the instrumentalized person who reasons, or paints, or makes movies.

For a work of art to defy the catalytic effect of *Herausfarden*, it must first dismantle the temporal embeddedness of (cinematic) narrative, and generate and sustain a cybernetic trajectory entirely its own. Above all else, *Once Upon a Time, Cinema* is a virtuoso performance in creative editing, elevated to the level of a reconfigurative narratology. The pace and tempo of Makhmalbaf's editing in *Once Upon a Time, Cinema* is inspired by a cinematic presence in the idea of history rarely imagined or dared before in Iranian cinema. The cutting blade of his splicing sharpness has the daring violence of the moment when he reached for his knife to attack that police officer. He has the entirety of the history of the Iranian encounter with colonial modernity and the entirety of the history of Iranian cinema before him to cut and paste in any way he wants. The result is an effective visual history of Iranian modernity that is not quite like anything else we may have heard or seen before. The swift editing of the visual testimony mixes fact and fantasy, cinematic inter-textuality and ahistorical textualization, all deliberate and evident, to manufacture a manner of telling a story that is an end unto itself, and yet it places a mirror in front of all else we have known about our colonial history. This is the way a work of art resists being put to use, instrumentalized, *Herausfarden*.

The contrast between the actual history of the Iranian cinematic encounter with colonial modernity and Mohsen Makhmalbaf's *Once Upon a Time, Cinema* is the contrast between 'The Rhine' as 'dammed up into the *power* works,' and as 'uttered out of the *art* work, in Hölderlin's hymn by that name,' which for Heidegger sums up 'the monstrousness that reigns here.'[23] With the reference to Hölderlin, Heidegger points to the possibility of the poetic release from that technological monstrosity. Far more immediate is his contrast between a pre-Modern linking of the two banks of the Rhine by way of a bridge that might facilitate the traffic of people or even the transportation of goods and the far more insidious logic of a capitalist mode of production, distribution, and consumption that makes the very physical scenery of the river 'an object on call for inspection by a tour group ordered there by the vacation industry.'[24] This is no longer a Greek conception of *technê* as *epistêmê*, Revealing, and Truth. This is *instrumental rationalism* carried *ad infinitum, ad nauseum,* to its own catastrophic results, a completely new phenomenon traceable exclusively to the project of capitalist modernity. Heidegger takes issue with Hegel's definition of *machine* as 'an autonomous tool,' and considers it only applicable 'to the tools of the craftsman.' Hegel, as a result, becomes the last technological metaphysician of feudal productivity, standing at the threshold of modernity. Between Hölderlin and Makhmalbaf, as it were, there is a structural link that balances, as it opposes, the structural link between the presumed centers and the delegated peripheries on the capital–colonial axis of capitalist modernity and artistic response to it.

Above and beyond all such reflections, *Once Upon a Time, Cinema* is a long love letter to the history of Iranian cinema, a beautiful ode to all its hopes and aspirations, a note of apology to all masters of his profession that Makhmalbaf ever insulted or hurt. Loving, visual quotations from Bahram Beiza'i, Amir Naderi, Abbas Kiarostami, Mas'ud Kimiya'i, and a host of other filmmakers come together, in a finale of embracing scenes (very much reminiscent of Giuseppe Tornatore's *Cinema Paradiso* [1989]), where in the wide publicity of the screen Makhmalbaf reaches for the older generation of his craft to kiss and hug them all and apologize.

The Perils and Promises of a Post/Colonial Artist

The poetic shattering of *the real* releases the knowing subject from the global subjugation of labor to capital and the concomitant de-subjection of the historical person. This de-subjection is integral to the mode of operation between labor and capital and thus far more brutally evident and operative at the dispatched colonial peripheries of capital than in its presumed cosmopolitan centers – the dangers there as perilous as promising.

On the colonial edges of modernity, the artist will have to give birth to her/himself – in the absence and deletion of all *traditions* invented for her/him. S/he will have to be born out of the wedlock. The script that Mohsen Makhmalbaf wrote in the summer of 1989, *Nan va Gol/Bread and Flower* (1989), which is not to be confused with the one that he made into a film in 1995, *Nun-o-Goldun/Bread and Flowerpot,* aka *A Moment of Innocence* (1995), reads in a mode of giving an immaculate birth to himself, a kind of birth that is far more into his art than into his physical body, more into his fiction than to his reality, or to his reality in its projected promises.[25] It is crucial to keep in mind that the public persona of Mohsen Makhmalbaf by the late 1980s is still very much as a Muslim theorist and practitioner of art, hand-in-glove with the custodians of the nascent Islamic Republic. His singular claim to fame are still his worst films ever: *Tobeh-ye Nasuh/ Nasuh's Repentance* (1982), *Este'azeh/Seeking Refuge* (1983), and *Do Chashm-e Bi-Su/Two Sightless Eyes* (1983). To be sure, his *Bycote/Boycott* (1985), *Dastforush/The Peddler*

(1986), *Bicycle-ran/The Cyclist* (1987), and *Arusi-ye Khuban/The Marriage of the Blessed* (1988) have created considerable critical acclaim for him. But while the world outside takes note of the birth of his third child, Hana (born 1988), no one paid much attention to the fact that he was reading ferociously in psychology and philosophy and that at the same time his creative mind was giving birth to himself.

Bread and Flower, written in the summer of 1989, in which a character is in fact called Hana, is a testimony to what is happening in the mind of the 32-year-old artist. *Bread and Flower* is the story of a re-birth, of an immaculate conception, of a childish figure called 'Isa,' Jesus in its Persian and Arabic (Qur'anic) pronunciation, who is born out of wedlock to Hana, who is a drug addict and makes a meager living by selling flowers in the street, and a father who is in jail pending trial. Isa is the breadwinner to his small and large family, taking care of both his mother and an array of other homeless vagabonds. Isa rescues a young girl from the horror of seeing her mother stoned to death and the two of them roam through the streets of Bombay, where the story takes place, in search of a modest living by selling flowers. Isa and his young mate eat, drink, go to the movies, take care of their friends and even smuggle flowers into a prison. Isa has a recurrent nightmare in which he is trying to sell flowers in a busload of people ranging from infants to the very old, a bus that is headed for a catastrophic head-on collision in a tunnel. In one of the police raids on the band of vagabond kids, Isa's young companion is kidnapped by a group of strangers and raped. She cuts her hair short afterwards and soils her face so that she is not kidnapped and raped any more. The two of them find a baby whose mother is dead and the three seek refuge in a stable where a flock of sheep is slaughtered. In the stable, the baby nurses from Isa's breast. Isa is finally arrested for illegal street vending and put in jail where he meets his father. His father asks him to bring him jasmine flowers so that he can ask Isa's mother Hana to forgive him. Isa is released from jail. He brings jasmine flowers for his father, but it is too late. He has already been executed. Isa's mother is also stoned to death because of a presumed adultery. So Isa and his young companion are both bastards whose mothers have been stoned to death. They are freed into the world, an Adam and Eve, born out of a sin that will re-define the very nature of whatever it is that defines a 'sin.' Hana and Isa are as much Makhmalbaf's fictive children as his creative parents.

Drawing from his earliest memories of child-like conceptions of love, Makhmalbaf here narrates a story of paradisiacal simplicity. This time he is not oblivious to the physical brutalities of the real world, and yet he manages to sublimate them to parabolic brevity. As his self-projected image, Isa becomes a parable of having been born out of legitimate social bonds, entering the world from the angular corner of a repressed denial. From this bundle of denial beauty is given to the world, as are all pain and suffering taken from it. Isa is a soothing breath of forgiveness upon the world, sent to set it ever so gently and in ever so minuscule measures to rights, all in the small parameters of a finite and limited slice of life. With a pun on the figure of Christ, Isa in *Bread and Flower* projects one of the closest self-images of Makhmalbaf as an autodidactic artist. With no formal training in anything, least of all in cinema, and having arisen from the poorest quarters of his homeland, Makhmalbaf's self-projection becomes the promise of an artist who is born out of the wedlock of social bonds and in the creative domains of his own art. He is an artist with no border, with no territorial, familial, ancestral, or cultural claims on his in/authenticities: a rebel of every cause.

In *Seh Tablo/Three Pictures* (fall 1989), yet another script that Makhmalbaf never made into a film,[26] he considers the oscillation between an artist's creative work and his physical and mundane presence in a family and a society. An artist keeps painting a young girl in a red dress, and a cow she is taking to the pasture, and gives the picture to his son. He instructs him to sell it in the city and buy a chicken for his mother to prepare for the supper. After the owner of the gallery has refused to buy any more pictures of a young girl and a cow, and the painter has been harassed by his wife for failing to fulfill his duties to his family, he yields to paint the picture of his wife in pursuit of a running chicken to behead it and cook it for dinner. He paints three pictures of this tumultuous scene, which result in a whole flock of chickens coming to the painter's home. Now with his family satisfied, the painter gets up from his habitual slumber on a bed and joins the young girl and her cow in his favored picture, embracing the cow and nursing on its milk.

Perhaps the most remarkable aspect of this script is its palpable brevity. Makhmalbaf here is mastering the art of suspending all superfluous narrative and reaching for a parabolic precision that defies time and space and yet its visual diction pulsates with tangible contemporaneity. There is a surreal meticulousness in Makhmalbaf's narrative. He knows what he wants to say and he engineers his narrative movements with a laser-beam concentration on visual details. The cuts are swift, the tempo measured, the sound effects almost audible even in the script. There is an almost total absence of dialogue in *Three Pictures*, except for the artist's wife's audible but incomprehensible bickering in a language that no one can understand. The camera is complacent with the artist, as it is evident in camera instructions which are integral to the script. This complacency gives an almost satirical awareness of how artists are harassed by their spouses. The narrative engineering of the tale is also predicated on a calculated repetition of the scenes of the wife busy with her household chores, the husband waking up to paint, and their son Elias taking the pictures and getting on a boat to go to the city to sell them. This numbing repetition is deceptively routinized so that when it breaks down at the end it is visually stunning. The success of Elias' last trip to the gallery shop is announced by a countless number of birds flying and moving toward the artist's cottage in a beautiful long shot.[27]

At the heart of that brevity, and the very soul of that parabolic narrative, is the pendulum swing of the artist between the *manner* of his art (painting a pastoral scene) and the *matter* of his survival (chasing after a chicken to make a soup and stay alive). In the humor and brevity of this story, Makhmalbaf has a wonderful medieval antecedent in a story recorded in *Kuliyyat-e Chahar Maqalah* of Ali al-Nizami al-'Arudi al-Samarqandi, the sixth/thirteenth century Persian litteratus. In his chapter 'On The Nature of Courtly Literature (*Dabiri*) and the Qualifications of a Litteratus (*Dabir*),' al-Samarqandi reports that one day a Dabir at the service of the Abbasid court was composing a beautiful letter on behalf of his patron prince for the governor of Egypt, for which he had summoned all his concentration and eloquence. Suddenly his servant arrived and said, 'we just ran out of flour.' The Dabir was so lost in his literary art that quite unknown to himself he wrote down 'we just ran out of flour' in the middle of composing that flowery letter.[28] Eloquence and poetry, here and in Makhmalbaf's case, is not a superfluous luxury born out of what Thorstein Veblen (1857–1929) called the 'leisure class.'[26] In this respect, another great contemporary of Makhmalbaf, Ahmad Shamlu (1925–2000), made a poetic career out of lyrically celebrating precisely that borderline where beauty is rooted in the soil of material reality.

Experiment Perilous

The thematic and stylistic combination of an immaculate conception and a parabolic narrative, deeply entrenched in an aesthetic manner that is rooted in the material soil of reality (by 1989 successfully articulated in Makhmalbaf's films and fiction), mark his successful passage from a committed ideologue to a restless artist. The passage is full of dangerous terrains – with Makhmalbaf's *A Time for Love* (1990) the most perilous trap on that road.

Makhmalbaf wrote the script of *Nobat-e Asheqi/A Time for Love* (winter 1989) right before he made it into a film, also *Nobat-e Asheqi/A Time for Love* (1990). Love is by far the most difficult subject for an Iranian artist to deal with, precisely because the Persian literature is so inundated with it, and precisely because that literature is so deeply afflicted with an ethereal irreality that is constitutionally mystical, metaphysical, and incapable of celebrating love in its immediate material glory (until the advent of the 'New Poetry' – *She'r-e No* – in the twentieth century). This one particularly powerful trap Makhmalbaf cannot escape and he falls squarely into its distorting ensnare. In *A Time for Love*, Makhmalbaf mobilizes everything that he has to launch a new conception of love. Yet he fails to achieve anything but to add yet another distorting gyration to the classical Persian penchant for mystifying the irreducibility of physical love.

A Time for Love is an attempt at narrating a ménage à trois in whose amorous triangulation love is to yield to an alternative, presumably superior, conception to the one operative in Makhmalbaf's culture. Gazal is married to a black-haired man but is in love with a blonde-haired man in the first episode of the film. There is a deaf old man who spies on Gazal while watching birds and trying to capture a mate for his canary who has lost its companion. The old man tells Gazal's husband about her infidelity. The husband attacks the two lovers and Gazal is hospitalized. In the second episode, it is now the blonde-haired man who is the husband and the black-haired man who is the lover of Gazal. The blonde-haired man did exactly as the black-haired man does, and Gazal is again hospitalized. After both hospitalizations, Gazal commits suicide when she hears that her lover has been murdered and her husband punished by death. The third episode picks up where the first episode had left off. The old man now harasses Gazal and admonishes her husband the black-haired man as to why he is not punishing his wife, which is now exactly what he does by beating Gazal twice and taking her to hospital. When he is finally about to kill the blonde-haired man in the third episode, the latter grabs the knife from him, puts it against his own throat and asks the husband to kill him if he wants but he cannot not love the woman he loves. The black-haired man is now admonished. The next thing we see is a wedding ceremony in which Gazal and her lover the blonde-haired man are getting married, the host being none other than Gazal's former husband, the black-haired man. As the wedding gift he gives the newly weds his cab, which was the only reason that Gazal's mother had given her daughter to the black-haired man in the first place. As the former husband leaves the newly-wed lovers alone, Gazal recognizes that now she loves the black-haired man more than the blonde-haired man, and so does the blonde-haired man recognize that he wants to reciprocate the black-haired man's generosity and return Gazal to him. On his way to do so he runs into the deaf old man, who confesses that he too is in love with Gazal. The end.[29]

A Time for Love is Makhmalbaf's attempt first to break the cliché-ridden pattern of melodramatic triangulation of an evil husband and a heroic lover. When the lover is put in the position of the husband he acts exactly as the husband does. Makhmalbaf equally manages to humanize the husband by showing him in both cases to be in love with his wife. Even the eavesdropping, snoopy, deaf old man at the end is a man who is in love. So is the judge who condemns the two successive husbands to death. He does so reluctantly because he understands love. The only culprit thus seems to be the woman, Gazal, who falls in love always with the wrong man only to dismiss him at the end when she actually possesses him. She is always attracted to the forbidden fruit, a sort of Biblical/Qur'anic leitmotif re-narrated.

This implicit demonization of Gazal, however, is not the only serious problem with *A Time for Love* − nor is the abundance of such misogynist traits in the film as incessant wife-beating and invocations of 'defending my honor' by both the husband and the judge. Yet another problem with the film is its getting away with such atrocities as the husband having just killed a man and maimed his wife, then defending himself in the court by saying: 'I was defending my honor (namus). If I had not done anything, I could not forgive myself. I did as my duty commanded. I am content with what I have done. I am fortunate.'[30] Here the very notion of 'the crime of passion' goes without the slightest critical examination in A Time for Love. These are all pathological signs of a social disease, however, that are as much revelatory as diagnostic. The major problem with A Time for Love is Makhmalbaf's nose-dive collapse into a sea of abstraction in which he sucks all the life out of the physical reality of love and tries to give it a metaphysical sublimity that in its pathology is squarely out of the old Persian penchant for mystifying the material physicality of love. As a result, A Time for Love is anything but a love story. It is a pathologically mechanical and clumsily awkward automation of gestures and movements that unfolds more like the gawky roster of a bureaucrat's report to his superior officials at the Ministry of Ethics, of his having witnessed a crime, than anything remotely graceful and appropriate for a love story. There is not an iota of love and affection, or a trace of grace in Gazal's relations with her lover, not even the hint of an awareness of a courage or conviction constitutional to the experience of being in love. The result is that her flirtations with another man remain at the abysmal depth of a deeply humiliating 'affair' of a married woman with a philandering man. She is constantly referred to as 'ma'shuq,' the 'beloved,' that ghastly Persian patriarchal annotation of a woman who is condemned to be 'passively loved' and never allowed or ennobled to attain the active agency of an 'asheq,' a 'lover' – a rebellious transmutation that happens much later in Persian poetry of the twentieth century.

In his own reflections on A Time for Love, Makhmalbaf insists that the 'meaning' of this film is not love, but that its 'case' is a love story – its 'meaning' being a 'philosophical examination of "free-will and pre-destination".' Makhmalbaf then articulates the point of a philosophical problem to be the nature of 'good' and 'evil,' and whether or not we are free or predestined to commit one or the other.[31] But the unfortunate thing is that the more Makhmalbaf insists on a 'philosophical' reading of this film, the more he digs his own grave into a frightfully metaphysical distortion of the nature and disposition of love. He is in the public domain of his printed page and he does not quite know he is speaking from the depth of his blind spot. There is a telling moment in his own reflection on A Time for Love when he says, 'there is no such thing as love. All we have is a person who is in love.'[32] But the Persian mystical proclivity to distort the material evidence of physical attraction and love ultimately catches up with Makhmalbaf, and by the end of his essay he again collapses into such mysticism as: 'It is absolutely natural that I have solved one problem for myself, and that is the fact that I consider sexual needs to be material and earthly and I will not give them the name of "love," while that which remains in the domain of loving someone I will call "love," considering its material to be non-material.'[33] It is crucial to catch Makhmalbaf here at a moment of his resounding defeat by the culture he has inherited in order to be able to celebrate his art when it triumphs over that culture (in his *Gabbeh* in particular). It is difficult for any Iranian artist to deal with the subject of love precisely because the idea of love is so suffocated with haughty and hollow (but beautifully elaborate) abstractions about the non-materiality of love. It is Makhmalbaf's innate aesthetic honesty that ultimately pulls him up toward the recognition that there is no such thing as love in abstraction, and that love is to be grasped in its material locality in an individual agency. But then the enduring culture of abstraction into which he is born pulls him back into the quagmire of first over-philosophizing the experience and then abstracting its reality into irreality, materiality into non-materiality, and its momentary matter-of-factness into a useless diffusion in the realm of the beyond. 'You mean you don't believe in soul?' I remember he once asked me rather abruptly. 'Yes I do,' I said, 'It is the greatest invention of the body – and the body is beautiful, and it is the body that loves. Even in its decadence body is beautiful, and that's why Forough Farrokhzad says, "zaval-e ziba-ye golha dar goldan/the beautiful decay of flowers in the pot".' He smiled and looked at me: 'I ascended the ladder of religion', do you remember, I asked him, that part of Sepehri's poem in *The Sound of the Footsteps of Water?*

> Until the end of the alley of doubt,
> Till the cool breathe of satisfaction,
> All the way to the end of the wet night of kindness I traveled.
> I went to visit someone on the other side of love.
> I went, I went until I reached woman,
> Until the light of pleasure,
> Till the silence of desire,
> Till the full sound of emptiness.

'There,' I said, 'you have the corporeal erotics of religious sentiments and the metaphysical pretensions of lovemaking shaking hands and dismantling all the fictive valleys that have sought to separate them.' He looked at me in silence for a while and then we resumed our walk.

Tackling a Taboo

Part of the problem that Makhmalbaf faces is the cultural conservatism that severely objected even to an attempted re-modulation of the taboo question of love. In his essay, we see him struggle to quote passages from the story of Youssef

25 *Shaghayegh Jowdat in the lead role in Mohsen Makhmalbaf's Gabbeh (1996). Gabbeh soon emerged as an ode to the flamboyant joy of color in a republic of juridical darkness. (Photograph: Mohammad Ahmadi; courtesy of Makhmalbaf Film House.)*

and Zoleikha in the Qur'an in order to point to the significance of his film. The same sort of confrontational anxieties are evident in Houshang Hesami's effort to rescue *A Time for Love* by reading into it a materiality that one wishes existed in the film. But even in Hesami's admirable attempt, still the trope of denial and shift is paramount. Gazal, Hesami insists, is not 'just the concept of "love," but that of freedom and choice.'[34] It is as if there is something embarrassing in trying to deal with the subject of love, physical love in particular, unless it is sublimated to some ethereal level of lofty ideals, divine aspirations, heavenly purposes, metaphysical import, or political significance. Hesami rightly detects a dialectic of historical agency to be operative in *A Time for Love*. But his examination remains so utterly mechanical that the result is constitutionally alien to the very spirit of a work of art. The outcome is a serious confusion on the part of both Makhmalbaf and Hesami about the difference between 'philosophical' edification and aesthetic practice. Art is not supposed to be a mechanical exercise in moral edification, metaphysical altercation, or presumed philosophical speculation. The failure of *A Time for Love* is more than anything else a matter of aesthetic recognition, a precision of moral balance, a quality that Makhmalbaf will gradually learn not by reading into the literature but by allowing his art to speak far more eloquently than he himself can narratively pontificate. Very much of Makhmalbaf the combatant social activist is still evident in *A Time for Love*, a perhaps admirable quality in which Hesami also shares, and an obstacle that they both fail to see as distinct from the mutating effect of a work of art.

The atmosphere that surrounded the screening of *A Time for Love* becomes even more evident in the short essay that Abdolkarim Soroush has written on *A Time for Love*. Soroush is categorical in his denunciation of elements in the Iranian government that had condemned Makhmalbaf because of the presumed illicit 'love affair' in *A Time for Love*. Soroush comes to the defense of love and protects Makhmalbaf's effort to attend to it in the context of contemporary Iranian life. But he too feels obligated to assert that in fact love is not the issue of this film.[35] The apparent paradox that *A Time for Love* is not about love and yet it is to be defended by the assertion that there is nothing wrong about love is only the tip of the iceberg of a systemic denial when it comes to dealing with the issue of physical love. Soroush in fact has a crucial point in his essay that remains much under-developed. He says that the only objection he has to *A Time for Love* is that it does not deal with the issue of human choice from the vantage point of 'humanity.'[36] Although he raises this objection in the cocoon-like denial of the centrality of love in the film, Soroush points to the central problem of metaphysical abstraction in Makhmalbaf's treatment of love. It is precisely the active agency of the human subject that would have, as it will in Makhmalbaf's future work, saved him from the pitfalls of the culture against whose impediments he revolts.

Against an avalanche of attacks on Makhmalbaf because of *A Time for Love*, even when people come to his support, they seek to exonerate him from any (what they consider to be) lowly, mundane affiliation with matters of physical love. 'In the course of his political activities, Makhmalbaf lived honorably and with an impeccable reputation,' pointed out Seyyed Ebrahim Nabavi in a review of *A Time for Love*. 'But today speaking of love undoubtedly results in nothing but ill-repute, even though this love has nothing to do with the material world and human relations.'[37] In Nabavi's estimation, 'love dies in its fulfillment. When it is diluted with the physical form it dies. What keeps a human being warm and alive in the path of love is the soul of love and not the beloved, because the beloved is only an excuse, an excuse in order to give warmth and to cause transcendence, and to enable him to go further.'[38] In the words of yet another reviewer of *A Time for Love*, one should not look at love through 'the opaque eyeglasses of materiality.'[39]

This curious insistence on the immateriality of love by Makhmalbaf himself, and by people who have either taken issue with his film on love or (even worse) by those who have actually come to his defense, exposes the endemic absence of any conception of bodily reality, corporeal presence, physical love, and above all fragile humanity. There is thus a direct correspondence between such systematic denials of the physicality of love and the innate attraction to metaphysical abstractions that can (and did) result in political authoritarianism. Much of the charismatic fixation with Ayatollah Khomeini as a mystical revolutionary is rooted precisely in such numinous notions of love – corroborated and returned by Khomeini's own attraction to mystical love, in praise of which he in fact composed his own voluminous poetry, published only posthumously.

At the conclusion of his essay on *A Time for Love*, Seyyed Ebrahim Nabavi quotes a story from the ninth/fifteenth century Persian mystic Abd al-Rahman Jami's (1414–92) *Nafahat al-Uns* – the famous story of Ruzbahan Baqli who once in Mecca falls in love with a woman. In his regular Sufi gatherings he begins to sing and dance with a passion that he had hitherto reserved only for God, but shich this time he knew was for the woman he loved. He stopped, took his Sufi cloak out, and publicly declared that he was in love with a woman and that the passion in his demeanor was all because of that woman and not for God. He had to be truthful to himself. His companions told that woman of the incident. She regretted the unfortunate reality and became a disciple of Ruzbahan. Ruzbahan lost his love for the woman and resumed his Sufi habit. The moral of the story the way Jami narrates it in the ninth/fifteenth century and Seyyed Ebrahim Nabavi in the fourteenth/twentieth is that the love of God is superior to the love of a woman. But then we have to deal with this poem that comes immediately after the story:

> Thy love is carved on my heart, or else I would have sold it.
> Thou art in mine eyes, or else I would have sewed them both.
> My life is thy abode, or else a hundred times every day,
> I would have burned myself in front of you like an incense.

If Ruzbahan composed this poem for God and not for that beautiful woman, then he could have been accused of anthropomorphism, with far graver juridical consequences.

Not even the interface between *Eros* and politics can rescue Makhmalbaf from this insurmountable urge to let physical love metastasize into divine love. In the short story *Mara Bebus/Kiss Me* (winter 1989), he tried to grapple with the crossing-point between love and political activities. Mustafa and Marziyeh are two political activists who are also in love with each other. In Mustafa's letters to Marziyeh we read the same pathological escape from physical love and a seeking of refuge in a 'heavenly love.' Mustafa is a religious revolutionary, committed to his political cause and determined to keep his attraction to Marziyeh 'pure and undiluted.' He describes his love to Marziyeh in a letter as 'a love that will not collapse into the corruption of sex. A sacred feeling that makes my soul burn with the desire to remain pure for ever.' To Mustafa, Makhmalbaf's hero in this short story, physical love – and thus sex – is 'impure, corrupt, and devilish.' He confesses to Marziyeh that 'I have just discovered that I am much more in need of being thirsty than in drinking water. I am much more in need of love than to have my love, much more

26 *Abbas Sayyahi teaching color to young eyes in Mohsen Makhmalbaf's* Gabbeh *(1996). Color, color, and then more color — color transcended to the allegorical mutation of reality to shapes, shades, and pigmentation. 'Life is color,' cries a voice from the heart of darkness. (Photograph: Mohammad Ahmadi; courtesy of Makhmalbaf Film House.)*

in separation than in being with you.'[40] And then he adds, 'let the earthly bed of this heavenly love be the mattress of my eyes.'[41] Marziyeh, on the contrary, is far more physical in her expression of love to Mustafa:

> I wish you were not a political activist. I wish I were your wife, and every night you would have come to me and to our house, tired from a day's work. You would have put your head on my chest, and told me whatever you had done, said, or wished for on that day. I wish you would have put your lips on my ears and whispered to me your innermost words. I would have listened to you, and caressed your disheveled hair, and I would have told you my own wishes, the wishes that were all in you. You were all I had, and you were all that I wished for.[42]

But finally Mustafa's revolutionary asceticism distorts Marziyeh's physical love too:

> You have taught me that love is different from lovemaking. Love is inevitable. It comes un-announced, and involuntarily. But lovemaking is

voluntary. Love has made me so magisterial that I can no longer lower myself to sleep with my love in the same bed. My love and I are but one being. We sleep in each other. I feel sorry for those who are attached to such loves that are to be proven in lovemaking. I have found love. The beloved is but an excuse.[43]

At this point, Mustafa and Marziyeh can no longer even write their own prose and begin to quote famous poems of their favored poet to each other. Both Marziyeh and Mustafa are finally arrested, put into jail, and tortured. Marziyeh's love for Mustafa and her inability to conceal it and be singularly devoted to her politics ultimately contributes to her execution.

A Time for Love is the weakest link between Makhmalbaf's early and later cinema. But precisely in its failure as a film it succeeds in bringing out some of the most troubling aspects of an ethic of bodily denial that is dangerously close to political totalitarianism. This vacuous and superlative metaphysics of bodily denunciation borders perilously with ethical absolutism and ideological fanaticism, and above all with a persistent puritanism that stays aloof from the messy majesty of the crowded, confused, and gloriously rambunctious life itself. Once again, and halfway through his career, Makhmalbaf needs a miracle to save him from this deadly trap.

Visions of the Invisible

The creative combination of an imaginative self-conception and a parabolic proclivity in story-telling, successfully articulated by 1989 in Makhmalbaf's films and fiction, finally survives its hazardous road to salvation and almost a decade later – with the death of Ayatollah Khomeini in the same year in between – comes to full fruition in *Gabbeh* (1995). Every single shot of Makhmalbaf's camera in this film is alight with the visions of what had remained invisible to him – the sheer materiality of life. *Gabbeh* is a love story that comes together in its astonishing visual formalism without ever suspending its erotic energy. The story is told by the two lovers in their old age, and they draw each other from the carpet that has visually narrated them. The lovers are cantankerous and irritable but tenderly reminisce about their love affair – their bodies having grown, matured, and now nearing dissolution in each other's proximity. The sub-plot, the flirtation of the uncle with the daughter of Allahdad, is replete with erotic energy; and in their verbal conversations and Makhmalbaf's visual mise-en-scène, comes closest visually to depicting sexual intercourse in an Islamic Republic.

In the *visual formalism* of *Gabbeh* ultimately dwells its colorful celebration of life. The sequence of the uncle entering the tribal classroom will remain a seminal scene in Makhmalbaf's *virtual realism* completely at the service of his unique *visual* formalism. The uncle enters the tent that functions as a makeshift classroom, and turns his back to the blackboard and faces the children, who are now looking at him through Makhmalbaf's tightly framed close up. 'What color is this?' he asks the children, while extending his right hand out of the blackboard frame and into a long shot of a prairie full of red field-poppies. The hand picks up an imaginary bunch of poppies and brings it back into the close up frame of the blackboard; and as if magically the flowers are for real now! 'The red of the field-poppies,' the uncle exclaims joyously, and asks again, 'Now what color is this?' – while extending his right hand out of the close up of the blackboard frame and right into the long shot of a golden wheat-field; and we hear the kids equally joyously exclaim 'yellow!', while the uncle's hand collects an imaginary bunch of yellow flowers and brings it back into the close up frame of the blackboard. Again as if magically the flowers are for real! 'The yellowness in-between the wheat-field,' the uncle says. He repeats the same colorful cycle of joy and magic with blue from the sky, yellow from the sun, green of the grass-field, and orange from the sunset – all negotiated in a traffic between the close up of a passive reality and the long shot of an active imagination.

The rest of the love story is an equally playful conversation between the close ups of the young girl in love and the long shots of her beloved. In one single cinematic narration the male–female dichotomy of the lover and the beloved in the entire spectrum of Persian literature is reversed. In the rich texture of Makhmalbaf's close up frames, and as they play their pendulum swings with the equally meticulous long shots, dwells the cinematic salvation of a verbal malaise of a culture that incessantly talks too much but invariably says very little. While the young Gabbeh (Shaghayegh Jowdat) is the center of Makhmalbaf's close up attentions, her beloved is cast aside to a very far away long shot – thus casting a woman in love in the lead role of desiring (not just the object of someone else's desires) and the man at the heart of her attention in the secondary role of being desired (not in the sovereign role of desiring).

In its forceful delivery of Makhmalbaf from the dungeon of his entrapment in a metaphysics of abstractions and irreality, *Gabbeh* is a symphonic celebration of life in colors, compositions, forms, shapes, and all other shades of reality. It is the picture of a romance seeking the very essence of beauty in the rugged lives of a nomadic people. Makhmalbaf began shooting *Gabbeh* initially as what might have developed into a documentary. While shooting his film, he began to be attracted to a carpet-weaving tradition among the nomads in which the carpet was at once the object of their communal sentiments and the subject of their collective stories. Men desired women in these carpets, women fell in love with men, children were born to them, lives were formed, destinies shaped, labor holding the vagaries of daily routines together to form a people, a culture, a universe. The lead character of the film, Gabbeh, is in love with a man riding on a horse at a distant, a man whom we never see, of whose identity we can never be sure – for all we know he might be the figment of Gabbeh's own imagination, an image she is weaving into a carpet to mark her days, emotions, existence. The rhythm of this love story is the melodic harmony of a people in peace with a land they never claim, a climate they habitually accommodate, a universe they inhabit without possessing, a landscape on which they are as gentle and accidental as a beautiful tree here, a roaming stream there, a silent lake somewhere else. Coming out of the subterranean domains of his philosophical abstractions, Makhmalbaf rediscovers in *Gabbeh* his own wandering soul, his nomadic disposition, while visually claiming a landscape he never knew existed in the barren desires of his own soul. *Gabbeh* restores materiality to Makhmalbaf.

Halfway through *Gabbeh*, its narrative texture becomes evident. This is no ordinary way of telling a story: the start of the story is *memorial* – as the two lovers are found in their old age reminiscing their love affair. It soon evolves into the texture of a carpet-weaving narrative, where the story comes to life literally from the figurative designs of the carpet. From there, the story takes a detour to collect its rather radical visual formalism – with the uncle as its discursive vehicle. And finally, as the young Gabbeh recollects her love story, *Gabbeh* becomes creatively folkloric, partaking in all forms of Persian storytelling. The result is a parabolic universe where things become the figurative suggestion of themselves – and as the tribe passes by a lake, with the surrounding mountains, valleys, ponds, and springs in full jubilant presence, we see a bird nesting in the palm of a young girl's hand. She takes her hand and the egg outside of Makhmalbaf's frame, and another frame catches it in the palm of another girl. The girl exclaims, 'It's time now!' The fog has completely covered the passing tribe. Sakineh, the uncle's sister-in-law, is in labor. Other girls are weaving the story. The uncle disappears into the thick fog and we hear:

The Uncle:	*Life is color.*
The Girls weaving their Gabbeh:	*Love is color.*
The Uncle:	*Man is color.*
The Girls weaving their Gabbeh:	*Woman is color.*
The Uncle:	*Child is color.*

Through his visual formalism and the virtual realism that it generates, Makhmalbaf has rescued the arrested erotics of his culture.

Chapter Six

The Gnostic Simplicity of Silence:
Makhmalbaf as an Ascetic Revolutionary

In the preceding chapter I guided you through Makhmalbaf's *Once Upon a Time, Cinema*, by showing how a cinematic manipulation of the binary opposition presumed between Tradition and Modernity can lead to an emancipation of the subservient (obsequious) subject, and how in fact the filmmaker might be posited in a moment when s/he is re-enchanting the world beyond its historic stalemates. Through a close reading of Makhmalbaf's *A Time for Love*, I also argued that this necessary emancipation of the subject is not final and its achievement is in fact fraught with dangerous pitfalls, such as an endemic mysticism that can completely annihilate the subject by liberating it. But I concluded the chapter by a reading of *Gabbeh*, in which I believe Makhmalbaf has successfully rescued the arrested erotics of the vanished body and with it the agential historicity of the (re-gendered) subject. On the post/colonial site, what we must, by definition, look for is not a 'sovereign' but a 'defiant subject,' for it is only in that defiance that subjectivity can assume historical agency.[1]

In this chapter, I wish to examine the precise opposite of cine-mysticism and explore a singularly important moment in Makhmalbaf's cinema. This is when he successfully demonstrates his innate, or cultivated, penchant for *gnostic simplicity* and *ascetic minimalism*, both of which are constitutional to his *parabolic narrative* and to by now his trademark *virtual realism*. I propose that these character traits of Makhmalbaf's mature cinema give his vision a Spartan disposition, a lean and crisp mannerism, that vacates his pictures of all superfluous busy-ness. This austere precision, in its parabolic deference to simplicity, prepares and levels the ground on which the creative consciousness of a globalized artist can give his native land to an audience beyond the reach of that domesticity. He can thus craft an agency beyond the pale of 'Tradition and Modernity,' 'Islam and the West,' 'The West and the Rest.'

We can speculate about any number of cultural and literary sources for this visual asceticism in Makhmalbaf's mature cinema. For example, in his poetic disposition he is deeply connected to Sohrab Sepehri (1928–80), and one can make a direct link between their mutual penchants for gnostic simplicity. Deeper in his cultural memory, the visionary recitals of Shihab al-Din Yahya al-Suhrawardi (1154–91), such as his *Avaz-e Par-e Jibra'i'l/ The Song of Gabriel's Wing* or *Ruzi ba Jima'at-e Sufian/ A Day in the Company of Sufis*, have striking similarities with Makhmalbaf's parabolic narratives.[2] One can also cite Shaykh Muslih al-Din Sa'di Shirazi (1200–92), whose proverbial command of a graceful brevity of diction in his *Golestan* has had an enduring effect on much of Persian literature and Iranian culture.[3] There is something in Makhmalbaf's best films deeply reminiscent of Jalal al-Din Rumi's (1207–73) proverbial admonition: *Ay Baradar, Kaqaz-e Espid-e Na-benveshteh bash!/Oh Brother! Be an un-written piece of white paper!*. But perhaps more immediately, Makhmalbaf's ascetic minimalism is rooted in his years of imprisonment, when he had to learn the art of brevity, summation, minimalism, memory, precision, survival by the mere minimum of necessities. In prison he was also severely tortured to the point beyond hurt, where the body no longer responds to pain, where consciousness has to fare for itself beyond the domain of its habitat.

Whatever immediate or distant source for the gnostic simplicity of his visual diction we might imagine, its effect on his *virtual realism* finds one of its finest expressions in *Sokut/Silence* (1998), a meticulously crafted parable that marks a major turning point in Makhmalbaf's cinema. There is something about the uncommon brevity of *Silence* that defies received conceptions of cinematic narrative. Without reaching for the deliberately modulated tempo of its narrative, *Silence* will be lost as a parable that puts an effective question mark in front of the temporality of all other narratives. Via an aesthetically cadenced suspension of that temporality, Makhmalbaf reaches and grabs a manner of being in the un-time of history, a mode and manner of aesthetic consciousness, which vicariously slows down the course of history and remaps the world. I remember the first time I saw *Silence* (it was in a small theater in the Paris offices of MK2, Makhmalbaf's producer – and I was the only one in the theater), I sat there completely disoriented, knowing not where in the world I was, until Makhmalbaf and his children showed up and we all went out for lunch. 'So what do you think?' he asked me casually as we walked out of the MK2 building. 'It's parabolic,' I mumbled. 'It's what?' I searched for the word 'parable' in Persian, and gave him a few suggestions and began to explain. We chatted as we were walking toward a small café, when I stopped him and said, 'Never mind what's "parable" in Persian. There are numerous words for it – Qesseh, Masal, Matal, Hekayat, etc. They are not what I mean. I tell you what I mean. Do you remember Sepehri's poem, *Posht-e darya-ha/Beyond the Seas?*' Of course he did – and we began to recite the poem almost simultaneously, one correcting the other if we mis-remembered a line, until we reached the final stanzas, when we continued in complete sync:

Behind the seas
There is a city
Where windows open
To Epiphany.
Where on the rooftops
Pigeons stare at the fountains
Of human intelligence, and where
In the hand of every ten-year old child
There is a branch of knowledge, and where
The inhabitants of the city stare
At a clay-wall as if
They are beholding a flame of fire,
Or watching a beautiful dream – and where
The Earth can hear
The music of your emotions,
While in the wind
There is an echo of mythical birds.
Behind the seas
There is a city
Where the vastness of the sun
Is in the size of the eyes of the early-risers, and where
Poets have inherited water, wisdom, and light.
Behind the seas
There is a city –
We must build a boat!

'That's a parable,' I said and we went inside the café.

Gnostic Simplicity

In *Silence*, Makhmalbaf narrates a parable from the depth of his unconscious presence in the Persian art of story-telling (*Qesseh-gu'i*). Once upon a time, he tells us, there was a young blind boy who lived with his mother. They were poor and could not afford to pay their rent, living in fear of their landlord evicting them from their abode. They would be wakened every morning by their landlord demanding his rent or else threatening to throw their belongings out. Blind, poor, and unschooled, the young boy, Khorshid (the Sun) his mother calls him, was gifted with a pair of impeccable ears, undiluted by corrupt noises. For precisely this pair of accurate ears, perfectly tuned, a *tar-maker*[4] has hired Khorshid to come to his shop and tune his musical instruments. Every morning, as soon as she is awakened by the landlord's knocking at the door (to Beethoven's Fifth Symphony opening bar, *ba-ba-ba-baam*), Khorshid's mother wakes him up and sends him off to the tar-maker's shop. The young boy gets up and in the gesture of saying his morning prayers sends his pet bee, held in an empty jar which echoes its buzzing, off to its daily routine of sitting on flowers:

> Ey Khoda Jan, Elahakom!
> Ta zanbur beh khaneash bargardah,
> Rahash safid bashah.
> Rah gom Nazanah.
>
> [Dear Lord —
> My dearest sweetest God —
> May the bee return safely
> To its home,
> And may it not get lost!][5]

His pet bee having been safely sent away, the young blind boy gets up and goes with his mother first to the local market, where several beautiful young girls are selling fresh bread and baskets of fruit. Here Makhmalbaf is at his Gauguinesque best. He relishes playing with the varied composition of beautiful faces, colorful scarves, and round pieces of bread. Khorshid cannot see these faces, nor the splendid roundness of the fresh pieces of bread they sell by holding them against their faces. But he can feel their beauty by touching their faces, and he prefers dried bread because it sounds better when he chews on it. The scene is highly stylized, barely realistic, and suggestively invokes the still-life paintings we know biographically that Makhmalbaf has studied carefully.

With the opening shots and the first sequence of *Silence*, it becomes immediately evident that we are in the presence of a parabolic manner of story-telling, where time and space modulate on a logic domestic to the mood of the story they invoke. An almost deliberately registered use of still-life traditions gives *Silence* the look of still photography, borrowing from that sedate energy to lend it to the poetic diction of the melodic Persian flowing out of Khorshid and his mother's mouths. Paramount in Makhmalbaf's vision here is the poetic presence of an elusive *awareness*, very much akin to when in his poem *The Palpitations of the Shadow of the Friend*, Sohrab Sepehri, Makhmalbaf's soul-mate, reports a nocturnal journey:

> There was still a distance
> To walk
> To the outskirt of the village.
> Our eyes were filled
> With an interpretation

of the native,
living moon.
Up in our sleeves we carried
The night.[6]

From the landlord's rhythmic banging at the door to the poetic diction of Khorshid and his Tajiki dialect, to the carefully choreographed gestures of the young girls selling bread and fruit, to the deliberate dwelling of Makhmalbaf's camera on crafted cuts and captured corners of the young girls' faces, we know that we are no longer in the Copernican world, we have entered the dream-world of a formalized, ritualized, inflected mannerism that casts the visual narrative into a deliberately modulated tempo. Time is no longer temporal, space no longer topographic. We are choreographed along the visual tempo and carried into a twilight zone, the crepuscule of an imaginative recital. The first sequence, therefore, not only introduces the chief protagonist Khorshid but sets the narrative mood, defines the visual disposition, and weaves the sacramental texture of the recital, of the ritual, and thus pulsating the liturgical disposition of what we are about to see.

With a bundle of fresh bread and red cherries, Khorshid's mother sends him off to the bus station with a pretty young girl as his guide. The young girl hands him and his bundle over to the bus driver who will drive him to his work. The young boy must stick his two fingers into his ears lest his sensibilities to pure music be corrupted by confusing voices. There is a biographical note here that is worth remembering. When Makhmalbaf was a young boy he would be regularly and ritually taken to the local mosque in their neighborhood to attend religious services. On their way to and from the mosque they would pass by a record shop from which the sound of music poured onto the pavement. He was instructed by his pious grandmother to stick his fingers into his ears so that he would not hear any music – so sinful was the inadvertent hearing of a pleasing melody. The temptation to listen must have been buzzing under those two impatient fingers. If we add to that childhood memory the fact that the most famous record shop in the Tehran of Makhmalbaf's early childhood and youth was called 'Beethoven,' we may have a biographical clue for the opening bar of *Silence*.

Summarized into the most irreducible simplicity of his character, Khorshid is the remembered childhood of a man who has a universe of political imagining as the site of his revolt and is now taking a journey toward the virtual, for the sake of the bare necessity that will make life beautiful and trustworthy. Khorshid is Makhmalbaf as he wishes to remember himself, reconfiguring himself back into a history he wants re-written for a whole nation.

As Makhmalbaf's alter-ego in *Silence*, Khorshid, sitting in the bus, is lured by the temptation of two young schoolgirls trying to memorize a quatrain of the seminal Persian poet, Omar Khayyám, giggling and frolicking the poem out-loud.

27 Nadereh Abdollah Yeva in Mohsen Makhmalbaf's Sokut (Silence, 1998): *ascetic realism at its height, space vacated of all its unnecessary clutters, reduced to the virtual evidence of all but itself. The closest that Makhmalbaf will come to the poetry of Forough Farrokhzad, quoting and characterizing her visually.* (Photograph: Meysam Makhmalbaf; courtesy of Makhmalbaf Film House.)

28 Nadereh Abdollah Yeva in Mohsen Makhmalbaf's Sokut (Silence, 1998). *Makhmalbaf works mostly through visual suggestions in this film, citing the side-effects of his camera angles, looking for or detecting implied intentions, ocular innuendos, sub-senses of the evident, suppositions with which reality negotiates.* (Photograph: Meysam Makhmalbaf; courtesy of Makhmalbaf Film House.)

29   Nadereh Abdollah Yeva in Mohsen Makhmalbaf's Sokut (Silence, 1998). A rare but effective combination of Cubism and Fauvism has consistently fascinated and influenced Makhmalbaf in his latest films, in which an increasing number of close ups become paramount. He looks for evident painterly qualities in his framing, accentuating deep colors that may or may not correspond to reality, all by way of positing exaggerated perspectives with bright and capricious colors. (Photograph: Meysam Makhmalbaf; courtesy of Makhmalbaf Film House.)

The young boy is now Makhmalbaf himself remembering his grandmother's inhibition: 'This sinful sound you don't want to hear.' That 'sinful sound' is now the thematic cohesion of this pious homage to music by quoting and celebrating the most famous opening bars in the forbidden and foreign music of Makhmalbaf's childhood. Here, in the figure of the young metaphoric boy, Makhmalbaf continues to keep his fingers in his ears but happily succumbs to the irresistible temptation of taking them out. Given to the temptation of the joy he senses in the presence of the two young girls, the young boy takes his two fingers out of his ears and hears them sing Omar Khayyám's quatrain:

> Az dy keh gozasht hich az ou yad makon
> Farda keh nayamadast faryad makon
> Bar namadah o gozashtah bonyad makon
> Hali khosh bash o omr bar bad makon.

> [Yesterday's gone, forget and never mention't.
> Tomorrow's not here, waste not your time on't.
> That which is not come, that which is yet to come, forget them all,
> Be happy now and waste not your life.][7]

This is a critical moment in Makhmalbaf's own cinematic psycho-genetics, where and when his creative act of *autobiographical remembrance* becomes an occasion of *collective deliverance* for his nation at large. This is the story of a boy who was not allowed to listen to music, is thus effectively deaf to music (and thus Khorshid is deaf), and yet his soul yearns for and listens to a perfect music (and thus Khorshid's ears are pitch-perfect). What would have happened had Makhmalbaf pulled his two tiny fingers out of his ears against his grandmother's inhibition? Here, it is crucial to remember that for Makhmalbaf his grandmother was the closest figure he had that he identified with God. In the course of one of his recorded conversations with me, he once said:

> If I have been a religious person, its roots can be traced to my grandmother. My grandmother was a very interesting character. She was incredibly kind. I think that the greatest love of my life has been my grandmother, because at the very time when I was most afraid that my father would kidnap me, and I was caught up in this madness [of a custody battle between his parents], when I slept beside her I felt more secure than any place in the universe. All the stories she told me at night, all the bedtime stories, were tales of the prophets. In these conditions, the tales of the prophets would give me such peace-of-mind that I would feel practically invisible to the world. My grandmother was so kind that God and my grandmother merged into one in her stories. When I think of God, I think that this is still the case ... the God that rests in the depths of my heart looks like my grandmother. When I was younger, there was a cabinet in our house, and when I opened it, there was a picture of my grandfather, and he had a hat on his head. I used to think that God was an old man. But later, God became an old woman. The affection my grandmother used to show me, and her religious talk, at that age ... [8]

In this scene in the bus, Makhmalbaf remembers that cultural inhibition, which is also a sacred inhibition, and this time around transgresses it in full view of the camera and for the whole world to see. The result is the sudden gushing-forth of a transgressive act that collectively curates a potential possibility should that inhibition be broken – the effect is as a result at once exhilarating and dangerous, accented here by the innocence of the young girls trying out loud to recite Khayyám's poem.

The two young girls cannot manage to memorize the quatrain, but they are living it. Khorshid is disturbed by the lack of harmony in their recitation of the poem. The whole world is a distorted harmony to him, and he is sent to set it right. He sets the two schoolgirls right, but they miss their stop. They miss their school. They need no school. All of Makhmalbaf's own children have dropped out of school and the regimented routine of official learning. Makhmalbaf has decided to teach them himself. He has regular classes for them (for which he at times hires college professors) on art, music, poetry, photography, painting, cinematography, directing, and editing – even on how to ride a bicycle and how to swim.

As Khorshid takes his fingers out of his ears, Makhmalbaf hears two simultaneous things: a mesmerizing poem but recited out of tune. The task is to keep reciting and listening to that liberating poem that Khorshid hears from these joyous young mouths but have it recited and received properly, harmoniously, to a rhythmic order of a conclusive attendance on its meaning. From the depth of his silence, the muted meadows of his gnostic simplicity, Khorshid has discovered the perfect pitch and Makhmalbaf wants to give the harmonious order of that melody to this poem. Makhmalbaf envisions a prophetic mission for Khorshid, which is not from the violent metaphysics of an order or a conviction, but from the silent simplicity of an ascetic dismissal of all violent metaphysics, of all certainties, absolutes. The boy is blind. He has to be blind because his vision has to be equally undiluted by the vision of evil in the world.[9] One reason that this film is so beautiful to look at is because we see it as the mental image of the world that Khorshid carries in his blinded memory. Makhmalbaf's camera is located, as it were, inside Khorshid's head.[10] We see through this blind boy, and he sees the world not as it is but as he wants to see it, in perfect pitch. He also listens to this world and what he hears is a beautiful poem recited badly. His mission in life is to synchronize a melodious voice to a vision of the world he carries in his mind. This whole film is a dream of the blind boy, as if the opening bar of Beethoven's Fifth Symphony did not wake him up at all.

Makhmalbaf's *Silence* detects the world caught up in mis-singing a beautiful song and a young blind boy is sent to have it sung right. Schooling of children is a distraction because we are born, as it were, with that harmony innate to our inner ear – and schooling is a way of forgetting what we knew. Remembrance as deliverance is the instinctive organicity of that song. Makhmalbaf's temptation to transgress translates into the young boy's temptation to listen to songs out of tune, to be registered against his perfect pitch. There is a gnostic simplicity about the world, and to see it, Makhmalbaf's *Silence* sends a blind, pitch-perfect, boy to be the measure of its resonance. *Silence* as a result appears as a silent cry of a deaf boy (Makhmalbaf himself denied the subversive pleasure of music) for a beautiful music – and thus in this film he transforms a debilitating private inhibition into the transgressive joy of a collective emancipation, his own personal ailment into a public moment of catharsis for his nation at large.

Ascetic Minimalism

Waiting at the young musician's stop is another young girl. Nadereh is her name and she is singularly beautiful – Makhmalbaf's camera is in Khorshid's mind and we see Nadereh through his blind eyes and vivid imagination. Nadereh is to take Khorshid to the music shop where he is to fine-tune the recently built instruments. The owner of the shop is angry with Khorshid for being late as usual, and for having opened his ears to outside noises. Khorshid sits down to work, and the young girl dances to his melodic music. This particular scene was objectionable to the authorities in the Islamic Republic, but Makhmalbaf managed to restore it and the final version premiered in Venice in September 1998.[11]

The sequence is pure cinematic joy. That joy conceals and reveals the function of the fabulous (the fable-like) in any metaphoric narrative. Here, the fabulous does not as much transcend reality as tease out its virtuality. From *A Moment of Innocence* forward, Makhmalbaf has mastered this art of ascetic minimalism that he has not just aesthetically assumed but practically lived. Ahmad Shamlu once in a poem said of a cultural icon, 'he was his own summation.'[12] One is often reminded of this poem of Shamlu when witnessing the asceticism with which Makhmalbaf lives. Day in and day out, he wears the same clothes and the same pair of shoes that his severely tortured and deformed feet can tolerate; nor does his tortured backbone allow him to sleep peacefully at night. *Zohd ro dost daram* ('I love asceticism'), he once said to me. That asceticism has now become integral to his cinematic aesthetics.

The minimalism that is evident in all Makhmalbaf's films after *A Moment of Innocence* reflects a gnostic simplicity that pervades his life in its entirety. It is precisely from that gnostic simplicity that the function of 'the fabulous' ought to be understood in Makhmalbaf's mature cinema. It is a simplicity that he has reached from the depth of his own maximalist confusion with the world as perhaps best represented in his *Once Upon a Time, Cinema*. Whereas *Once Upon a Time, Cinema* was the crescendo of his maddening presence in the midst of Iranian religious politics, from *The Cyclist* forward he begins to circumambulate away (just like the Afghan cyclist on the periphery of Iranian society) from the crowded center of Iranian political culture and develop a peripheral vision of his own place in the world. From *The Cyclist* forward, a pervasive minimalism begins to define Makhmalbaf's gnostic simplicity, precisely at a time that he begins gradually to distance himself from his natural habitat in Tehran. If *The Cyclist* (1989) marks his circumambulatory and centrifugal falling away from the center of his Iranian urban disposition, through an increasing identification with Afghan refugees, *Gabbeh* (1996) marks the height of his migratory and nomadic soul. In the vast and variegated domain of that peripheral, nomadic, and migratory disposition, Makhmalbaf has discovered and cultivated his ascetic minimalism.

The gnostic simplicity operative at the heart of Makhmalbaf's ascetic minimalism is outlined on the site of pure sensibility, which is interchangeable with that simplicity, sight for sound, visual for vocal, aural for tactile. In the scene that Nadereh dances to Khorshid's tuning behind a glass door, the old man who is the owner of the music shop cannot hear Khorshid and yet he can tell if he makes a mistake by looking at Nadereh dancing. He has a visual record of Khorshid's vocal registrations. This symbolic approximation of the visual and the vocal thematically coheres and effectively virtualizes the senses back to their originary sites. On these sites, even the very function of memory is re-originated. Notice that when the old man is to memorize a phone number he actually notes it on his abacus, or as Makhmalbaf puts it in the script, 'commits it to the memory of the abacus.'[13] Wood, in other words, has a capacity for memory, a remembrance of its function as a tree. A similar contraction of senses is evident when Khorshid falls down in the rain and the raindrops begin to play on the strings of his tar. Moments later when we see that Khorshid and his musical instrument are neck-deep in the lagoon, the contraction of the audile and the tactile is visually overwhelming. In Makhmalbaf's own words in the script, 'It is as if Khorshid, the musical instrument and the water have merged together.'[14] It is immediately after this scene that we see Khorshid practicing his conducting skills and witness the flying of birds emanating from his harmonious hands. The result is a cosmic ordering of evident chaos, from audile to tactile, visual to vocal, earthbound to heavenly.

There is yet another visual and vocal assimilation of the audile and the tactile memory into each other. When Khorshid finds his way into the music conservatory and is admonished by the instructor for the poor quality of instruments that his factory has produced, he notices a correspondence between the modular movements of the conductor's hands and the rhythm of music that he hears. The result is a contraction of his audile and tactile senses into a singular harmonic memory. It is also precisely on this site of de-codification of human memory that we need to read Khorshid's poverty. He is portrayed as poor, but not as in a class-based kind of a political criticism. He is poor as in divested from material investment in an implicated memory. Makhmalbaf narrates Khorshid as a template site of gnostic simplicity, a narrating back from all sight, sound, memory, and matter, so that he becomes a measure, a tabula rasa, a memory for all other acts of remembrance.

This collapsing of all perceptive categories is done squarely at the service of a translucent approximation of senses in Khorshid's mind. The Gauguinesque sequence in the row of bread- and fruit-sellers approximates all natural fruits of the earth, bread, and human faces to each other. 'Khorshid grabs the loaf of bread and bites into it,' Makhmalbaf explains in his script, 'as if biting into the bread-seller.'[15] This is all happening in Khorshid's mind and memory, the measure and measuring of all remembrances. The virtual site of clairvoyance that is thus assayed in Khorshid's mind's eyes charts the cultural memory of a people back to their inaugural pre-moment, before their history begins, before their topography is graphed. This virtual realism, at once real and evident and yet prototypical and ideal, by now is definitive to Makhmalbaf's cinema.

The constitution of that site is not drafted with an ignorance of evil. Addressing his pet bee, Khorshid admonishes it severely:

> Don't you ever talk with those shit-sucking bees! Do you hear me? Your voice will turn shitty. When you were flying away yesterday such a zigzaggy nonsense, bull-shitty noise was coming out of you – and now you have returned with more zigzagging bullshit. I will throw you out of this house. Do you hear me?[16]

The same dis/attraction to the material world is equally evident in moments of Khorshid getting lost in the market. His initial dis/attraction begins with a melodic sound (a poetic recitation, a young musician playing his instrument), but it inevitably leads him to confusion and anarchy, as is best evident in the coppersmith market. There is a marked and palpably noticeable difference between the gnostic simplicity of Khorshid's measuring site and the world at large. His bringing the two little schoolgirls into a harmonious recitation of Khayyám's quatrain is nothing in comparison and there only to accentuate the overwhelming monstrosity of the coppersmith market. Now *that* is a cacophonous confusion of noises that constitutes a Herculean task, a jarring challenge, for the birth-blind and then decidedly deaf boy. From that cacophonous confusion of noises he is determined to create a harmonious music. This music is decided on the opening bar of his material condemnation, the fateful banging on his door, the call of reality that wakes him up. It is a *material order* that he wants to give to the *real*. It is not accidental that the second young coppersmith he approaches and asks to follow his harmonic instructions takes him for a beggar and wants to dismiss him with a coin or two. 'I don't have any use for money,' he objects, 'I am asking for a beautiful sound.'[17] There is an organic link, a material connection, between *the immanent danger of the real* that he faces and *the sensual virtualization of the real* that he is after.

The ascetic minimalism I detect here in Makhmalbaf's mature cinema has successfully worked itself out toward a fabled vision of reality that without distorting it sublates and distills it to its constitutional core, having arrived at it from the material basis of its worldly manifestations. Notice, as a point of comparison and affinity, how in the following stanza Sepehri creates an existential moment of pure creative connection to consciousness, but from the very harsh reality at the roots of worldly experiences:

We were passing through
A dried out patch of water –
Our ears saturated
With the words of the prairies,
As our backpacks filled
With the echo of distant cities:
The rough logic of the earth
Running under our feet.[18]

I believe that there is precisely such a correspondence between 'The rough logic of the earth/Running under our feet' and 'Our ears saturated/With the words of the prairies' in Makhmalbaf's ascetic minimalism, in fact constitutional to it.

Parabolic Narrative

One must also add an element of imminent danger that threatens the young boy. Through the intermediary voice of Khorshid's mother, we are aware that they are about to be evicted and thrown out of their dwelling. Khorshid does not have much time. He is charged with an impossibility: to provide for a roof over his and his mother's head by a full ab/use of his auricular capabilities. Cornered by the imminent danger of eviction, confused by the cacophonous cascade of noises that comes at him relentlessly, Khorshid is and has to remain the plain site and sight, while birth-blind and decidedly deaf, of the virtually real, the plainly true. The task of providing for a roof over their heads is an impossible duty, not because Khorshid is incapable of working and earning a living but because his task in life, his mission manifest, is to bring peace and harmony to the chaos and cacophony that he senses in the world. What prepares us from here, halfway through the film, for the final sun-bathed crucifixion scene is the Christ-like figure of Khorshid – the auricular citation of his oracular vocation.

The symphonic banging of the landlord at the door of Khorshid's home echoes its threatening announcement in yet another moment of despair when the Old Man fires Khorshid and asks Nadereh to give him the news:

Nadereh: *Khorshid!*
Khorshid: *Hum?*
Nadereh: *The Old Man has fired you. He said he is not going to pay you any wages.*
        Get up. We have to go to the bus station.
Khorshid: *No.*
Nadereh: *Why?*
Khorshid: *Every day a man comes and bangs at our door. Ba-ba-ba-baam. Ba-ba-ba-*
        baam. The man says that if we don't pay him his rent he will throw out our

belongings. I have only four days left. My mother said that I should get my salary from the Old Man one month in advance so that we can pay the landlord.[19]

Khorshid soothes his own anxiety by playing the opening bar of Beethoven's Fifth Symphony on his *robab*, and Nadereh begins visually to modulate her face and body with what she hears. The scene of Khorshid's playing and Nadereh's dancing is mesmerizing for those who now see the image of Nadereh as the juvenile personification of one of the most famous stanzas of one of the most endearing poems of Forough Farrokhzad (1935–67), a poet for whom Makhmalbaf has unsurpassed love and affection:[20]

> *gushvari beh do gusham mi-avizam*
> *az do gilas-e sorkh-e hamzad*
> *va beh nakhon-ha-yam*
> *barg-e gol-e kokab michasbanam.*[21]

> [I will hang from my ears
> Earrings from a pair
> Of twin cherries and I will
> Stick petals of dahlia
> To my fingers.]

It is right at this moment that the vocal attenuation of Khorshid and the visual accompaniment of Nadereh, reaching a perfect fusion, is suddenly and brutally interrupted by the Old Man banging on the glass barrier encasing the young couple: ba-ba-ba-baam! This is a parable announced by danger – it is as if Khorshid and Nadereh are the young Adam and Eve at the first dawn of history, before history. We have been watching a dream, dreamt before time began.

Virtual Realism

Makhmalbaf's planted hope in the middle of this oscillation between *the immanent danger of the real* and *the gnostic virtualization of the real* is the ritual birth that he gives to this new Adam and Eve. The suggestion that these two creatures are the simulacrum of a new Adam and Eve is already evident in the fact that we know nothing of Khorshid's father. The husband of his mother who has gone to Russia to work may or may not have been Khorshid's father. We never see Khorshid in the company of a father. Nor is the Old Man Nadereh's father. 'The Old Man looks after me. He is not my father,' she tells the vagabond musician.[22] The autobiographical fact of Makhmalbaf growing up with his mother, aunt, and grandmother, and in

30   A shot from Mohsen Makhmalbaf's Sokut (Silence, 1998). Facial and bodily dispositions become the visual alphabet of Makhmalbaf's parabolic narrative in Silence – fruits and faces interchange, as do shapes and shadows, angular perspective and Fauvist fixation with color, all detected and narrated in search of a vernacular of the commonplace. (Photograph: Meysam Makhmalbaf; courtesy of Makhmalbaf Film House.)

the total absence of his father, is quite crucial for reading the loaded emotional cadence he invests in Khorshid. Makhmalbaf himself grew up under the debilitating fear that his father might kidnap him. Judicious attention to this bit of biographical data gives the necessary accent to this absence of a father for Khorshid and Nadereh and their narrative visualization as the first paradisiacal mates. The result, though, is not an active re-mythologization of *the evident* the way we see Bahram Beiza'i, for example, confront the particulars of Iranian culture. Makhmalbaf is an entirely different visionary. He is merciless in cutting the unnecessary fat from around the factual evidence of the real and reaching for its sheer virtuality. In Khorshid and Nadereh, as a result, Makhmalbaf generates a virtual couple, simplified to the bare necessity of re-presenting *the evident* in a way that can now draw and chart an entirely different reality, predicated on a renewed normative subjectivity for the authors of a whole new agential history.

The visual finale of this *virtual union* is the sequence immediately after Nadereh gives Khorshid the sad news that the Old Man has fired him. Nadereh invites Khorshid to go with her to the spring and Makhmalbaf leads them like two paradisiacal figures into the site. On their way, Makhmalbaf plants a danger straight out of the streets of the revolutionary Tehran with the morality police keeping vigilance on every corner:

> Nadereh: *I am afraid Khorshid.*
> Khorshid: *Afraid of what?*
> Nadereh: *An armed man sits over there. He fights with every young girl who doesn't have a scarf on. Let's go the other way.*
> Khorshid: *Let's go.*

They change their direction. But Nadereh is still terror-stricken.

> Nadereh: *This is the wrong way. The armed man is still sitting there. What are we to do?*
> Khorshid: *Let's walk fast by him. Don't look at him.*[23]

The irony, of course, is that Khorshid cannot look at anything. But there is more to his paradoxical injunction than meets the eye, as it were. He has just *heard* of an evil thing, of a man who is armed, from Nadereh. He instructs both himself and Nadereh to close their eyes on evil, pretending that he does not exist. What we see next is again firm confirmation that this entire film is a figment of Khorshid's imagination. We see the armed man playing a musical instrument. In his mind (with Makhmalbaf sitting there with his camera), Khorshid changes the man's gun into a musical instrument and his potential act of violence into an actual act of beauty.

Beyond this danger, now visually pacified and surpassed, the young paradisiacal birds enter their Edenic site. Nadereh pulls out a mirror and begins to admire her beauty – Narcissus unbound. The exquisite movements of Nadereh here are meticulously measured. Notice Makhmalbaf's own wording in the script: 'They reach the spring. Nadereh pulls out a mirror from under her dress, looks at herself and hands it over to Khorshid.'[24] This is an undressing scene, done with exceptional visual precision. A spring is always a site of bathing in classical Persian literature. We have it since the bathing of Shirin in the medieval Persian poet Nezami's *Khosrow and Shirin* (composed in 1209), deeply planted in every Iranian's coded sensuality. Nadereh reaches for the mirror from under her dress with the memory of her naked body still on its translucent mind. She first looks and admires herself in the mirror and then submits it to Khorshid. What does Khorshid do? He cannot see. Makhmalbaf here begins to assimilate the visual into the tactile. Again Makhmalbaf's precise camera instructions: 'He touches the mirror.'[25] Now Khorshid asks, in a muted moment of wonder, 'What is this?' The rest of the conversation is too beautiful to be missed, too self-evident to need explanation:

> Khorshid (touching the mirror): *What is this?*
> Nadereh: *Mirror.*
> Khorshid: *What is this for?*
> Nadereh: *For seeing. I see myself in it.*

She sits down and picks flower petals and puts them on her fingernails:

> Khorshid: *Am I in the mirror too?*
> Nadereh: *Uhuum.*
> Khorshid: *Where am I?*[26]

The scene here assumes a mythic melody. Nadereh now turns from child-Eve to mate-Eve to mother-Eve. She begins to give visual birth to Khorshid. Notice the pregnancy and the birth: they are now both looking at the mirror. Khorshid asks Nadereh 'Am I in it too?' She says yes. Khorshid asks, 'Where am I?' Nadereh gets up and draws a circle with her finger onto the surface of the mirror – the womb of creation. 'This is your face,' she says, and we know that we are now witnessing the moment of conception and that we are looking at the fetus, with the caressing finger of the mother-Eve in full magical control. 'This is your face,' she says and then she draws two horizontal lines: 'These are your eyebrows.' The face is taking shape. The fetus-Adam is being born. Mother-Eve moves one more time. The caressing finger draws yet another vertical line: 'This is your nose.' Another short strike, this one horizontal: 'This is your mouth.' Makhmalbaf's camera is now fully obedient. Khorshid's face appears on the mirror and Nadereh announces the cosmic nativity in the sweet voice of a confident mother who has just given birth: 'This is you Khorshid!'

Having just given birth to Khorshid in the mirror, Nadereh retires to a corner and busies herself with picking flowers. Suddenly we hear the mirror broken. The first murder. Abel killed. Cain confused, baffled, guilt-ridden, guilty. The Biblical is also Qur'anic. Both cosmic. 'Did you break it?' Nadereh asks, disappointed: 'Bakhshesh-e kalan miporsam.' Makhmalbaf knows how cosmically exquisite the Tajiki dialect of Persian sounds to our ears: 'I deeply apologize.' We are now out of Eden and moving toward the Eastern moment of history. Nadereh moves toward the broken mirror, the *tabula rasa* of her creation. The mirror is broken into two pieces. Creation mutation. On one piece we now see Nadereh's face. On the other Khorshid's. Two faces. Exposed. Moment of their innocence passed, possessed, prepositional. Nadereh picks up the broken piece with Khorshid's face on it. Masculinity in the feminine. Khorshid picks up the other piece with Nadereh's face on it. Femininity in the masculine. One pregnant with the other. History delivering itself, from the mythic into the material.

Having come to maturity here in *Silence*, Makhmalbaf's trademark *virtual realism* works its magic from ground up. Nothing in *Silence* is unreal. Its 'Sur/realism,' if we can call it that, is deeply rooted in the material evidence of its origin. No other film of Makhmalbaf is so close in its soul to the spirit of Sohrab Sepehri's poetry. The cosmic nativity that Makhmalbaf generates and invests in Khorshid and Nadereh has its most immediate roots in the gnostic serenity of a presence in the world that does not forfeit its harsh realities. In *Silence*, Makhmalbaf is a companion of Sohrab Sepehri in the following journey:

> Under our teeth
> The taste of being carefree
> Was moving around.
> Our shoes,
> Which were made of prophecy,
> Lifted us from the ground
> Just like a breeze.
> The poles we were carrying
> In our hands, bore
> Upon their shoulders
> A permanent spring.
> Each one of us had a whole heaven
> Hidden in every turn of thought.
> Every motion of our hand
> Was singing

With the fluttering of a wing
(Mesmerized by the dawn).
From our pockets
We could hear the
Cheeping and chirping
Sounds of the sparrows
Of our early childhood mornings.
We were a band of lovers
And our path
Was stretching
From the side of villages
Familiar with poverty
All the way
To the green grace of infinity.[27]

Sight Unseen

Khorshid is desperate. He has to find the vagabond musician and take him to his employer to prove that he was distracted by his music so that the Old Man may forgive him and hire him again. This desperation is accented by the conversation (in Russian) between Khorshid's mother and the fisherman, revealing more of their predicament. The situation reaches a critical point when Nadereh informs Khorshid and the vagabond musician that the Old Man has locked up his shop and gone to find a new person to replace Khorshid. The vagabond musician now becomes the sole source of solace and leads Khorshid and Nadereh to his band of musicians. The vagabond musicians decide to come to Khorshid's home the following day, play their music for the landlord, and hope that this might dissuade him from evicting Khorshid and his mother. Nadereh is pessimistic that this is going to have any effect, but Khorshid has run out of options. All he can do is to gallop like a horse to the music of the vagabond musician, in pursuit of giving order and rhythm to the tempo of a reality he cannot see but must muster. The following day, now the fifth day of the event, the vagabond musicians and their attending flock of sheep, dog, and horse gather with Khorshid and Nadereh in front of Khorshid's home and begin to perform their music. They cannot, however, dissuade the landlord from evicting the mother and son. Nadereh informs Khorshid that the landlord has thrown out their belongings and his mother has collected everything in a boat and is headed toward them, holding their huge mirror in her hands. Khorshid is defeated. He turns to the musicians and says: 'I am going to a long journey. Play the gallop of the horse.' They play the gallop of the horse and he gallops away.

Where else but to the coppersmiths market. Khorshid has now finally succeeded in giving perfect harmonious order to that cacophonous confusion of noises. He conducts the entire guild of coppersmiths into one orchestral, harmonic composition, walks erect and clad in black toward the center of the arena and under the full rays of the sun drops his clothes and stands erect, naked, with his hand raised toward the heavens: crucifixion.

The very last shot of *Silence* is the visual mutation of the auricular fixation of Khorshid into his oracular resolution of all cacophonous noises: The prophetic, the portentous – the mission Makhmalbaf having assigned him accomplished. All in the creative subconscious of Makhmalbaf. But why, how, and to what end?

In his tribute to Hölderlin's elegy *Bread and Wine*: '... and what are poets for in a destitute time,' Heidegger locates the time of the poem after 'the appearance and sacrificial death of Christ' when 'Night is falling.'[28] Heidegger's own prophetic words, uttered at a moment of particularly acute crisis at the heart of instrumental rationality (the speech was delivered on the tenth anniversary of Rilke's death, in 1936), is valid well into the post/colonial edges of Europe:

> The world's night is spreading its darkness. The era is defined by the
> god's failure to arrive, by the 'default of God' ... The default of God
> means that no god any longer gathers men and things unto himself,
> visibly and unequivocally, and by such gathering disposes the world's
> history and man's sojourn in it. The default of God forebodes
> something even grimmer, however. Not only have the gods and the god
> fled, but the divine radiance has become extinguished in the world's
> history. The time of the world's night is the destitute time, because it
> becomes ever more destitute. It has already grown so destitute, it can
> no longer discern the default of God as a default.[29]

If the Christian God at the heart of instrumental rationality foreclosed the world at the dawn of Enlightenment modernity, the Islamic God had to account for the consequences of this foreclosure. Makhmalbaf's cinema, the cinema of a committed Muslim activist turned into an artist, begins to build its case precisely at the moment when that night had long since spread its darkness. It is from the depth of that darkness, as he now creatively remembers it, that he makes his luminous films – in part to pay penance for his own share in the heart of that darkness. In the depth of that darkness, historical memories, code-named *culture*, are *ipso facto* implicated in a history that has been set against its own course. Khorshid's *poverty* in *Silence* cannot be read too literally and must be considered as the simulacrum of an active divestment from that invested memory in the making of an historical narrative, all the way back to its inaugurating moments. Material poverty, not having enough to pay the rent, approximates a *tabula rasa* of re-crafting *the real* from *the virtual* in order to make a renewed historical agency possible.

The Christian and the Islamic Gods come together in the title and theme of Mohsen Makhmalbaf's *Silence* and its (perhaps) namesake, Ingmar Bergman's *Tystnaden/The Silence* (1963). Makhmalbaf's gnostic simplicity in *Silence* becomes more evident if we compare it with its Swedish counterpart. What we see in Bergman's *The Silence* is a vacuous space generated by and in a young boy's memory of a trip with his mother Anna (Gunnel Lindblom) and aunt Ester (Ingrid Thulin). Except for the two sisters, no other two characters in this film have an affinitive relationship with any other – to the degree that the whole story is an act of remembrance on the part of the young boy, Johan (Jorgen Lindstrom). All the homoerotic suggestiveness between the two sisters, incestuous innuendos between Anna and her son, or sexual obsession on the part of Anna, are represented entirely through tacit implications, imperceptive suggestions. As such they are all generated and sustained in a negative space that Bergman creates in between his characters, which is in its entirety the figment of the young boy's memory. This negative space is peopled by absented presence of the two sisters, and as witnessed by an outside world that is on the brink or in the midst of war, or an inside world peopled by a troupe of dwarf entertainers. The world that is created is not so much eerie as dreamlike, reminiscences of an adult man of his childhood memories. The dream begins on a train ride with Ester, Anna, and her young boy, crescendos in an almost vacant hotel, and concludes on another train ride back home but minus Ester.

While in Bergman's *The Silence* the emotive universe is generated in and by the negative space in between the absented characters, in Makhmalbaf's *Silence* the emotive universe is virtually sublated from the mundane routines of daily life. Both their spaces are conspicuously vacated, their frames and forms tightly controlled – but in Bergman's case we almost feel the weight of the negative space generated *among* these absented characters, whereas in Makhmalbaf's case we visibly see the surfacing of the *virtual* (neither *actual* nor *factual*) properties of things, emotions, people, their relations, and our awareness of them. In Makhmalbaf's film, *silence* is suggested by the young boy's deafness; in Bergman's conspicuously by the absence of anything to be said between the two sisters (while one of them, Ester, is a literary translator from several languages), and by their residence in a hotel in a country with a (strange) language that none of them speaks. But the *silence* of Bergman's film can also be understood as the silence in the memorial recollection of the young boy from this strange trip (dream) that he once took with his mother and aunt. The element of music, central to Makhmalbaf's *Silence*, is not entirely absent from Bergman's film: 'I began work on *The Silence* at Christmas time after I'd just finished *Winter Light*,' Bergman has said in an interview. 'My original idea was to make a movie that should obey musical laws, instead of dramaturgical ones. As I was putting it together, I thought much more in musical terms than I'd done before ... .'[30]

That is where the similarities and differences between Bergman's *The Silence* and Makhmalbaf's *Silence* end. The gnostic simplicity that we detect in Makhmalbaf's minimalism in this and in many of his latest parabolic films is a visual strategy to reach out for the *tabula rasa* that clears any historical memory. Makhmalbaf has effectively set for himself the task of mapping out the *virtual* evidence of that cultural memory, reducing it to its quintessential forces, at once historically particular and yet culturally universal. If Makhmalbaf has the audacity to reach for the cosmic re-ordering of the chaos that he sees and hears in the world, it is because of his creative ability to cut to the chase so quickly and effectively that we no longer yearn for the time when God could 'gather men and things into himself.' In the bosom of the harmonic memory that is thus virtually constituted, Makhmalbaf turns his autobiographical recollections into collective deliverance – working toward an active re-subjection of the post/colonial person in a way that makes historical agency possible. Nadereh giving visual birth to Khorshid in *Silence* is the peculiar way in which Makhmalbaf has learnt to re-mythologize his culture but not (like Beiza'i's equally effective way) by taking us back into the myth. Instead, he reduces *the evidently real* to its *virtuality* – and that is the key operative leitmotif of his best films. He can make of that virtuality the *quintessential* (we may read it as *mythological*) re-constitution of the real. The broken mirror that Nadereh and Khorshid pick up and look into is the gateway through which Makhmalbaf has effectively delivered a whole nation of possibilities into history, out of the Biblical Eden, squarely in the earthly shape of our self-creative being.

At the conclusion of that journey, Sepehri is already awaiting Makhmalbaf:

> Upon a pond
> Our head involuntarily
> Turned down (looking):
> On our face the night
> Was evaporating – as friends
> Could hear the voices of friends.[31]

Close Up

Chapter Seven

The Beauty of the Beast:
From Cannes to *Kandahar*

In the previous chapter I used the occasion of a close reading of Makhmalbaf's *Silence* to examine the particular features of his *virtual realism*. To see how the gnostic simplicity of his parabolic narrative is constitutional to the production of a material subjectivity, I traced it back to his mythic reading of reality, where he teases out the virtual matter-of-factness at the root of that reality. I concluded by suggesting that Makhmalbaf's *ascetic minimalism*, now a trademark of his cinema, is integral to his creative re-subjection of the post/colonial person. In my search for the cinematic particularity of that objective, I have always assumed that there is an autonomy of purpose to a work of art, that it can do any number of things independent of the political context in which it is manufactured, presented, and contextualized. In this final chapter, I would like to take that assumption to task and via a close reading of the origin and fate of Makhmalbaf's *Kandahar* (2001) examine the way unanticipated political circumstance can in fact turn a work of art against itself. I will conclude, however, by demonstrating how a work of art has at times uncanny abilities to 'take revenge' on its historical abuses. My purpose in doing so is to demonstrate that a work of art derives its emancipatory energy from the very depth of darkness it exposes in order to liberate its darkened promises of vision. I identify a manner of *visual improvisation* in Makhmalbaf's cinema that I propose is central to his ability to go inside a political predicament and come out with a work of art that liberates it from its contradictory forces. In this respect I will have occasion to take issue with Jean Baudrillard's assumption that ours is a *transaesthetics of indifference* – suggesting that from the depth of the darkness a work of art exposes it is perfectly possible to tell the beautiful from the ugly, truth from falsehood.

What are Poets for in Dire Circumstances?

'We must work out a new legitimation for art,' says Hans-Georg Gadamer in his essay on 'The Relevance of the Beautiful.' One of the most enduring insights of

Gadamer in this essay is his attempt to articulate the varied functions of *the beautiful* by covering the distance – the 'chasm' as he calls it – between *the real* and *the ideal*. Something in Gadamer's insistence that 'the essence of the beautiful does not lie in some realm simply opposed to reality' resonates with a work of art that promises otherwise than the real without betraying it in the realm of the fantastic by way of making and delivering that promise – articulating a vision of the beautiful in the belly of the beast, as it were, rather than in some other-worldly abode. 'On the contrary,' Gadamer insists, 'we learn that however unexpected our encounter with beauty may be, it gives us an assurance that the truth does not lie far off and inaccessible to us, but can be encountered in the disorder of reality with all its imperfections, evils, errors, extremes, and fateful confusions.'[1] That paradoxical breaking of the beast, by having the hidden beauty in it rise against it, is of crucial consequence in what I have tried to articulate in this book on Makhmalbaf's cinema. One of the principal points of my attraction to his cinema is precisely because he was once a fanatical Islamist who served the brutal establishment of an Islamic theocracy in Iran. My interest in his cinema is not despite that fact but because of it. I have always sought to see how did one (Islamic revolutionary zeal) lead to the other (cinematic visionary emancipation). If we are to follow Gadamer's wisdom that 'the truth does not lie far off and inaccessible to us,' then we have to see how it dwells in 'the disorder of reality with all its imperfections, evils, errors, extremes, and fateful confusions.'

The darkness from the midst of which this light emerges is not just local. It has a decidedly global disposition. Paramount in Makhmalbaf's *Kandahar* (2001) is the presence of a testimony as to how a work of art transcends reality by teasing out its emancipatory forces – particularly in a colonial context where historical agency is to be articulated against an Enlightenment modernity that has categorically denied it, and in fact made itself possible by doing so. More than in and of itself, Iranian cinema can be seen as a set of creative tropes of imaginative explosions emerging out of critical circumstances, where artists have been able to re-subject the categorically de-subjected in and through a colonially militated modernity. In trying to see how they could wrest their conception of *the beautiful* from rather bestial circumstances, one can detect a kind of Manichean cosmogony at work where artists seek to rescue the light of subjective emancipation from the very cruel heart of colonial darkness they have inherited. Under these circumstances, art emerges as the wresting of the otherwise of reality out of reality, not phantasmagorically hallucinating an outlandish *ideal* against the brutality of *the real*, but in fact acknowledging and even celebrating *the real* by teasing out its hidden and concealed otherwise. The global appeal of Iranian cinema in general, one might argue, is precisely because of the global disposition of the bondage (denial of agency) from which it seeks to emancipate a nation.

31   Nelofer Pazira *as Nafas in Mohsen Makhmalbaf's* Kandahar (2001). *Soon after the premier of this film in Cannes, 9/11 happened and the burka became a matter of global attention in the aftermath of the US invasion of Afghanistan in October 2001 to topple the government of the Taliban. (Photograph: Mohammad Reza Sharifi-nia; courtesy of Makhmalbaf Film House.)*

Many of these assumptions were to be critically tested in the immediate aftermath of 9/11, when issues of imperial hubris and neo/colonial arrogance assumed unparalleled proportions in contemporary history. Until 9/11, and when by sheer historical serendipity Mohsen Makhmalbaf's *Kandahar* became a public spectacle far beyond its intended audience, it appeared that such articulations of art as a site of creative resistance to colonialism – in its widest sense, as the global abuse of labor by capital, whether domestic to the operation of national capital or external to it – was a one-way proposition, left in peace to do its work. Faced with the amorphous operation of capital, one might have hoped that art could articulate a site of creative resistance that crafted an historical agency against the monstrosities of capital. After 9/11, however, it became clear that such assumptions were entirely naïve: that the globalizing operation of capital has created its own amorphous culture in the body of an enormous propaganda machinery that spans the news and the culture industry, from CNN to Hollywood. This multifaceted propaganda apparatus scourges the expectant face of reality with blinding speed and inundates it with an unfathomable force and ferocity. What the immediate aftermath of 9/11 made clear was the battle-line between the news and culture industry on one side and creative and critical art on the other: one the globalizing ideology of the already globalized capital, charged to abuse reality at the service of the will to power, the other the aesthetic practice of wresting out of reality a will to resist power. Between Mohsen Makhmalbaf's *Kandahar* and the US propaganda preparations leading to the October 2001 invasion of Afghanistan had become evident two defining moments: art as the creative reconstitution of reality, wresting an arrested light in the heart of its darkness; and a globalized expansion of the news and culture industry as absenting that reality at the service of the domination of globalized capital. There is a thoroughness with which the propaganda machinery of the culture and news industry, at the full disposal of globalized capital, gobbles up, chews to pieces, and spits out everything that comes its way with a massive transaesthetics of indifference, as Jean Baudrillard puts it,[2] in effect re/producing a hyper-reality that in its tasteless banality corresponds to the amorphous – shapeless, baseless, and certainly nation-less – operation of capital.

' ... and what are poets for in a destitute time?'[3] They are here to shame the world.

From Cannes to *Kandahar*

'Sir,' the Prince of Denmark's wisdom was not always tragic, but at times even celebratory in its own evidentiary matter-of-factness:

> *in my heart there was a kind of fighting,*
> *That would not let me sleep: methought I lay*
> *Worse than the mutines in the bilboes. Rashly,*
> *And praised be rashness for it, let us know,*
> *Our indiscretion sometimes serves us well,*
> *When our deep plots do pall: and that should teach us*
> *There's a divinity that shapes our ends,*
> *Rough-hew them how we will.*

That playful wisdom (in *Hamlet*, Act 5: Scene 2) presides royally over my mind whenever I think of the fate of Makhmalbaf's *Kandahar*, from its obscure premier at Cannes Film Festival in May 2001 and its spectacular rise to global attention in the immediate aftermath of 9/11.

The example of *Kandahar* and how its fate (as an obscure art film suddenly thrown into the global scene) has faltered with the ups and downs of the politics of its reception points to the precarious place of art and the uses and abuses to which it is susceptible. Makhmalbaf had already shot, edited, and mixed *Kandahar*, and submitted it to Cannes for their consideration, when he visited New York in March 2001 to accompany his wife Marziyeh Meshkini for the US premier of her debut, *The Day I became a Woman* (2000), and for us to hang out together. When

I rescheduled a meeting I had at Columbia to go to JFK Airport in New York to pick them up, they did not utter a word to me that they had just been subject to a systematic harassment at the border. Between catching up with the personal and professional news, there was not much to say about the vagaries of a bureaucratic banality. Makhmalbaf had shot *Kandahar* in the fall of 2000, after some initial hesitations, when Nelofer Pazira, who would end up acting the lead role, had originally proposed the idea of a documentary to him. He was still in New York, and we had resumed our prolonged conversations and walking up and down Manhattan, when he received the news that *Kandahar* was chosen for Official Selection in Competition in the Cannes Film Festival. He, of course, had to deal with the usual Cannes predicament of cutting a scene here and dubbing a voice-over there. This time the scene had to do with the surreal dropping of artificial legs from the heavens while an excited group of amputees chase after them in the barren desert. In his typical virtual realism, Makhmalbaf had carefully cut out the helicopter, so that the parachuted legs appear to be heaven-sent. That visual suggestion carries a kind of metaphysical metaphor that is integral to Makhmalbaf's virtual realism. The suggestion had apparently escaped the Cannes authorities. Be that as it may, *Kandahar* was accepted at Cannes primarily on the strength of its cinematic significance. Afghanistan and its predicament were far from the minds of people who make such decisions. September the Eleventh had not yet happened. It was now March 2001. Makhmalbaf's wife was screening *The Day I became a Woman* at The Museum of Modern Art (MoMA). Makhmalbaf's own *Kandahar* had just been accepted at Cannes – and Osama bin Laden and George W. Bush were yet to lock horns.

Come May 2001, Cannes did not have much to offer Mohsen Makhmalbaf except for the premier of *Kandahar* in the highly visible Competition section. On my way back from Cairo and Beirut, where I was giving a series of lectures, I went to Cannes and spent a few days with Makhmalbaf for the premier of *Kandahar*. He was obviously quite happy for the selection of his film by Cannes – which in and of itself is a singular recognition. But the Jury, headed by Liv Ullmann and featuring such luminaries as the Tunisian filmmaker Moufida Tlatli and the Taiwanese director Edward Yang, favored Nanni Moretti's *La Stanza del Figlio / The Son's Room* (2001), a moving deliberation on the moral collapse of a father after the sudden death of his son. An obscure award by a council of ecumenical Christians was the only consolation prize that Makhmalbaf received that year at Cannes. That and the equally inconspicuous exhibition on the second floor of Palais du Festival of the photographs that his daughter Samira had taken while he was shooting *Kandahar*. The Cannes officials arranged for a second screening of *Kandahar*, as they did for all the other films in Competition. It was screened at Salle Louis Buñuel on Sunday 20 May, at 8:00 a.m. That might as well have been 3:00 a.m., the way people frolic on the Boulevard Croisette into the wee hours of the night. Makhmalbaf was quite nonchalant about the lukewarm reception of *Kandahar* at Cannes. He had written a long essay, 'The Statues of Buddha in Afghanistan were not Demolished: They Collapsed out of Shame,' which he distributed to reporters by way of sharing with them his concerns about the fate of Afghanistan. But he could hardly convince anyone to take the matter seriously – notwithstanding the suggestive title of his essay, referring to the destruction of two giant Buddha statues in Bamiyan by the notorious Taliban. Some took the essay politely, others shrugged it off, all thought he was barking up the wrong tree. Drawn from his poetic formalism, *Kandahar* itself (in a first viewing) appeared as a politically alerted variation on Makhmalbaf's virtual realism. Both thematically and formally he had hit a creative plateau after *Silence*, I remember I thought at the time, and his turn to training his wife and children as filmmakers could have been interpreted as a necessary pause to give himself time to figure out where he would go next. *Kandahar*, as a result, appeared in Cannes as perhaps advancing a worthy social cause, but it did not much move Makhmalbaf's cinema beyond what he had already achieved.

At the end of the Cannes Film Festival in late May, Makhmalbaf returned to Iran to read the poetry of Rumi and Hafez with his wife and children, while working on the website he was putting together for the Makhmalbaf Film House. His French distributor, The Wild Bunch, was equally busy launching *Kandahar* internationally on the quite impressive ticket of 'Selection Officiel' at the Cannes Film Festival. By the end of August, Makhmalbaf was happy with the black and blue background of his website, while The Wild Bunch was mapping out the commercial topography of a run-of-the-mill 'art-film' for international distribution.

September the Eleventh would change everything – from millenarian imperialism to cultural criticism.

Much to its credit, it was before September the Eleventh that UNESCO in Paris had decided to award Makhmalbaf its Federico Fellini Award for *Kandahar*. Makhmalbaf's daughter Samira was the previous recipient of that same award for her *Blackboard* (2000), in which she had addressed the predicament of the Kurds in Iran and Iraq. She too was optimistic at the 2001 Cannes Festival, where she premiered her second feature. But she lost to Lars von Trier and his *Dancer in the Dark* (2000). The Kurdish catastrophe remained moot and mute in the global power gaze, and only UNESCO's bureaucratic humanism would pay any attention to the young filmmaker and her concerns. The same would have been the case with Mohsen Makhmalbaf had September the Eleventh been yet another ordinary day on Wall Street, with Dow Jones and NASDAQ waking every money manager in the neighborhood up with indigestion, heartburn, headache, and the calamitous miracle of round-the-clock electronic capitalism.

The Fellini award brought Makhmalbaf back to France. But by the time he arrived in Paris on 4 October, September the Eleventh had already shaken the globe. What a difference between the modest gathering in a small room in Palais du Festival when Makhmalbaf received that ecumenical award in May and the global gaze on him in October when he received the Fellini Award. On the first occasion, I was among a handful of close friends of Makhmalbaf's, plus a few cameramen and photographers who had surrounded him and Nelofer Pazira, the inspiration behind and the star of *Kandahar*, in a short ceremony in a back room of Palais du Festival where he delivered the same speech that he would have if he had won the Palm d'Or, speaking on behalf of the poor and the forgotten of Afghanistan, with nobody listening except those who knew, who sympathized, who agreed – with an air of resignation. On the second occasion, though, the whole world was listening to Makhmalbaf and what he had to say about Afghanistan. 'For years,' he exclaimed, 'bombs have dropped from its sky and mines planted in its land.'

> Afghanistan is a country where its people are flogged in the streets by its government. Afghanistan is a country whose neighbors expel its refugees. Afghanistan is a country where nature kills its inhabitants with famine. Although the name of God is mentioned in Afghanistan more than in any other, it seems that even God has abandoned this place. Until the events of September the Eleventh in the US, Afghanistan was an entirely forgotten land. Today that Afghanistan has attracted much attention it is far more for revenge than for humanitarian help. If during the last twenty-five years, superpowers had dropped books instead of bombs, there would have remained no room for ignorance, ethnic tribalism, or terrorism in Afghanistan. If instead of mines, under their feet wheat had been planted, millions of people would not have perished from hunger or been made into refugees. Under such circumstances, awarding 'Kandahar' the Federico Fellini Award is a sign of hope. But I wish that this award were bread that could be distributed among the hungry Afghanis. I wish that this award were rain that would pour over the arid land of Afghanistan. I wish that this award were the breeze of freedom casting away the Afghan women's burka. But now that this award is not bread, or rain, or the breeze of freedom, and it is just a sign of hope, I keep it with me with much anticipations for the people of Afghanistan, and before you, distinguished emissaries of nations, promise the tyrannized people of Afghanistan that after their emancipation I will build a school in the city of Kandahar in the name of Federico Fellini and on your behalf will dedicate this medal to the students of that school.[4]

Now the world listened, read, and watched what Makhmalbaf had to say, write, and show. The essay that he wrote when making *Kandahar* – 'The Statues of Buddha in Afghanistan were not Demolished: They Collapsed out of Shame,' which he could hardly convince a reporter at Cannes to read beginning to end – was now serialized in the French daily *L'humanité*, and subsequently published in whole as a supplement, complete with the pictures that Makhmalbaf's daughter Samira had taken while accompanying her father in Afghanistan. Now in the oversized pages of the *l'Humanité* supplement, they had assumed more urgent and ominous proportions. Soon a French publisher, One Thousand and One Nights (what else?), printed 10,000 copies of the French translation of Makhmalbaf's essay, along with Samira's pictures. Another outlet bought her pictures for 100,000 French francs. Makhmalbaf placed the proceeds from these sales in a fund at the disposal of UNICEF for the education of Afghan refugee children in Iran and Pakistan. His arithmetic mind was at work, and he had found a cause that had rekindled his earlier revolutionary zeal:

> I sat down and calculated that for every cruise missile that Americans fire at Afghanistan some 130,000 Afghan children can be educated. Just this one comparison is enough to see to what depths humanity has collapsed.[5]

Makhmalbaf put his offices in Tehran at the disposal of the UNICEF project and established a foundation so that others could contribute too. He would do the groundwork and UNICEF would implement an ambitious project for the education of Afghan children. He committed himself to making a short documentary about the schooling of the Afghan children in Iran for UNICEF.

On 8 October, the day after the USA invaded Afghanistan, Makhmalbaf left Paris for Rome and the Italian premier of *Kandahar*. Prime Minister Silvio Berlusconi (soon to be echoed by Oriana Fallaci) had already publicly boasted of the superiority of 'the West' for having produced Mozart and Michelangelo and denounced 'Islam' for having produced Bin Laden.[6] Italians themselves, though, spoke differently. By the time Makhmalbaf left Rome in mid-October, some 80 movie theaters were screening *Kandahar* throughout Italy. By the time he was in Zahedan making his documentary about the Afghan refugee children, more than 100 movie theaters were showing *Kandahar* in Italy. The silent response of ordinary Italians, soon to be followed by that of the British (where *Kandahar* broke the per-screen record of *Harry Potter*), was a referendum, showing that Berlusconi and Blair, like Bush and Bin Laden, represented nothing and nobody – except the worst nightmares of our planet. Fallaci, meanwhile, betrayed the discrete c/harm of the European intellectuals in such moments of crisis, when their worst fears reveal their most carefully guarded racism.[7]

Makhmalbaf's plans to meet with Zaher Shah, the deposed Afghan king, in Rome fell through. In Paris he was fascinated by the idea of meeting with the old monarch: 'Thirty years ago he was deposed, and since then he has taken some 80,000 pictures. He is a photographer of some note. I will make a documentary about him and give the money to UNICEF.' Makhmalbaf is always statistical, accurate in his diction, and at this point he used to pronounced UNICEF in Persian (YOU-KNEE-SEFF) with a solidity of purpose to the intervening 'S' sound, a factual assurance to the final 'F.'

After his Italian sojourn, Makhmalbaf returned to Tehran to get ready to shoot a documentary for UNICEF on the status of Afghan children refugees in Iran. By mid-October 2001, he was in Zahedan and Zabol on the border between Iran and Afghanistan shooting his documentary, *Alefba-ye Afghan/Afghan Alphabet*, which was ready by November of the same year. On his behalf I submitted a copy of this short film to UNICEF officials in New York and met with them several times. But the project ultimately fell through because UNICEF officials did not approve of a scene in the film where a young Afghan girl is cajoled to take off her veil. Before the year ended Makhmalbaf wrote an open letter to President Khatami proposing an ambitious literacy program for Afghan refugee children; soon after that he and Nelofer Pazira went to meet with Grand Duchess Joséphine-Charlotte of Luxemburg, who promised to help out with the education of children in Herat. He spent the entire month of December 2001 lobbying the Iranian parliament to change the law to allow the Afghan children to be educated in Iran. By the end of the month he was on his way to Herat for some on-site visits for a school he wanted to establish inside Afghanistan.[8]

As Makhmalbaf was busy with the human subject of his *Kandahar* rather than its commercial and political fate in the world, events in New York had taken a more ominous turn. Soon after 9/11, and while Makhmalbaf was still in Paris to receive his Federico Fellini Award, I solicited his permission for a screening of *Kandahar* at Columbia University in New York, where I teach. Given the angry and vindictive disposition of the Bush administration, it was a matter of days before the US would attack Afghanistan. *Kandahar* had not made it through the selection committee of the New York Film Festival, in session when September the Eleventh came about. My initial attempts to have a special screening of *Kandahar* immediately after September the Eleventh at the Lincoln Center were not successful. Meanwhile, Makhmalbaf's French distributor, The Wild Bunch, was still deciding between Avatar and its rivals as the distributor of *Kandahar* for the US market. The US mass media was now the principal source of sight and sound of Afghanistan in New York and the rest of the country. The drums of war were now blasting loudly and clearly. These were days after 9/11 and it would be years before a national anti-war movement were to take shape. The most belligerent were loud and clear; the more cautionary and progressive minds were yet to collect their wits and speak out. Even the screening of a film that would underline the humanity of the Afghans was deemed unacceptable.

Professor Rosalind Morris, my Columbia colleague who at the time was the Director of our Institute for Research on Women and Gender, agreed to view *Kandahar*, and once she saw it (from a bootleg copy Makhmalbaf had brought for me in March) she agreed to host a screening of it at Columbia. The US attack against Afghanistan started on 7 October, before the Columbia University screening of *Kandahar*. But our preparations went ahead apace anyway. To participate in a panel discussion after the screening of the film, we invited Nelofer Pazira, whom I had met in Cannes in May, and she flew to New York from Ottawa, Canada, where she resides. By the time she had asked Makhmalbaf to make a film about the predicament of 20 million Afghans inside their country, she was already a dedicated activist. By the time *Kandahar* was up and about, she had become one of the most eloquent voices telling the world of the horrors of her homeland. We also invited my old friend and colleague (from the time I was a graduate student at the University of Pennsylvania) Margaret Mills, then the Chair of the Department of Middle East Studies at Ohio State University and the most distinguished American folklorist specializing in Afghanistan. Margaret Mills' years of patient recording of storytelling among the Tajiks, the Pashtuns, and the Hazaras had turned her into an acute observer of the rugged region she had visited regularly over many decades.[9]

I also thought of inviting Makhmalbaf himself. But when he had come to New York in March 2001, he and his wife were subject to humiliating behavior by the US immigration and custom officers – and he swore he would never come to the USA anymore.[10] When I asked him to consider coming to New York for our Columbia screening, he suggested quite casually that the best person to speak on this occasion was in fact the UNESCO representative who had given him the Fellini Award. 'Her name is Marisa Berenson,' Makhmalbaf told me on the telephone. 'She lives in New York.' He gave me Marisa Berenson's New York telephone number and I called and invited her without quite knowing who she was. After she had accepted our invitation I discovered that she was not just a UNESCO Goodwill Ambassador and, after September the Eleventh, its Artist for Peace, but that she is in fact the surviving sister of Berry Berenson Perkins, a passenger on one of the hijacked airplanes that was crashed into the World Trade Center.[11]

Having also secured permission from its French distributor The Wild Bunch and its US distributor Avatar, we proceeded with our Columbia screening of *Kandahar* (from the same bootleg copy I had, where the name of the film was still *The Sun behind the Moon* – its original title, which was subsequently changed during its premier at Cannes). That Wednesday evening, we had a riot on our hands in front of the Altschul Auditorium on Columbia campus. We had grossly

32 *A scene from Mohsen Makhmalbaf's* Kandahar *(2001). The fate of Afghan refugees preceded and was soon exacerbated after the US-led invasion of Afghanistan. (Photograph: Mohammad Reza Sharifi-nia; courtesy of Makhmalbaf Film House.)*

underestimated the crowd that would gather after Judith Kempfner of WNYC, the New York affiliate of National Public Radio, did a piece on our event. Some 1500 people showed up, forming a belt around the central atrium adjacent to Altschul. We could not seat more than a few hundred. The rest had to be sent away. The campus security got into some rough exchanges with the rambunctious crowd. The New York Police Department had to be called in. But things were brought under control and the crowd dispersed when we promised them additional screenings the following night at two adjacent halls in our Law School. Rosalind Morris, Nelofer Pazira, Margaret Mills, Marisa Berenson, and I introduced and discussed Makhmalbaf's *Kandahar* in what was the first exposure to a visual and analytic vocabulary available at a public domain independent of the banalities of CNN and Co.

As we were getting ready for our second Columbia screening, the news of our event soon spread around the country and I received a phone call from the Search for Common Ground, asking if I could take the film to Washington, DC, adding 'with a possible screening at the White House.' But they first wanted a video copy of the film to see if it was suitable. I made a duplicate of my solitary copy and sent it to the Search for Common Ground, and then I called Makhmalbaf in Iran and told him about the intentions of the Search for Common Ground. He asked me to call The Wild Bunch in Paris to request a copy with English subtitles and proceeded to put the news on his website. I called The Wild Bunch and they sent the only English subtitled copy of *Kandahar* available – and en route to London – to New York. But The Wild Bunch refused to release the copy to Avatar because they had not yet officially signed a contract. The copy was kept with a French carrier until such time as we were to hear back from the Search for Common Ground and call the carrier to send it to Washington, DC. Soon after I sent the duplicate of my copy to the Search for Common ground they called me back and said regretfully they had decided against their original idea because 'this film is too intellectual for this White House.'

Meanwhile reporters from around the world were picking up the news off Makhmalbaf's website that President Bush was 'asking to see *Kandahar*.' To this day the world is under the impression that President Bush 'asked' to see *Kandahar*, and that he in fact saw it! *After* the US invaded Afghanistan, Robin Lim, the late President of Avatar, told me in the course of a telephone conversation that Mrs. Bush's and Secretary of State Colin Powell's offices had contacted him and requested a screening of *Kandahar* – at which point the Bush administration was eager to use the film in order to justify their Afghan campaign.

This is not the end of the story – it had just begun. If politics has a way of abusing a work of art, a work of art has a way of abusing politics. At about 3:30 p.m. on Friday 14 December 2001, I received a phone call from Robin Lim, who called me at home, which meant there was an emergency. Since September, we had been in regular e-mail and telephone contact to promote *Kandahar*. Robin Lim had successfully bid against Avatar's rivals to get the US rights of *Kandahar* from The Wild Bunch, which had its global rights. Robin Lim, meanwhile, was quite nervous about *Kandahar*, at once excited about its potential commercial success and fearful of his rivals who he thought were trying to rob him of his potential bonanza. He was convinced that they were out to damage *Kandahar*, and were using their influence to delay or even thwart his big theatrical release in New York in December.[12] Had it not been for the New Yorker Films and Lincoln Plaza Cinemas, he believed that he would probably have not even had a New York outlet to release *Kandahar*. He had been given a huge commercial boost by two successive pieces about *Kandahar* on the front page of *The New York Times* art section. National public radio had given the film major coverage. In addition, on Monday 10 December, my friend and Columbia colleague Richard Peña, the director of programming at New York Film festival, had hosted a special screening of *Kandahar* at Walter Reade in the Lincoln Center to launch the publication of my recently released book on Iranian cinema, *Close Up: Iranian Cinema, Past, Present and Future*. Cine-clubs around the country were screening *Kandahar*, and the buzz around it was unprecedented. Robin Lim was set to open that Friday at the Lincoln Plaza Cinemas and witness the spectacular success of his first major acquisition for Avatar. But the story still had many more nasty and bizarre twists.

The point of Robin Lim's calling me at home was quite urgent. A reporter from *The Washington Times* had just called him about a story she was writing concerning Hasan Tantai, the Black American who had acted as Tabib Sahib in *Kandahar*. According to this reporter, this Hasan Tantai was none other than a certain David Belfield, aka Dawud Salahuddin, a fugitive from law for having committed a murder in the USA and who had then fled to Iran. 'She wants to link this to Mr. Makhmalbaf's own violent past,' Robin Lim was now almost entirely incomprehensible on the phone. When later I checked my phone messages at my office, the same reporter had called and left me a message, wishing to talk to me about the same issue. I did not return her phone call.

It gradually emerged that in a screening of *Kandahar* in Washington, DC, an Iranian in the audience had noted the resemblance between Hasan Tantai and David Belfield, the apparent assassin of his twin brother soon after the 1979 Islamic Revolution. David Belfield, evidently, is an African–American Muslim who had disguised himself as a mailman and assassinated the man on behalf of the nascent Islamic Republic, before fleeing to Iran. He was now on the FBI wanted list, and at some point in fact had given an interview to ABC News program '20/20.' Robin Lim wanted Makhmalbaf to issue a statement dissociating himself from Hasan Tantai/David Belfield. In response, Makhmalbaf wrote a scathing account, 'The Trial of Che Guevara in Gandhi's Court,' and put it on his website, in short saying that he chose his actors from people in the street, and thus knew nothing about their lives before or after their appearance in his films.[13] The story gradually died away, and it turned out to be a bizarre combination of facts and fantasies fueled by the petty professional rivalries among filmmakers in Iran and lucrative enmities among film distributors in the USA. But the fact, that exactly at a moment when *Kandahar* was being politically appropriated and abused to justify the US invasion of Afghanistan, suddenly a 'terrorist' surfaced from its Trojan belly is a telling example of how a work of art can gently disabuse itself from its abusers.

Visual Improvization

In the realms of aesthetics, art faces the same double-bind that afflicts it politically. If in the realm of the political, art is abused and disabused, in the domain of aesthetics, art oscillates between its domestic and global bipolarities. What is happening to Iranian cinema in terms domestic to its immediate culture is globally opaque; what is happening to Iranian cinema globally is domestically docile. If the two angles were to be brought together, the vision would be radically revolutionary. Here are the parameters of the two lenses – first the local, then the global:

'The improvising jazz musician must work right in the heat and the pressure of the moment, giving form and order in a mobile environment, where choices must be constantly assessed and reacted to in one way or another. The success of jazz is a victory for democracy ....' I was reminded of these sentences in Stanley Crouch's *Blues to be Constitutional*, in my colleague Bob O'Meally's edited volume, *The Jazz Cadence of American Culture* on 1 November 2001, when while giving a talk at Middlebury College in Vermont I was invited to attend what is now invariably called a 'classical Persian concert.' It was a duet between a master *santur* player and a novice *tunbak* player. I sat there in that hall with a group of moderately amused, but largely bewildered, people watching and listening to this concert with Stanley Crouch's phrase in my mind: 'The demands on and the respect for the individual in the jazz band put democracy into aesthetic action.' Right in front of me I was witnessing *tyranny* put into aesthetic action, and the aesthetic was no longer so beautiful to hear, let alone to watch. The master *santur* player would begin and sustain a piece with full and solitary control over its melodic and harmonic elements, with his attention and gaze totally fixated on his instrument. After a complete exhaustion of the melodic trajectory of the piece, he would feel the need for some rhythmic intervention so he could re-modulate. At that point he would ever so royally lift his head, look to his right toward the novice *tunbak* player, all the while fully attentive and immobile, and then deign to give a royal nod. The young tunbak player would ever so gently (timidly, even with an innate hesitation) begin to introduce a shy number that was almost immediately taken over and dominated by the omnipresent master who now took the lead again and began a new round of melodic improvization. The *tunbak* player would soon retreat back into silence and immobility, never given a chance to have a complete solo. Every once in a while you could feel the hopeful young man have a go at a solo. But not a snowball's chance in hell. The master would not allow it. The thing was just too brutal to watch.

This phenomenon is not limited to obscure Iranian musicians in remote corners of the USA. Even (or particularly) the most prominent and revolutionary minded musicians, master vocalists like Mohammad Reza Shajarian and Shahram Nazeri, brilliant instrumentalists like Mohammad Reza Lotfi and Abbas Alizadeh, or groundbreaking composers like Fereydun Shahbazian and Houshang Kamkar, have failed to transform the tyrannical texture and disposition of Persian music. At the height of the Iranian Revolution of 1977–1979, before it was completely taken over and Islamicized, Shajarian and Nazeri were pioneering figures of revolutionary events in Persian music. Though in lyrics and sentiment their music participated in the democratic aspirations of their nation, in composition and improvisation it remained constitutionally undemocratic and patriarchal. The patriarchal dimension of this music has now become even more evident in such prominent musicians as Mohammad Reza Shajarian and Shahram Nazeri, and the manner in which they promote their own sons as the next generation of Persian vocalists. On Sunday 5 March 2006, I attended a concert of Mohammad Reza Shajarian at Alice Tully Hall at the Lincoln Center in New York. Accompanying Shajarian were master musicians Keyhan Kalhor on *kamancheh* and Hossein Alizadeh on *tar*, all accompanied by Shajarian's own son, Homayun Shajarian, on *tunbak*. What was frightful about this particular performance is when Mohammad Reza Shajarian actually allowed his son Homayun Shajarian to sing. The son began to sing while playing the *tunbak* and his voice was absolutely indistinguishable from that of his father. You could (and I did) close your eyes and not be able to tell if this was Shajarian the father singing or Shajarian the son. They started doing a duo, and the mimicking became even more evident. What a terror is that? Where was the son's own voice, his own inflection, tonality, accent, reverberation, his own take on the song, his own grasp of the poem – all brutally suppressed under a parroting practice that only extended his father's legendary diction. It seemed that the aging Shajarian had effectively cloned himself, metamorphosed into a rejuvenated extension of himself, entering the young body of his son, soliciting immortality – a ventriloquist mummifying his own son, so his own voice can continue to sing. At that revelatory moment Mohammad Reza Shajarian was indistinguishable from the Shah and Khomeini combined. This was an even more brutish scene to watch. I came home and for days could not hear anything but Charlie Parker and Louis Armstrong and their glorious bands. 'So, what would America be without jazz?'[14]

The miracle of Iranian cinema is precisely in its emancipatory possibilities that have become evident in the creative freedom it has given its creators. Despite the fact that cinema is a solitary act of creation, with the director in full control of the creative vision, in the democratic dignity that it invests in its creators it has begun to cure a whole culture of the malignant disease of undemocratic improvisation. Even the most authoritarian directors have to yield their vision to the expertize and mercy of their cinematographers, actors, sound engineers, special effects technicians, editors, and then to producers, distributors, film festival directors, film critics, and most disconcerting of all to the unseen and unforeseeable public. Add to that unsettling circumstances, the frequent fact of unfair and artificial selection processes for major film festivals, in which – to add insult to injury – glamorous members of the jury end up giving outlandish prizes to bizarre films and permanently fracturing the already bruised egos of visionary filmmakers. It is very unfair – but it is very democratic.

What is important in Makhmalbaf's cinema, and in *Kandahar* in particular, is his uncanny ability visually to improvise with a full awareness of a democratic spirit that sustains the creative effervescence of the work of art. This democratic improvisation is constitutional to the polyfocality of a work of art – to its mysterious ability to sustain and solicit a full range of contradictory readings, all the way from abusive politics to speculative aesthetics.

Something exceptionally significant is happening in the creative disposition of a culture when it begins to sublate its undemocratic improvisations in democratic directions. But before we have had a chance to seize on that critical moment and reflect on a cinematic culture deeply embedded in that transformative mode and in terms domestic to its consequences, we need to attend the stage where that transformation is staged and see how it is read in terms alien to that domesticity.

Transaesthetics of Indifference

In his dispatch from Paris early in November, Alan Riding summed up the initial US and European reaction to Makhmalbaf's *Kandahar* as it was first premiered in Cannes 2001. 'Because its theme is essentially grim, several critics have been troubled by the beauty of some images, not least those of multicolored burkas floating across the arid landscape.' A.O. Scott of *The New York Times*, meanwhile, believes that *Kandahar* contains 'moments of sublime visual poetry that at once heighten and complicate their humanitarian messages,' while Christopher Ayad of *Libération* acknowledges 'pure moments of grace' in *Kandahar*, but objects that Makhmalbaf's 'message and camera go in opposite directions.' More specifically, Ayad interjects: 'The burka is an abomination, that's understood, but it does not prevent one from thinking that it is also photogenic.'[15] In a subsequent piece in *The New York Times*, A.O. Scott repeats these earlier views and then adds the six-letter word: 'The world it depicted [speaking of *Kandahar*] seemed, to me and to other Westerners in attendance, far away and even – in part because of the lyricism Mr. Makhmalbaf brings to his grimmest pictures of war and depravation – exotic.'[16]

The burka is *not* an abomination. It is an abomination to force women to wear (or not to wear) the burka (or any other piece of customary garment) against their will. What the self-absorbed pathology of bourgeois feminism, the US imperialism of gender politics, and the pathetic band of native informers that entertains and tickles its fancies[17] confuses are the varieties of cultural practices to which every people is entitled and the tyrannical power that forces them one way or another. One military thug, Reza Shah Pahlavi, comes to power in Iran and orders women to come out of their habitual veil – both beautiful and banal, neither beautiful nor banal – because of his inferiority complex with the Western side of his perturbed imagination. Another medieval tyrant, Ayatollah Khomeini, comes to power and says, 'Now, enough breathing! Go back under the veils.' It is this monstrosity of power that is abominable, not the burka, the chador, the purda, or the veil. But the good-hearted liberals get offended by the burka, on the generous side of their protestation, and yet titillated by its sexual suggestiveness, on the repressed side of their Oriental fantasies. And then those of us who were born and bred under those burkas, chadors, purdas, or veils, played hide-and-seek with our siblings or sought refuge from nasty mosquitoes under those multi-functional garments, now have to choose sides, either with the forbidden fantasies of film critics or else with mercenary bandits like the Taliban – either with tyrannous mullahs in Qom and Tehran or else with native informers who have dyed their hair Lolita-blonde and fancied themselves liberated in the company of such luminary liberators of Muslim women as Paul Wolfowitz and Bernard Lewis. The obscenity of this choice simply defies reason.

In an ideal world we would be allowed to request a moratorium on these Orientalist tropes and exotic fantasies. We would then be able to suggest that long, very long, before the beauty of Makhmalbaf's images and the visual poetry of his elegant framing *complicated*, as one puts it, or *contradicted*, as the other suggests, his message, he has been at work articulating the aesthetic parameters of that *beauty*, and the rhyme and reason of its *relevance*.

To make this point particularly clear, let us in fact *complicate* the situation even further. Look at the pictures that Samira Makhmalbaf took of Afghan women while her father was shooting his film. Look at them very carefully. They are all staged. Their mise-en-scène, choreography, rhetoric, and suggestiveness, all are manipulated and carefully staged. We have no way of knowing that these are even Afghan women under those burkas. They might as well be Makhmalbaf's camera crew! Now what? Such exploitative, photogenic, dishonesty!

The problem we are facing here is far worse than what Adorno more than half a century ago identified as 'culture industry.'[18] The problem has now mutated into a realm that can only be articulated with Jean Baudrillard's hyper-diction – when he becomes a detective and looks for the criminal who killed reality – in his unraveling of the technological and social processes through which the world has been transmuted into an amorphous constellation of emptied transparencies. In doing so, Baudrillard has demonstrated how the 'real time' of CNN and Co. has in fact killed reality. One particularly powerful result of that erosion of reality into 'real time' is the criminal constitution of some form of Other on the broken back of which the globalized Self can hang his Armani coat. 'Doomed to our own image, our own identity, our own "look," and having become our own object of care, desire and suffering,' Baudrillard observes at one point:

> we have grown indifferent to everybody else. And secretly desperate at that indifference, and envious of every form of passion, originality or destiny. Any passion whatever is an affront to the general indifference. Anyone who, by his passion, unmasks how indifferent, pusillanimous or half-hearted you are, who, by the force of his presence or his suffering, unmasks how little reality you have, must be exterminated. There you have the other resuscitated, the enemy at last re-embodied, to be subjugated or destroyed. Such are the incalculable effects of that negative passion of indifference, that hysterical and speculative resurrection of the other.[19]

33 '*Afghan Women*': while Mohsen Makhmalbaf was shooting Kandahar (2001), his daughter Samira did a series of photographs on the theme of Afghan Women. (Photograph: Samira Makhmalbaf; courtesy of Makhmalbaf Film House.)

What could be the function of art against this globalizing erosion of reality? Here Baudrillard's assumption that the postmodern has intimated a *transaesthetics realm of indifference* is too Eurocentric to be taken globally seriously. Right as he is that 'a strange pride incites us not only to possess the other but also to force the other's secret out of him, not only to be dear to the other but also to be fatal to him,'[20] he is a European nativist when he thinks that 'inasmuch as we have access to neither the beautiful nor the ugly, and are incapable of judging, we are condemned to indifference.'[21] This is *not* a description of Makhmalbaf's art. Baudrillard is right about what Cannes may do to Makhmalbaf's art, at once celebrating and destroying his otherness. But Baudrillard has scarcely anything to say about the substance of Makhmalbaf's art, and that precisely is the dignity limiting his theory, when and where he knows *not to try to possess* and thus rob an artist of his particularity.

And what precisely is Makhmalbaf's aesthetic particularity – the specifics of his local universe of imagination made universally valid, but short of any flirtation with a transaesthetics of globalized indifference? Rescued from its filmcrits international, Makhmalbaf's art is resistant to over-exhaustion into analytical nullity. You can never completely explain away his images. His cinema works through a visual brevity, a virtual realism that vacates the scene almost entirely of all its excessive paraphernalia, minimally reducing it to bare necessities. There is a rich *asceticism* in Makhmalbaf's cinema, and unless and until that deeply contradictory but effectively true aspect of his art is understood we will never get close to the magic of his realism. But even that recognition does not exhaust his aesthetic *modus operandi*. It is useful to remember that he (subconsciously) borrows that rich asceticism from the gnostic ('irfan) tradition of his Persian poetic ancestry. It would be equally important if we were to add a bit of biographical note that between 1974 and 1978, while in Pahlavi prison, Makhmalbaf mastered, perforce, the art of brevity, summarizing the political instructions operative among the group of revolutionaries incarcerated with him. But none of these will reveal or diminish the magic of his tabulated frames, perfectly syncopated shots, almost sinful suggestion of sounds, perfectly illegal breaking and entering of laser-sharp cuts, in all of which brevity, simplicity, and an epigrammatic elegance form the soul of his visual wit.

Makhmalbaf harbors, and allows for, no *transaesthetics of indifference*. His is a caring intellect, a vision of the otherwise, the sound and the fury of the im/possible. His is Baudrillard's dream of art, ' ... the soul of Art − Art, as adventure, Art with its power of illusion, its capacity for negating reality, for setting up an "other scene" in opposition to reality, where things obey a higher set of rules, a transcendent figure in which beings, like line and color on a canvas, are apt to lose their meaning, to extend themselves beyond their own *raison d'être*, and, in an urgent process of seduction, to rediscover their ideal form (even though this form may be that of their own destruction).' He nostalgically adds, 'in this sense, Art is gone.'[22] But it is *not* gone. What is gone is the hope that even in his dream of art, Baudrillard does not know how to wish for it. Art, the way Makhmalbaf practices it, is no *Aristotelian real* in search of its *Platonic ideal*, the way Baudrillard desperately conjures it. Baudrillard has too readily lost hope in the real. He does not know even how to dream. His Platonic soul! Too dulled by an Aristotelian contraction of reality, he wants art to transcend it, negate it, become illusory, to become completely other than the real, 'in opposition to reality, where things obey a higher set of rules.' This is a belated bourgeois banality that has no place in the harsh deserts of Afghanistan. Art, the way Makhmalbaf practices it, is manipulation of reality, not a negation of it. Art *uses* reality, manipulates it, steals its viciously guarded and concealed promises from the very depth of its madness. What are those beautiful burkas doing in Makhmalbaf's *Kandahar*? They are ab/using *the politics of concealment* by turning it against itself, into *an aesthetic of revelation. The politics of concealment* turned upside down into an *aesthetics of revelation* takes a look at the physical reality of burkas and the tyrannical rule of Taliban, forcing it against the wishes of those who do not wish to wear it. What about those who wish to wear it? Where have all these colors come from? Did the Taliban order those flamboyant colors too? Makhmalbaf uses their vivid reality against the Taliban and the so-called 'Tradition' they represent, turning the tyranny of their ugly reign into a site of hope − going into the belly of the beast to steal beauty.

In sublating the power of concealment into an aesthetics of revelation, Makhmalbaf takes his cues, whether he knows it or not, from the classical instance of Persian Gnosticism, the homocentric mutation of the juridical fear of God into the injudicious love of God. The Platonic sublation of the Aristotelian real into the ideal is simply too prosaic for the glorious accidentality of the real. Rethinking the Manichean cosmogony as light hidden in the heart of darkness is a far more accurate metaphor for art. Art, the way Makhmalbaf dreams and delivers it, does not escape reality. It takes reality too seriously to take it seriously. Art intuitively *knows* the fabricated disposition of the real. It de-fabricates and re-fabricates it at will, with a joyous sense of frivolity in its entirely child-like encounter with reality. Years ago, after the conclusion of a Locarno Film Festival Makhmalbaf and I traveled to Geneva. One day we went for a walk by Lake Geneva. We were walking and talking behind our daughters, his Hana and my Pardis. I remember I asked him about his interest in Persian Gnosticism. 'No,' he said, he was not interested in classical Persian Gnosticism. He was far more interested, he said, in *the ascetic impermanence of the moment* (my words, his sentiments), and how as children we were far closer to it than adults are: 'Look at Hana and Pardis!' They were both about eight at the time, walking playfully, entirely oblivious to their surroundings: 'They could not care less about time, about space, about obligation, commitment, responsibility. These are all alien, alienating, distractions. My entire cinema has been an attempt at getting close to that moment of childish carelessness, when reality is pliable on the edges of its presumed solidity.'

The Sun behind the Moon

Makhmalbaf's penchant for the *sur/real* is planted so well, so strategically accurately, in the middle of his narrative that every time his depicting reality threatens to collapse into a blasé documentary, evidencing a social catastrophe flattened in boredom, he manages to save it. The story behind and before Makhmalbaf's camera is simple enough. An Afghan woman is traveling through Iran to enter Afghanistan in order to get to Kandahar to save her sister, who has written her a letter that she intends to kill herself at the moment of the solar eclipse as it reaches Afghanistan. Around the bare thread of that non-narrative, Makhmalbaf narrates *Kandahar* into an allegory of limbless men and veiled women, the operatic protagonists of a drama set against the backdrop of the destroyed Afghan landscape. There is an arid desolation about *Kandahar*, a deserted emptiness, the barren nakedness of a Day of Judgment – the world vacated of all its excesses, stripped to its bare insignia.

In the midst of the catastrophe of a culture at war with itself, Makhmalbaf sends his camera scouting for signs of salvation. Afghanistan is now the nightmare that an Islamic Revolution turned Republic could interpret and deliver. Between Iran and Afghanistan, Makhmalbaf has found a no-wo/man-land where maladies hide their cures. It is perfectly apt that *Kandahar* is filmed on the border between Iran and Afghanistan, between the interpretation of a nightmare and the possibility of a dream, between a promissory note and a threatening notation, without us ever getting to know which is which, or what is particularly Republican about the Islamic, or Islamic about the Republic – with the Taliban the metaphoric proxy of the Mullahs who run the Islamic Republic. Makhmalbaf is in the twilight zone of his culture. He is out hunting for hope. Things are pregnant with their opposites. His camera has light-sensitive lenses on, un/like the ones that the US army uses to detect ghostly green apparitions in the depth of darkness. Makhmalbaf's camera teases those ghostly green apparitions out to bring them to life, the US army to kill them off. Makhmalbaf is among the legless men, faceless women, hopeless children, the land of make-believe: covered Afghan women are really liberated Canadian journalists, bearded Afghan men turn out to be beardless American idealists/assassins, militant Taliban seminary students are shy vocalists who prefer to sing a song than recite the Qur'an, and lead a beautiful woman through the desert to safety than launch a religious revolution toward misery. In Makhmalbaf's *Kandahar*, the pious are godless, the godless are idealists. In a land where for a quarter of a century people have screamed 'Death to America,' Makhmalbaf chooses an American to bring 'Life to Muslims,' bread for their belly, truth to their falsehood – so that the only true Muslim in a land of would-be Muslims was born Christian, the only physician a retired warrior. This is how art works: forcing the real to stand on its head and spin around its own tail, and out-emerges a reassuring truth from the depth of a systemic mendacity.

Revealing her face, Nafas is the will to beauty, the daydream of every woman imagining herself under the burka. Under every burka breathes the possibility of a beautiful woman. Makhmalbaf dreams and delivers that promise? The image of a woman under the burka is the walking embodiment of doubtful certainty? There is something there, but what is it? Who is under that thing? The question is asked as much by the onlookers as by the onlooked. Who is this woman under the burka? Makhmalbaf delivers the dream of every woman under the burka to herself. If she were to lift that burka this is what she would see, herself, breathing, beautiful, the object of her repression transformed into the subject of her own beauty, intelligence, autonomy, agency.

In this landscape of absenting realties, Makhmalbaf creates a fable of absented virtualities. Things are reduced here to their *having just been there*, and thus alerted to their *should be virtually there* – there, that is, in their mere matter of factness. Things here are their promises postponed, their hopes hollowed, their vistas blinded. Notice that there is a yellowness to this landscape of jaundiced hopes that is deserted and abandoned, blood of life sucked out of its visions of itself. In the no-wo/man-land of Makhmalbaf's Afghanistan, where men have no legs, women no face, children no future, far more tragic than limbless men is that they have nowhere to go. Far more dreadful than faceless women is that they have nothing to see. There is a deserted landscape of abandonment about Makhmalbaf's *Kandahar*. Nowhere to go, nothing to see. Where would these men go, even if they had legs? What would these women see even if they were allowed to lift their burkas? Nowhere. Nothing. Makhmalbaf's landscape is dreamy, vacated, abandoned, emptied of all the accouterments of life, perfectly set to re-narrate humanity as if from nothing. In this sisterly search for life, things lose their whereabouts. There exists nothing to go to, to see, to have, to hold, to claim or to call a culture. Makhmalbaf here is at the borderland, between two claims to authenticity, an Islamic Republic that is neither, and an Afghanistan that is worse.

With *Kandahar*, something critical about Makhmalbaf's cinematic narrative becomes incontrovertibly final. His strategic use of *virtual minimalism*, in order to offset the real, generates his trademark sur/realism (and not surrealism), where the porous borderline between fact and fantasy creatively caves into the debilitating reality and forces it to yield its otherwise. The otherwise is not dreamt out of some hallucinatory ideal in the tired streets of the cosmopolis. It is excavated like pure water out of a stubborn well in the hopeful deserts of Afghanistan. It is creatively negotiated, frivolously wrested, out of the obstinate reality itself. He patiently taps into the otherwise than reality out of the mulish seriousness of the real itself.

How precisely does a political revolutionary become a revolutionary artist? *Kandahar* contemplates that proposition. By his own recollection, Makhmalbaf failed to change the world in a way he thought it would be better off. The revolution for which he almost gave his life turned out to be a ghastly episode in modern world history. That political revolution having miserably failed, as a revolutionary artist Makhmalbaf reaches for the defining moment of history: the sense of reality that makes it move and mobilize, hope and change. The visual poetry he has now perfected to an art that distinguishes his cinema from miles away inevitably opts for a sur/realism that shakes down the hidden fantasies off all the evident facts, of reality itself, against itself: 'A Light descended upon the Earth.' Notice how Sohrab Sepehri, Makhmalbaf's kindred poetic soul, does that sur/realism verbally — it is entirely visual:

> *A Light descended upon the earth:*
> *I saw two footsteps upon the sands in the desert.*
> *Where did they come from?*
> *Where were they going?*
> *Only two footsteps were visible.*
> *Perhaps a mistake had set foot upon the earth.*
> *Suddenly the footsteps began to move.*

Light traveled with them.
The footsteps disappeared –
And I began to watch myself face to face –
A pit was filled with death;
And I began to walk in my own dead self.
I could hear the sound of my own footsteps from afar –
As if I was traveling through a desert,
A lost sense of expectation traveling along with me.
Suddenly a light descended upon my dead self
And I came to life in an anxiety:
Two footsteps filled my existence:
Where did they come from?
Where were they going?
Only two footsteps were visible.
Perhaps a mistake had set foot upon the earth.[23]

Rooted in the dream-like, self-referential, and kinetic commotions of Sohrab Sepehri's poetry, there is something *virtually archaic* about Makhmalbaf's *Kandahar*, something pre-eternal, post-eternal, about the anonymity of its faces, the open-endedness of its deserted landscape. Even though we hear Nafas speak English into her tape-recorder, see her aboard a Red Cross helicopter, and even though we run into parachutes, paramedics, and then into an idealist African–American out looking for God in the deserts of Afghanistan, a sentimental Afghan husband shopping for a pair of beautiful artificial legs that match his wife's shoes and dress, still the archaic texture of *Kandahar* remains intact, operative by virtue of the landscape it conjures up and occupies. The bare-minimum of a story-line gets completely lost in the vast desert with no beginning, no end, no rhyme, no reason. It is precisely in the *archaic virtuality* of that landscape that Makhmalbaf can reach for the bare, skeletal, bones of being-in-the-world without robbing it of its iconic proclivities. He fully recognizes the iconic components of life, before and beyond their particular codification into a 'culture.' One compelling reason that people across cultures and continents identify with *Kandahar*, and in fact with much of Makhmalbaf's cinema, is precisely because of his ability to bare the elemental forces in his (and thus any other) culture and there and then play and dance with them, take them to the party of their forgotten joys, and have them remember the hopeful promises they once made.

What makes the cultural universality of that appeal particularly powerful is rooted in the specific way in which Makhmalbaf has gradually expanded his cosmovision and in the process mutated the very idea of a national cinema, making it light and agile enough to combat the terrorism of globalizing capital and its news and culture industry. With *Kandahar*, Makhmalbaf has completed a cycle of films he has made around Iranian national territory: *A Time for Love* (1990) in Turkey, *Silence* (1998) in Tajikistan, and *Kandahar* set in Afghanistan. In addition, two of his recent short films, *The Door* (1999) and *Testing Democracy* (2000), were shot in Kish Island in the Persian Gulf, so southern to the Tehran-based imagination that it might as well have been in an island in the Indian Ocean or the Arabian Sea. Add to that constellation the third episode of Makhmalbaf's *The Peddler* (1985) and *The Cyclist* (1987), in both of which he addressed the plight of Afghan refugees, and you will have a more complete picture of his extra-territorial concerns. The result of this migratory filmmaking is an epicyclical expansion of the very idea of the *cinematic nation* and of *national cinema*. Except for a few propaganda uses to which cinema was periodically put in Iran in order to generate and sustain the idea of the monarchical nation, the schemata of the *cinematic nation* entirely disappeared from the best and most enduring aspects of Iranian cinema. An *Iranian cinema* was thus generated almost unbeknown to itself. The best that Iranian cinema could produce contributed to the collective making of this *cinematic nation*, entirely oblivious to itself. Now oblivious to himself, Makhmalbaf has made the idea of that cinematic nation palpably more evident by epicyclically identifying it, having its dominant assumptions cadence in expansive measures, via a remembrance of the Afghan, the Tajik, or any other hidden corners of its dominant repressions.

What exactly is an Iranian filmmaker doing in Tajikistan, Afghanistan, Turkey, circumambulating North, South, East, and West of the territorial imagination of his homeland? What happens to the idea of the *cinematic nation*, or *national cinema*, when its imperceptible boundaries are crossed over and thus made perceptible? The phenomenon becomes even more evident when we add the explosion of the very idea of the *center* as these peripheries are incorporated into its cosmovision. *The Cyclist* brought the question of the Afghan refugees into the center of the varied practices of the cinematic nation. Jafar Panahi's *The White Balloon* (1997), Hassan Yektapanah's *Jom'eh* (2000), and Majid Majidi's *Baran* (2001) can all be added to this central attention to peripheral boundaries. So can Samira Makhmalbaf's *Blackboard* (2000) about the Iraqi victims of Saddam Hussein's chemical warfare, and Bahman Qobadi's *A Time for Drunken Horses* (2000) about the predicament of the Kurds, a people without a homeland. As in these films, the very idea of the center sinks and its peripheries metamorphose, so is the very assumption of the *cinematic nation* challenged and with it the viability of a *national cinema*, of Iranian cinema as a case in point. A prominent Iranian filmmaker makes a film about the status of women in Afghanistan, finances it by a French producer and distributor, premiers it in Cannes Film Festival in France, and from there it starts circulating the world, with a stopover in Iran, before the events of September the Eleventh and October the Seventh make it a global sensation. The phenomenon is a textbook case of globalization, with the corresponding ideas of *cinematic nation, national cinema,* and ultimately *nation* itself completely collapsing and superceded. The event can make cinema as much an instrument of cultural pacification, aka globalization, as it can sublate cinema into a site of effective resistance against globalization. It is a guerilla tactic of planting a Trojan Horse in the belly of globalizing capital. Makhmalbaf received a couple of peanuts for *Kandahar* compared with the farm that The Wild Bunch now controls. Meanwhile *Kandahar* can be the template of the very vaccine that globalizing capital carries, like a pharmakon, which if not destroyed by the beast it may actually cure it.

So no – no *transaesthetics of indifference* here. Allow the *democratic improvisation* that is beginning to take shape in Iranian cinema, and through the Iranian cinema in the rest of its culture, to mark its global reception and it will be conducive to anything but a *transaesthetics of indifference.* For the Persian aesthetics operative in Iranian cinema to translate for a global reception, the Aristotelian mimesis at the core of the European reception of it will have to allow for a mode of mimetic modulation of reality that is neither real nor unreal, neither factual nor fantastic – it is a mimesis that takes reality too seriously to take it seriously.

Baring the Beautiful

Gadamer's insight that our encounter with *the beautiful* assures us that 'the truth does not lie far off and inaccessible to us, but can be encountered in the disorder of reality with all its imperfections, evils, errors, extremes, and fateful confusions'[24] points to a conception of the aesthetic more immediately accessible to mortal and fallible souls. But that conception of *the beautiful* implicates all of us, whether artists or mortals, in articulating a work of art as *will to resist power,* without collapsing it into the mere dialectical negation of power. Makhmalbaf comes from a culture whose enduring traits of charismatic terror he has now successfully sublated into blissful moments of *democratic improvisation.* The melodic agility and the imaginal opulence of that improvisatory genius does not allow itself to be completely digested by the culture and news industry it ordinarily mobilizes. Makhmalbaf uses the tyrannical forces of a culture against itself with the same alacrity that he gives imaginative indigestion to the operative machinery of the news and culture industry. The local culture provides him with a burka to conceal a woman's beauty, intelligence, and agency. He uses it to accentuate that beauty, exude that intelligence, and restore that agency. The global culture of violence, death, and destruction generates squadrons of legless men who can barely walk. He choreographs and conducts them through a ballet. Legless men dance, face-less women are shown to be stunningly beautiful, intelligent, and in charge of their own destiny. When reality is richer than fiction, when the deadly destruction of two towering buildings, gentle giants gracing a global cosmopolis, is staged as the operatic orchestration of a cosmic vengeance, when statues of Nirvanic serenity are violently destroyed and crumbled to dust, how else can art reciprocate except teasing beauty out of ugliness, sighting light in blinding darkness. This Makhmalbaf's art achieves by an orchestral choreography of signs that never collapse into signifiers, signs signating *ad glorium*, planting themselves in the imaginative topography of our future memories, never dissolving, always suggestive, now in our dreams, then in our hopes.

Baudrillard is wrong in his assessment that we no longer have access to the ugly or the beautiful, to truth or to falsehood – if we allow that 'we' to expand the geography of its imagination and re-map the planet. The 'we' that Baudrillard pronounces is too White, too European, too much trapped in the 'Western' delusions of its Enlightenment modernity and its catastrophic consequences in its presumed cosmopolitan centers. Linking the depth of its own vertical colonization and its alienated, horizontally colonized, otherness, is a solid base from which we – now expanded democratically to include a re-mapped planet – can tell and trace the beautiful from the ugly, the truth from falsehood. We are not condemned to a *transaesthetics of indifference* if we are not like Berlusconi and Fallaci, and can see and celebrate the beautiful in more than one geography of inherited reflexes. Instead of robbing Makhmalbaf of his aesthetics in Cannes, or shredding it to pieces elsewhere, for fear of indigestion, we need to allow for that in his art that defies augury. We have to open a space for it to show itself. It is the prophetic delivery of itself. *The rich asceticism* of his art reveals the mere matter-of-factness of being, the translucent gaze of the otherwise, ready to be stolen like light from the heart of darkness. We need not know that Makhmalbaf extends this feature of his art from the heart of Persian Gnosticism where the juridical fear of God is transmuted into the injudicious love of God. All we have to know is how he turns the fear of death into love of life, just like his poetic ancestor, Omar Khayyám, the brevity of whose poetic diction is now the soul of Makhmalbaf's wit.

There is a solitary space that a work of art occupies in the world from which it can soothe pains and grace hopes without falling into fear. A work of art is of the world but not in the world. There is something perilous about a work of art when it suddenly becomes an object of public curiosity. It is in danger of losing its touch, missing its point, abandoning its hope. Never in his entire prolific career will Makhmalbaf make another film that will so put every iota of his creative intellect on the line the way *Kandahar* did. The film is now a political football way beyond its creator's control, as indeed it is the insubstantial subject of a global and globalizing gaze. Whether or not it will endure under so much abusive attention is a question that points to something more than the creative powers of its maker. The question marks a cosmic repression of hope having returned to restore a nation to dignity, and with that nation oscillates the rest of the world.

Flash Back

Conclusion

There was a wandering dervish who would occasionally visit our neighborhood in Ahvaz when I was a child and to whom I had a frightful attraction. I was at once mesmerized by his appearance and demeanor – the way he walked, the melodic casuistry with which he sang the praise of our Shi'i saints and Imams, with his coarse and carefree voice – and yet I was frightened out of my wits by the very same apparition that every once in a while would appear out of nowhere and then as imperceptively disappear into the thin air. He wore black, top to toe, sported a thick black and free-flowing beard, and carried a *kashkul* (a sort of sturdy handheld bag) that was also black. Inside his *kashkul*, Dervish Mowla Ali, as he was popularly known, always had these white little sweets we call *noql* in Persian. My late mother had an unsurpassed belief in the miraculous properties of these *noqls*. 'Run along and give him this money,' she would say and dispatch me with some change she had handy – and I would do as she said, approach Dervish Mowla Ali politely, excitedly, carefully, almost reverently, say my greetings ('salaam arz mikonam Dervish Mowla Ali'), and gently dare to approach his *kashkul* and drop the coins my mother had given me without daring even to breath, let alone look inside it. What wondrous things he might have carried inside that *kashkul*, other than those sweet and miraculous *noqls*! A subterranean labyrinth, I always imagined, opened up from that *kashkul*, hanging loosely as it was from a chain handle, swinging gently on Dervish Mowla Ali's left wrist. 'Pir shi Pesaram,' he would say with a noble and lofty generosity to his voice, 'May you grow and become an old man, my son!' 'Mowlam Ali negahdaret/May my master Ali protect you!' And then as my mind was wandering on an imaginary journey through his *kashkul*, his eyes began to smile from the deep sockets of their whereabouts and without lifting his fearful and gentle eyes from me he would reach inside his kashkul, fish out a handful of *noqls* and hand them to me – 'Shirin kam bashi Baba Janam!/May you always taste sweetness in your life, my son!'

To this day, Dervish Mowla Ali remains in my mind the very definition of that moment of the uncanny when we are attracted to a person, a phenomenon, a memory, or a work of art and yet we have no clue exactly why, or that alternatively we are afraid of that person, phenomenon, memory, etc. and yet we cannot fathom exactly why. The uncanny disposition itself is not as important as the fact that it is productive, generative, proliferating – though not in its own terms. It is like the ignition key of a car. Once the engine starts, the ignition key has done its task and disappears from the scene – where we go with that car is almost entirely independent of the science and the technology that has started its engine. In that moment of bewilderment and curiosity that the uncanny upholds and subsumes, dwells much emotive and aesthetic mystery that must perhaps be left unraveled. A few years ago I spent many blissful days at Fundació Joan Miró in Barcelona looking at Miró's paintings incessantly – walking up and down the galleries, day after day, not knowing quite why, somewhat sleepwalking through the sinuous shapes, forms, and colors of his curiosities. I had a similarly fearful attraction to the entirety of Miró's paintings, but particularly to his very last works, and specifically to three huge canvases on which he had drawn three diagonal lines – one diagonal line per huge white canvas – and to me those three lines summoned the entirety of his work – the mystery and magic of his lifetime achievements. When I first went for a visit to Miró's museum it was an entirely innocent and casual visit. When I started going there day after day, I had no idea what I was looking for – and when I finally emerged with a vision of his lifework, from beginning to end, I had no clue how precious, how enduring, was the experience.

Mortality, immortality, fear of the unknown, joy of the unexpected – the unwarranted accidentality of discovering something you never knew existed: here the personal become public, the individual collective – and the work of art its artist. Come to think of it, I have been thinking, watching, reading, and writing Makhmalbaf soon after I met him in Locarno in August 1996, accelerated after my visit to Miró's museum in Barcelona in January 2001, and all by way of actively remembering Dervish Mowla Ali of my childhood in Ahvaz to whose enduring memory I still attach that unending sense of the uncanny – and for the life of me I still cannot remember where in the world he came from and into what ethereal space he disappeared.

Returning to Paris

On 6 December 2005 I flew from New York to Istanbul, and from there to Nicosia (or what the locals call Lefkosa) in northern Cyprus as the guest of the Rumi Institute in the Near East University – in the Turkish part of Cyprus. The Turkish Cypriots consider this part of Nicosia as the capital of what they call 'the Turkish Republic of Northern Cyprus,' which is actually a 'country' that no country in the world recognizes except Turkey. I was here as the guest of the Rumi Institute and as part of an international conference on the legendary mystic Mawlana Jalal al-Din Rumi. The highlight of my trip was meeting Neshat Celebi, the twenty-third descendent of Mawlana Jalal al-Din Rumi himself – a splendid young basketball and soccer fan full of wonders and joy. I had a relatively long and simple conversation with him about his life, his ancestry and how best he might put his new responsibilities as the leader of the Mevlevi Order to promote peace in major trouble spots around the world. There was a sizeable Palestinian student body at this university.

While I was in Cyprus, I called Makhmalbaf in Paris and once the conference was over, on 11 December 2005, I flew from Nicosia to Istanbul, and thence to Paris to spend a few days with him. I had not seen him for over two years, since Cannes 2003, when we were all there for the premier of Samira Makhmalbaf's *Panj-e Asr/At Five in the Afternoon* (2003) and Siddiq Barmak's *Osama* (2003). When I called him from Cyprus and asked for his Paris address, we were both reminded of Sohrab Sepehri's poem, *Vaheh-'i dar Lahzeh/An Oasis in the Moment*. It is strange how Sepehri has been with us all along: 'Beh Soragh-e Man Agar Mi-a'id/Posht-e Hichestanam,' Sepehri says in the first stanza of the poem, 'If you were to come visit me/I live just behind Nowhereville.'

Once I had arrived at Charles de Gaulle Airport, I took a cab and told him where to go – a suburban neighborhood called Montrouge, near a place called Place des États-Unis, about an hour or so from the airport. For about two years now, Makhmalbaf has effectively moved to Paris and lives in this neighborhood. This is of course as much as one can actually consider Makhmalbaf's life stationary, which it is not. He still navigates his days and life somewhere in the midst of Paris, European film festival circuits, Afghanistan, Tajikistan, India, and anywhere else around the globe (except the USA, where he has sworn never to go again) that care to show his films. The ascetic impermanence that has always been about him seems written into his character no matter where exactly he calls home. At this particular time, when in mid-December 2005 I was on my way to spend a few days with him, he was alone in Paris; his wife Marziyeh Meshkini and youngest daughter Hana were in Tehran, their elder daughter Samira and her husband were in London studying language, while his son Meysam was also in London taking courses in finance and business administration, effectively to run the financial aspects of the Makhmalbaf Film House. They all had a post-production studio in Dushanbe, Tajikistan, an assortment of facilities in Afghanistan for when they went shooting there, and an equally important post-production set of facilities in India, to which Makhmalbaf has always been attracted. His most recent films have been written in Paris, shot in Tajikistan, Afghanistan, and India, with post-production mostly done in India, and then the finished product brought to Paris to submit to various film festivals, with The Wild Bunch still the production company mostly interested in their work. In

Makhmalbaf's film, fiction, and character, medieval Persian ascetic mysticism and postmodern globalization have a strange but palpable rendezvous.

When the cab reached Place des États-Unis neighborhood and as I started looking around for street signs for where he lived, I suddenly saw Makhmalbaf himself walking toward my cab. I got out of the cab, we exchanged greetings, went to his home, dropped off my small green backpack and went immediately out for our habitual long and brisk walk, where our words and steps commingle and interchange pace and purpose. The weather was quite cold, the sky gray and tight, and the neighborhood strange and alienating. But as always, our surroundings soon disappeared into the thicket of our conversations – about art, politics, cinema, literature, poetry, our children – his involvements with Afghanistan, my preoccupations with Palestine. 'What sort of a neighborhood is this?', I asked him casually. 'It's a subway ride away from Quartier Latin,' he said. 'Looks like Sepehri's Nowhereville', I prompted him, and we were at it before we knew it:

> Just behind Nowhereville
> There is a place –
> Just behind Nowhereville
> The veins of the air are full
> Of flying dandelion seeds
> Bringing the good news
> Of the flower
> Of the most distant bushes of the earth –
> Having just bloomed.[1]

We both had much to report and much to catch up. He had made two long feature films and a short since I saw him last, which I had not yet seen. We went to a restaurant in his neighborhood, near the subway station, had a quick meal, and then decided to go back to his apartment to start watching his films that I had not seen. But before we did that, he suggested we go out to a nearby sauna and swimming pool. 'You look too tired. You need to relax before watching my films.' His long-time friend and now neighbor in Paris, Kazem Moussavi, drove us to a swimming and sauna place – an amazing in- and outdoor pool, hot and splendid in the dead of winter. We entered an indoor pool, warm and inviting, and then through an opening we swam into an open-air pool, in the dead of winter – the outside temperature was subzero, but the water in the pool kept your body pleasantly warm. We swam, chatted, reminisced, and relaxed. There was a childish frivolity about it all – a sense of suspended animation, a light-heartedness and a joy I had not quite felt for a long time. From the pool we went to a small sauna cubical inside the same facility. 'You know my father was a public bath attendant,' he said, as we looked for a place to sit down in the sauna room. 'Yes I do.'

After the swimming and sauna, we drove back to his home and over a splendid feast of nun-o-panir-o cha'i (baguette, feta cheese, and sweetened tea) we sat down on the floor of his living room and together watched his most recent film Faryad-e Morchegan/Scream of the Ants (2006). He had a huge, flat television in his living room, with an assortment of DVD and video equipment, all connected through a panoply of anarchic and rebellious wires – but the picture was perfect, the sound crystal clear, and the neighborhood quite calm and quiet. As I put a cushion under me to be more comfortable when watching the movie, he went to the kitchen and brought me a cup of tea and handed me a fistful of noqls. 'These just came from Iran.'

Scream of the Ants was yet to be premiered. Makhmalbaf had an initial cut ready, which we were about to watch together. Scream of the Ants returns to Makhmalbaf's earliest cinema – full of passionate intensity – but this time it projects an absolutist and flamboyant metaphysical break with Islam, let alone with any Islamic Revolution or an Islamic Republic; and thus as all acts of metaphysical break ups it becomes exceedingly metaphysical itself. For all intents and purposes, in Scream of the Ants Makhmalbaf protests too much. A newly-wed couple travel to India for their honeymoon. A religiously attuned and yet erotically assertive bride, and a groom who is professedly atheist but consistently preoccupied with religious doctrines make for quite a colorful but ultimately self-indulgent journey through a metaphysical encounter with India. Mahnour (Mahnour Shadzi) and Mahmoud (Mahmoud Chokrollahi) are two young Iranians who have come to India for their honeymoon, and yet they end up spending their precious time searching for Ensan-e Kamel ('the perfect human being') – a mystical designation at once abstract and vacuous, and yet imaginatively compelling and curious. While in India, the couple decide to renew their marriage vow and pursue their quest, probing into each other's soul – leaving each other's bodies terra incognita – and thus revealing Makhmalbaf's own renewed preoccupations with abstract metaphysics, however visually more compelling, but still quite disconcerting for an artist at the height of his craft.

Perhaps the most jarring aspect of Scream of the Ants (a problem Makhmalbaf acknowledged and sought to address soon after this viewing by making an additional set of cuts throughout the film) is the almost unwatchable bad acting of the two lead actors – particularly the husband. A bit of behind-the-scene information that Makhmalbaf gave me about these actors and their off-screen background may in part account for this really terrible acting. But the trouble with Scream of the Ants is only exacerbated by their bad acting, and is rooted in Makhmalbaf's own post-Kandahar uncertainties, undoubtedly confounded by his circumambulatory (I hesitate to call it exilic) life. The aesthetic formalism of

Makhmalbaf, to be sure, is still at its absolute and most mature best here in *Scream of the Ants*. The opening shot of the film, with a black glove covering the eyes of Mahnour while she is sitting on a chair over a railroad track, will remain among the best that Makhmalbaf has ever shot – and there are many such shots scattered throughout the film. Such sublime moments of formalism, however, are not consistent; the middle part of the film, when the couple reaches Bombay, breaks into an unseemly realism that jars the visual registers of the story and reveals the absence of any visionary awareness of the film in its entirety, which minutes into its beginning, slides ever so deeply into a self-indulgent crisis of faith of which no-one could care less from where it has originated or where it is going.

After we watched *Scream of the Ants*, Makhmalbaf also showed me a short film he had made, *Sandali/Chair* (2006), while he was making *Scream of the Ants*. In *Chair*, the same couple who are in *Scream of the Ants* appear in a single sequence of equally compelling, almost breathless, metaphysics – mostly overwhelmed by the young groom's preoccupation with God, His presence, absence, necessity, or moral requisition. Again, there are some stunning shots of sands and dunes in this short as well, and there are an uncanny number of occasions when Makhmalbaf's camera has fun with these two 'ants' running along the sands. But ultimately the short fails precisely on the same grounds where the longer version fails – two hopeless, graceless, boring, and banal people stranger to themselves than they are to us, doing as Makhmalbaf's renewed fixation with absolutist terms of belief, conviction, truth, and reality tells them to do. They all fail – Makhmalbaf, his actors, his story – and no matter how his by now perhaps intuitive camera catches moments of pure cinematic bliss, they do not gel, will not come together, and scatter for a yard-sale in the backyard of an otherwise astonishing cinematic career. Judged by this film, here in Paris, there in Afghanistan, or else in India, Makhmalbaf did not seem to be at home in his own craft anymore. He was perhaps intuitively repeating himself – and his creative courage seemed to have shied away from his worldly whereabouts. He has always been not at home at home. Exile is an innate, not an acquired, condition to him. Paris here or Afghanistan, Tajikistan, and India there are all extensions of farther circumambulatory distances he has always kept from his childhood neighborhood in Iran. But the crisis of faith that preoccupied Mahmoud in *Scream of the Ants* was simply too prosaic to amount to a worldly awareness.

I was now very tired, but because we were 'on a roll' we decided to watch the other film of Makhmalbaf that I had not seen yet, *Sex-o-Falsafeh/Sex and Philosophy* (2005), premiered at the Montreal International Film Festival in Canada earlier that year. *Sex and Philosophy* is by far the most sensually throbbing film of Makhmalbaf today. It is a romantic film of unusual contemplative texture. It is the most sustained visual reflection on the nature and function of love in Makhmalbaf's oeuvre – carrying to their formalist conclusions themes that he had

34   *Maryam Gaibova as Maryam in Moshen Makhmalbaf's Sex va Falsafeh (Sex and Philosophy, 2005). A taboo subject, dealt with in a film made outside the boundaries of the Islamic Republic. (Photograph: Hana Makhmalbaf; courtesy of Makhmalbaf Film House.)*

first initiated in *A Time for Love* (1991). A middle-aged man, celebrating his fortieth birthday all by himself, decides to invite four women with whom he has had romantic involvements to his dance class. On the premise of this simple plot, and as each woman enters and exists in the man's dance class, Makhmalbaf seeks to reach for a manner of bodily reflection on the nature and disposition of love and sensuality – and by extension life and death. *Sex and Philosophy* is infinitely more successful than *Scream of the Ants* and exudes a probing confidence on part of Makhmalbaf in exploring bodily reflections. The film in effect thrives on a corporeal manner of thinking, turning the human body, as *corpus eroticus*, into an instrument of contemplative reflection. *Sex and Philosophy* still suffers from Makhmalbaf's over-intellectualization of love – that it is impermanent, transitory, relative, withering, and such – but this time the film is saved by an accidental curiosity on the part of Makhmalbaf when he lets his visual uncertainties dance freely with his fascination with the moving, mobile, and dancing human body. That directorial curiosity effectively saves the film, no matter how self-indulgent the middle-aged man might appear in testing the boundaries of love and lust, and with that the patience of his audience. There is an elegant quietude about the film, perhaps best evident in a virtuoso aerial long shot where Makhmalbaf's camera chases after the middle-aged man and one of his lovers, which piously studies the sinuous corners of silence, where the human body begins to exude a different significance.

We chatted a bit more after *Sex and Philosophy* was over, and then said goodnight. I went to bed tired and exhausted, but oscillating in my mind between hope and despair as to what was happening to Makhmalbaf's cinema. After *Kandahar* (2001) and Makhmalbaf's increasing attention to Afghanistan, his territorial connections to Iran had been radically uprooted. He was incessantly shedding skin, one layer after another, a normative and emotive mode of successive ecdysis, exuviating one shade of ideas and sentiments, affiliations and convictions, after another. Constant, however, it seemed to me, was this bizarre fixation with the metaphysical, with the presence or absence of a God he desperately sought to ascertain, and the more he tried the less convinced or convincing he had become. Was his lost and forsaken faith, his Islam, coming back to haunt his cinema? Did he ever get over his Islamism? Was this the memory of his grandmother – foreboding, lovingly tyrannical, fanatical, forbidding him ever to go see a movie – coming back to avenge his disregard? These questions were unsettling. Oscillating between politics and aesthetics, it now seemed to me, can be as much reinvigorating and life-affirming as it might degenerate into a mode of escapism, not knowing quite where to call home. I remembered Sepehri again:

> Just behind Nowhereville
> There is a place . . .
> There upon the sands
> March the traces of horses' hoofs –
> Horses of delicate riders
> That early in the morning
> Have galloped high
> To the top of the hill
> There to witness
> The nocturnal ascends of poppy flower
> To the heavens.[2]

Oh! Incurable metaphysicians that we are – even in the most sacrosanct moments of our impieties!

The following day, 12 December, soon after breakfast, we started watching *Sag-ha-ye Velgard/Stray Dogs* (2003), Marziyeh Meshkini's astounding second feature. The small girl and her dog at the center of Meshkini's film, very much reminiscent of Vittorio De Sica's *Umberto D.* (1952), will remain in world cinema. Two Afghan kids, a brother and a sister, their mother in prison for having married a man thinking her first husband dead, while their father was a Taleb and in jail, all come together to make a perfect film. Premiered at the Venice Film Festival in 2004, *Stray Dogs* is the story of these two homeless kids who report to jail in the evening both to be with their incarcerated mother and to have a roof over their head. When they finally are refused entry to the prison unless they commit a crime, they go about town, wondering how to get back to the jail. Taking their clue from another Vittorio De Sica masterpiece, *The Bicycle Thief* (1948), they try to steal a bicycle but in a manner that they are caught and sent to jail to their mother. The extraordinarily balanced and poised mannerism of Marziyeh Meshkini's *Stray Dogs* is very much reminiscent of Makhmalbaf's best cinema, in close vicinity of which his wife has now perfected her own unique and perceptive cinema. We spent the rest of the day with Mamad Haghighat in Quartier Latin, where he runs a movie theater, and had dinner at a French–Algerian café – talking mostly about Makhmalbaf's recent visit with Mohammad Khatami, the ex-president of the Islamic Republic.

The next day, 13 December, I saw a series of behind-the-scene documentaries that various European, Japanese, and Korean television networks have made about Makhmalbaf, his family, and their collective work, particularly in Afghanistan. As I was watching these documentaries, I noted that altogether we now have the following films made by Makhmalbaf and his family about Afghanistan: Mohsen's *The Cyclist* (1989), *Kandahar* (2001), and *Afghan Alphabet* (2002); Samira's *At Five in the Afternoon* (2003); Marziyeh Meshkini's *Stray Dogs* (2003); and Hana's *Joy of Madness* (2003) – to which we can then add Siddiq Barmak's *Osama* (2003).[3] This is quite a unique phenomenon – a complete transplantation of an entire family of filmmakers from their own homeland into another country as the site of their socially responsible filmmaking career. The project has a dual character to it: first and foremost, for Makhmalbaf and his family Afghanistan is a simulacrum of Iran, where their collective endeavors still have a social purpose and a global audience; equally important is the role that Afghanistan plays as a surrogate of the Islamic Republic, where the Makhmalbafs cinematically contemplate what they cannot articulate inside their own homeland. Afghanistan in many significant ways is still a *terra incognita* where things can go one way or another, and as such it is the no-man's-land of Makhmalbaf's revolutionary disposition, where his life and career finds meaning and purpose, and where he is hoping to get right what he missed in Iran.

On the same day we had a luncheon meeting with Reza Deghati, the legendary Iranian photographer, whom I did not know personally. I had no clue that he was in fact a good friend of Makhmalbaf's. The two of them were cellmates in Pahlavi prison. Having just received France's highest cultural distinction, the Légion d'Honneur (a recognition that Makhmalbaf had also received years earlier), Reza Deghati's camera has been the eye of the world's conscience in some of the most troubled spots, including, most recently, Lebanon and Afghanistan. Makhmalbaf and I first took the subway to Reza Deghati's office at Rue Haxo, where I met him and his staff, including his assistant Roshanak Bahramlou, and where we learned about their extraordinary project in Afghanistan, through a forum called *Ayeneh* –

an educational enterprise dedicated to the education of children and young adults in Afghanistan. The image of Mohsen Makhmalbaf and Reza Deghati having come together in Pahlavi dungeons first, and then their paths separated only to come together again in their mutual work in Afghanistan, pretty much sums up an entire generation of Iranian political activists whose work easily mutated into the realm of art, education, and cultural struggles. After a tour of Reza Deghati's office and archives, the three of us went out to lunch at a nearby restaurant (where we all ordered identical pizza). Makhmalbaf and Deghati began reminiscing about their time in jail together. One of the most memorable stories that Deghati told us that day, when he learned that I lived and taught in New York, was how the very first word he had learned in English was 'torture;' the reason for that was because while they were in prison he wanted to tell a Red Cross official who was visiting them that they were being tortured in the Pahlavi dungeons. '*Shekanjeh beh Engelisi chi misheh, Bacheh-ha,*' he had asked his cellmates, 'Hey guys, what's "torture" in English?' Once he learns the word, he keeps repeating it to the Red Cross official – 'torture, we are being tortured, torture.' The way that Deghati and his friends kept repeating the word 'torture' with their Persian pronunciation was very close to something like 'torcheh,' which in turn sounds very similar to the way Azari-speaking Iranians pronounce the word 'Torkeh' which means 'the Turkish one.' As it happened, they had a warden who was in fact Azari Iranian, to whom the Tehranis (in a condescending and derogatory manner) referred as 'a Turk,' and who took the word torture/torcheh as referring to him, thinking that the prisoners were complaining to the Red Cross official about him personally. 'What's wrong with Torcheh [with being a Turk]?' the warden had wondered, which to the Red Cross official amounted to 'What's wrong with torture.' The comedy of errors, predicated on a macabre sense of arrested humor, now years after their boyish imprisonment was exceedingly funny to both Deghati and Makhmalbaf, as they now remembered such incidents in the autumnal grayness of their sedate manners and memories. The nobility of their continued causes and noble struggles seemed to have kept them both forever young.

In the evening of that day we sat down together and saw several short Afghan films that had just been sent to Makhmalbaf from Afghanistan. These were mostly by young filmmakers whom he had taken under his wings and trained in a variety of ways. These films ranged from rudimentary to astoundingly competent and well-crafted.

The next day, 14 December, we both got up quite late in the morning. Soon after breakfast, Makhmalbaf began reading to me a seemingly endless number of scripts he had written over the past couple of years. This is a ritual we have done many times. He first tells me a one-line synopsis of a script, then he reads it out loud to me, and at the end he asks me to rank it in comparison with others he has just read and who I think should make it: Marziyeh, Samira, Hana, or he himself. The first time we did this together, in the summer of 1997 in his home in Tehran, I remember I fell asleep halfway through a script, and kept dreaming the rest of the script while still hearing his voice.

Later that day we went to Quartier Latin to have coffee with Mamad Haghighat. We saw a Korean film in his theater, but we left halfway through it. Makhmalbaf and I have never been able to sit in a movie theater and see a single film together completely, even (or particularly) when we are at Cannes. We become fidgety, start talking to each other, soon lose the plot and then interest, and we leave the theater and resume whatever conversation we were having before. It seems to me that he and I have always watched various works in progress, his or someone else's. The finished product, a completed and polished film, seems to be too much of a done-deal to engage with in any sustained manner. While I was in Paris, Mamad Haghighat also brought a film by a student of Amir Naderi in New York, which Naderi wanted us all to see. Halfway through the film, though, Makhmalbaf's system did not like the DVD and we lost the pictures.

The following day, 15 December, we went down to Institute du Monde Arab at Rue des Fossés-Saint-Bernard and got several Palestinian films for Mohsen to see. Ever since my involvement with Palestinian cinema, this has emerged as a major point of conversation between us. In particular, I was quite anxious for him to see Elia Suleiman. Years ago we had seen Michel Khleifi's *Wedding in Galilee* (1987) in New York and Suleiman's *Chronicle of a Disappearance* (1996) in Paris together. But I was anxious for him to see other Palestinian films as well. We purchased the films and went back to his apartment to watch them. But still his system did not work. There was something the matter with it. Makhmalbaf called his son Meysam in London to see if he could tell us how to fix it. Meysam is something of an engineering guru. But we still could not get the system working. We would have audio but no pictures. Later that evening, we went back to Quartier Latin and had dinner with Mamad Haghighat at a local Iranian restaurant. The owner was so excited that Makhmalbaf was there that he did not tell us that his kitchen was down – he went out and bought us Lebanese *shwarma* for dinner. It was a cold *shwarma*, in a cold restaurant, in the company of a quiet conversation, with the owner of the restaurant and what appeared to be his family overlooking our reluctant bites. I looked at Makhmalbaf and we remembered:

> Just behind Nowhereville
> The umbrella of desire is wide open:
> And as soon as the very breathing suggestion
> Of thirst
> Runs through the stem of a leaf
> The chime of rain starts ringing.[4]

35 *Mohsen Makhmalbaf directing* Faryad-e Morchegan (Scream of the Ants, 2006). (*Photograph courtesy of Makhmalbaf Film House.*)

The next day, 16 December, we stayed mostly at home and worked. We went out for a brief walk and coffee, and then came home and waited for Makhmalbaf's daughter Samira and her husband Mehrdad Zonnur, who were coming for a visit from London. I spent the next two days mostly catching up with Samira's news. Her cinematic career was now much less of a priority, and she was attending to her personal and private life.

On Sunday 18 December, I woke up very early in the morning, packed, and said goodbye to Makhmalbaf, Samira, and her husband. As I hugged and kissed Makhmalbaf goodbye, I remembered (but kept it quiet to myself) the final stanza of Sepehri's poem:

> Humans are lonely here —
> And in this loneliness
> The shadow of an elm tree
> Runs all the way to eternity.
> If you were to come visit me,
> Come gently and softly — and do
> Beware lest the delicate china of my solitude
> Be cracked![5]

I collected my green backpack, jumped into a cab that had been ordered for me the night before, headed to Charles de Gaulle Airport, and from their flew home to New York. In my pocket, I had a fistful of noqls Makhmalbaf had given me just before I left. 'These are for your tea in the airplane.'

The Discoverer of the Mine of Morning

Midway to New York and suspended in the air, I woke up from a short but sweet nap thinking that the aesthetic emancipation at the heart of Makhmalbaf's generation of filmmakers, even at their most political moments, is rooted in a poetic realism that has defined the entire cultural character of Iran in the twentieth century. I asked a stewardess for a cup of tea and started sipping it with the handful of noqls Makhmalbaf had put in my pocket just before I left. In that poetic realism, I thought, beauty and banality, poetics and politics, the manners of aesthetics and the matters of history, are all invariably intertwined, inseparable, metamorphic. And then I remembered the following part of Sepehri's magnificent poem, To the Garden of Fellow Travelers (1967):

> In these dark alleys
> I am frightened
> By the multiplication of suspicion and matches.
> I am frightened
> Of the concrete surface of this century.
> Come
> So I won't be afraid of cities
> Whose dark soil is the prairie of heavy-duty cranes.
> Open me
> Like a door opening
> To the descent of a pear
> In the age of the ascent of steel.
> Put me to sleep
> Under the branch of a tree
> Far from the night of the striking of metals
> Against each other — and
> Wake me up
> If the discoverer of the mine of morning
> Comes along — and
> I will wake up
> In the dawn of a jasmine flower
> That will grow on the back of your fingers.
> And then tell me
> About the bombs that were dropped
> While I was asleep —

And tell me
About the cheeks that became wet with tears
While I was asleep –
And tell me
How many seagulls were frightened
And flew away over the sea
When the tanks rolled over the dreams of children – or
Upon what emotion did the canary tie the thread of its song?
And then tell me
What innocent goods arrived in the waterfront – and
What science was it that discovered
The positive music in the smell of dynamite – or
What understanding of the mysterious taste of bread
Was it that spread in the palate of prophecy?
And then I –
Like a faith warm by the heat of the equator –
Will sit you at the gate of the garden.[6]

Like a Ray of Light Through the Thick of Darkness

Like a ray of light through the thick of darkness, a light integral to that darkness, the darkness definitive to that light: that is how I have always thought of Mohsen Makhmalbaf and his cinema, a life and an art that are the autobiography of a nation at war with itself, at odds with its own destiny – and rightly so.

To me, Mohsen Makhmalbaf will always remain a paradox, and it is precisely that paradox that has first and foremost attracted me to his film and fiction. Early in his cinematic career, he represented the most fanatical devotion to an Islamism that categorically denied and repressed the Iranian cosmopolitan culture, a fanaticism that went fascist in its derive for power, murdering cold-bloodedly all its ideological alternatives. From the depth of that hell-hole, Makhmalbaf emerged in his cinema as a beacon of hope for a nation he could not but call his people.

It is in the way that Makhmalbaf's film and fiction is deeply rooted in the historical fate of his people that I think his career as a revolutionary artist will have to be assayed. From the early nineteenth century and well into the first decade of the twenty-first, Iran as a nation-state and Iranians as a people inhabiting this domain have been caught in a major paradox. While their society, polity, economy, and culture at large have become increasingly and incessantly globalized and cosmopolitan, their state apparatus and civil society are yet to achieve the most basic institutions of a liberal democracy. The gap between the two opposing sides of this paradox is increasingly pulling it toward a universal awareness of its cosmopolitanism in one direction, while the other holds it rooted in a recalcitrant authoritarianism with a false claim to authenticity. The gap is filled by a creative imagination mapping out the contours and the creative character of phantom liberties that hold the very idea of 'Iran' as a nation afloat and moving. Radical revolutionaries, liberal reformists, tyrannical monarchs, theocratic clerics have all come along and joined poets, novelists, filmmakers, dramatists, and artists alternating between visions and nightmares of how to overcome this paradox. Makhmalbaf happened to Iranian cinema at a time when his restless and phantasmagoric creative imagination vastly navigated from the depth of all its basest denomination to the height of all its aspirations. With one film after another – some the vista of a metaphysical culture of anger and alienation and others the ecstasy of an aesthetic of emancipation – Makhmalbaf has produced a variegated landscape of the fears and aspirations of Iranians as a people. He emerged from the very depth of his nation, and the further he has traveled in the world the closer he gets to the dreams and nightmares of his own people. The limits of his imagination are the parameters of his people's fear of the material history and hopes to transcend and overcome it. One revolution after another, one military coup succeeding another, one dreadful monarchy giving way to one more horrid theocracy, it is a miracle that Iranians as a people can still dream and call their interpretations an Abbas Kiarostami one day or a Mohsen Makhmalbaf another. We Iranians remain a people – connected, cantankerous, divergent, and miasmatic – precisely because of these creative egos we keep naming, calling, coding, decoding, and interpreting. If for millennia and for generations we have dreamed and dared our cultural elements in Persian, Arabic, Kurdish, or Turkish, nowadays we have also learned to dare even more uncharted elements in visual and performing terms, in languages we never knew how to learn, speak, read, or write – and in that very vein, as our cinema has become globalized, English too has become one among many other Iranian languages.

The ultimate appeal of Makhmalbaf will always remain far more as a rebel rather than merely as a filmmaker. As a filmmaker, his cinema ebbs and flows. As an artist, he will remain significant only to the degree that we can connect his art to his earliest and enduring revolutionary aspirations. 'I have found in cinema,' he is fond of saying, 'what I failed to find in the mosque.' His cinema from beginning to end is an unfolding tableau of his rebellious and restless dreams. He was too impatient with the world to be an effective partisan revolutionary. Having paid his penance for his earliest revolutionary rashness and zeal with four and a half years in prison, he immediately turned to art, where in his cinema he could continue to dream, interpret, and fix the world in a much more viable environment. Perhaps he is the very last revolutionary that Iran will ever produce. Perhaps his cinema is the visual simulacrum of all the feasible, potential, and plausible revolutionaries dreaming and projecting themselves out into the unfolding history. Perhaps running out of historical energy, the tired wisdom of all revolutionaries who have for decades and centuries sought to change and managed only to mar the world even deeper, has finally opted to transcend the evident violence in all revolutionary utopias into the hidden synergy that holds every one of Makhmalbaf's films together. 'There is something of that 17-year-old daring rashness that once tried to knife a police officer in your cinema,' I once told Makhmalbaf, while we were having tea at a café in Paris. He smiled. 'How so?' he wondered. 'He cuts to the chase,' I said. I have seen Makhmalbaf actually cut. Once I looked over his shoulder while he was re-editing a scene in *Silence*. He cuts with a staccato whipping between his hands and his eyes, slicing the scene and pacing the frame with the swift determination of a pointed and purposeful strike. That revolutionary violence that once moved him to attack and strike a police officer is now sublated, metamorphosed, syncopated, and then spread evenly in the hidden assuredness with which he frames his shots, decides his camera movements, instructs his director of photography, commands 'Action!' and then 'Cut!' – and then goes about pasting a long shot here, a close up there, and thus seamlessly sells his dreams for a living.

'I have always thrown in my lot with the hard-livers,' says Scott Nearing (1883–1983), who lived to become 100 years old in a rich and fulfilling life dedicated to his noble ideals. 'I was not born to enjoy myself or to live on the labor of others. I came here to do a job, do it early and late, with might and main.'[7] Scott Nearing was a formidable American activist, fighting against a whole host of evil in his country, from child labor to imperialism. His steadfast determination to oppose injustice wherever he saw it finally made it impossible for him to appease his employers at various university teaching jobs he held. Throughout the depression era he traveled and lectured extensively around the country. Remaining true to his dignity, he and his wife Helen Nearing finally quit New York City, moved to Vermont in 1932, and for the rest of their beautiful, noble, and joyous lives farmed on their own land, read, wrote, and labored and thus lived the ideal they most cherished. One need not think of ancient or medieval mystics when one thinks of the simple, noble, and ascetic life that Makhmalbaf leads today. To me he sometimes appears as a Scott Nearing, with his gaze never dimmed as to what is noble, necessary, sublime, and beautiful.

A Glimpse and a Vista

Beginning with my Introduction and then throughout the rest of this book, I have discussed Makhmalbaf's cinema in terms of his varied attempts at an aesthetic articulation of moral and normative agency beyond the inherited limitation of a colonial subject. In my reading of Makhmalbaf's cinema, I have tried to see how his creative imagination defies the critical condition of the post/colonial subject by breaking through its epistemic and narrative limitations. In writing this book,

I hope to have given a glimpse of what has happened in post-revolutionary Iran once its Islamic Revolution failed to liberate it from the colonial disposition of its ideological imagination. I have also tried to link this structural failure at the presumed periphery of global capitalism to its privileged center. I believe and propose that there is a structural similarity between the crisis of the subject (and with that the material conditions that occasion and sustain that crisis) endemic to the colonial edges of capitalist modernity and a similar crisis specific to the moments of anxiety at its presumed centers.

My single ambition in this book has been to detect and articulate the evident aesthetics at the heart of Makhmalbaf's cinema. My objective has been to navigate through Makhmalbaf's cinema and get closer to its revolutionary aesthetics, articulated by the artist himself almost unconsciously. The aesthetic mutation of violence into an assertive reconstitution of a defiant subject, as I have tried to show in this book, is evident throughout Makhmalbaf's cinema, but perhaps most visibly in *A Moment of Innocence* (1996). In the final scene, where Makhmalbaf brings the police officer and the would-be assassin together, one with a gun and the other with a knife, imaginatively re-narrating a critical moment in Makhmalbaf's own history into a creative reconstitution of agency, instead of the assassin's knife and the officer's gun we see their extended hands bringing forth a piece of bread and a flowerpot into the graceful embrace of a beautiful woman's gaze – the would-be accomplice in an assassination attempt. This is the re-enactment of a moment in Makhmalbaf's own militant history when he took a knife to attack a police officer to steal his gun; and when he failed the police officer almost killed him on the spot, except that the trigger in his gun was stuck. The visual mutation of the knife and the gun into a flowerpot and a piece of bread does not erase the fact of their memorial history – that in fact that piece of bread is a knife (for the knife was raised to secure bread for the hungry), and that flowerpot is a gun (meant to be stolen in no less a sign of love for a brutalized nation). Throughout his cinematic career, Makhmalbaf has remained that 17-year-old rebel, reaching for his knife (now metamorphosed into the slicer on his editing machine) to take a stab at history and slice a diagonal cut into the side of its brutal verdicts – healing the wounds of humanity on the very edge of that cut. The gun that he would have stolen if he were successful in his initial attempt is now his camera, successfully shooting one vision of his nation's emancipation after another. He has hidden that violent reach for justice in the graceful choreography of a cinema that still resonates with an emancipatory violence, no matter how beautifully you slice it.

The year after Makhmalbaf had made *A Moment of Innocence*, we were both at Cannes for the premier of his daughter Samira's *Apple* (1997). After that festival was over, Mohsen, Samira, Meysam, and I went to Paris and spent a couple of weeks watching films and cooking Persian food together. Makhmalbaf had rented an apartment in a suburb of Paris. One day, we went shopping at a nearby supermarket. Among various items we purchased I also bought a small potted geranium. Makhmalbaf looked at me bewildered but did not say anything. Back in our small kitchen, as we were preparing the meat and vegetables we had purchased for me to teach Samira how to cook a simple pasta, I placed the geranium on the window-sill where there was sunshine and watered it a bit. 'What's that for?' Makhmalbaf asked, 'We are here only for a few days?' The geranium looked really pretty and happy – smiling joyously at the generous Paris sun and wet to the core of its roots in the flowerpot. 'We will take turns watering and taking care of it,' I said as I cleaned up around the green flowerpot with a wet napkin, 'it will teach us discipline and caring.' Makhmalbaf laughed: 'I will sooner make a film about you,' he said laughing, 'than you finish your book about me.'

Notes to Chapters

Introduction

1 Although after 9/11 in New York I have become increasingly more adamant about the fact that I am a Muslim, more so than I ever thought I was, as indeed a stubborn Muslim suddenly sneaked out of my New York demeanor when I visited occupied Palestine and went to visit al-Haram al-Sharif.

2 In specifically cinematic terms, I have had three consecutive occasions to reflect on this question. First, in my book on Iranian cinema, *Close Up: Past, Present and Future* (london and New York: Verso, 2001), then in my edited volume on Palestinian cinema, *Dreams of a Nation: On Palestinian Cinema* (Verso, 2006), and finally in my *Masters and Masterpieces of Iranian Cinema* (Mage, 2007). For a more theoretically expansive account of this concern about post/colonial agency, see the Postscript to my *Iran: A People Interrupted* (The New Press, 2007).

3 For the best example of this encounter, see Jürgen Habermas' *The Philosophical Discourse of Modernity*, translated by Frederick G. Lawrence (Cambridge, MA: MIT Press, 1990).

4 See Gayatri Chakravorty Spivak's 'Can the Subaltern Speak?', in Cary Nelson and Lawrence Grossberg (eds), *Marxism and the Interpretation of Culture* (Chicago: University of Illinois Press, 1988).

5 See Nasrin Rahimieh's 'Marking Gender and Difference in the Myth of the Nation: A Post-Revolutionary Iranian Film,' in Richard Tapper (ed), *The New Iranian Cinema: Politics, Representation, and Identity* (London and New York: I.B. Tauris, 2002): p. 252. This essay, in my judgment, is the best theoretical reading of the critical issue of gender in Iranian cinema.

6 Susan Buck-Morss, *Thinking Past Terror: Islamism and Critical Theory on the Left* (London and New York: Verso, 2003).

7 I have published a small portion of this chapter in an earlier incarnation as an essay on Tehran for *Sight and Sound* (January 2002).

8 An earlier version of this chapter has appeared as the text of a catalogue that the National Gallery in Washington, DC – in association with Lens to Lens, Inc.

and the American Film Institute – published on the occasion of a major retrospective on him from 17 May to 15 June 2002.

9 An earlier version of this chapter was published in Richard Tapper's edited volume, *The New Iranian Cinema: Politics, Representation, and Identity* (London: I.B. Tauris, 2002).

10 See Frantz Fanon, *The Wretched of the Earth* (New York: Grove Press, 1963): p. 35.

11 An earlier version of this chapter was published in Rose Isa and Sheila Whitaker's edited volume, *Life and Art: The New Iranian Cinema* (London: National Film Theatre, 1999).

12 The best example of such futile exercises in cultural anthropology, reducing Iranian cinema to objects of useless speculations, is to be seen in Michael M.J. Fischer's *Mute Dreams, Blind Owls, and Dispersed Knowledges: Persian Poesis in the Transnational Circuitry* (Durham, NC: Duke University Press, 2005). The fundamental problem with such exercises in speculative futility is that their authors could not care less about the historical fate of a nation, so far as they get theoretically to play fast and loose with their cultural artifacts – and thus they fail to see or suggest the slightest connections between those artifacts and the collective fate of the nation that has, in the final analysis, produced them.

13 For the original formulation of the notion of a 'transaesthetics of indifference,' see Jean Baudrillard, *The Transparency of Evil: Essays on Extreme Phenomena*, translated by James Benedict (London: Verso, 1990): pp. 14–19.

Chapter One

1 For more details of Makhmalbaf's early life, see his autobiographical reflections in the course of an interview with me in my *Close Up: Iranian Cinema, Past, Present, Future* (London and New York: Verso, 2001): pp. 1156–1212.

2 For preliminary studies of Makhmalbaf's life and work in Persian, see Abass Baharlou (Gholam Heidari), *Mo'arefi-ye Mohsen Makhmalbaf va Asarash* ('Introducing Mohsen Makhmalbaf and his Work'). (Tehran: Qatreh, 1997 (2000)); in Italian, see Alberto Barbera and Umberto Mosca, *Mohsen Makhmalbaf* (Festival Internazionale Cinema Giovani, 1996); in English, see Lloyd Ridgeon, *Makhmalbaf's Broken Mirrors: Analysis of the Socio-Political Significance of Modern Iranian Cinema* (Durham, UK: Centre for Middle Eastern and Islamic studies, University of Durham, 2000); in Korean (and English translation), see Kim Ji-Seok (ed), *Salam Cinema: Films of Makhmalbaf Family* (Pusan: Fifth Pusan International Film festival, 2000). There is also a Japanese translation of a collection of my essays on Makhmalbaf. See Hamid Dabashi, *Yami Karano Kobo* ('The Light Arisen from Darkness') (Tokyo: Sakuhin-sha, 2004). See also the excellent study of Eric Egan, *The Films of Makhmalbaf: Cinema, Politics, and Culture in Iran* (Washington, DC: Mage Publishers, 2005). Two excellent books on Iranian cinema in general have extensive references to Makhmalbaf. One

is Natalia L. Tornessello's *Il Cinema Persiano* (Rome: Jouvence, 2003); the other is Mamad Haghighat (with the collaboration of Frédéric Sabouraud), *Histoire du Cinéma Iranien* (Paris: Centre George Pompidou, 1999). The veteran American anthropologist Michael M.J. Fischer has also written a book on Iranian cinema, *Mute Dreams, Blind Owls, and Dispersed Knowledges: Persian Poesis in the Transnational Circuitry* (Durham, NC: Duke University Press, 2005), with extensive references to Makhmalbaf's work.

3 Houshang Golmakani has made an excellent documentary film on Makhmalbaf and his cinema called *Gong-e Khabdideh/A Dumb-man's Dream* (1996), documenting many of these developments.

4 There are several perspectives on the idea of national cinemas, from which I have benefitted and to which I address my perspective here. For a few recent samples, see Sarah Street, *British National Cinema* (London: Routledge, 1997); Millicent Marcus, *After Fellini: National Cinema in Postmodern Age* (Baltimore, MD: Johns Hopkins University Press, 2002); Pierre Sorlin, *Italian National Cinema* (London: Routledge, 1997); Yingjin Zhang, *Chinese National Cinema* (London: Routledge, 2004); Sabine Hake, *German National Cinema* (London: Routledge, 2001); Karl G. Heider, *Indonesian Cinema: National Culture on Screen* (Hawaii: University of Hawaii Press, 1991); and Ernesto R. Acevedo-Munoz, *Buñuel and Mexico: Crisis of National Cinema* (Santa Barbara, CA: University of California Press, 2003).

5 On the historical vicissitude of Arab cinema, see the excellent work of Viola Shafik, *Arab Cinema: History and Cultural Identity* (New York: Columbia University Press, 1998).

6 On Soviet cinema, see David Gillespie, *Early Soviet Cinema* (New York: Wallflower Press, 2001).

7 On Italian Neorealism, see Peter E. Bondanella, *Italian Cinema: From Neorealism to the Present* (New York: Continuum International Publishing Group, 2001).

8 See Sabine Hake, *German National Cinema*, op. cit.

9 See Chris Wiegand, *French New Wave* (London: Trafalgar Square Publishing, 2001).

10 On Cuban cinema, see Michael Chanan's *The Cuban Image: Cinema and Cultural Politics in Cuba* (London: BFI Publishing, 1986).

11 For more on Palestinian cinema, see my edited volume, *Dreams of a Nation: On Palestinian Cinema* (London and New York: Verso, 2006).

12 For more on Chinese Cinema, see Kwok-Kan tam and Wimal Dissanayake's *New Chinese Cinema* (Oxford, UK: Oxford University Press, 1998).

13 For more on Iranian cinema, see my *Close Up: Iranian Cinema, Past, Present and Future* (London and New York: Verso, 2001). See, also, Richard Tapper (ed), *The New Iranian Cinema: Politics, Representation and Identity* (London: I.B.Tauris, 2002). For the most recent works on Iranian cinema, see Shahla Mirbakhtyar, *Iranian Cinema and the Islamic Revolution* (New York: McFarland & Company, 2006); and Reza Sadr, *Iranian Cinema: A Political History* (London: I.B. Tauris, 2006).

14 For more on these and other major Iranian filmmakers, see my *Masters and Masterpieces of Iranian Cinema* (Washington, DC: Mage Publications, 2007).

15 For more on the Islamic Revolution, see my *Theology of Discontent: The Ideological Foundation of Islamic Revolution in Iran* (New York: New York University Press, 1992); Said Amir Arjomand, *Turban for the Crown: The Islamic Revolution in Iran* (Oxford: Oxford University Press, 1988); and Ervand Abrahamian, *Iran Between Two Revolution* (Princeton, NJ: Princeton University Press, 1982). For the censorial policies of both the Pahlavi regime and the organs of the Islam Republic, see Jamsheed Akrami's essay on 'Censorship' in *Encyclopedia Iranica*.

16 For an account of the social condition of the post-revolutionary Iran, see Fariba Adelkhah, *Being Modern in Iran* (New York: Columbia University Press, 1999).

17 To learn more about Abdolkarim Soroush, see the excellent selection in Ahmad Sadri and Mahmoud Sadri (eds), *Reason, Freedom, and Democracy in Islam: Essential Writings of Abdolkarim Soroush* (Oxford, UK: Oxford University Press, 2002). On my own preliminary assessment of Soroush's ideas, see my 'Blindness and Insight: The Predicament of a Muslim Intellectual,' in Ramin Jahanbegloo (ed), *Iran: Between Tradition and Modernity* (Lexington: Lexington Books, 2004). For a more comprehensive treatment of Iranian intellectuals, see Mehrzad Boroujerdi, *Iranian Intellectuals and the West: The Tormented Triumph of Nativism* (Syracuse, NY: Syracuse University Press, 1996). More specifically on the post-revolutionary intellectuals, see the groundbreaking work of Farzin Vahdat, *God and Juggernaut: Iran's Intellectual Encounter With Modernity* (Syracuse, NY: Syracuse University Press, 2002).

18 See my *Theology of Discontent: The Ideological Foundation of the Islamic Revolution in Iran*. New edition, with a new introduction (New Brunswick, NJ: Transactions, 2005).

19 I have now carefully examined this historic process of anticolonial re-subjection through a close reading of the works of 12 major Iranian filmmakers, from Forough Farrokhzad to Jafar Panahi, in my *Masters and Masterpieces of Iranian Cinema* (Washington, DC: Mage Publications, 2007).

20 For more on Kiarostami's cinema, see my chapter on him in *Close Up*, as well as Mehrnaz Saeed-Vafa and Jonathan Rosenbaum's *Abbas Kiarostami* (Chicago, IL: Illinois University Press, 2003), and Alberto Elena's *The Cinema of Abbas Kiarostami* (London: Saqi Books, 2005).

21 On the reformist movement, see my 'The End of Islamic Ideology,' *Social Research*, June 2000. For excellent analysis and eyewitness accounts of the reform movement, see Genevieve Abdo and Jonathan Lyon's *Answering Only to God: Faith and Freedom in Twenty-First-Century Iran* (New York: Henry Holt and Company, 2003). For a more comprehensive account of post-Khomeini developments, see Mehdi Moslem, *Factional Politics in Post-Khomeini Iran (Modern Intellectual and Political History of the Middle East)* (Syracuse, NY: Syracuse University Press, 2002).

22 See Jean Baudrillard, *The Transparency of Evil: Essays on Extreme Phenomena*, op. cit.

23 By far the best example of such useless anthropological studies, full of pointless insights, is to be read in Michael M.J. Fischer's *Mute Dreams, Blind Owls, and Dispersed Knowledges: Persian Poesis in the Transnational Circuitry* (Durham, NC: Duke University Press, 2005).

24 See Jean Baudrillard, 'Transaesthetics,' in his *Transparency of Evil: Essays on Extreme Phenomena*, op. cit: p. 17.

Chapter Two

1 To see who is capable of the sublime and the beautiful and who is not, see Immanuel Kant, *Observations on the Feeling of the Beautiful and Sublime*, translated by John T. Goldthwait (Berkeley, CA: University of California Press, 1960). 'The Negroes of Africa,' the father of the European Enlightenment modernity believes and states, 'have by nature no feeling that rises above the trifling. Mr. Hume challenges anyone to cite a single example in which a Negro has shown talents, and asserts that among the hundreds of thousands of blacks who are transported elsewhere from their countries, although many of them have even been set free, still not a single one was ever found who presented anything great in art or science or any other praiseworthy quality, even though among the whites some continually rise aloft from the lowest rabble, and through superior gifts earn respect in the world.' (Ibid.: p. 111).

2 Kant's exclusion of the non-Europeans from his aesthetics is so categorical, so visceral, that it leaves no room, no hope, for any other way of reading him at the colonial edges of his philosophy than simply closing his book and looking for alternative sites of reflecting on the ennobling effects of the sublime and the beautiful. 'And it might be,' Kant once came close to exempting a colored person from his general rule, 'that there were something in this which perhaps deserved to be considered; but in short, this fellow was quite black from head to foot, a clear proof that what he said was stupid.' See Kant, *Observations on the Feeling of the Beautiful and Sublime*: p. 113.

3 On Musaddiq era and the CIA coup, see James A. Bill and W. Roger Louis (eds), *Musaddiq, Iranian Nationalism, and Oil* (Austin, TX: University of Texas Press, 1988); and Homa Katouzian, *Mussadiq and the Struggle for Power in Iran* (London: I.B. Tauris, 1999). For the specifics of the CIA-engineered coup, see the account given by its principal operator in Kermit Roosevelt's *Countercoup: The Struggle for the Control of Iran* (New York: McGraw-Hill, 1979). For the most recent research into the British and American coup that toppled Musaddiq, see Stephen Kinzer, *All the Shah's Men: An American Coup and the Roots of Middle East Terror* (New York: John Wiley & Sons, 2004).

4 For more on Ayn al-Qudat, see my *Truth and Narrative: The Untimely Thoughts of Ayn al-Qudat al-Hamadhani* (London: Curzon Press, 1999).

5 The periodization of Makhmalbaf's career as a filmmaker that I offer in this chapter is somewhat different from what he sees in his own work, for which see his interview with me in my *Close Up: Iranian Cinema, Past, Present and Future* (London and New York: Verso, 2001). For an alternative periodization, see also the excellent work of Eric Egan, *The Films of Makhmalbaf: Cinema, Politics, and Culture in Iran* (Washington, DC: Mage Publishers, 2006).

6 There are no good English translations of Makhmalbaf's works of fiction. The existing translation of *The Crystal Garden* (Tehran: Ney Publishing House, 1989) is useless. But there is an excellent French translation of *The Crystal Garden*. See Mohsen Makhmalbaf, *Le Jardin de Cristal* (Paris: Calmann-Lévy, 2002).

7 I am sounding a cautionary note about Makhmalbaf's literary achievements here because in a recent volume of otherwise half-decent translations of Abbas Kiarostami's poems, the translators make the rather unfortunate and outlandish claim that Kiarostami's poetry has achieved for modernist Persian poetry what no other poet has done – identifying Kiarostami as 'the most radical Iranian poet of his generation, perhaps of the century.' They are even more emphatic and clear: 'even Nima Yushij (1897–1960), the poet most often cited as the modernizer of Persian poetry,' in the estimation of these translators, achieve what Kiarostami has in his poetry. (See Abbas Kiarostami, *Walking with the Wind*, translated by Ahmad Karimi-Hakkak and Michael Beard [Cambridge, MA: Harvard Film Archive, 2002]: p. 8.) This is categorical nonsense. As a major Iranian filmmaker, Kiarostami is as accidental and negligible a figure in the Persian poetic pantheon of the twentieth century as Makhmalbaf is in its fiction. Both Kiarostami and Makhmalbaf are gifted but entirely amateurish poets and novelists, respectively. It is principally as filmmakers that we need to consider their work. The unknowing outside world attracted to the magnificence of Kiarostami and Makhmalbaf's cinema, and yet entirely innocent of Iranian intellectual history in general and the giants of Persian poetry and fiction of the twentieth century in particular, should be spared such irresponsible nonsense and not be abused by outlandish remarks that if uttered in Persian and in front of a learned literary community would cause ridicule and embarrassment. Nima Yushij (poet) and Houshang Golshiri (novelist) are both dead, but the libraries of groundbreaking work they have left behind make a mockery of any such gothic and grotesque remark. Kiarostami is no Nima, nor is Makhmalbaf a Golshiri. We need to keep things in perspective.

8 Some of these former prisoners have started writing their memoirs – though mostly in Persian and thus very limited in their distribution and reading by the larger public. See, for example, Nasrin Parvaz, *Zir-e Buteh-ye Laleh Abbasi* (Stockholm: Nasim, 2002), Fariba Marzban, *Tarikh-e Zendan: Haghayeghi az Zendan-ha-*

ye Zanan dar Jomhuri Islami Iran (n.p. 2005), Vida Hajebi Tabrizi, *Dad-e Bi-Dad* (n.p. 2003). Several of these former prisoners have also started making documentaries about their experiences. See, for example, Masoud Raouf, *The Tree That Remembers* (2002), as well as Pante A. Bahrami's *From Scream to Scream* (2005).

9 The criminal activities of the Islamic Republic continue apace and have survived the initial stages of Makhmalbaf's career as a filmmaker. The serial murder of scores of Iranian public intellectuals and political activists by the agents of the Ministry of Information during Khatami's presidency (1997–2005) were the subject of the investigative journalism of Akbar Ganji, a heroic figure in exposing, at great risk to himself, the criminal atrocities of a regime whose power he in fact once helped to consolidate.

10 'The inhabitant of the Orient,' in Immanuel Kant's critical judgment, 'is of a very false taste in this respect [the relation of the sexes]. Since he has no concept of the morally beautiful which can be united with this impulse, he loses even the worth of the sensuous enjoyment, and his harem is a constant source of unrest. He thrives on all sorts of amorous grotesqueries ...' See Kant, *Observations on the Feeling of the Beautiful and Sublime*: pp. 112–113. This is Immanuel Kant, the author of the groundbreaking three critiques that change the course of European philosophy, and the author of 'What is the Enlightenment?', which is the foundational text of European Enlightenment modernity. If I am hoping for your patience to bear with me in this book as I try to configure the particular aesthetic parameters of the sublime and the beautiful at the colonial edges of that globalized modernity, it is in part because Kant, alas, has no room at his gracious, sagacious, and elegant table for us – his Orientals. We must fend for ourselves.

11 For more on Adorno's critic of logical absolutism, see Theodor W. Adorno, *Against Epistemology: A Metacritique* (Cambridge, MA: MIT Press, 1982): pp. 41–88.

12 See Theodore W. Adorno, *Kant's 'Critique of Pure Reason'* (Stanford: Stanford University Press, 2001): pp. 57–58.

13 See Mohsen Makhmalbaf, *Gong-e Khabdiddeh/A Dumb-Man's Dream*, three volumes, Tehran: Nashr Ney, 1375/1996. In my interview with Makhmalbaf in my *Close Up: Iranian Cinema, Past, Present and Future* (op. cit.), Makhmalbaf reviews and comments on the content of these three volumes: the first volume is a selection of the stories he wrote in the 1980s; the second volume a selection of his plays and film scripts during the same decade; and the third volume a selection of his interviews and comments at the same time.

Chapter Three

1 See Martin Heidegger, 'The Question Concerning Technology,' in Martin Heidegger, *The Question Concerning Technology and Other Essays*, translated and with an Introduction by William Lovitt (New York: Harper Torchbooks, 1977): p. 34.

2 Ibid.: p. 19.

3 Ibid.: p. 14.

4 Ibid.: p. 34.

5 Ibid.: p. 34.

6 Ibid.: p. 34.

7 Ibid.: p. 34.

8 Ibid.: p. 35.

9 Ibid.: p. 35.

10 There is a prolonged tradition of reading poetry as *technê* in medieval Islamic theories of poetry, of which the Heidegger generation of European philosophy remained entirely innocent. 'Poetry is an art form (*sinâ't* = literally *technê*),' says the medieval Muslim literary theorist Ali al-Nizami al-Arudi al-Samarqandi, 'by virtue of which technique (*sinâ't*), [the poet] links a set of imaginative foregroundings to certain inevitable syllogisms, in such a way that can make small matters appear as grand, grand matters small, beautiful things ugly, and ugly things evidently beautiful' (see Ali al-Nizami al-Arudi al-Samarqandi, *Chahar Maqalah* [Leiden: E.J. Brill, 1909]: p. 26). The book was composed circa 550 AH/1155 AD.

11 Ibid.: p. 35.

12 See Jürgen Habermas, 'Modernity: An Unfinished project,' in Maurizio Passerin d'Entreves and Seyla Benhabib (eds), *Habermas and the Unfinished Project of Modernity* (Cambridge, MA: MIT University Press, 1997): p. 45.

13 Ibid.: p. 35.

14 I have made an extensive case for the categorical rootedness of Islamism in the project of colonial modernity it has faced and opposed in my *Theology of Discontent: The Ideological Foundation of Islamic Revolution in Iran*. An updated edition with a new Introduction (New Brunswick, NJ: Transactions, 2005).

15 See Frantz Fanon, 'Algeria Unveiled,' in his *A Dying Colonialism* (New York: Grove Press, 1965): pp. 23–34.

16 For more, see the chapter on Ali Shari'ati in my *Theology of Discontent*, op. cit.

17 The Chicago-based American sociologist Thorstein Veblen coined the phrase 'leisure class' in his now classic study, which was originally published in 1899 and sought to theorize the rise of conspicuous consumption as a marker of social prestige in the *fin de siècle* America. See Thorstein Veblen, *The Theory of the Leisure Class* (New York: Dover Publications, 1994).

18 See Stanley Kubrick and Frederic Raphael, *Eyes Wide Shut* (New York: Warner Books, 1999): p. 65.

19 Heidegger, 'The Question Concerning Technolog.' Ibid.: p. 15.

20 For more on the subterranean consciousness of Victorian morality, see the groundbreaking work of Steven Marcus, *The Other Victorians: A Study of Sexuality and Pornography in Mid-Nineteenth-Century England* (New York: W.W. Norton, 1985).

21 See Philip Rieff, *The Triumph of the Therapeutic: Uses of Faith after Freud* (Chicago: Chicago University Press, 1987). Philip Rieff (1922–2006) was my own teacher at the University of Pennsylvania, with whom I wrote my doctoral thesis on Weber's theory of charisma.

22 Kubrick and Raphael, *Eyes Wide Shut*. Ibid.: p. 25.

23 Kubrick and Raphael, *Eyes Wide Shut*. Ibid.: p. 57.

24 Schnitzler in Kubrick and Raphael, *Eyes Wide Shut*. Ibid.: p. 221.

25 Kubrick and Raphael, *Eyes Wide Shut*. Ibid.: p. 52.

26 Michel Foucault, *The History of Sexuality, Volume 1: An Introduction*, translated by Robert Hurley (New York: Pantheon, 1978): p. 6.

27 Foucault, *The History of Sexuality*. Ibid.: p. 7.

28 See Mohsen Makhmalbaf, *Bagh-e Bolur/The Crystal Garden* (Tehran: Nashr-e Ney, 1374/1995 – ninth printing). There is an English translation of this novel. See Mohsen Makhmalbaf, *The Crystal Garden*, translated by Minou Moshiri (Tehran: Ney Publishing House, 1989). There is also a French translation of this book. See Mohsen Makhmalbaf, *Le Jardin de Cristal* (Le Serpent a Plumes, 2003). All the passages translated from the original in this chapter are mine. All the page references are to the original Persian text.

29 For more of this interview, see the chapter on Makhmalbaf in my *Close Up: Iranian Cinema, Past, Present and Future*. Ibid.

30 I have extensively discussed and elaborated Makhmalbaf's *virtual realism* in the context of other forms of realism in Iranian cinema in my *Masters and Masterpieces of Iranian Cinema* (Washington, DC: Mage, 2007).

31 It is imperative not to reduce the 'cosmopolitan' disposition of Iranian political culture to a 'secular' designation. The binary opposition manufactured between 'religious' and 'secular' does far more harm in distorting both sides of this presumed binary than revealing anything definitive about either of them. Aspects of whatever we understand by 'religious' or 'secular' is perfectly evident on the opposite side of the dichotomy. The term 'secular' is a nervous category full of Eurocentric racist tendencies, blindly adopted by lapsed and militant Muslims alike – though for two entirely opposite ends. The Iranian, as indeed that of many other cultures in the region, political culture was *cosmopolitan* in its historic disposition and not secular. That cosmopolitan culture had room for both sacred and profane – to use the more accurate terms of Mircea Eliade – components of the social, civil, and moral imagery.

32 Makhmalbaf, *The Crystal Garden*. Ibid.: pp. 95–96.

33 Makhmalbaf, *The Crystal Garden*. Ibid.: pp. 149–150.

34 Makhmalbaf, *The Crystal Garden*. Ibid.: p. 137.

35 Makhmalbaf, *The Crystal Garden*. Ibid.: p. 142.

36 Makhmalbaf, *The Crystal Garden*. Ibid.: p. 135.

37 Makhmalbaf, *The Crystal Garden*. Ibid.: p. 185.

38 Makhmalbaf, *The Crystal Garden*. Ibid.: pp. 250–251.

39 Makhmalbaf, *The Crystal Garden* (ibid.): pp. 261–262. The last scene of Makhmalbaf's *The Crystal Garden* (1985) is very much reminiscent of the final scene of John Steinbeck's *Grapes of Wrath* (1940), where Rose of Sharon, the eldest Joad daughter, who has just given birth to a stillborn child, breastfeeds a starving old man. In the case of *The Crystal Garden*, this is reversed – and an old woman is feeding a starving child. Years ago, when I mentioned this similarity to Makhmalbaf, he was startled, said he had never read Steinbeck's *Grapes of Wrath*, and thought its ending was positively beautiful.

40 This conclusion reminds me of the precise moment when, once in Cannes Makhmalbaf and I were having dinner together and toasting his health, I recited this passage of Sepehri: 'Give me the wine,/We must hurry:/I am coming back from having been through an epic/And know/The story of Sohrab and Panacea/By heart.' Sepehri's reference is to the story of Sohrab and Rostam in Ferdowsi's *Shahnameh*, where Rostam has just inadvertently killed his own son and in vain is looking for the panacea (*Nushdaru*). Sepehri's allusion, and thus my remembering the passage then (and now), is to the purgatorial passage through which the vision is clarified and the outlook uplifted.

41 Pierre Bourdieu, *The Political Ontology of Martin Heidegger* (Stanford, CA: Stanford University Press, 1991): p. 8.

42 Bourdieu, *The Political Ontology of Martin Heidegger* (ibid.): p. 10. Bourdieu further refers to Siegfried Krakauer's *From Caligari to Hitler, a Psychological History of German Cinema* (Princeton, NJ: Princeton University Press, 1947) as singularly expressive of the phenomenon. For a more detailed examination of German cinema of the period, see Anton Kaes, *From Hitler to Heimat: The Return of History as Film* (Cambridge, MA: Harvard University Press, 1989).

43 Oswald Spengler, *Man and Technics* (London: Allen & Unwin, 1932).

44 Spengler, *Man and Technics* (ibid): p. 97. In Bourdieu, *The Political Ontology of Martin Heidegger* (ibid.): pp. 11–12. Notice also the origin of German Orientalism here in Spengler's reading of post-war Germany.

45 Bourdieu, *The Political Ontology of Martin Heidegger*. Ibid.: pp. 25–26.

46 See Luc Ferry and Alain Renaut, *Heidegger and Modernity*, translated by Franklin Philip (Chicago, IL: Chicago University Press, 1990).

47 In addition to Bourdieu's book, see Hans Sluga, *Heidegger's Crisis: Philosophy and Politics in Nazi Germany* (Cambridge, MA: Harvard University Press, 1993). While Sluga's study seeks to place Heidegger in the political predicaments of his time, Richard Wolin in his *The Politics of Being: The Political Thought of Martin Heidegger* (New York: Columbia University Press, 1990) traces the origin of Heidegger's attraction to Nazism right into *Being and Time*. In all these cases, without any exception, the alternately vindictive or apologetic tones of the account prevents the simple

recognition that Heidegger's attraction to Nazism makes his critic of Modernity more, rather than less, legitimate.

48 William V. Spanos, *Heidegger and Criticism: Retrieving the Cultural Politics of Destruction,* foreword by Donald E. Pease (Minneapolis, MN: University of Minnesota Press, 1993): p. 3.

49 See Victor Farias, *Heidegger and Nazism,* translated by Paul Burrell and Gabriel Ricci (Philadelphia: Temple University Press, 1989). Ibid.: p. 3.

50 Bourdieu, *The Political Ontology of Martin Heidegger.* Ibid.: p. 26.

51 Bourdieu, *The Political Ontology of Martin Heidegger.* Ibid.: p. 28.

52 Bourdieu, *The Political Ontology of Martin Heidegger.* Ibid.: p. 28.

Chapter Four

1 See the Conclusion of my *Theology of Discontent.* Ibid.

2 See Gayatri Chakravorty Spivak, 'Can the Subaltern Speak?', in Cary Nelson and Lawrence Grossberg (eds), *Marxism and the Interpretation of Culture* (Chicago, IL: University of Illinois Press, 1988).

3 I have given a fuller account of this theoretical articulation of the anticolonial subject in the Postscript of my *Iran: A People Interrupted* (New York: The New Press, 2007).

4 See Michel Foucault, *The Order of Things: An Archeology of the Human Sciences* (New York: Vintage Books, 1970): p. 387.

5 See Michel Foucault, *The History of Sexuality, Volume 1: An Introduction.* (London: Allen Lane, 1979): p. 70.

6 See Michel Foucault's *I, Pierre Riviére, Having Slaughtered My Mother, My Sister, and My Brother ... A Case of Parricide in the Nineteenth Century* (Nebraska: University of Nebraska Press, 1982); and Herculine Barbin, *Being the Recently Discovered Memoirs of a Nineteenth-Century French Hermaphrodite* (New York: Pantheon Books, 1980).

7 See Steven Marcus, *Other Victorians: A Study of Sexuality and Pornography in Mid-Nineteenth Century England* (New York: Basic Books, 1977).

8 Following Philip Rieff, here I take the notion of 'transgression' not merely in a moral but more effectively as a normative category – the way Rieff articulated it in his theory of culture. See Philip Rieff's *Fellow Teachers: Of Culture and Its Second Death* (Chicago: University of Chicago, 1973/1985): *et passim.* Between *transgressions* and *interdictions,* Rieff posited a *remissive* realm of normative behaviour that made what he called *the sacred order* at once inhibitive and operative. Foucault's attraction to the notion of *transgression* in the formation of a defiant subject remained aloof from Rieff's far more ambitious theory that was not merely satisfied with either interdictory or transgressive extremities, but sought to engage them in an animated dialectic that was facilitated by way of a remissive mechanism that held them together.

9 I take this lead from Paul Ricoeur's *Time and Narrative* (Chicago, IL: Chicago University Press, 1990). Two volumes. I have further extended Ricoeur's theory of narrative in my *Truth and Narrative: The Untimely Thoughts of Ayn al-Qudat al-Hamadhani* (London: Curzon Press, 1999).

10 For the script of *Silence*, see Mohsen Makhmalbaf, *Sokut/Silence: A Film on Music*. Pictures by Meysam Makhmalbaf (Tehran: Nashr-e Ney, 1377/1988). In Persian and English. For the script of *Gabbeh*, see Mohsen Makhmalbaf, *Gabbeh*. Pictures by Mohammad Ahmadi (Tehran: Nashr-e Ney, 1376/1996). In Persian, English, and French. For the script of *A Moment of Innocence* see Mohsen Makhmalbaf, *Nun-o-Goldun/Bread and Flower Pot*, in Mohsen Makhmalbaf, *Zendegi Rang Ast/Life is Color* (Tehran: Nashr-e Ney, 1376/1997): pp. 299–354.

11 Hans-Georg Gadamer, *The Relevance of the Beautiful and Other Essays*, edited by Robert Bernasconi (Cambridge, UK: Cambridge University Press, 1986): p. 53.

12 I attribute this fact to the inorganic nature of cinematic writing on Iranian cinema. By and large, most non-Iranian commentators on Iranian cinema cannot even read, let alone read and incorporate, what Iranians themselves write about Iranian cinema in Persian. The globalized nature of spectatorship has further helped to mutate the specific items of Iranian cinema to fetishized commodities entirely divorced and isolated from their culture and process of production. The best example of this fetishization of Iranian cinema is evident in Michael Fischer's *Mute Dreams, Blind Owls, and Dispersed Knowledges: Persian Poesis in the Transnational Circuitry* (ibid.). The hidden and/or operative aesthetics of Iranian cinema is as a result not the subject of conversation in a hermeneutic circle that includes and consists of the theorists and practitioners of Iranian cinema. This, I believe, is very much evident in other national cinemas as well. The Palestinian cinema in particular is another example that best comes to mind in this respect – though this time around in a politically far more brutal way.

13 Costanzo Costantini (ed), *Conversations with Fellini*, translated by Sohrab Sorooshian (New York: Harcourt Brace & Company, 1995): p. 778.

14 For a classic study of the reasons for the retardation of capitalist mode of production in Iran, see Ahmad Ashraf, *Mavane'-e Tarikhi-ye Roshd-e Sarmayeh-dari dar Iran/Historical Obstacles to the Rise of Capitalism in Iran* (Tehran: Zamineh, 1359/1980). Ashraf articulates a series of domestic and foreign causes that have historically prevented the formation of a modern bourgeoisie and a fully fledged mode of capitalist production. The particular relation between the cities and the rural areas and the function of the tribal formations domestically, and the semi-colonized relation with the colonial powers, are the principal reasons that Ashraf offers in his analysis.

15 To learn more about these intellectuals, see my *Theology of Discontent* (op. cit.), and my essay 'Blindness and Insight: The Predicament of a Muslim Intellectual,' in Ramin Jahanbegloo (ed), *Iran: Between Tradition and Modernity* (Lexington: Lexington

Books, 2004). See also Farzin Vahdat, *God and Juggernaut: Iran's Intellectual Encounter with Modernity* (Syracuse, NY: Syracuse University Press, 2002).

16 What I propose here is a modification of Gramsci's famous distinction between what he called 'traditional' (by which he meant the ecclesiastical) and 'organic' (or class-based) intellectuals. The conditions of subalternity are identical at the presumed center and designated peripheries of the capital so far as the material conditions of production are concerned. But at the colonial edge the manufacturing of a comprador bourgeoisie and inorganic intellectuals is predicated on a false ideological consciousness that places them both on the tropical edges of the metropole. This colonial condition was not part of his parameters when Gramsci theorized the difference between 'traditional' and 'organic' intellectuals. See Antonio Gramsci, *Selections from the Prison Notebook* (New York: International Publishers, 1971): pp. 5–23.

17 Makhmalbaf, of course, is not the only director who has also acted as 'himself' in his own films. From Charlie Chaplin to Jacques Tati to Elia Suleiman, other directors have done the same, and in a more systematic way – though with differing implication. For my reflection on Elia Suleiman's cinema, see my chapter on him in my edited volume, *Dreams of a Nation: On Palestinian Cinema* (London: Verso, 2006).

18 The hermeneutic function of a 'multi-significatory' (*mushtarik al-dilalah*) manner of signification was first discovered and articulated by the medieval Persian mystic, Ayn al-Qudat al-Hamadhani. For more detail, see my *Truth and Narrative: The Untimely Thoughts of Ayn al-Qudat al-Hamadhani* (London: Curzon Press, 1999).

19 Martin Heidegger, *Being and Time*, translated by John Macquarrie and Edward Robinson (New York: Harper & Row Publishers, 1962): p. 164.

20 Michael E. Zimmerman, *Heidegger's Confrontation with Modernity: Technology, Politics, Art* (Bloomington: Indiana University Press, 1990): p. 22.

21 *The Qur'an*, vii: 172.

22 Sa'di, *Bustan*, edited by Gholamhossein Yusefi (Tehran: Khwarazmi Publishers, 1359/1980): p. 101.

23 See Mohsen Makhmalbaf, *Salam bar Khorshid/Greeting the Sun* (Tehran: Nashr-e Ney, 1372/1993).

24 I have developed the particulars of this pararealism in Iranian cinema in my *Masters and Masterpieces of Iranian Cinema* (Washington, DC: Mage, 2007).

25 The origin of such narrative techniques can be traced back to a Persian passion play, *Ta'ziyeh*, whose mimetic techniques are quintessentially different from Aristotelian mimesis, and in which such time warps can be instantaneously created and discarded without any forewarning. I have argued this point in several places, most recently in my essay, 'Ta'ziyeh: The Theater of Protest' (*The Drama Review*, 2005).

26 Michel Foucault, *Discipline and Punish: The Birth of the Prison*. New York: Pantheon Books, 1977: p. 23.

27 Ibid.: p. 29.

28 Ibid.: p. 30.

Chapter Five

1 On the inherently temporal nature of narrative, see Paul Ricoeur's *Time and Narrative*. Three volumes (Chicago: University of Chicago Press, 1990). For theoretical conversations with Paul Ricoeur in an Islamic (gnostic) context, see my *Truth and Narrative: The Untimely Thoughts of Ayn Al-Qudat Al-Hamadhani* (London: Curzon, 1999).

2 On the origin and critic of ocularcentricism, see Martin Jay's *Downcast Eyes: The Denigration of Vision in Twentieth-Century French Thought* (Berkeley, CA: University of California Press, 1994). In this book, Martin Jay examines the recent criticism of the primacy of vision in European modernity, as put forward by such philosophers as Jean-Paul Sartre, Maurice Merleau-Ponty, Michel Foucault, Jacques Lacan, Louis Althusser, Guy Debord, Luce Irigaray, Emmanuel Levinas, and Jacques Derrida.

3 *The Qur'an*, II: 3. For an extensive discussion of the visual implications of this Qur'anic doctrine, see my 'In the Absence of the Face,' in *Social Research*, Spring 2000.

4 For more on early Iranian cinema, see Jamal Omid, *Tarikh-e Cinema-ye Iran, 1279–1357 (History of Iranian Cinema, 1900–1978)* (Tehran: Rozaneh Publishers, 1374/1995): pp. 20–22.

5 On 'Absolutism of Reality,' see Hans Blumenberg, *Work on Myth* (Cambridge, MA: MIT Press, 1985).

6 On Max Weber's concept of the 'disenchantment of the world,' on which I predicate this proposal of a 're-enchantment of the world,' see Max Weber's 'Science as a Vocation.' In Hans Gerth and C. Wright Mills (eds), *From Max Weber: Essays in Sociology* (Oxford, UK: Oxford University Press, 1946): p. 148. I have extended the Weberian conception of the 're-enchantment of the world' in its ideological domain in my introduction to *Theology of Discontent* (op. cit.).

7 For more on this period of Nasser al-Din Shah's reign and the circumstances of his assassination, see the chapter on Constitutional revolution in my *Iran: A People Interrupted* (New York: The New Press, 2007).

8 See the text of *Once Upon a Time, Cinema* in Mohsen Makhmalbaf, 'Nasser al-Din Shah, Actor-e Cinema,' in his *Gong-e Khabdiddeh* (op. cit). Volume II: p. 663.

9 See Frantz Fanon, *A Dying Colonialism* (New York: Grove Press, 1965): p. 42.

10 See Frantz Fanon, *The Wretched of the Earth* (New York: Grove Press, 1963): p. 36.

11 For more on the Iranian Constitutional Revolution of 1906–1911, see Janet Afary's *The Iranian Constitutional Revolution, 1906–1911: Grassroots Democracy, Social Democracy, and the Origins of Feminism* (New York: Columbia University Press, 1996).

12 BP, the abbreviation for British Petroleum, was sold to Iranians (especially in the oil-rich southern province of Khuzestan, where I was born and raised) as standing for *Benzin-e Pars* (Persian Oil)! Recently I have seen British Petroleum advertisements in New York subway cars, dubbing BP as standing for 'Beyond Petroleum,' appealing to the environmentally conscious riders. BP has become a traveling signifier chasing after the changing colors of colonialism – as I have lived through that changing signifier from southern Iran to North America.

13 For example, see the collection of reviews on Makhmalbaf's *The Peddler* (1987) in Ebrahim Nabavi (ed), *Film-nameh va Naqd-e Film-e Dastforush/The Script and Reviews of 'Peddler'* (Tehran: 1368/1989): pp. 101–210. Usually, *The Peddler* is considered a turning point in Makhmalbaf's career. For my own periodization of Makhmalbaf's films, see Chapter Two of this book.

14 One of the most persuasive arguments in periodizing Heidegger's thoughts that is inclusive of his turn to Nazism but not anchored on it is Fred Dallmayer's *The Other Heidegger* (Ithaca, NY: Cornell University Press, 1993). Fred Dallmayer's later attention to Abdolkarim Soroush is itself indicative of this structural similarity, I suggest here. See Fred Dallmayer's 'Islam and Democracy: Reflections on Abdolkarim Soroush' (*Proceedings of the Center for the Study of Islam and Democracy, Second Annual Conference,* 2001): pp. 132–144.

15 For more on these two films, see Jamal Omid, *Tarikh-e Cinema-ye Iran* (op. cit.): pp. 41–70.

16 See Jamal Omid, *Tarikh-e Cinema-ye Iran* (op. cit.): p. 69. Among the documentary shown at this theater was the coronation of Reza Shah.

17 Martin Heidegger, 'The Question Concerning Technology' (op. cit.): p. 5.

18 Heidegger's insistence that there was an original link between *craft* and *poetry* in Greek *technê* was not unknown in medieval Arabic and Persian poetics. In his chapter on poetics, Ali al-Nizami al-'Arudi al-Samarqandi, the sixth/thirteenth century Persian literary critic, clearly identified poetry as a 'sinâ't,' which literally means 'technique,' and which he might have very well taken from its Aristotelian origin. See Ali al-Nizami al-'Arudi al-Samarqandi, *Kuliyyat-e Chahar Maqalah*, edited with an Introduction by Muhammad Qazvini (Leiden: Brill, 1909): p. 26.

19 Heidegger, 'The Question Concerning Technology' (op. cit.): p. 10.
20 Heidegger, 'The Question Concerning Technology' (op. cit.): p. 12.
21 Heidegger, 'The Question Concerning Technology' (op. cit.): p. 14.
22 Heidegger, 'The Question Concerning Technology' (op. cit.): p. 15.
23 Heidegger, 'The Question Concerning Technology' (op. cit.): p. 16.
24 Heidegger, 'The Question Concerning Technology' (op. cit.): p. 16.

25 For the text of *Bread and Flower*, see Makhmalbaf 'The Dumb Man's Dream' (op. cit.), volume II: pp. 557–580.

26 Over the years, Makhmalbaf must have read me scores of scripts that he has written but never made into a film. His mind seems to be a boundless fountain of stories, most of which emerge from accidental encounters in his daily life, something that he reads in the newspaper, hears on the radio, watches on television, or just sees in the street. We are walking in the street in Paris, for example, or roaming through its subway, and we come across a scene, an old man trying to ascend the stairs, a young woman anxiously waiting for a cab, a child holding her mother's arm and gazing at the window of a pastry shop, anything, and he abruptly says, 'You see that child?' and he grabs me by my arm and we interrupt what we were saying. 'Yes,' I say. 'You can make a beautiful short film about her and her mom and that pastry shop. The opening shot must be from inside the shop, the camera looking at the child, a close up of her eyes, then the camera opens its frames as it starts slowly to dolly-in and around and come outside ... .' Then we resume our walk and he forgets about the whole scene. He writes his scripts in his own Persian handwriting first in a rough draft, then he prepares a clean copy and files it in neatly held dossiers. 'What do you think?' he often asks me after reading a script for me, 'Should Samira make this or Marziyeh?' Then we drop everything and go to have a tea or a meal: 'Do you see that tree out there from the window? You can make a beautiful little scene, just a scene, like a video installation ... .'

27 See Mohsen Makhmalbaf, 'Seh Tablo' in his *Nobat-e Asheqi* (Tehran: Ney Publications, 1375/1976): pp. 9–17.

28 For the original story, see al-Samarqandi, *Kuliyyat-e Chahar Maqalah* (op. cit.): pp. 16–17.

29 See Mohsen Makhmalbaf, 'Nobat-e Asheqi' in his *Nobat-e Asheqi* (Tehran: Ney Publications, 1375/1976): pp. 41–70.

30 Ibid.: p. 51.

31 See Mohsen Makhmalbaf, *Gong-e Khabdideh* (op. cit. III): p. 300.

32 Ibid.: p. 310.

33 Ibid.: p. 312.

34 See Houshang Hesami's review of Makhmalbaf's *A Time for Love*. Ibid.: III: p. 316.

35 See Abdolkarim Soroush's review of *A Time for Love*. Ibid.: III: p. 325.

36 Ibid.: III: p. 326.

37 See Seyyed Ebrahim Nabavi's review of *A Time for Love*. Ibid.: III: p. 331.

38 Ibid.: III: p. 332.

39 See Hossein Hadavi's review of *A Time for Love*. Ibid.: III: p. 340.

40 See Mohsen Makhmalbaf, *Mara Bebus (Kiss Me)* in his *Nobat-e Asheqi* (Tehran: Nashr-e Ney, 1375/1996): p. 75.

41 Ibid.: p. 76.
42 Ibid.: p. 76.
43 Ibid.: p. 79.

Chapter Six

1 Again, I have given a detailed account of this argument in the Postscript to my *Iran: A People Interrupted* (op. cit.).

2 For more on these treatises, see Shihabuddin Yahya Suhrawardi, *The Mystical & Visionary Treatises of Suhrawardi*, translated by W.M. Thackston, Jr. (New York: Octagon Press, 1982). For more on his philosophy of illumination, see Shihab al-Din Suhrawardi, *The Philosophy of Illumination*, translated by John Walbridge and Hossein Zia'i (Provo, UT: Brigham Young University, 2000).

3 For more on Sa'di, see Homa Katouzian, *Sa'di: The Poet of Loving and Living* (London: Oneworld Publications, 2006).

4 A *tar* is a double-bowled string instrument usually made of mulberry wood and covered with a thin stretch of animal skin. The extended fingerboard has a set of strings that range about two and a half octaves.

5 See Mohsen Makhmalbaf, *Silence: A Film on Music*. Photographs by Meysam Makhmalbaf (Tehran: 1998): p. 3. The original script of *Silence* in this book includes an English translation. All translations in this chapter are my own.

6 See Sohrab Sepehri, *The Palpitations of the Shadow of the Friend*, in his *Hasht Ketab* (*Eight Books*) (Tehran: Tahuri, 1363/1984): p. 366. All translations of Sohrab Sepehri's poetry in this and other chapters are my own.

7 See Makhmalbaf, *Silence* (op. cit.): p. 7.

8 For the full account of this conversation, see my chapter on Makhmalbaf in my *Close Up: Iranian Cinema, Past, Present and Future* (op. cit.).

9 In one of the earliest versions of *Silence*, when Makhmalbaf described it to me while we were walking one day in Geneva in Switzerland, this abstinence from looking at evil was far more central to the story. In its subsequent and final version that theme became subsumed in the rest of the story.

10 A similar clairvoyance of camera is evident in Majid Majidi's *Rang-e Khoda/Color of God* (in the USA released as *Color of Paradise*, 1999).

11 He simply cut that scene from the version he submitted to Islamic authorities, took the censored version and the cut scene outside the country and re-edited it back into the original print.

12 The poem is called *Song for the Man of Light who Went into Shadow*, and the full stanza reads: 'A Man with the flow of water/The Summary of a man/Who was his own summation.' See Ahmad Shamlu, *Majmu'eh-ye Ash'ar*. Two volumes (Gießen, West Germany: Bamdad Publisher, 1989): II: p. 970. When this poem first appeared, everyone assumed that it was dedicated to the cultural icon of the

1960s generation, Jalal Al-e Ahmad (1923–69), and Shamlu did not deny that attribution. But after the Islamic Revolution he retracted that attribution because of his ideological differences with Al-e Ahmad. For Shamlu's denial of this attribution, see ibid.: p. 1153.

13 Makhmalbaf, *Silence* (op. cit.): p. 190.

14 Ibid.: p. 15.

15 Ibid.: p. 4.

16 Ibid.: pp. 12–13.

17 Ibid.: p. 19.

18 See Sepehri's *The Palpitations of the Shadow of the Friend* (op. cit.): p. 367.

19 Makhmalbaf, *Silence* (op. cit.): p. 16.

20 For Makhmalbaf's reflections on Forough Farrokhzad, see Mohsen Makhmalbaf's *Forough Khwahar-e Ma Bud/Forough was our Sister* (1995) in his *Zendegi Rang Ast/Life is Color* (Tehran: Ney Publishers, 1376/1997): pp. 77–95.

21 See Forough Farrokhzad, *Tavallodi Digar/Another Birth* in *Tavallodi Digar* (Tehran: Morvarid, 1363/1984): p. 153. My translation.

22 Makhmalbaf, *Silence* (op. cit.): p. 24.

23 Makhmalbaf, *Silence* (op. cit.): p. 20.

24 Makhmalbaf, *Silence* (op. cit.): p. 20.

25 Makhmalbaf, *Silence* (op. cit.): p. 20.

26 Makhmalbaf, *Silence* (op. cit.): p. 20.

27 Sepehri, 'The Palpitations of the Shadow of the Friend' (op. cit.): pp. 367–368.

28 See Martin Heidegger, 'What are Poets for?', in *Poetry, Language, Thought*, translated by Albert Hofstadter (New York: Harper and Row, 1971): p. 91.

29 Ibid.: p. 91.

30 As reported in an essay on Ingmar Bergman's *The Silence* in *Geocities.com* (see: http://www.geocities.com/SunsetStrip/Venue/3825/thesilence.html, accessed on 15 November 2006).

31 Sepehri, *The Palpitations of the Shadow of the Friend* (op. cit.): p. 368.

Chapter Seven

1 See Hans-George Gadamer, *The Relevance of the Beautiful and Other Essays*, edited by Robert Bernasconi (New York: Cambridge University Press, 1986): p. 15.

2 See Jean Baudrillard, 'Transaesthetics' (op. cit.): *et passim*.

3 This verse of Hölderlin is the subject of Heidegger's essay, 'What are the Poets for?' See his *Poetry, Language, Thought*, translated by Albert Hofstadter (New York: Harper and Row, 1971): pp. 91–142.

4 The text of Makhmalbaf's speech as he delivered it on 3 October 2001 at UNESCO in Paris – from a telephone conversation with me on the following day.

5 From a telephone interview with Makhmalbaf while he was in the Iranian border town of Zahedan on 28 October 2001.

6 'We must be aware of the superiority of our civilization,' declared the Italian Prime Minister Silvio Berlusconi, 'a system that has guaranteed well-being, respect for human rights and – in contrast with Islamic countries – respect for religious and political rights, a system that has as its value understanding of diversity and tolerance.' As reported by BBC. See http://news.bbc.co.uk/1/hi/world/europe/1565664.stm (accessed on 25 November 2001). Radio Netherlands further reported: 'The Western civilization is superior,' Mr. Berlusconi added, because 'it has at its core – as its greatest value – freedom, which is not the heritage of Islamic culture.' The Italian prime minister predicted that 'the West will continue to conquer peoples, even if it means a confrontation with another civilization, Islam, firmly entrenched where it was 1400 years ago.' See http://www.rnw.nl/ hotspots/html/italy010927.html (accessed on 25 November 2001). The prominent Italian journalist and writer Oriana Fallaci (1929–2006) soon echoed her president on Islam: 'It is the Mountain. That Mountain which in one thousand and four hundred years has not moved, has not risen from the abyss of its blindness, has not opened its doors to the conquests of civilization, has never wanted to know about freedom and democracy and progress. In short, has not changed. That Mountain which in spite of its shameful richness of its retrograde masters (kings and princes and sheiks and bankers) still lives in scandalous poverty, still vegetates in the monstrous darkness of a religion which produces nothing but religion.' See Oriana Fallaci, *The Rage and The Pride* (Rome and New York: Rizzoli, 2002): p. 30. This book was an expansion of Fallaci's article, 'La rabbia e l'orgoglio,' which she wrote for *Corriere della Serra*, published on 29 September 2001. The distinguished Italian philosopher, semiotician, and novelist Umberto Eco subsequently challenged Berlusconi and Fallaci's comments in his 'Le guerre sante passione e ragione' (*Repubblica*, 5 October 2001). But in Eco's own comments even more hidden blind spots were revealed. This cycle of spiteful utterances went around Europe and the USA incessantly, exposing some of the most frightful shadow lines of European and American intellectuals. Edward Said in 'The Clash of Ignorance' (*The Nation*, 22 October 2001: pp. 11–13) traced these ideas to Samuel Huntington's thesis of 'The Clash of Civilization.' For a reading of the causes and consequences of Huntington's theory and its place in the rise of the recent US imperial imagination, see my essay 'For the Last Time: Civilization,' in the *Journal of International Sociology*, 16(3) (September 2001).

7 In his response to Fallaci's article, Umberto Eco's 'Le guerre sante passione e ragione' (op. cit.) revealed very troubling signs of the self-absorbed European intellectuals. Eco, echoing Huntington, believes that differences between 'Islam and the West' are a matter of cultures and civilizations (he prefers to be hospitalized in Milan than in Baghdad, as he puts it) – and further adds, echoing

Bernard Lewis this time, that only 'the West' has been curious about other cultures. These comments are critically important not just because of the politics of their racism, but far more importantly for the shadow of doubt they cast on the theories and philosophies of prominent European public intellectuals – all reasoned and articulated in the parochial provincialism of their 'Europe,' which as Fanon noted is itself an invention of the Third World.

8 Makhmalbaf proceeded to help change the Iranian law to allow the Afghan children refugees attend school, did massive fundraising to make this project possible, and then moved inside Afghanistan to build a school in Herat. That project became the cornerstone of a far more ambitious plan he has now brought to fruition – his Afghan Children Education Movement (ACEM). For the details of ACEM project visit Makhmalbaf's website: www.Makhmalbaf.com.

9 See Margaret A. Mills' *Rhetorics and Politics in Afghan Traditional Storytelling* (Philadelphia, PA: University of Pennsylvania, 1991). See also Margaret A. Mills *et al.*, *South Asian Folklore: An Encyclopedia: Afghanistan, Bangladesh, Nepal, Pakistan, Sri Lanka* (London and New York: Routledge, 2003).

10 Makhmalbaf never made a public case of his treatment at JFK airport in New York in March 2001 because he did not want the Islamic Republic to use it in its own propaganda machinery. But the atrocious treatment of Iranians (among other Muslims) when entering the USA came to world attention when on 15 April 2001 Ja'far Panahi, one of the most distinguished Iranian filmmakers en route from Hong Kong Film Festival to Montevideo and Buenos Aires, was chained to a chair at Kennedy airport, while a year later Bahman Qobadi and Abbas Kiarostami were denied a visa altogether. In the case of Kiarostami, even *The New York Times* was outraged: 'It's a mystery what the Bush administration thought it was protecting us from when it denied a timely visa to Iran's leading film director, Abbas Kiarostami. Surely not international embarrassment. The idea that the United States government is incapable of distinguishing between a potential terrorist and a renowned 62-year-old filmmaker who has been here seven times before without incident is not flattering to America's intelligence capacities or its reputation for cultural literacy' (*The New York Times* editorial, 2 October 2002). The distinguished Finnish director Aki Kaurismaki cancelled his trip to the New York Film Festival in sympathy. 'Not with anger (which has never brought anything good),' he said in a press release, 'but with deep sorrow, I received the news that Abbas Kiarostami, a friend of mine and one of the world's most peace-loving persons, is prevented from participating at the New York Film Festival because, being a citizen of Iran, he was refused a visa. I had also been invited to the festival, which is one of the best in the world. Under the circumstances I, too, am forced to cancel my participation – for if the present government of the United States of America does not want an Iranian, they will hardly have any use for a Finn. We do not even have the oil. However, what concerns me more is that if Abbas

Kiarostami is being treated like this, what will happen to nameless prisoners? I consider the Geneva Convention as the last hope of mankind, and as a private citizen of Finland, I accuse the Government of the United States of violating it.' (For the full text, see the Human Rights Watch Film Festival website, http://www.hrw.org/iff/2002/kiarostami.html, accessed on 22 October 2002.)

11 Berry Berenson Perkins, 53, was the widow of Anthony Perkins (died 1992) and lived in Los Angeles, California. She was an actress and a photographer, and was survived by two sons, Osgood and Elvis. Berry Berenson had appeared in such films as *Remember my Name* (1978), *Winter Kills* (1979), and *Cat People* (1982). Marisa Berenson herself is an actress and a model who lives between New York and Europe. She has acted in such classics as Luchino Visconti's *Death in Venice* (1971), Bob Fossey's *Cabaret* (1972, for which she was nominated for a Golden Globe Award for Best Supporting Actress), Stanley Kubrick's *Barry Lyndon* (1975), Blake Edwards' *S.O.B.* (1981), and Clint Eastwood's *White Hunter, Black Heart* (1990). After September the Eleventh, UNESCO nominated her as 'Artist for Peace'.

12 There were even press reports that presidents of major distribution companies in competition with Avatar had hired other Iranian filmmakers to go inside Afghanistan and make a quick film as a rival to *Kandahar*. These reports were not altogether inaccurate.

13 *The New Yorker* subsequently published an article on David Belfield in its issue published on 5 August 2002, 'An American Terrorist,' by Ira Silverman, who went to Iran and interviewed him.

14 From Robert O'Meally's Preface to his edited volume, *The Jazz Cadence of American Culture* (New York: Columbia University, 1995): p. xiv. The exception that proves the rule is Dariush Dolat-shahi, the virtuoso Iranian composer, musician, and master performer whose happy, joyous, and democratic conversations with classical Persian music have always been sources of utter musical delight. For an example, listen to his 'When the Moon Whispers: Improvisations on Tar' or 'The Third Eye: Improvisations on Tar'.

15 See *The New York Times*, Monday 5 November 2001, 'The Arts' section.

16 *The New York Times*, 23 November 2001, 'The Arts' section.

17 The prime example of which is Azar Nafisi's *Reading Lolita in Tehran* (New York: Random House, 2003). For a critical review of this book, see Negar Mottahedeh, *Off the Grid: Reading Iranian Memoirs in Our Time of Total War* (MERIP, September 2004). For another examination of this book in the larger context of the US imperial project, see my 'Native Informers and the Making of the American Empire' (*Al-Ahram*, 1–7 June 2006).

18 On Theodore Adorno and Max Horkheimer's conception of 'culture industry,' see their *Dialectic of Enlightenment* (New York: Continuum, 1993 – originally published as *Dialektik der Aufklarung* in 1944). See also Adorno's *The Culture Industry: Selected Essays on Mass Culture* (London: Routledge, 1991).

19 See Jean Baudrillard's *The Transparency of Evil* (op. cit.): p. 156.

20 Ibid.: p. 156.

21 Ibid.: p. 18.

22 Ibid.: p. 14.

23 Sohrab Sepehri, 'Encounter,' in his *Hasht Ketab* (op. cit.): pp. 121–123. My translation.

24 Gadamer, *The Relevance of the Beautiful* (op. cit.): p. 15.

Conclusion

1 From Sohrab Sepehri's *Vaheh-'i dar Lahzeh* (*An Oasis in the Moment*) in his *Hasht Ketab* (op. cit.): pp. 360–361. My translation.

2 From the same poem of Sohrab Sepehri, *Vaheh-'i dar Lahzeh/An Oasis in the Moment* in his *Hasht Ketab* (op. cit.): pp. 360–361. My translation.

3 Siddiq Barmak is an Afghan filmmaker. But his emerging cinema is deeply influenced by Makhmalbaf, while his film crew is almost indistinguishable from Makhmalbaf's and those of his wife and children. They have all worked in close proximity with each other.

4 From the same poem of Sohrab Sepehri, *Vaheh-'i dar Lahzeh/An Oasis in the Moment* in his *Hasht Ketab* (op. cit.): pp. 360–361. My translation.

5 From the same poem of Sohrab Sepehri, *Vaheh-'i dar Lahzeh/An Oasis in the Moment* in his *Hasht Ketab* (op. cit.): pp. 360–361. My translation.

6 From Sohrab Sepehri's *Beh Bagh-e Ham-Safaran/To the Garden of Fellow-Travelers* in his *Hasht Ketab* (op. cit.): pp. 394–397. My translation.

7 See Scott Nearing, *The Making of a Radical: A Political Autobiography* (White River Junction, VT: Chelsea Green Publishing Company, 2000): p. viii. I have never seen this extraordinary and inspiring autobiography in any chain bookstore. I bought my copy from a grocery store in Middlebury, Vermont.

Index